The Politics of
European
Integration

About the website

This book has a companion website containing a range of resources created by the author for students and other readers using this book. Features include:

- Web resources
- Web links for additional resources on the EU
- Flashcards
- Independent study questions
- Consolidated glossary
- Consolidated references
- Consolidated further readings

You can access these resources at: www.wiley.com/go/glencross

The Politics of European Integration

Political Union or a House Divided?

Andrew Glencross

WILEY Blackwell

Registered Office
John Wiley & Sons, Ltd, The Atrium, Southern Gate, Chichester, West Sussex, PO19 8SQ, UK

Editorial Offices
350 Main Street, Malden, MA 02148-5020, USA
9600 Garsington Road, Oxford, OX4 2DQ, UK
The Atrium, Southern Gate, Chichester, West Sussex, PO19 8SQ, UK

For details of our global editorial offices, for customer services, and for information about how to apply for permission to reuse the copyright material in this book please see our website at www.wiley.com/wiley-blackwell.

Library of Congress Cataloging-in-Publication Data

Glencross, Andrew.
  The politics of European integration : political union or a house divided? / Andrew Glencross.
    1 online resource.
  Includes bibliographical references and index.
  Description based on print version record and CIP data provided by publisher; resource not viewed.
  ISBN 978-1-4051-9394-8 (Paperback) – ISBN 978-1-4051-9395-5 (cloth)   1. European Union–Politics and government–21st century.   2. European Union countries–Politics and government–21st century.   I. Title.
  JN30
  341.242'2–dc23
                                        2013040257

A catalogue record for this book is available from the British Library.

Cover image: European union flag © Ramberg / iStock; European Parliament, Strasbourg, France © GAUTIER Stephane / SAGAPHOTO.COM / Alamy; Protestors demanding a referendum on Europe, London, 2008 © Guy Bell / Alamy; Anti Europe Union graffiti, Zagreb, Croatia © CroatiaPRESS / Alamy; Protests over EU plans to liberalise service sector, Strasbourg 2006 © Peter Stroh / Alamy.
Cover design by Simon Levy Associates

Set in 10/12.5 pt Minion by Toppan Best-set Premedia Limited
Printed in Singapore by Ho Printing Singapore Pte Ltd

1   2014

Contents

Contents

List of Figures

List of Tables

List of Timelines

List of Boxes

Acknowledgments

Although a solo-authored textbook, this volume has benefited immensely from the input of a number of friends, students, and family. I consider myself extremely lucky to have been able to draw on the scholarly wisdom of Stine Andersen, Matej Avbelj, Patrick Bernhagen, John Cronin, Igor Guardiancich, Xymena Kurowska, Alex Wilson, and Michael Wycherley. Alex, Igor, Michael, and Xymena deserve special thanks for their extensive feedback on particular chapters. At the University of Pennsylvania, where writing began in earnest, Laura White, Jonathan de Jong, and Katrina Youssef proved able research assistants. Karolina Raudsepp, at the University of Aberdeen, contributed bibliographical assistance. Frank Churchill was both a sounding board and a continuing source of encouragement during the years of writing this book. My father, Michael Glencross, did so much to improve the quality of the writing (including roping in my mother, Michèle, for proofreading) that words cannot do justice to his unstinting support for this project. Lastly, Janou was there for me from the first word to the last: my alpha and omega.

It has been a pleasure working with the editorial team at Wiley: Louise Butler, Annie Rose, Justin Vaughan, and Ben Thatcher. Louise and especially Annie provided outstanding feedback on the work in progress as well as prompt answers to my many queries. During the final stretch, I benefited greatly from the input of a superlative copyeditor, Manuela Tecusan, who remedied all sorts of syntactical infelicities. The anonymous reviewers are also owed a major debt of gratitude, as their thorough and challenging feedback was the source of constant improvement to both the structure and content of the book.

Finally, researching and writing this book was assisted in part by a European Commission Jean Monnet Module Grant "The Politics of European Integration" (Grant Decision Number 2011–3244).

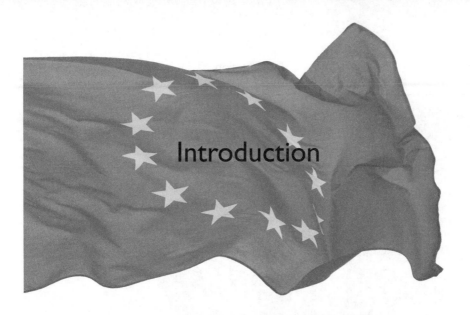

Introduction

The Purpose of This Book

The European Union (EU) is often said to be in crisis. It is criticized by journalists, politicians, non-governmental organizations (NGOs), citizens, and scholars for not doing enough or for doing the wrong things. Yet European integration – the process whereby Europe's countries formally coordinate their laws, economies, and policies – is now over 60 years old. Despite the crises and the criticism, the EU now undertakes many of the same tasks as a national government. Politics – meaning contestation over how resources are allocated (the economy), who can make binding decisions (institutional design), how authority can be held to account (democracy), how society should be organized (social policy and justice), and how to conduct relations with other countries (foreign policy) – is thus at the heart of the EU.

Twenty-eight different countries make up the member states of the EU, as depicted in Figure 0.1; all have agreed to be bound by a common system of law and to formulate together a variety of policies. Specially created political institutions are used for cooperation on matters such as the economy, the environment, foreign policy, agriculture, and justice. Many of the countries involved also share the same currency, the euro, which is administered cooperatively and is the second most important global currency behind the US dollar. The EU represents nearly 20 percent of global wealth and is the largest

The Politics of European Integration: Political Union or a House Divided?, First Edition. Andrew Glencross.
© 2014 Andrew Glencross. Published 2014 by Blackwell Publishing Ltd.

Figure 0.1   Map of contemporary EU

exporter and importer of goods and services in the world. Thanks to the set of international treaties creating EU institutions, citizens and firms have the right to work, live,
and do business unhindered across the EU's member states. At the same time, EU law
also prohibits discrimination based on gender, race, and disability. Today there are over
500 million EU citizens who benefit from these legal arrangements.

Brussels, the capital of Belgium, hosts some of the most important EU institutions,
which makes it the political center of a united Europe. Integration has had a transformative impact on member states, whose leaders meet regularly in Brussels to decide
important economic and political issues. Countries beyond Europe recognize this power
shift too. Powerful states such as the United States, China, and Russia pay close attention
to what the EU does, each having a permanent diplomatic mission in Brussels. A
country seeking recognition from the international community now targets diplomatic
relations with the EU. Meanwhile neighboring countries seek to join the EU club, which

is conditional on their meeting certain democratic standards and on the agreement of all existing member states.

With all these policy responsibilities, it is no surprise that the EU's performance is often called into question. As members of the EU, individual countries lose a certain degree of autonomy over important political decisions such as how to run the economy, how to control their borders, and how to conduct foreign policy. These countries agree to be bound by EU law, which trumps national law, and they also accept the possibility of being outvoted when it comes to important policy decisions. In return, politicians and citizens across Europe expect policy solutions and material benefits, notably an improved standard of living. With such expectations, some form of dissatisfaction is inevitable.

In fact, there is a laundry list of complaints about the EU. Some argue that the EU is trying to do too much, seeking to expand its competences even when current policies struggle to achieve their objectives. Others claim that member states need greater autonomy because compromise policies agreed upon by 28 countries are not always in the best interests of a particular state. Since the EU relies on national governments to administer EU policies, another complaint is that the mechanism for ensuring that all countries play by EU rules is not sufficiently robust. Finally, there is a concern that EU integration creates winners and losers in economic terms: this means that some groups, and even countries, benefit more than others. The criticism here is that the EU is not doing enough to mitigate the social inequalities that greater economic competition and globalization engender. Indeed some citizens and political parties blame the EU for imposing constraints that prevent national governments from doing more to fight unemployment or from resisting the harmful effects of globalization.

The aim of this book is to make sense of the politics of European integration, which is precisely an exercise in understanding the politics of dissatisfaction by disentangling the strengths and weaknesses of the EU. To accomplish this goal, it is necessary to make sense of what the EU does, as well as of why it functions as it does. The book also examines in detail the often heated debates not only on whether the EU has the right policies and institutions, but also on whether it is sufficiently democratic. That is a lot for a relatively compact introductory textbook. However, since all these questions are interconnected, it is necessary to cover them together, as a whole: doing so systemati-cally is what makes this textbook distinctive. In this way the book is not explicitly tied to a single disciplinary or theoretical approach. Rather the aim is to draw together scholarly insights from comparative politics, international relations, law, and democratic theory so as to provide a thorough survey of the politics behind the creation and func-tioning of the EU.

Why European Integration Matters

In the first half of the twentieth century Europe was very much at the center of world politics, given that it was the setting for two conflicts that became global wars. Today Europe is at peace, thanks in large part to the institutions created through European integration. It is thus interesting to explore how political and legal integration has helped overcome conflict and produce cooperation between countries. Another fundamental reason why integration matters is that it is a mechanism for Europe to remain a global player, especially in economic affairs.

Europe's global importance has undoubtedly decreased – EU inhabitants represent only 7 percent of the global population, while economic power has shifted dramatically eastwards. Yet European integration is relevant globally because the EU constitutes the world's most powerful trading bloc, representing a fifth of world trade. Firms from other countries want to sell goods to the EU's 500 million consumers and to make investments there. As a $16 trillion economy (2012), as large as that of the USA, the EU has great clout in the world economy, providing it has the right policies and institutions to take full advantage of its size.

The EU is also the most successful model of regional integration, a process that continues in Asia, Africa, Latin America, and North America. On these four continents, the Association of South-East Asian States (ASEAN), the African Union (AU), the Southern Common Market (Mercosur), and the North American Free Trade Association (NAFTA) respectively are pursuing cross-border cooperation. These global efforts at regional integration illustrate how international politics is increasingly regulated by a rich array of international organizations and international law. Institutions such as the EU and other regional organizations affect the policy choices available to national governments. Thus, by studying the EU, it is possible to assess the successes and failures of developing policy-making and law beyond the nation-state. It also becomes possible to assess the extent to which these developments help or hinder democracy. From this broader perspective, the EU is perhaps less an anomaly in world politics than a harbinger of the future.

Finally, as governing human societies becomes more complex, political institutions like the EU are expected to do more and more. Tackling policy problems such as migration, climate change, economic development, and human rights protection puts the EU at the heart of global efforts to address fundamentally interconnected issues that cross borders. Hence what the EU does – not just in economic policy but also in environmental matters, foreign affairs, immigration policy and so on – has consequences far beyond Europe, and this leaves it also vulnerable to criticism from outside. That is why understanding the politics surrounding the EU is a matter of importance for students, teachers, and citizens across the world.

The Basic Structure of the EU

As this book assumes no prior familiarity with the EU, it is helpful to lay out some important background facts about what constitutes the political system born of European integration. The easiest way to make sense of the EU is to understand it as a set of institutions trying to make the whole greater than the sum of its parts (individual member states). Unfortunately the result is not something that fits the standard categories of federal state or international organization.

Like a federal state, the EU has a well-integrated legal system, overseen by an independent court that is supreme over national law. Like in any international organization, member states play a key role in decision-making. Unlike a federal state, the EU is not a sovereign entity, which means that its member states continue to have their own foreign relations and sit in the UN. Unlike an international organization, the EU has its own elected parliament, with real power to amend and reject legislation. There is also a powerful independent authority, the European Commission, which proposes laws, administers policies associated with an annual budget of €150 billion (in 2013), and brings legal cases to the EU's independent court, the Court of Justice of the European Union (CJEU), when member states fail to comply with EU rules. Figure 0.2 represents a simplified model of the interactions between the various institutions constituting the EU system.

This is a simplified depiction of the EU's five main institutions and of the interactions between them that ultimately produce EU policies and law. A more complex explanation is offered in Chapter 4, but a brief discussion of Figure 0.2 is useful at this stage. At the top of the diagram is the European Council, an assembly of all 28 heads of state or government (prime ministers and presidents) that meets periodically in Brussels to set the overall EU policy agenda, coordinate EU foreign policy, negotiate new EU treaties, and generally address big problems of the day. As well as being a major agenda-setter, this body is also in charge of appointing two presidential figures. It appoints the president of the European Council itself, who helps prepare the Council's work and establish consensus among heads of state or governments. The European Council also selects the president of the European Commission, who serves a five-year term, as does the whole College of commissioners.

The Commission itself is an unusual institution, which not only oversees EU policies but also proposes legislation in line with the European Council's overall objectives. These two responsibilities have been delegated by EU countries for the sake of improving cooperation and coordination. The Commission is formed of 28 commissioners (one from each country, including the president), who are in charge of different policy areas, like a cabinet government, although collectively they are referred to as a college. Commissioners are national politicians selected to serve by their governments (not elected by citizens), although the Commission itself is independent of member state control and is tasked with promoting European interests alone. This independence is designed to prevent policies that favor individual member states as well as to enable the Commission to monitor, in a politically neutral fashion, whether countries are meeting all their obligations. The European Commission has three main activities: overseeing existing EU policies, proposing legislation in those (ever increasing) areas where the EU has the power to act, and ensuring member state compliance with EU rules and law.

Whatever the Commission proposes in the form of legislation has to be approved by two decision-making bodies, which are made up of different kinds of representatives. One of the bodies that decide whether to accept a policy proposed by the Commission is the Council of the EU (formerly called the Council of Ministers) – not to be confused with the European Council discussed previously. This institution represents national governments, whose ministers (one from each country) sit in the Council of the EU according to what policy area is being discussed (that is, agriculture ministers discuss agriculture, justice ministers are present when discussing justice). At any one time, an EU country holds the presidency of the Council of the EU for a period of six months.

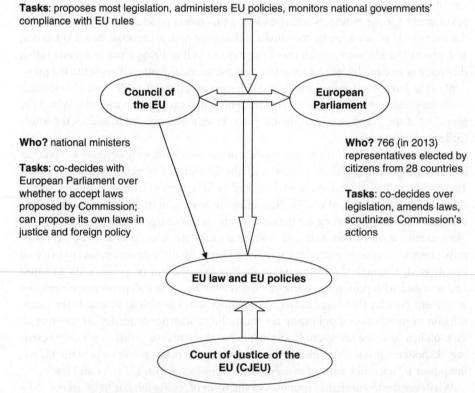

Who? heads of government or state from 28 EU countries

Tasks: sets overall EU policy agenda, coordinates foreign policy, negotiates new EU treaties, appoints president of European Council and president of the Commission

Who? 28 Commissioners chosen by member states but who serve EU interests

Tasks: proposes most legislation, administers EU policies, monitors national governments' compliance with EU rules

Who? national ministers

Tasks: co-decides with European Parliament over whether to accept laws proposed by Commission; can propose its own laws in justice and foreign policy

Who? 766 (in 2013) representatives elected by citizens from 28 countries

Tasks: co-decides over legislation, amends laws, scrutinizes Commission's actions

Who? 28 independent judges

Tasks: to give definitive interpretation of EU law, to decide whether countries have broken EU law, and determine whether EU institutions act in accordance with their legal mandate

Figure 0.2   Diagram of EU institutional decision-making

Leaders from that country are then responsible for arranging and chairing meetings of the Council, thereby providing political leadership that is a source of prestige for national politicians. In the sensitive areas of justice and foreign affairs, the Council of the EU can propose its own legislation, without relying on the Commission to act (as depicted by the arrow in Figure 0.2).

The other political decision-making body is the European Parliament, whose members, called MEPs (members of the European Parliament), are elected directly by citizens within the different member states. The allocation of MEPs per country is based on population. The parliament also needs to approve the president of the Commission chosen by the European Council as well as give its approval to the entire College of commissioners once the latter has been selected. Moreover, during the five-year term of the Commission, the European Parliament can issue a vote of censure that, providing it has a two-thirds majority, forces the commissioners to resign. So it is a crucial institution for holding the Commission to account. It also plays a fundamental role in scrutinizing and shaping legislation, as no law, except in the area of foreign policy, can pass without its approval. This means that the Parliament is a co-legislator alongside the Council of the EU, both bodies co-deciding on whether to pass laws. Although it has no power to initiate laws itself, the Parliament can amend legislation (a majority of MEPs suffices) as well as ask the Commission to legislate on a particular issue.

The final EU institution on the diagram is the Court of Justice of the European Union (formerly called the European Court of Justice), depicted at the bottom of Figure 0.2 to illustrate its independence from political decision-making; in this it is just like the US Supreme Court. This court is made up of 28 senior judges from across the EU. As the supreme interpreter of EU law, the CJEU is in charge of resolving competence disputes about whether a policy can legally be carried out at the EU level. It also makes a major contribution to EU politics by deciding whether member states meet their EU legal obligations. If the court finds a state in breach of its obligations, it can fine that country's government in order to compel compliance, and governments also have to adapt their laws in response to court rulings. Additionally, the CJEU arbitrates disputes between EU institutions over whether these have acted within their legally defined mandate or not.

Having introduced a description of what the EU looks like, it is also important to grasp what it does. A crucial starting point for getting to grips with the EU's various policies is to understand the division of competences between member states and the EU, which is similar to the division between the powers reserved to the federal government and those left to state governments by the US constitution. Instead of having a document called a formal constitution, the EU is founded today on two international treaties of equal value, signed by all 28 heads of state and government as well as ratified by parliaments in each member state. Articles from each of these treaties are referred to at various points in this book, but both have the same legal weight. One is the Treaty on European Union (TEU) and the other is the Treaty on the Functioning of the European Union (TFEU). Together they set out the EU's values, its decision-making procedures, and, most significantly, its competences.

The EU wields three types of competences: *exclusive*, *shared*, and *supporting*. *Exclusive* means that the EU political system makes all the relevant decisions in the following six areas: the customs union (e.g. tariffs on imports), monetary policy for countries using the euro (the currency used in 2013 by 17 countries in what is referred to as the "Eurozone"), competition laws relating to the EU single market (e.g. anti-trust actions, mergers, and acquisitions), common commercial policy (i.e. international trade deals through the World Trade Organization), conservation of marine resources, and the conclusion of certain international treaties. Exclusivity prevents member states from making any independent policy decisions in these policy areas, although the domain of exclusive competences is rather restricted in scope. *Shared* competences are very wide, covering the internal EU market, certain areas of social policy (e.g. worker rights and non-discrimination), agriculture and fisheries, the environment, consumer protection, transport, energy, border control, immigration, justice, and finally common safety concerns in public health. In these policy areas member states can still make their own policies, but any such national legislation has to conform with EU legislation; EU rules in these areas supersede national law, a situation closely monitored by the Commission, which can bring prosecutions for non-compliance with EU rules to the Court of Justice. Finally, *supporting* policy competences allow the EU to provide funds or policy initiatives supporting national policies in areas such as education, research, tourism, and sport. These measures do not constrain how governments legislate in these areas.

Plan of the Book and Learning Objectives

As suggested by the above presentation of what the EU looks like, European integration is a complex topic. Decision-making rules and policy processes are convoluted, and also inherently related to complicated as well as heated political debates. This is because politicians, parties, interest groups, and scholars fight over what European integration should achieve and how it should work. The analytical survey provided in this book is thus designed to supply the tools for understanding the politics of European integration in both theory and practice. Readers can then judge for themselves where they stand on any of the many controversies surrounding this process.

The approach adopted to explain the politics of European integration is to separate this process into its different components and debates. Hence the book is organized into four parts: The History of European Integration; Analyzing Integration; Debating the EU System and Its Policy Outputs; and Democracy and Integration. Each part consists of three chapters that focus on a particular aspect of integration, while the sum of the parts combines to provide a detailed overview of the many complexities behind this political project.

The historical side of integration is covered in Part I, with chapters that explore early proposals for uniting the European continent before detailing the institutional construction of integration that occurred after 1945. Part II provides the analytical framework for understanding how the institutions of today's EU function, what policies they produce, and how this political system can be compared with others, such as federations and international organizations. Debates about the EU system and the policies it produces are treated in the three chapters constituting Part III. These explore the politics behind EU laws, its foreign policy, and proposals to reform the way integration is actually organized. Finally, Part IV deals with the interconnection between democracy and integration. Two chapters examine, respectively, how democratic the EU is and what impact integration is having on the functioning of democracy within member states. This part concludes by analyzing the origins of and the response to the Eurozone sovereign debt crisis as indicative of this complex relationship between democracy and integration. This final chapter on the EU's latest crisis thus serves as a conclusion to the book, allowing for a reflection on the state of integration today and on the ongoing political debates it engenders.

What, then, should readers expect to gain from this book? They should attain the following four learning objectives, based on the four sections:

- detailed knowledge of the trajectory and politics behind integration, from early ideas about European cooperation to the present-day EU;
- the ability to analyze how the EU functions, how its institutions interact, and how it compares with other political systems;
- a theoretical and practical understanding of the strengths and weaknesses of EU economic regulatory policy, foreign policy, and its institutional design;
- the analytical tools to consider whether the EU is sufficiently democratic, how integration affects national politics, and how well the EU responded to the Eurozone sovereign debt crisis.

Overall, this means providing a broad coverage of issues, analytical depth, a balanced reflection on the strengths and weaknesses of integration, and the most up-to-date coverage possible. Each chapter also integrates scholarly debates on the various topics covered. Hence the references and further reading provided at the end of each chapter constitute a starting point for individual research, for example for projects and essays. The text also identifies key concepts, key debates, and case studies: these are presented in separate boxes throughout the chapters. Finally, a glossary of key terms accompanies each chapter: this is the place to look when there is a word or concept whose meaning is unclear.

To complement the material presented here and enhance individual research as well as understanding, this book is supported by a companion website, which can be found at www.wiley.com/go/glencross. On the website you will find a list of the web links referred to throughout the book chapters wherever there is a "Web" icon in the page margins. In addition, the website contains a list of further relevant online resources – such as websites for EU institutions, political groups, archives, and think tanks, information on studying abroad, and the biographies of key figures. You will also find self-assessment tools in the form of flashcards and independent study questions, all organized by chapter. As European integration is a moving target, the companion website will be updated periodically, to keep track of current developments.

Part I

The History of European Integration

I

The Idea of Europe
Foundations and Justifications for Unity

Contents

Learning Objectives

- to identify different political definitions of Europe;
- to analyze the reasons why thinkers called for European unity to replace the balance of power;
- to evaluate why plans for European unity all failed prior to 1945;
- to distinguish between different justifications put forward for European unity;
- to analyze the reasoning behind three different justifications for European unity;
- to evaluate why the idea of uniting to strengthen state capacity is controversial in the context of European social democracy.

The Politics of European Integration: Political Union or a House Divided?, First Edition. Andrew Glencross.
© 2014 Andrew Glencross. Published 2014 by Blackwell Publishing Ltd.

Timeline of Key Events 1.1: The Historical Background to European Integration

circa 50–400 CE	Roman Empire provides common political and legal order for much of Europe
circa 800	Charlemagne, king of the Franks, unites Western Europe by conquest
1095	Pope Urban II calls for Christian crusade to help Byzantium in war with Turks
circa 1460	George of Podiebrad, king of Bohemia, calls for Christian kings to unite to drive Turkish forces out of Europe
1648	Peace of Westphalia establishes sovereign state as basic political unit in Europe
1693	William Penn writes *An Essay towards the Present and Future Peace of Europe*
1700–1800	Europe as a political concept (continent of sovereign states) replaces earlier notion of Christendom (continent with a common religious identity)
1713	Abbot Saint Pierre writes *Project for Perpetual Peace in Europe*
1789	French Revolution challenges monarchical rule throughout Europe
1795	Immanuel Kant publishes *Perpetual Peace: A Philosophical Essay*
1815–circa 1890	Concert of Europe whereby powerful European countries try to manage their disputes cooperatively, in *ad hoc* conferences
1914–1918	First World War
1919–circa 1939	League of Nations, collective security organization established for peaceful resolution of inter-state conflicts
1923	Count Coudenhove-Kalergi publishes *Pan-Europa*
1929	Aristide Briand, president of France, calls for a European Union
1939–1945	Second World War

1.0   Introduction: What and Where Is Europe?

Europe is a commonly used geographical term, referring to the western part of the Eurasian land mass. In the Atlantic Ocean, the Mediterranean, and the Arctic Ocean it has clear maritime boundaries respectively to the west, the south, and the north. This peninsula lacks an equivalently clear boundary to the east – a fact that remains a source of controversy to this day, since uncertainty over Europe's borders means uncertainty over which countries can become members of the European Union. As a result, who and what counts as European is contested, especially in the case of Russia and Turkey, countries with territory in both Asia and Europe (see Box 1.1).

The notion that Europe is a geographical and cultural entity separate from Asia was articulated already by the ancient Greeks, who sought to distinguish themselves from their fierce rivals and neighbors, the Persians. Indeed the very word "Europe" derives from a Greek myth recounting how Zeus, father of the gods, abducted a princess named Europa. So, as well as being a continent, Europe is a concept used to explain and justify separateness. Hence this chapter first sets out the reasons behind the development of Europe as a political idea indicating separateness from Asia – which, by the seventeenth

Box 1.1   Key Debate: Where Are the Boundaries of Europe?

With 28 current member states, the EU clearly does not encompass all the countries that make up modern Europe. For instance, the Council of Europe (a human rights organization) consists of 47 countries, thereby including Armenia, Azerbaijan, Georgia, and Turkey in its definition of Europe. Identifying a geographical boundary between Europe and Asia is inherently problematic. Physical features of the landscape have been used to this end, notably the Caucasus mountains and the Urals in Russia. Yet relying on these features means excluding Turkey, which actually has a land border with the EU, and splitting Russia into two. Moreover, for many centuries the Mediterranean was a common cultural and economic space, with North Africa and the Levant closely tied to Southern Europe – a tradition begun under the Roman Empire, which called this body of water *mare nostrum*, "our sea." Morocco's unsuccessful application to join the EEC in 1987 suggests that the possibilities of EU enlargement south of the Mediterranean are slim. However, the EU is ambiguous about how it defines Europe; the founding treaties do not provide a formal definition as to which countries are considered European, and hence potential EU member states. Hence the EU's frontiers in the East remain rather uncertain, at least until one reaches Russia – which, for reasons of size, prestige, and sovereignty, can realistically only be an EU partner rather than a member state. Many of the countries in post-Soviet Eastern Europe, the Balkans, and the Caucasus would like to reap the economic and political benefits of EU membership. Moreover, Turkey has been negotiating to join since 1987 – so far without success (see Section 5.6 for a discussion of enlargement).

century, also meant a common political space with unique characteristics. In fact, as explained in Section 1.1, this political vision replaced an earlier religious definition, which based separateness on a common religious identity.

Historically, the political understanding of Europe arose in tandem with proposals for uniting the continent. Early ideas and pioneers of integrating rival European countries into a single political system were concerned with security, for states and citizens alike. A continent divided into rival states was free from the menace of absolute rule by one leader or country, but this carried a high cost. States frequently resorted to war in order to defend their territory, the dynastic claims of their princely rulers, or the freedom of religious expression. Section 1.2 outlines how schemes for integration were designed to put an end to violent competition between those countries. Through the creation of common political institutions, European unity came to be seen as a way to keep a certain degree of autonomy without suffering the depredations of inter-state warfare. These proposals continued until the 1930s, just before Europe tore itself apart again, in the Second World War.

Although the idea of European unity has always presupposed building institutions to allow cooperation beyond the state, different justifications for integration have been put forward. Hence, in addition to charting early models for uniting Europe that predate the institutional developments after 1945 discussed in Chapter 2, this chapter surveys the history of different ideas about what integration is actually for. As analyzed in Section 1.3, the oldest justification for unity is the concern to bring peace, or to civilize a continent that has struggled to protect citizens' rights. Beginning in the period between the two world wars, another justification was articulated. This was the idea that looking beyond the nation-state would bring not only peace but also economic benefits. This prosperity justification, examined in Section 1.4, also played a key role after 1945, as states sought economic reconstruction. Finally there is the justification that common institutions can actually equip national governments to tackle complex cross-border problems more effectively. This idea, discussed in Section 1.5, grew in popularity as the Second World War was coming to an end and states were looking to new instruments for governing complex societies. Indeed, to various degrees, all three justifications have been present during the institutional development of integration examined in the subsequent two chapters.

1.1   The Historical Background to Thinking about European Unity

In ancient times, Europe was a cacophony of tongues spoken by a multitude of ethnic groups with differing religious and cultural practices – a rich diversity still reflected in the heterogeneity of EU member states today. There were certain notable periods of unity, as during the Roman Empire, which at its peak (around 100 CE) ruled the greater part of Europe, and at the time of King Charlemagne's conquests (768–814 CE). These were short-lived though, and they left religion – not a common ruler – as the principal object for European self-identification (Le Goff 2005).

Christianity began to form the basis of European identity as the Germanic and other tribes that overran the Roman Empire converted to the religion of the cross. The Christian element of Europe was underscored in 1095, when Pope Urban II called for volunteers to travel to Byzantium (Constantinople, modern-day Istanbul) to wage a holy war – that is, a crusade. Muslim warriors had for several centuries taken control of Jerusalem and were now threatening the chief city of the Byzantine Empire, formerly the Eastern capital of the Roman Empire. Kings, princes, knights, and even peasants across Western Europe participated in crusades to the Holy Land until the thirteenth century. Crusaders set out with the intention not just of preventing the fall of Byzantium but also of "liberating" Jerusalem and other biblical lands from under non-Christian rule.

Religion thus served to differentiate Europe from the peoples further east. Even after the end of large-scale crusading, Catholic popes such as Pius II (1458–1454) renewed calls for a holy war to fight non-believers in the East. With the fall of Constantinople to Turkish forces in 1453, the Muslim Ottoman Empire began its incursions into Greece and the Balkans, eventually reaching what is today Hungary. The Europe the Popes wanted to defend against this invader was the *respublica christiana*, the "Christian republic" also known as **Christendom** (den Boer 1993). Indeed it was in this period that George of Podiebrad, the king of Bohemia, appealed to his fellow monarchs to unite in order to protect Christianity – a plea sometimes seen as the first project of European union (Le Goff 2005, 158–159).

If Christendom was considered separate on religious grounds, a secular political interpretation also came to be attributed to the geographical expression Europe. As the Ottoman threat receded, European Christianity was further divided by the sixteenth-century Reformation, so that it was not until the seventeenth and eighteenth century that thinkers discussed the "natural republic of Europe" (Deudney 2008, 136–160). By this they meant that the territorial units into which Europe was divided produced a sort of republican order, whereby no single state dominated. Like in a republic rather than in a monarchy, there was no single ruler, and combinations of states could check the hegemonic ambitions of a powerful monarch such as the French King Louis XIV – a process resembling institutional checks and balances found in republican constitutions. Of course, this so-called order contained a great deal of violence: states, led mostly by kings, would often resort to war in their disputes. Nevertheless, this understanding of Europe as a shared political space with unique characteristics – notably territorially bounded states led by secular leaders – replaced the older notion of Christendom (Schmidt 1966).

The seventeenth century also gave rise to the first projects for uniting the European continent under a common political system. Thinkers and statesmen grappled tentatively with the question of how to overcome the division of Europe into rival territorial units, often in bloody conflict with one another. This timing was no coincidence: the rise of a new political unit, the sovereign state, brought about constant preparation for war, ushering in more instability and violence.

The European sovereign state, organized as a hierarchical order of rule whereby all citizens in a certain territory owed allegiance to one ruler alone, was largely a product of the Peace of Westphalia (1648). This peace settlement was an attempt to end the religious warfare sparked by the sixteenth-century Reformation, when Protestant cities and territories sought to gain independence from Catholic rulers in order to obtain the freedom to exercise their reformed version of Christianity. Under the terms of the peace settlement, the dynastic rulers of various territories (kings, princes, emperors) agreed not to interfere in the affairs of the others and to respect their religious convictions.

In theory, rulers were supposed to recognize one another's sovereignty – that is, territorial independence. In practice, states such as France, England, Spain, Sweden, and the Dutch Republic engaged in an often violent competition for land, wealth, and even prestige. Joined eventually by new powers such as Prussia and Russia, this inter-state competition took place under a framework known as the balance of power, whereby the most powerful states cooperated to prevent any one great power from becoming so strong as to be able to impose its will on the whole continent (see Box 1.2). Typically this arrangement took the form of shifting diplomatic alliances. Just as often, the process of balancing power required military action to counter the hegemonic ambitions of a Louis XIV or Philip IV (the Spanish king). It was this process of power balancing that made certain thinkers see Europe as possessing features of a common political system, albeit a highly dysfunctional one, which privileged state sovereignty over peace.

Box 1.2   Key Concept: The Balance of Power

Both international relations theorists and political leaders have long argued that the key to a stable international order – in the absence of a world government – is the balance of power between the most powerful states (Nexon 2009). This theory holds that no single major power must become stronger than the others put together, otherwise the strongest could impose its will on the others, causing them to lose their sovereignty. Balancing implies the possibility of using force to stop a state from becoming too powerful, and it is often indifferent to the plight of weak states, whose territory could be carved up between major powers in order to preserve an equilibrium between stronger states. The First World War (1914– 1918) showed that relying on power balancing was little better than anarchy and that an alternative was necessary. The **League of Nations** was supposed to replace balancing with a legal framework for resolving disputes between states; but it failed to prevent states' pursuit of power through force, and this led to a new global conflict. What the two world wars also demonstrated was the fact that the balance of power system makes for mutual suspicion, which fosters tension. When each state has to maintain a large army, spend greatly on defense, and craft diplomatic alliances, a **security dilemma** emerges, as one country's enhanced security comes at the cost of making another feel more vulnerable (Jervis 1978). This situation is especially pernicious for democracies, since politicians will ask citizens to sacrifice individual freedoms for national security, as happened in the 1930s in Germany. Abandoning this reliance on armies and alliances for balancing against rival states was thus the shared objective of the leaders and citizens of post-1945 Western Europe.

1.2   Early Ideas and Pioneers of Unity

Once war was a common occurrence among the sovereign states of Europe, thinkers trained in philosophy and law examined the conditions upon which a lasting peace could be founded. This objective had to be reconciled with the need to preserve individual freedoms, especially freedom of religious worship. Hence the aim of figures such as William Penn, the Abbot Saint Pierre, and Immanuel Kant was to improve Europe's political system by finding a mechanism to avoid war. They did not wish to see unity imposed by force or through a return to a common religious identity. Rather these authors sought to overcome the deficiencies of the balance of power system by limiting states' right to make alliances or use force to settle their disputes. This objective was not realized, and the First World War, which left 30 million dead in Europe alone, revealed the atrocious cost of relying on war to settle inter-state disputes. Statesmen led by French President Aristide Briand began to question the very value of state sovereignty in this context. However, Briand's plan for European unity was not put into practice; the first institutions capable of overcoming balancing and attenuating sovereignty were only established in the second half of the twentieth century.

1.2.1   William Penn

William Penn, an English landowner after whom the US state of Pennsylvania is named, was by religion a Quaker, a breakaway group of the Church of England strongly associated with pacifism. In 1693, as war was raging in continental Europe, Penn proposed a system for a congress of nations designed to procure peace. His *An Essay towards the Present and Future Peace of Europe by the Establishment of an European Dyet, Parliament or Estates* spoke of Europe's "harassed inhabitants" and criticized the doctrine that "peace is the end of war." In the absence of a common government between states, leaders across Europe traditionally defended war as a legitimate means of enforcing their rights to foreign territories or of installing a friendly ruler on a foreign throne. Penn dismissed this notion that war was a proper instrument for bringing peace in disputes over territory or dynastic succession. Instead, his proposal called for Europe's states to send delegates (on the basis of a country's wealth) to a general assembly or parliament, which would meet yearly to arbitrate disputes, settling them by a three-quarters majority.

Penn was not a utopian; he did not expect sovereign states to yield to this arbitration without some means of enforcement. This is why his plan called for a **collective security** approach. That is, if any country refused to abide by the decision of the European parliament, all the countries, "united as one strength," would enforce compliance. Joint military action was thus threatened against violators of this system. Although this sounds potentially violent, Penn did not expect disputes to end in military conflict, because the great characteristic of Europe was that no single state was more powerful than the rest combined. In this situation he envisaged peaceful dispute resolution, as no state would dare challenge all the others. Anticipating objections, he argued that this same logic would mean that even the most powerful European country would feel obliged to join this parliamentary system rather than stay on the margins of a united continent. Moreover, limiting the use of war did nothing to diminish domestic sovereignty (e.g. over religious matters), so concerns about loss of autonomy would be no excuse for non-participation either.

1.2.2   Abbot Saint Pierre

Penn's visionary project failed to make an impact on European politics. Yet this did not stop others from trying to design similar systems for the unification of the continent. Abbot Saint Pierre, a French cleric who served his country as a diplomat, was another thinker determined to help the pacification of Europe. His participation in the negotiations of the Treaty of Utrecht (1713), which put an end to more than a decade of warfare involving all the region's major powers, helped inspire his most famous work, *Project for Perpetual Peace in Europe* (1713). Responding to the jealousies between states over territory and trade – the causes of the wars that ended at Utrecht – Abbot Saint Pierre proposed a European Union designed not only to remove war but also to stimulate trade via free commerce (Hont 2005, 27–28).

Abbot Saint Pierre's project of union was intended to remedy the deficiencies of the balance of power. He also assumed that peace treaties like that signed in Utrecht were only ever temporary expedients, bound to be broken as a result of the jealousies and fickleness of rulers. European Union in his eyes needed to be set on a permanent basis, through a treaty establishing a congress of all the leading rulers. Again, the purpose of this union was to provide the weakest state with the backing of all, so that even the most powerful state would have to accept the binding decisions of this congress. The most important matters Abbot Saint Pierre expected the congress of this union to settle were territorial and dynastic claims as well as commercial disputes. The latter were increasingly important in Europe, as warring states were not only cutting off trade with one another – beggaring themselves – but also trying to restrict neutral trade, bringing more states into conflict (Hont 2005, 31).

Like Penn's plan, therefore, the Project for Perpetual Peace in Europe was a collective security scheme for waging war on any state that broke its treaty promise to accept collective dispute settlement. Living under the shadow of this collective use of force would be far preferable to relying on *ad hoc* balancing alliances, continuously made and unmade, for security. From a rational perspective, kings and princes capable of understanding their true interest in stable trade relations and secure rule over their territories would have to sign such a treaty. Moreover, Abbot Saint Pierre thought this model of political military union was universal, meaning other regions should adopt it.

1.2.3 Immanuel Kant

The treaty envisaged by Abbot Saint Pierre was stillborn. Republican critics of monarchy thought they knew exactly why such schemes faltered: kings did not share subjects' interest in peace and prosperity. Instead, kings and other unelected rulers were motivated in their foreign relations by lust for conquest and glory regardless of the toll exacted from ordinary citizens. Hence, when the German philosopher Immanuel Kant envisioned a plan for European peace, he advocated the need for each state to become a republic as a precondition for a federal-style union.

Kant's *Perpetual Peace: A Philosophical Essay* was written in 1795, at a time when the French Revolution threatened the existence of monarchical rule throughout Europe. This plan for peace proposed abolishing not just war, but also the custom of rulers inheriting, exchanging, or purchasing other territories. These practices, which entailed treating the state as the personal property of a ruling family, went against the new, revolutionary language of individual rights and popular sovereignty. The latter meant that citizens had the right to government by consent and were not subject to the whims of monarchs.

By extension, Kant argued that perpetual peace rested on each state having a republican constitution where the people was sovereign – not the king. Popular sovereignty, he claimed, prevents states from going to war for a trifle, as when kings did so for glory or to avenge their honor. Monarchs could make these decisions and pass the costs on to their subjects, who would do the actual fighting and suffer the civilian privations of being at war. Republican governments responsive to the needs and preferences of citizens would instead be more self-restrained with citizens preferring self-defense over aggression – a proposition now known as "democratic peace theory," which remains highly influential in international relations (Doyle 1983). Once organized as republics, European states would be able to form a federation and take further steps toward a peaceful future. This included the gradual abolition of standing armies and the prohibition of external public debt, both of which Kant saw as facilitating conflict. Hence his scheme meant circumscribing state sovereignty per se by limiting precisely what made states such efficient instruments for waging war.

Again, these radical proposals for eradicating the causes of war among European states fell on deaf ears. After the Napoleonic wars (1803–1815), which were an indirect result of the French Revolution, the most powerful states did try to manage their affairs without resorting to war. Known as the **Concert of Europe**, this arrangement involved the leaders of Austria, Britain, France, Prussia, and Russia meeting in *ad hoc* conferences to settle their differences (Elrod 1976). Although the arrangement was successful in minimizing great power conflict within Europe, by the early twentieth century the major countries in Europe had abandoned this system and resorted to classic balancing behavior. Two rival sets of alliances, the Triple Entente and the Triple Alliance, came into conflict in 1914, sparking the beginning of the First World War.

Ironically, this horrendous conflict occurred when European governments had become far more republican than ever before. Each major belligerent relied on mobilizing its people, civilians as well as soldiers, on an unprecedented scale, which was achieved through **nationalism**. This ideology promoted national unity and the sense that armies were of the people fighting for their people. The devastating consequences of inter-state war fuelled by nationalistic antagonism made Winston Churchill's remark in 1901 that 'the wars of people will be more terrible than the wars of kings' truly prophetic (quoted in Gilbert 2012, 54). In response, peace between the warring parties was accompanied by a bold collective security project: the League of Nations.

The League of Nations shared the design of some of these earlier projects for unity. Based as it was on a global membership that included states beyond Europe, the League depended on all member states agreeing to arbitration in case of disputes. Decisions that were not respected would be enforced through economic sanctions imposed by other members, and ultimately it was possible to use force collectively in order to uphold the League's rules, for instance in the event that one member invaded another. This arrangement signified an unparalleled restriction on state sovereignty. Members of the League committed themselves to accepting binding arbitration for their disputes and to participating in collective action to enforce the decisions of the League when broken.

1.2.4 Aristide Briand

It was the catastrophe of the First World War that persuaded European and other states to accept this project. This global conflict had shown that war was an intolerable price to pay for state sovereignty; it was preferable to limit sovereignty in order to create a system for managing inter-state disputes more peaceful than balancing. Sadly, the failure of the League of Nations to prevent the Second World War has made this institution a byword for fanciful utopianism. However, the inter-war period in Europe was actually the first time when statesmen (rather than philosophers) actively considered taking measures for political union.

French President Aristide Briand, already a Nobel Peace Prize winner for his willingness to pursue reconciliation with Germany, proposed a plan for a European Union as a form of federation. Known as the Briand Memorandum, this document was sent in 1929 to all the region's governments, to canvas their opinion. Culturally the inter-war era was a period of grave European self-doubt, reinforced by the obvious strength and dynamism of the United States, and also by the looming presence of the alternative Soviet socio-economic model (Heater 1992, 116–130). Briand's proposal thus came at a time when the idea of European unity seemed to offer a preferable alternative to crass materialism or the abolition of private property. Numerous writers put forward this

ideal. Chief among them was Count Coudenhove-Kalergi, whose book *Pan-Europa* (1923) and the Pan-European Movement it spawned advocated unity as a form of moral and economic regeneration.

Despite the popularity of this idea, Briand's memorandum – admittedly short on details – fell on deaf ears. Although it proposed a customs union to promote free trade, this project put political objectives above economic ones at a time when Europe's suffering economies were the main preoccupation for citizens and governments. Following the 1929 stock market crash, countries reverted to **economic protectionism**, thereby reducing intra-European trade. In 1930 the League of Nations did establish a Study Commission for European Union, even though governments had shown little enthusiasm for Briand's project. With diminished expectations from the League itself, in the 1930s Europe's states returned to a balancing behavior based on diplomatic alliances and stoked up nationalism to justify territorial and other claims against neighboring countries. Unsurprisingly, this system resulted again in violent conflict, beginning in 1939. Consequently, when politicians debated European integration after 1945, the emphasis was placed on economic reconstruction alongside pacifying the continent by restraining both state sovereignty and nationalism.

1.3 The Peace or Civilizing Justification for Unity

Historically the primary motivation for European unity has been peace, as seen in the schemes for unification described in Section 1.2. After 1945 this justification assumed an even greater moral dimension, in response to the egregious human rights crimes, including genocide, committed during the Second World War. In this context the "never again" spirit meant the priority was to find an institutional mechanism for abolishing the absurd national rivalries that led to bloodshed. Integration was thus considered an end in itself, a way to civilize Europe's nations and citizens that balance of power could not achieve.

The integration pursued after 1945 was thus intended to have a civilizing effect, because cooperation via shared institutions would allow countries to become more tolerant and respectful of their neighbors. Moreover, the idea of integration through economic coordination was also designed to encourage citizens as well as governments to consider their mutual interests. This would prompt them to set aside selfishness and national boundaries in favor of an expanded conception of identity, a phenomenon known as cosmopolitanism (Beck 2006). Cosmopolitanism, the ability to put oneself in the shoes of someone in another country, was essential to reduce the appeal of nationalism.

Another benefit of eliminating national rivalries that appealed after 1945 was the positive impact this would have on democracy. By providing an institutional framework for peace and reconciliation, integration could make Europe safe for democracy. Prior to the Second World War, democratic states entangled in balancing strategies were obliged to spend heavily on defense rather than welfare and other socially useful ends. In addition, the security imperative facing states after 1918 had undermined new democracies in Europe. Democratic regimes in Italy and Germany were toppled by extremist leaders who promoted nationalism and did away with constitutional limits on the exercise of power. These ideas were popular among citizens frightened that democracy was ill equipped to provide security and prosperity in a hostile international climate. Hence reducing inter-state rivalry was a means to encourage democratic consolidation, allowing governments to help citizens' wellbeing rather than prepare for possible war (Mazower 1998).

This peace justification for unity has proved very potent, especially among the six West European states that took the first concrete steps toward integration after 1945 (see Section 2.2). Belgium, the Netherlands, Luxembourg, and Italy had suffered repeatedly from Franco-German rivalry; all six thus understood the need to limit state sovereignty and nationalism. Yet this justification continued to prove important in the development of integration in the second half of the twentieth century. This can be seen in the period after the end of the Cold War, when membership of what became the EU expanded greatly.

The fall of the Berlin Wall in November 1989, which marked the ideological division of Europe between the capitalist West and the communist East (to be discussed in detail in Section 2.1), left a question mark over the future of Germany – which had been divided into two since 1945 – and of the former Soviet satellite states in Eastern Europe. In this novel context, European leaders again made the case for European integration as a means to prevent the re-emergence of nationalism. As the then French President François Mitterrand explained, "nationalism is war." Tightening the bonds of integration was thus promoted in this period as a means to keep Europe at peace. Indeed, in 1992 French citizens – who had a direct vote on whether to accept the treaty creating the EU – were told by politicians that spurning integration would mean Germany going it alone. Without more integration to accompany German reunification, the latter process could revert to continental dominance – or worse (Criddle 1993). Similarly, the 2004 enlargement of the EU so as to include in it Central and Eastern European countries was commonly justified in terms of its pacifying or civilizing effects. Spreading integration eastwards was seen as

a way to stabilize countries that had little democratic experience and in some cases har-
bored unresolved territorial claims and grudges over the treatment of national minorities
living abroad (Schimmelfennig 2003).

Up until the 1990s, European leaders came from generations that had either lived
through the Second World War – if not also through the First – or experienced firsthand
the ruined lives and shattered societies left behind after 1945. Today's generation of
leaders is remote from the horrors of warfare, something also true of their electorates.
Indeed, such has been the success of reconciliation and of leaving behind the balance
of power system that it is easy to forget that Europe was once the most militarized part
of the globe (Sheehan 2008). Nevertheless, the peace justification still plays a role in the
political discourse accompanying integration. During crisis talks in 2010 over emergency loans to Ireland, Herman Van Rompuy, president of the European Council,
argued that "the biggest enemy of Europe today is fear. Fear leads to egoism, egoism
leads to nationalism, and nationalism leads to war" (EU Observer 2010). Indeed, in
recognition of what the EU has accomplished and also in order to give it support in a
time of crisis, the Nobel Prize Committee awarded it the 2012 Nobel Peace Prize.

One flaw in this justification, though, particularly from a citizen's perspective, is that
it neglects certain positive features of national identity in Europe. For instance, whereas
nationalism in Germany in the first half of the twentieth century was military and
antagonistic, national pride in Nordic countries is associated with protecting democracy
and promoting social equality. Pride in what their own countries have achieved in the
past – whether **social democracy** in Scandinavia, secular education in France, or fighting Nazi Germany in Great Britain – means that few EU citizens are as anti-national as
the Irish author Colm Tóibín. Writing in 2008, he explained: "I support the European
project as a way of protecting me from Irish politicians. I voted for [the] Lisbon [Treaty],
not because I wanted to follow the Irish political establishment but because I despise it
and need protection from it" (Tóibín 2008). Since national identity and patriotism still
matter in Europe, there is a limit to how far integration just for the sake of peace can
be justified. Another persuasive justification regarding the instrumental benefit of unity
exists: the way in which it helps improve prosperity.

1.4   The Prosperity Justification for Unity

One of the most powerful and successful justifications for European unity is the claim
that it is a unique mechanism for enhancing prosperity across Europe. This argument
was used at the end of the Second World War, when Western Europe urgently needed
economic reconstruction. Since then it has remained extremely pertinent: in the 1970s,
when Europe suffered from the oil crisis; in the 1980s, when national economies stag-
nated in comparison to those of the US and Japan; in the 1990s, when enlargement to
include the struggling but low-wage cost economies of Eastern Europe became possible;
in the 2000s and beyond, when globalization and the financial crisis squeezed both
ordinary citizens' standard of living and government spending. Improving growth in
Europe has thus been a central political preoccupation for several decades, a feeling
reinforced by anxious comparisons with major rival economies (see Table 1.1).

Table 1.1 Average GDP growth of large economies, 1970–2009

	1970–1980	1980–1990	1990–2000	2000–2009
EU (15 until 2000)	3.02	2.42	2.02	1.5
USA	3.28	3.20	3.21	1.82
Japan	4.47	4.01	1.27	0.7
India	-	5.7	5.5	7
China	-	9.2	9.7	10.2

Source: data from EUROSTAT, World Bank

National politicians have thus looked to integration when they wanted to provide opportunities for improving economic growth through participation in a bigger free market area. The idea of creating a continental-sized economy by abolishing national customs barriers was already present in Briand's plan for European Union (see Section 1.3). The 1930s were a decade when European countries turned their backs on free trade – a move seen as detrimental to growth and prosperity, which further under-mined inter-state relations (Mazower 1998, 104–137). On the basis of this historical experience, economic justifications for unity became particularly persuasive and have been used repeatedly (see Box 1.3).

Box 1.3   Case Study: The Prosperity Justification in Action

EU officials are very active in making the economic case for European integration. This was perhaps most evident in the 1988 Cecchini report for the European Commission, which specified the costs of "non-Europe" – in other words the productivity and growth benefits lost by not having a fully integrated market. The report predicted that Europe's gross domestic product (GDP) could grow by an extra 4–7 percent, if the EEC dismantled national practices discriminating against foreign trade and introduced Europe-wide regulatory standards for making and selling goods. British Prime Minister Margaret Thatcher – not ideologically inclined to transfer powers away from her government – accepted this kind of argument. She signed up to the Single European Act (1986), which was designed to help complete a single market. This meant giving up national control over the economy in certain areas in return for benefiting from enhanced economic growth and better prospects for British businesses (George 1998). In this context, integration was preferred to national sovereignty on the basis of economic ben-efits otherwise unavailable, a logic that also applied to the creation of the euro. Of course, citizens and governments do not always find this logic convincing. Denmark, Sweden, and the United Kingdom have chosen to retain their national currencies, in order to keep greater control over fundamental aspects of economic policy such as interest rates and devaluation. This example shows there are limits to how persuasive the prosperity justification can be.

After 1945 the removal of customs barriers was promoted as a way of making European economies more competitive, as well as more interlinked. That is, economic competition within an expanded market area was associated with positive developments such as allowing firms to innovate, improved access to capital, and creating a better business environment generally. Indeed in certain countries politicians, as well as citizens and firms, have tended to see integration as a means of stimulating domestic socio-economic reforms. The economic justification here, then, is about the benefits of adapting national practices to a more competitive and rule-based order. For instance, generations of Italian leaders have promoted integration as a means of modernizing socio-economic relations and thereby overcoming clientelism, or even corruption (Ferrara and Gualmini 2000).

The single European currency, the euro (used by 17 EU countries in 2013), is perhaps the best practical example of this idea that integration can stimulate European economies into becoming more competitive globally. The prosperity justification behind the euro was that a shared currency would spur growth by removing the transaction charges associated with converting currencies when trading goods or services and by stimulating price competition across an integrated market. In turn, this would help control inflation, allowing for lower interest rates and further boosting investment. Additionally, the new currency came with a Stability and Growth Pact designed to prevent countries from running large budget deficits and thereby forcing them to control public spending (see Section 5.2). Hence the euro was expected to provide long-term beneficial changes that politicians otherwise could not implement (Marsh 2009). Of course, the results in practice have not necessarily lived up to these expectations (see Chapter 12 for a discussion of the Eurozone crisis).

The prosperity justification is further complicated by the fact that participation in European integration can actually be expensive for governments. All EU member states contribute to a common budget, which is used to finance common policies. This spending, notably the subsidies to farmers and the money spent on infrastructure in poorer regions, is not spread evenly across Europe. Consequently some countries end up as net beneficiaries of EU spending, while others are net contributors (see Section 5.1). In the latter there is heated political debate as to whether integration represents good value for money. Scandals involving EU money – such as the €720,000 of EU regional development funds intended to pay for an Elton John concert in Naples and subsequently paid back – get a lot of attention. This perception that EU money is not necessarily well spent makes citizens in net contributor countries wary about financing integration through their taxes.

Hence, while there is a shared desire for economic growth through integration, this attitude has yet to translate into a great deal of financial solidarity across European countries. Citizens and governments want the economic benefits of integration but, especially in the wealthier countries, they remain skeptical about redistributing prosperity from richer to poorer regions.

1.5   The Strengthening State Capacity Justification for Unity

As opposed to moral (peace) or economic (prosperity) justifications, another way of explaining the merit of European unity is to point to what it allows countries to achieve that they otherwise cannot manage alone. Hence this justification concerns the way in which creating shared institutions to manage common policy issues permits national governments to do more for their citizens. This argument has been put forward most forcefully by the British historian Alan Milward, who claims that integration effectively rescued the nation-state in Europe. Prior to integration, small and large countries alike had struggled to remain politically independent and prosper economically – that is, to actually succeed as sovereign states. So transferring a limited set of policy competences to institutions like the European Commission has definitely been worth it, as all EU countries are now in a position to achieve both (Milward 1992).

This justification is not just about economic growth, but about the overall policy effectiveness made possible by unity in all manner of important administrative tasks. In many policy areas, as a result of integration, EU member states now have instruments to meet the needs of their citizens. This is illustrated by examples such as the European Arrest Warrant, which expedites the return of suspected criminals from other EU countries; the Blue Card visa, which permits the recruitment of highly skilled immigrants; or the Community Trade Mark system, which protects intellectual property across national borders and globally. A small European country acting alone on the global stage would find it harder to perform all these tasks. These examples thus highlight how unity provides states with new capacities for delivering policies that concern citizens in areas such as justice, immigration, and global trade.

Yet there are important political disagreements within and across EU countries about what integration can best achieve with regard to strengthening state capacity. That is, politicians and parties are split over what state capacities integration should strengthen. On one side there are those who think that integration should help EU countries resist globalization and protect existing social policies; on the other side, there are those who believe that integration is the best way for Europe to adjust to the new realities of a globally interconnected world.

In France, for instance, European integration has traditionally been justified as a way to limit the effects of globalization on the social policies of the French state (Schmidt 2007). French politicians thus see integration as a means of reducing the pressure to lower taxes and social spending. This pressure exists because countries compete for investment and jobs in a globalized world where capital and highly qualified labor are very mobile. By uniting their forces, countries can promote common rules – for instance European-wide standards of social protection, or taxes on financial transactions to raise funds – rather than accept shedding government programs. Nicolas Sarkozy (France's president, 2007–2012) illustrated this attitude of using integration to protect jobs and standards of living by calling for a "buy European" law to compel governments to purchase only European-made goods in public procurement.

This idea of strengthening state capacities through measures associated with economic protectionism is usually articulated by social–democratic or left-of-center political parties. These parties support integration via the creation of a shared economic space, which involves a loss of national autonomy over economic and social policy. However, in return, they wish to see that European-level social regulation helps preserve national welfare traditions such as generous pension rights, job protection, subsidized health care, as well as high standards of sickness and housing benefits. Their ambition is thus to use integration as a means of preserving social democracy – something that individual countries cannot sustain if European countries compete on lowering taxes and on attracting investment through lower social protection. Strengthening state capacity via integration, on this understanding, depends on limiting how far EU countries can compete among themselves, so as to avoid achieving unity at the expense of social–democratic principles. Keenly aware that integration means giving up certain powers over economic and social policy, left-of-center parties face a dilemma over whether to accept integration if it is not accompanied by concrete attempts to extend social democracy in Europe (Dimitrakopoulos 2010).

Liberal and center-right parties hold a different perspective on which state capacities integration should benefit. They want EU rules and increased inter-state cooperation actually to reduce protectionism and to stimulate reform of the European **welfare state**, which they argue makes firms uncompetitive in a globalized world. Whereas social democrats want to strengthen the state's capacity to prevent the phenomenon of globalization from increasing socio-economic inequalities, those on the other side of the political divide want to strengthen the state's ability to adapt to globalization by embracing open markets. Free market liberals and the center-right see the ability to use the EU to reform national policies on employment rights, pensions, labor mobility, as the best way to adapt to globalization, that is, allowing EU countries to remain prosperous and fund more suitable welfare policies. Liberal and right-of-center parties face their own dilemma over integration, because there is a risk that pooling competences means sharing control over key economic policies with countries and governments that want protection from rather than adaptation to globalization. This is the quandary spelled out by former British Prime Minister Margaret Thatcher, when, already in 1988, she observed that "we have not successfully rolled back the frontiers of the state in Britain, only to see them re-imposed at a European level."

Consequently there is no shared consensus about what exactly European unity should do to strengthen the state. What matters, though, is that politicians and citizens across party divides see integration as a mechanism for achieving something that individual countries cannot do on their own. As in the peace and prosperity justifications, here too the idea of European unity constitutes a political objective for transcending state sovereignty.

1.6   Concluding Summary

Europe as a geographical term exists alongside a political definition, indicating what is different about this western tip of Eurasia. The oldest political definition of Europe was in terms of a common religious identity based on Christianity. Hence Christendom denoted separateness from the peoples to the east, notably the powerful Muslim Turks. With the development of the territorial sovereign state in the seventeenth century, a secular definition of Europe arose. This distinguished Europe in terms of a continent divided into sovereign states, none being more powerful than the rest combined. Europe was said to function as a republic because states balanced against one another to prevent the complete dominance of any single country.

The balance of power between these states was not a peaceful order. Thinkers such as William Penn, Abbot Saint Pierre, or Immanuel Kant thus developed plans for a more peaceful system based on European unity. They looked to collective security to overcome the deficiencies of balancing. This meant that states would lose the right to resort to force; in its place would come mutual dispute settlement, enforced through collective action if a state refused to play by the rules. Such projects relied on the fact that even the most powerful European state could be kept in check by the combined strength of the others. However, these proposals came to naught – states prized their sovereignty too highly, while monarchs, unlike ordinary citizens, were in any case insulated from the sufferings wrought by war.

It was only after the horrors of the First World War that governments accepted to implement collective security, which they did in the form of the League of Nations. In 1920s' Europe there was a cultural and political movement in favor of unity. This was seen as a means of moral regeneration, but also as one of economic reconstruction, designed to help fend off communism and avoid losing influence to the New World. Aristide Briand's call for a European Union in 1929 suited the zeitgeist; but other states, already concerned about the weakness of the League of Nations, did not muster much enthusiasm. This project, like the League itself, foundered and Europe returned to war.

Hence the need for peace is the original justification for uniting the continent. From this perspective, European unity is a way to overcome the balance of power system – which requires constant preparation for war, engendering a security dilemma. In addition, a peaceful order based on states working together enables civilized relations between citizens and governments, thereby overcoming the artificial enmities inspired by nationalism. Circumscribing sovereignty and nationalism are not the only justifications put forward for unity. Stimulating economic growth by eliminating obstacles to trade between European countries is another powerful justification. This prosperity justification sees economic benefits as a central component of unity. Finally, there is a justification for unity in terms of strengthening state capacities. That is, working together not only allows for peace and prosperity but also enables governments to tackle complex problems in a world where individual European states are no longer so powerful. Acting together permits states to implement better policies in areas such as justice, immigration, and global trade, although there is stark disagreement about whether unity should help sustain national welfare provisions or encourage reform.

Guide to Further Reading

Heater, D. 1992. *The Idea of European Unity*. Leicester: Leicester University Press.
    Comprehensive historical account of the actors and motives behind European unity; concise and highly accessible.
    Mazower, M. 1998. *Dark Continent: Europe's Twentieth Century*. New York: Knopf.
    A provocative work chronicling how and why democracy in Europe was constantly under threat in the first half of the twentieth century before finding a successful institutional form after 1945.
    Milward, A. 1992. *The European Rescue of the Nation-State*. London: Routledge.

A bold, historically based thesis about how integration provided a means to reinvigorate the state, allowing national governments to satisfy the socio-economic needs of citizens.

Discussion Questions

1   How and why has Europe been defined as a separate continent? What do these definitions imply about the question of which countries are considered European?
2   What were the characteristic features of the balance of power in Europe prior to integration and why did they make for a violent inter-state order?
3   What remedy did European thinkers propose for overcoming power balancing? How similar were the proposals of William Penn, Abbot Saint Pierre, and Immanuel Kant?
4   Why is nationalism also considered deleterious for inter-state relations in Europe? How is integration supposed to minimize the negative facets of nationalism?
5   In what way can European unity be said to strengthen the state and how does European integration affect social democracy?

Web Resources

This book is supported by a companion website, which can be found at www.wiley.com/go/glencross. There you will find a list of the web links referred to in this chapter wherever you see a "Web" icon in the page margins. In addition, you will find a list of further relevant online resources such as websites for EU institutions, political groups, archives, and think tanks, information on studying abroad, and biographies of key figures. You will also find self-assessment tools in the form of flashcards and independent study questions developed specifically for this chapter.

Glossary

Christendom
   An historical definition of Europe as a continent united by a shared Christian identity. In the Middle Ages, the notion of a *respublica Christiana* ("Christian republic") served a political end: to distinguish Europeans from Muslim Turks and to encourage crusaders to fight the latter.

Collective security
   Inter-state arrangement whereby members agree to resolve their differences through negotiation. This system rests on a joint pledge to combine forces in order to deter, or even defeat, a member that fails to abide by collective decisions.

Concert of Europe
   Informal arrangement (1815–circa 1890) between major European powers to manage inter-state disputes peacefully, so as to avoid domestic political unrest like that occur-

ring during the Napoleonic wars. The system functioned for a while through *ad hoc* conferences, but consensus among major powers eventually broke down.

Economic protectionism

Government policy of shielding domestic firms from foreign competition via high import tariffs and other trade barriers. It is done for the sake of protecting jobs or politically favored industries, but it invariably produces a counter-response leaving nations worse off.

League of Nations

Collective security organization established in 1919 to manage inter-state conflict peacefully. After some initial successes, it failed to restrain states from resorting to war, notably in 1939.

Nationalism

Political ideology that sees the state as the territorial expression of a particular nation, whose people share a common national identity. More extreme versions see inter-state rivalry as a competition between nations over which ethnic group or national values will prevail.

Security dilemma

Phrase used in international relations to refer to the insecurity produced when countries seek to make themselves safer through alliances or arms build-ups. Such moves encourage other states to do the same, thereby potentially creating a spiral effect that renders all countries less secure.

Social democracy

Center-left political ideology, highly successful in post-war Western Europe. Advocates social rights (good healthcare, pension, and sickness provisions) and full employment as an essential element of a healthy democracy. It is based on the principle that government must intervene in the economy to attain these goals and prevent capitalism from creating extreme inequalities.

Welfare state

An economic order based on government providing essential services such as healthcare, pensions, or sickness benefits. Welfare is typically redistributive, i.e. dependent on transfers from the wealthy to the less well off, funded through taxation.

References

Beck, Ulrich. 2006. *The Cosmopolitan Vision*. Cambridge: Polity.

Criddle, Byron. 1993. "The French Referendum on the Maastricht Treaty September 1992." *Parliamentary Affairs*, 46: 228–238.

Den Boer, Pim. 1993. "Europe to 1914: The Making of an Idea." In Kevin Wilson and Jan van der Dussen eds., *The History of the Idea of Europe*, 1–59. London: Routledge.

Deudney, Daniel. 2008. *Bounding Power: Republican Security Theory from the Polis to the Global Village*. Princeton, NJ: Princeton University Press.

Dimitrakopoulos, Dionyssis, ed. 2010. *Social Democracy and European Integration: The Politics of Preference Formation.* London: Routledge.

Doyle, Michael W. 1983. "Kant, Liberal Legacies, and Foreign Affairs." *Philosophy and Public Affairs*, 12: 205–235. Available at http://www.jstor.org/stable/2265298 (accessed July 15, 2012).

Elrod, Richard B. 1976. "The Concert of Europe: A Fresh Look at an International System." *World Politics*, 28: 159–174. DOI: 10.2307/2009888.

EU Observer. 2010. "EU President Issues Stark Warning against Nationalism." *EU Observer*, November 10. Available at http://euobserver.com/institutional/31240

Ferrara, Maurizio, and Elisabetta Gualmini. 2000. "Italy: Rescue from Without?" In Fritz W. Scharpf and Vivien A. Schmidt, eds., *Welfare and Work in the Open Economy, Volume 2: Diverse Responses to Common Challenges*, 351–398. Oxford: Oxford University Press.

George, Stephen. 1998. *An Awkward Partner: Britain in the European Community.* Oxford: Oxford University Press.

Gilbert, Martin. 2012. *Churchill: The Power of Words.* London: Transworld Publishers.

Heater, Derek. 1992. *The Idea of European Unity.* Basingstoke: Palgrave Macmillan.

Hont, Istvan. 2005. *Jealousy of Trade: International Competition and the Nation-State in Historical Perspective.* Cambridge, MA: Belknap Press.

Jervis, Robert. 1978. "Cooperation under the Security Dilemma." *World Politics*, 30: 167–214. DOI: 10.2307/2009958

Le Goff, Jacques. 2005. *The Birth of Europe.* Oxford: Blackwell.

Marsh, David. 2009. *The Euro: The Politics of the New Global Currency.* New Haven, CT: Yale University Press.

Mazower, Mark. 1998. *Dark Continent: Europe's Twentieth Century.* London: Allen Lane.

Milward, Alan S. 1992. *The European Rescue of the Nation-State.* London: Routledge.

Nexon, Daniel H. 2009. *The Struggle for Power in Early Modern Europe: Religious Conflict, Dynastic Empires, and International Change.* Princeton, NJ: Princeton University Press.

Schimmelfennig, Frank. 2003. *The EU, NATO and the Integration of Europe: Rules and Rhetoric.* Cambridge: Cambridge University Press.

Schmidt, H. D. 1966. "The Establishment of 'Europe' as a Political Expression." *The Historical Journal*, 9: 172–178. DOI: 10.1017/S0018246X00026509

Schmidt, Vivien. 2007. "Trapped by Their Ideas: French Elites' Discourses of European Integration and Globalization." *Journal of European Public Policy*, 14: 992–1009. DOI: 10.1080/13501760701576494

Sheehan, James J. 2008. *Where Have All the Soldiers Gone? The Transformation of Modern Europe.* New York: Houghton Mifflin.

Tóibín, Colm. 2008. "A Godsend to Every Crank in Ireland: On the Left or on the Right." *The Guardian*, June 14. Available at http://www.guardian.co.uk/world/2008/jun/14/ireland.eu (accessed July 16, 2012).

2

The Institutional Development of European Integration, 1945–1973

Contents

Learning Objectives

- to identify the key problems facing Western Europe after 1945;
- to analyze the role played by the USA in post-war European security;
- to contrast the different national interests behind Franco-German reconciliation;
- to assess the impact of the failure of the EDC on the trajectory of integration;
- to distinguish between the policy objectives of the ECSC and those of the EEC;
- to evaluate why de Gaulle wanted to change the EEC from within and rejected British entry.

The Politics of European Integration: Political Union or a House Divided?, First Edition. Andrew Glencross.
© 2014 Andrew Glencross. Published 2014 by Blackwell Publishing Ltd.

Timeline of Key Events 2.1: End of Second World War to UK Accession to EEC (1945–1973)

1945 May	Nazi Germany surrenders; war in Europe ends; Germany occupied by France, Great Britain, the Soviet Union, and the USA
1945–1947	Soviet Union takes control of Eastern Europe
1947 March	US President Harry Truman launches official doctrine of containing communism
1948 May	Congress of Europe meets in The Hague to discuss European integration
1949 April	Creation of NATO to provide security for Western Europe
May	Creation of the Federal Republic of Germany by merging French, British and American-occupied zones
1950 May	Schuman Declaration calling for Franco-German reconciliation
	Outbreak of Korean War
1951 April	European Coal and Steel Community Treaty signed in Paris
1952 May	Signature of European Defense Community (EDC) Treaty
1953 March	Announcement of European Political Community (EPC) plan for common foreign policy
1954 August	EDC and EPC projects collapse as French Parliament refuses to ratify EDC
1955 May	West Germany joins NATO
June	Six ECSC states meet to discuss common market project
1957 March	EEC Treaty and EURATOM Treaty signed in Rome
1960 May	European Free Trade Association (EFTA) launched as rival free trade agreement
1962 July	Common Agricultural Policy launched
1963 January	French President Charles de Gaulle vetoes British membership of the EEC
1965 July	De Gaulle provokes "empty chair crisis," resolved in January 1966 through "Luxembourg Compromise"
1970 June	Membership negotiations open with Great Britain, Denmark, Ireland, and Norway
1973 January	Great Britain, Denmark, and Ireland join EEC

2.0   Introduction: Uniting for Peace

Europe is not unique in having a history of intense rivalries among its peoples and frequent inter-state warfare. Rather the specificity of Europe since the last great military conflict – the Second World War – is the ability of its states to establish political institutions for lasting cooperation on an ever increasing range of policy issues. The growth and striking success of these supranational institutions – meaning that they are beyond the state – is what makes European integration stand out. Other instances of regional cooperation have not gone as far as the EU in creating a binding legal and political framework that reduces member states' policy autonomy.

The unprecedented atrocities and catastrophic cost of the Second World War provided the impetus for Europe's countries to begin supranational cooperation, as explained in Section 2.1. With the defeat of Nazi Germany in May 1945, most of Europe's leaders and citizens felt an acute need for a genuine alternative to balance of power politics (for which see Box 1.2). This meant finally accepting limitations on states' sovereignty, that is, on political independence. Unfortunately this premise was not accepted by Stalin, the ruler of the Soviet Union, whose army then occupied most of Eastern Europe. Distrustful of German intentions and of western capitalism, he preferred to continue relying on the strength of his country to dissuade aggression. Thus he blocked Soviet and Eastern European participation in new institutions for peace that would inevitably mean sharing decision-making with others, including defeated Germany and capitalist regimes. This is why European integration first took root only in Western Europe.

Integration in Western Europe was preoccupied with economic considerations as well as with security. With the USA accepting to help with the latter, leaders in France and West Germany looked to create institutions to enhance prosperity and rebuild shattered economies. As explained in Section 2.2, integration initially took the form of the European Coal and Steel Community (ECSC), an organization aimed at building trust between former belligerents by pooling control over the material resources used to wage war. Security issues returned to the agenda, however, as western diplomats and statesmen debated the need for West Germany to rearm in order to join the **North Atlantic Treaty Organization (NATO)**, the defensive alliance against the Soviet Union. In this context, a bold proposal for political and military union – a **European Defence Community (EDC)** and a **European Political Community (EPC)** – in Western Europe was floated, as discussed in detail in Section 2.3.

The failure of this radical idea of union did not spell the demise of integration. Instead, building on the ECSC, a plan was launched to create a single market, free of tariffs and other impediments to the free movement of goods, services, people, and capital. Named the European Economic Community (EEC), this ambitious treaty again relied on **Franco-German reconciliation** and on member states' willingness to cede sovereignty to supranational institutions. The incentive, as analyzed in Section 2.4, was again economic: unshackling intra-European commerce to stimulate economic growth and benefiting governments, businesses, and citizens alike. Furthermore, participation in the EEC was designed to build trust and to cement linkages between the peoples and politicians of Western Europe, making a return to hostilities an unthinkable proposition.

These developments proceeded without the participation of the United Kingdom, although its leaders began trying to join the EEC in the 1960s. This same decade was a formative period during which the EEC faced internal challenges about designing a major policy, the **Common Agricultural Policy (CAP)**, and about finding a way to implement supranational decision-making – key topics discussed in Section 2.5. The president of France, General Charles de Gaulle, not only refused to countenance the entry of the United Kingdom but also tried to reconfigure EEC decision-making so as to keep control over integration. It was only after these struggles were resolved – facilitated as they were by de Gaulle's fall from power – that supranational integration could continue and gain new participants. Hence the chapter ends with the first enlargement of the EEC in 1973.

2.1   The Struggle to Resolve Post-War Security and Economic Issues, 1945–1951

The context for organizing the uniting of Western Europe after the war involved two fundamental security quandaries alongside the pressing need to rebuild shattered economies. Both security questions revolved around the future status of Germany, which was occupied by French, British, US, and Soviet troops. Finding a cooperative solution was problematic given Stalin's deep split with its wartime allies, the USA and Great Britain, over how to reorganize liberated Europe, including the lands to the east of Germany as well as allied-occupied Germany itself (Judt 2006). Originally, Great Britain and the USA wanted to see free elections held in the formerly German-occupied countries of Hungary, Poland, and Czechoslovakia. As democracies, Great Britain and the USA wanted citizens in these countries to decide freely what kind of political system to adopt. This policy was unacceptable to Stalin, who believed that capitalism was inherently aggressive and who wanted to impose communism on the countries close to and bordering the Soviet Union. Installing friendly communist regimes there was intended to create a huge buffer zone with the capitalist West.

Stalin's plan was rendered possible by the fact that the Soviet Union's enormous Red Army (numbering over 10 million) had effectively gained control of Eastern Europe during its successful campaign against Nazi Germany. By late 1945, the USA and Great Britain reluctantly acquiesced to the Soviet Union's often bloody imposition of communist rule throughout Eastern Europe. Ideological rivalry and mistrust between Stalin's Soviet Union and the capitalist world – which turned into an unofficial Cold War by the time of the adoption of the Truman Doctrine in 1947 – rendered East–West cooperation over Germany impossible (Gaddis 2006). Consequently the country was divided into two: East Germany under Soviet rule, and West Germany under shared British, French, and American rule.

The first security dilemma facing the US and its West European allies, therefore, was over the role that West Germany would play in moves to form a defensive alliance against a Soviet bloc perceived as inherently aggressive. Here it was the US that pushed for a security arrangement that would enable West Germany to participate militarily in such an alliance. Many West European countries were worried by this proposal; they wanted an American security commitment to Western Europe without necessarily allowing for German re-armament. This issue was further complicated by a second security issue: the persistence of French claims over resources in the area of Germany called the Ruhrgebiet, Europe's most industrialized region, and territorial claims over the Saar region, a former French province. As the heart of Germany's industrial might (coal, steel, and chemicals), the Ruhrgebiet was also the key to its military power. France, a country that had experienced three hugely costly German invasions in less than a century (1870–1871, 1914–1918, 1940–1945), was understandably wary of its great rival's potential resurgence. Hence French politicians were not only diffident about incorporating West Germany into a common defense system; they also sought to exercise control over Germany's industrial heartland, especially the Saar, which became a French protectorate in 1947 (Gillingham 2003).

Alongside these two security issues, the countries of Western Europe were grappling with the question of how best to rebuild their shattered economies. The US plan for global post-war prosperity was based on the opening up of international trade. This would be done by reducing tariffs on the exchange of goods (through the Global Agreement on Tariffs and Trade, precursor to today's World Trade Organization) and by creating a system for monetary stability (via the International Monetary Fund). The overall arrangement for an open world economy was known as the Bretton Woods system (Ikenberry 2001, 163–214). Ultimately this economic agenda was linked to improving relations between states, because free trade fosters interdependence and shared interests.

Global economic interdependence could thus hopefully prevent a return to the economic nationalism seen in the 1930s. Yet this interdependence was conditional on European economies being strong enough to participate in global trade. This was far from a given, with Europe suffering from poverty, destroyed infrastructure, and weak agricultural production. To remedy this problem, the US launched its 1947 Marshall Plan of financial assistance to Europe. The aim was, on the one hand, to anchor Western European countries into the system of international trade as quickly as possible. On the other hand, the plan aimed to stimulate economic growth in order to prevent citizens from turning toward communism in order to relieve their economic woes – communist parties being particularly strong in France and Italy. Officially known as the European Recovery Program, the Marshall Plan provided 13 billion US dollars (the equivalent of 90 billion today) in the knowledge that support for democracy in Western Europe depended on a speedy return to prosperity (Schain 2001). Cementing the division of East and West, Stalin blocked the US offer of extending this aid to countries in Eastern Europe.

Despite the success of the Marshall Plan, by the late 1940s plans for uniting Western Europe were blocked. This was due to three differing national interests. The United States wanted a strong West Germany to help share the burden of deterring the Soviet Union; at the time many US policy-makers thought their country should avoid entangling alliances in Europe (Lundestad 1998). France desired lasting control over West Germany's industrial might and was wary of accepting German rearmament. Finally, leaders in West Germany – especially Konrad Adenauer, the founder of the important Christian Democrat Party – advocated the end of military occupation and the creation of a sovereign state (Granieri 2003).

While political elites disputed Western Europe's future, there were various civil society initiatives that tried to seize the moment for reorganizing Europe. Advocates of creating a federally united Europe were particularly prominent in this period (Burgess 2000). Much of the impetus for this European federalist movement came from Altiero Spinelli, a leading anti-fascist in wartime Italy. In 1941 he co-authored the *Ventotene Manifesto*, a call to arms for opposing fascism and creating a European federation that would end the violent inter-state rivalry inevitably produced, he argued, by balance of power. During the Second World War, this message was warmly received among resistance groups throughout Nazi-occupied Europe, eventually spawning the Union of European Federalists founded in 1946. Many of these federalist activists participated in the 1948 Hague Congress in the Netherlands – a private meeting of politicians, labor union leaders, and intellectuals from both East and West. Federalists hoped to use this meeting to design a constitution for Europe; but this goal was only shared by a minority of participants.

Although it did not lead to a federally united Europe, the Hague Congress achieved lasting significance. It provided the inspiration for the **Council of Europe**, a human rights organization, and for its European Convention on Human Rights, which was designed to protect citizens throughout Europe against mischief done by their own state. This Convention has 47 state signatories (covering most of the continent) and allows individuals to bring cases against a state, for alleged violations of fundamental rights, to the European Court of Human Rights. The latter is not an EU institution, although it is often confused with the Court of Justice of the EU (CJEU), the top EU court.

Notwithstanding the accomplishments of the Hague Congress, the need for a diplomatic settlement to resolve Western Europe's security and economic issues remained pressing. In response to both US calls to foster West German economic development and Adenauer's campaign for restoring sovereignty, France accepted the creation of the German Federal Republic in May 1949. At this point, however, the Saar remained a French protectorate subject to future diplomatic negotiations. The counterpart to this deal was a formal American pledge for the USA to remain a guarantor of West European security via NATO. This reassured Britain and France: they considered it was imperative to have a US military presence in Europe in order to coordinate the defensive posture against the Soviet Union and to keep watch over West Germany's rearmament. The North Atlantic Treaty was signed in 1949 and marked the first peacetime American military alliance. Whereas after the First World War the US Senate had refused to participate in stabilizing the international system through the League of Nations, the creation of NATO proved America's new determination to play a global role (Trachtenberg 1999, 95–145).

Reliance on this unprecedented US security guarantee – based on collective defense in case any alliance member is attacked – was controversial from the outset and remains so to this day (see Box 2.1). Then as now, the guarantee was considered by some (on both sides of the Atlantic) a sign of Europe's weakness and unwillingness to solve its own security issues. Britain and France were also concerned about the reliability of the USA's military commitment. To hedge against possible US withdrawal, these two countries eventually developed their own nuclear weapons. For France, fears of the US reneging on its commitment to defend Europe were mixed with an awareness that NATO offered no political mechanism for supervising West Germany's economic reconstruction. This was seen as a crucial weakness, given the close relationship between economic and military power. Moreover, French plans for modernizing the country's own economy depended on privileged access to German resources, especially fuel coke essential for the production of steel. Consequently, to solve the problem of economic reconstruction and further cement a peaceful inter-state order, France proposed a bold initiative: to create a European Coal and Steel Community (ECSC) in order to make war "materially impossible."

2.2   The Creation of the European Coal and Steel Community (ECSC) in 1951

The signature of the ECSC Treaty in 1951 provided the institutional framework for settling the Ruhr and Saar problems and established a precedent for Franco-German

Box 2.1   Key Debate: European Integration and NATO

Since day one European integration has taken place under the umbrella of an American security guarantee. Originally, NATO was intended to secure Western Europe from Soviet aggression. The benefit of this arrangement was not only that the US underwrote a large proportion of the cost of deterring the Soviet Union. Additionally, the US military presence in Europe (numbering in the 100,000s at the height of the Cold War) served as a safeguard against possible German military resurgence and made it redundant for Germany to acquire nuclear weapons. However, reliance on NATO has been seen by some as enfeebling and as a constraint on Europe's freedom of foreign-policy action, even though not all NATO members belong to the EU and vice versa. During the 1960s, French President Charles de Gaulle wanted Europe to formulate an independent foreign policy that would break the superpower duopoly between the US and the Soviet Union (Bozo 2001). To achieve this, he withdrew France from NATO's integrated military command (the planning and organizational part, not the mutual assistance pledge) in 1966. But he failed to persuade other countries to follow his lead in creating a more independent European foreign policy, which was seen primarily as a cloak for French interests. After the fall of the Berlin Wall in 1989, NATO remained a crucial institution as the countries of Eastern Europe, including former Soviet republics in the Baltic, sought a security guarantee against Russia. This led to the eastward expansion of NATO, which proved highly controversial because Russia perceives it as a form of encirclement and interference in its backyard. Europe's continuing military reliance on the US was obvious in the 1990s, when ethnic conflict in the former Yugoslavia (1991–1995) and Kosovo (1999) required a US-led NATO effort to enforce the peace. These Balkan crises illustrated the continuing absence of a coordinated European security policy and the military ability to enforce it (Rathbun 2004). The EU's current relationship with NATO is explored in greater detail in 8.2.

cooperation that, it was hoped, would extend into other fields (Gillingham 2003). The ECSC resolved the Franco-German problem by creating more than mere institutions tasked to manage matters of economic policy in common. Its competences were very marginal compared to the ordinary business of government – the goal was a common market in coal and steel, but these were highly strategic industries underpinning military strength and economic modernization. The ECSC's key success was the creation of new precedents and expectations regarding the conduct of international politics in Western Europe. Indeed, its institutional architecture provided the blueprint for the future European Economic Community Treaty (1957).

The idea of creating a common market for steel and coal was first announced by French Foreign Minister Robert Schuman on May 9, 1950. The context for Schuman's announcement was the establishment of the German Federal Republic, the sovereign democratic country ruling West Germany, led by Konrad Adenauer. The return of German sovereignty led France to seek a further safeguard against possible future German economic and political domination of Europe.

Much of the credit for the ECSC plan belongs to Jean Monnet, a French entrepreneur and public servant, who as a key government planner of French economic modernization sought to increase West German trade with Europe. It was Monnet who insisted that the institutions of the ECSC should be *supranational* rather than *intergovernmental*, for the sake of decision-making efficacy (Dinan 2004). That is, the ECSC institutions were designed to be independent (supranational) and not controlled directly by representatives of the signatory states (intergovernmental), although ultimately a compromise arrangement mixing both was agreed upon (see Section 2.3). In the subsequent development of European institutions there has remained a fundamental tension between these two principles. Supranationalism, in the sense of institutional autonomy for proposing and monitoring policies, ensures that governments do not renege on their treaty commitments, while intergovernmentalism relates to national governments seeking to control decision-making (see Box 2.2).

The announcement of the ECSC plan, now known as the **Schuman Declaration** and celebrated annually in the EU as "Schuman Day" on May 9, was a bold appeal for inter-

---

Box 2.2   Key Concept: Supranationalism and Intergovernmentalism

The EU is distinguished by the strength of its supranational institutions, notably the Commission and the CJEU. The former scrutinizes EU member states' respect for treaty obligations and EU law. If a state is considered to be in breach of these rules, the Commission will bring a case against it to the CJEU, whose rulings are legally binding and must be followed by national courts and government. Failure to do so can result in financial penalties. These two bodies thus act independently of states' preferences. However, member states have insisted on retaining an important component of intergovernmentalism in the EU system in order to stay in control of policy-making. For instance, treaty reform or the admission of new members can only happen if all member states agree. The Council of the EU, which represents national governments, also votes by unanimity on matters of utmost national importance such as taxation, social security, and foreign policy: in other words all countries must agree, giving each a potential veto. Yet over time the number of policy areas in which states have a veto has been greatly reduced. Instead of vetoes, each national government has an allocated voting weight (ranging from 29 to 3, depending on population). Legislation requires a qualified majority vote in order to pass, representing, from 2014, 55 percent of the total national votes, as long as this accounts for 65 percent of the total EU population. By removing national vetoes, the spread of qualified majority vote marks a further stage in the development of supranationalism.

national cooperation, but there was no certainty that this would be well received in Europe's capitals. Schuman's plan called for Western Europe's coal and steel production to be placed "under a common High Authority, within the framework of an organization open to the participation of the other countries of Europe" (Schuman 1950). The text made specific reference to "the elimination of the age-old opposition of France and Germany" as the reason why control of coal and steel – the lifeblood of war – needed to be shared so as to make conflict "not merely unthinkable but materially impossible" (Schuman 1950). The more immediate aims were to modernize production in both industries, improve their supply on equal terms to member states, promote exports to third countries, and enhance coal and steel workers' standards of living. Creating an independent institution that would treat states equally but would nevertheless be binding on all of them represented "the first concrete foundation of a European federation." Hence the declaration recognized explicitly that "Europe will not be made all at once, or according to a single plan" (Schuman 1950), implying the need for piecemeal progress toward unity, which is exactly how the course of integration has proceeded since that time. Needless to say, advocates of a federalist Europe felt the ECSC plan was too timid. Federalists argued that the ECSC plan failed to appreciate that a more fundamental change to sovereignty was necessary in order to overcome the dysfunctionality of the state system in Europe (Glencross 2009).

The audience to whom the Schuman Declaration was addressed were the countries of Western Europe, especially Great Britain and West Germany, although neither had been consulted about the proposal. Great Britain, the country that had done most to safeguard democracy in Europe during the Second World War, was considered vitally important for ensuring the post-war stability of the continent. Small countries, such as Belgium and the Netherlands, looked upon Great Britain as a counterweight to potential French and West German dominance of supranational institutions. However, Britain's politicians were hostile to the principle of supranationalism per se, fearing a loss of sovereignty. Moreover, Britain's strategic orientation following the war was based on cultivating a privileged relationship with the USA and on transforming a decaying empire into a Commonwealth community of trade beneficial to British exports. European integration, it was feared, would interfere significantly with both these objectives. Thus Britain excluded itself from the ECSC, only joining the European Economic Community in 1973, although two earlier applications to join during the 1960s were vetoed by France (George 1998).

West Germany, by contrast, was very favorable to the Schuman plan. Adenauer was particularly struck by the fact that the ECSC promised to offer equal treatment to all states under the supervision of an independent, supranational authority. Given his struggle to establish a sovereign West German state, Adenauer realized that shared sovereignty was far better than limited sovereignty, since certain politicians in France still wanted political control over parts of the German territory should the ECSC fail. The benefits for West Germany's successful re-emergence in international politics were seen as so great that Adenauer was prepared to make the ECSC work even as a purely Franco-German institution. This was not necessary, as four other countries signed the ECSC Treaty in 1951: Italy, Belgium, the Netherlands, and Luxembourg. Three of these were small countries that had long been caught in the crossfire of Franco-German rivalry and so saw the obvious benefits of reconciliation and of abandoning the balance of power mentality; Italy, the weakest large state in Europe, believed that European integration offered the best chance for economic growth and for healing domestic political divisions. In all six member states, therefore, the goal of uniting for peace under a new supranational institutional framework coincided with perceived national interest (Milward 1992).

2.3   The Functioning of the ECSC and the Attempt at Full Military and Political Union, 1951–1957

The Schuman Declaration only contained an outline of what the ECSC institutions would look like; their definitive form was the product of nearly a year of hard-nosed diplomatic negotiations between the six member states. The first bone of contention concerned the principle of supranationalism. Monnet had insisted on this as the basis for an effective decision-making institution – the High Authority – to supervise the production and distribution of coal and steel, for which it could issue legally binding decisions. Members of the nine-member High Authority came from across the six ECSC countries. However, members had to pledge to defend the interests of the European whole rather than their respective nation states: they took the **Commissioner's Oath**, an oath EU commissioners still take to this day in front of the justices of the CJEU.

The Netherlands, however, strongly objected to leaving decision-making in the hands of the High Authority, which they expected to be dominated by Franco-German interests. At their insistence, the powers of the High Authority were diluted through the creation of a Council of Ministers (now called the Council of the EU) designed to represent member states' governments. This body would act as an intergovernmental counterweight supervising the decisions of the High Authority, to ensure the latter stuck to its purview over coal and steel matters. In addition to supervision from national governments, a Common Assembly drawn from national parliaments was created to provide additional oversight. Completing this trio of new institutions was a supranational court, the Court of Justice, designed to provide authoritative interpretations of the ECSC Treaty and its application, as well as to hear cases against member states involving ECSC law. Designing these institutions was complex, but deciding where to locate them was also politically sensitive. In an attempt to avoid chauvinism and show its sincerity toward reconciliation, West Germany did not stake a claim to having an institution on its territory. The Dutch negotiator walked out in frustration at the jockeying for national advantage when the matter was discussed. Consequently, the Common Assembly was established in Strasbourg, France, the Council of Ministers in Brussels, Belgium, and the Court and the High Authority in Luxembourg – Italy being too far from Europe's coal and steel heartland.

The ECSC Treaty was signed in Paris on April 18, 1951, to last for 50 years; Jean Monnet was appointed as the first president of the High Authority. By this time already, however, the treaty was overshadowed by global events. War had broken out on the Korean peninsula barely a month after the Schuman Declaration; communist North Korea, supported by Mao Tse-tung's China, invaded the Republic of Korea. The US immediately mobilized its resources and allies to put into practice the doctrine of containing communist expansionism. The aftershock in Western Europe was that, with the US now also heavily committed in the Pacific, the pressure was suddenly on for a remilitarization of West Germany, in order for it to share the burden of deterring the Soviet Union.

Remilitarization was extremely controversial, as, although the Federal Republic of Germany and NATO had both been created in 1949, the former was not yet a member of the latter. Integrating the allied-occupied parts of West Germany to create a sovereign state and to proceed with economic reconstruction – under the supervision of the ECSC – was one thing. Recreating Germany's army, the *Wehrmacht*, which had sowed terror throughout Europe, was another proposition entirely. Yet the Soviet Union had over 30 divisions across the border in East Germany. In response to US pressure to integrate a remilitarized West Germany into NATO, French Prime Minister René Pleven announced on October 20, 1950 an unprecedented plan to create a common European army as an alternative to West German membership in NATO (Parsons 2003, 67–89).

Known as the Pleven Plan, this project was, in fact, again the brainchild of Jean Monnet. It called for a European army, under the control of institutions analogous to those of the ECSC, in which all countries except Germany would contribute their national forces. West German battalions would then be mingled with each national contingent. The US rejected the plan outright, considering it a diversionary tactic that would never raise the number of German troops necessary for defending Western Europe. Returning to the drawing board, France devised a new plan that allowed for the creation of entire West German divisions, with the multinational army coming under supranational control. This concession carried favor with the US and also with West Germany, where it was seen as a means to return to full sovereignty – an important domestic political goal. The Soviets disliked the idea of rearming West Germany and even tried to derail negotiations by offering to reunite Germany in exchange for its neutrality.

The new plan was labeled EDC and was formalized as a treaty in May 1952, when it was signed by all six ECSC member states. France sought British participation in the EDC, but these overtures were swiftly rebuffed. With the signature of the EDC Treaty – which still needed to be ratified by the parliaments (see Box 2.3) in all six countries – Europe was closer than ever been before or since to a fully federal state. This is because, alongside the EDC plan, supporters of European federalism from within the ECSC's Common Assembly formed an *ad hoc* committee to draw up a constitutional project for a European federation. The proposed EPC was accepted by the ECSC's Common Assembly and sent for discussion to national governments. Behind the EPC project was the idea to unite the ECSC and EDC as part of a federally integrated union with both a directly elected assembly and a senate representing national parliaments.

Neither the EDC nor the EPC came into being. In August 1954, a particularly heated session in the French parliament resulted in the rejection of the EDC Treaty. Even though the other five signatory states had ratified the treaty in their own parliaments, French parliamentarians were willing to pull the plug on the project. A ceasefire in Korea, the death of Stalin, and France's difficulties keeping order in its colonial empire meant prioritizing French military and foreign policy independence over sacrificing

---

Box 2.3   Case Study: Treaty Ratification

International treaties between countries are often signed with fanfare, in front of cameras and the press. Yet the moment when a country's representatives sign the document does not mark the point at which it becomes national law, obliging the state to behave according to the terms of the treaty. Treaties have to be ratified as well as signed. In most countries ratification is the responsibility of the legislature, for example the US Senate or the French National Assembly. This is an accountability check designed to prevent governments from signing treaties that hurt national interests. The treaties that have been signed in the course of European integration have all been subject to national ratification in this way. Since legislatures do not always share the preferences of their governments, ratifying EU treaties is often highly fraught, and sometimes even fails. Governments try to anticipate legislative approval during treaty negotiations, and countries facing ratification obstacles sometimes gain more concessions. However, failed treaty ratification has huge repercussions, as under international law a treaty can only be revised if all signatories agree to the proposed changes. Thus ratification failure puts EU treaty revision on hold for all countries. Many EU countries have held referendums on a treaty (i.e. a national vote on whether or not to accept a treaty) alongside parliamentary ratification. Referendums, especially ones that fail to accept treaty ratification, bring a new set of problems to the ratification process (a problem discussed in detail in Section 11.3).

---

sovereignty to solve the quandary of West German remilitarization. Instead of a common European army and a federal political system, therefore, West Germany was integrated into NATO, in exchange for new US and British guarantees to station troops there. In addition, Germany renounced the right to acquire nuclear weapons in exchange for regaining full internal and external sovereignty.

The demise of the federal option was highly dispiriting for those who believed that only federalism could unite the continent in peace and create successful and accountable institutions for solving common policy problems. Yet a European federation was not high on the agenda of the majority of Western Europe's citizens; nor did many politicians think it a beneficial arrangement for their own countries. Instead, the priority for both citizens and political elites was economic growth, in order to continue post-war reconstruction. This explains the institutional path taken by European integration after the demise of the EDC, which resulted in the European Economic Community (EEC) Treaty in 1957. This new treaty represented a compromise agreement between advocates of growth through a common market designed to help nation-states rebuild and convinced federalists, who saw economic integration as another important step toward full political union.

2.4   The Continuing Pursuit of Economic Integration: Creating the EEC, 1957

By shelving the issue of a common European army and an associated project for federal union, West European states probably avoided fractious national debates about why and how to pursue integration. Economic integration was far less controversial, as it was not considered to require a significant surrender of national sovereignty. Also, citizens were less focused on the highly technical issues surrounding economic integration (e.g. common standards for producing and selling goods) than on a common army or the creation of a federation. The choice to pursue this economic path was made in the Sicilian coastal town of Messina in 1955. There ministers of the six ECSC member states met to discuss a plan for creating a common market based on the removal of barriers to trade, in order to stimulate economic growth and to increase interdependence between countries (Moravcsik 1998, 86–158). At this time West European countries protected their national industries and markets with high tariffs and quantitative restrictions on imports, leaving consumers with less choice and higher prices.

Great Britain was invited to participate in these talks – its presence was particularly sought by the Benelux countries (Belgium, the Netherlands, and Luxembourg) as a counterweight to Franco-German dominance. However, as in the case of the ECSC project, British politicians spurned this overture, preferring to concentrate on developing the Commonwealth trading bloc. They were also skeptical that France would agree to bind itself to opening up its markets and industries to foreign competition. No other European countries associated themselves with the common market project.

At this time Spain and Portugal were both dictatorships with few international ties and with underdeveloped economies, which explains their exclusion from both the ECSC and EEC treaties. On the Eastern side of Europe, Greece had just emerged from a bloody civil war that left it a virulently anti-communist state surrounded by members of the communist bloc, with an uncertain future and a primarily agricultural economy. In the center of Europe Switzerland saw no reason to sacrifice any of its sovereignty, since its historical tradition of neutrality had successfully spared it the horrors of two world wars. Neighboring Austria, annexed to Germany by Hitler in 1938, sought to reconfigure its international relations by pursuing a strict policy of neutrality that precluded even economic integration. This neutral streak was also present in Nordic countries such as Finland and Sweden. Norway, Denmark, and Ireland had economies strongly linked to Great Britain, and so they had little interest in a common market lacking their chief export market. Hence the signatories to the 1957 **Treaty of Rome** (signed that year but ratified and entering into force in 1958), which created the EEC, were the same six countries that participated in the ECSC.

The hybrid supranationalism and intergovernmentalism contained in the ECSC was enshrined in the EEC institutions created by the Treaty of Rome (see Table 2.1). This treaty reproduced the essential design of the ECSC: a supranational, unelected executive (the European Commission) to propose legislation; an intergovernmental decision-making body that would eventually, however, sometimes use **qualified majority voting (QMV)** rather than unanimity (the Council of Ministers); an independent court (the

Table 2.1 The EEC institutions

Name	Function	Membership	Decision-Making Principle
European Commission	Proposes policy, scrutinizes member state enforcement	College of commissioners drawn from each state, President appointed by European Council but college acts in European interest	Supranational
Council of the EU (formerly Council of Ministers)	Votes on Commission proposals	Representatives of national governments, country voting weights used for QMV based on population	Intergovernmental when voting by unanimity, supranational when using QMV
European Parliament	Scrutinizes work of Commission and Council; co-decision with Council (increasingly common after 1992)	Delegated from national parliaments (directly elected after 1979); number of MEPs based on population	Largely supranational. Although MEPs represent national parties, these aggregate as European party groups
Court of Justice of the EU	Settles competence disputes, oversees correct application of treaties and EEC legislation in member states	One justice appointed by each member state; justices are independent	Supranational

Court of Justice); and a representative assembly, composed of delegates from national legislature, lacking legislative powers (the European Parliament). Yet, whereas the ECSC regulated solely steel and coal companies and member states' policies toward those industries, the EEC Treaty created a legal framework based on "four **fundamental freedoms.**"

The four fundamental freedoms the EEC was designed to protect are the free movement of goods, workers, services, and capital. Removing obstacles to these freedoms, notably national regulations that protected certain industries or trades, was and remains at the heart of the integration project of creating a single pan-European market. An integrated market with shared rules is supposed to generate economic growth thanks to more efficient competition as well as interdependence through cross-border investments, profits, and even living. Not only was the single market an end in itself but, as the preamble to the EEC Treaty explains, it was also a means toward "an ever closer union among the European peoples." The EEC Treaty thus contained additional pledges of what states would do together. This included the establishment of a common tariff toward third parties, the need to harmonize member state law in line with common market rules, the creation of a common agricultural and transport policy, general economic policy coordination, and a Social Fund aiming to improve workers' employment prospects and raise their standard of living.

Not all of these objectives were realized immediately and some would only be achieved much later, after new treaties. Indeed, much of the detail for how these objectives would be implemented in practice was not fully specified – despite the treaty running to a lengthy 248 Articles. Thus it is best to understand the Treaty of Rome as a framework agreement for signatory countries to work together through common institutions. The policies these institutions would actually implement to establish a common market were contingent upon subsequent political and judicial decisions stemming from the complex interactions between EEC institutions.

If the four fundamental freedoms were the economic capstone of the EEC Treaty, the political foundation was Franco-German cooperation. Starting with the Schuman Declaration, which specifically appealed for West German participation, France sought to work with its neighbor and former rival, not only for the sake of reconciliation but also to make sure that its preferences shaped European integration. Leaders of the German Federal Republic accommodated French preferences as the price to be paid for being allowed to participate in shared institutions on an equal, sovereign basis. In fact France's support for the EEC Treaty was dependent on the signature of a parallel treaty, on scientific and industrial research and cooperation on civilian nuclear energy. This EURATOM Treaty, also signed in Rome in 1957, was intended to create a European Atomic Energy Community that would help share the costs of developing civilian nuclear energy, allowing France to allocate greater resources to its military atomic program. However, France's uncompromising focus on strategic imperatives and the availability of cheaper civilian nuclear technology from the US meant this project for industrial cooperation failed to provide any significant impetus to European integration, although the treaty remains in force. Nevertheless, French preferences would play a key role in the first two decades of the EEC, and not necessarily for the better.

2.5   Overcoming the First Tests: The Common Agricultural Policy and the Empty Chair Crisis, 1957–1973

The EEC Treaty entered into force in 1958. The first business of the incoming European Commission, the supranational quasi-executive body tasked with devising policy, was to cut tariffs on intra-EEC trade. Cutting tariffs as part of regional economic integration is the first step toward eventually achieving a single (also known as a common) market, as depicted in Table 2.2. Politically, removing intra-EEC tariffs was a real test of will, as France had just emerged from a constitutional crisis with a new president, Charles de Gaulle, who was strongly opposed to supranationalism. At the same time the British government tried to destabilize the EEC by launching a proposal for a rival free trade

Table 2.2 Forms of regional association

Form of Regional Association	Functions	Impact on Sovereignty
Free Trade Association (FTA)	Eliminates quantitative trade restrictions (tariffs, quotas) between members	Relinquishes unilateral right to set tariffs and quotas against fellow members
Customs Union	In addition to FTA, creates common external tariff on imports from third states	Relinquishes unilateral right to set tariffs and quotas for all imports
Common Market	In addition to both FTA and customs union, establishes free movement of factors of production (goods, services, capital, labor)	Reduced scope for independent policy affecting factors of production; pressure for policy harmonization among members

bloc, the **European Free Trade Association (EFTA)**, encompassing the rest of Western Europe. The aim of EFTA was to prevent the EEC from becoming a protectionist customs union by seeking to promote tariff reductions across Western Europe. However, this British initiative proved largely ineffective and failed to receive US support. The EEC proceeded to develop a customs union, as de Gaulle chose not to jettison integration. He saw the economic and strategic value of Franco-German reconciliation especially because of the potential benefits a CAP could offer France (Moravcsik 1998, 159–237).

2.5.1 The launch of the Common Agricultural Policy

The first test of economic integration, reduction in tariffs and increase in import quotas, was successfully passed in 1960. Immediately thereafter, negotiations for how agricultural products would circulate in the EEC began in earnest. Article 39 of the EEC Treaty provided for a CAP based on the principles of market unity, Community preference, and financial solidarity with the strategic goal of boosting food production across Western Europe. France's idea for realizing these objectives was to implement a system of guaranteed prices within the EEC and subsidies for exporting outside its borders. This plan was based on the fact that France already greatly subsidized food production, which resulted in domestic prices higher than those of competing agricultural exporters but lots of export capacity. A CAP that subsidized exports would allow French products to compete overseas, while fixed high prices within the EEC would ensure an expanded European market for French farmers – who in turn, de Gaulle hoped, would be compelled to modernize and reform in response to competition. Moreover, these farmers were, as in many countries, a highly organized and powerful lobby group that pressured de Gaulle to get the best possible deal.

Almost all states worldwide intervene in their domestic market for agricultural products in order to support farmers' incomes and secure supplies for consumers, both being considered crucial to economic and political stability. Thus the interventionism of the original CAP, a policy still in existence today, is by no means that distinctive. Rather the novelty of the CAP lies in the fact that it redistributes the costs of this intervention across national boundaries. In 1960 agriculture represented over 10 percent of GDP in the EEC six, as well as around 20 percent of the workforce; and ensuring a stable food supply was a high priority, given the recent experience of shortages during and after the Second World War. Consequently the agricultural negotiations were always destined to be a high-stakes affair.

France's insistence on intervention in order to maintain high prices (surpluses would be bought directly by the EEC) and on cancelling bilateral agricultural deals with non-EEC members met sharp West German resistance. West Germany preferred to have lower prices and to maintain bilateral deals, as its farmers were less productive than French farmers but were competitive globally on price, while access to cheap imports through bilateral deals would help keep prices low for consumers. In the face of a series of threats from de Gaulle to dismantle the EEC if the CAP was not finalized, in 1962 West Germany acquiesced to France's vision of the CAP. German leaders wanted to maintain the momentum of European integration and to open up a greater market for its advanced industrial exports. Yet the irony of the CAP, as sought by de Gaulle, was that it relied on substantial supranational involvement in order to function. The Commission set agricultural prices and oversaw the purchase of surplus produce as well as coordinating plans for modernizing the sector.

However, the method for financing for the CAP was only agreed upon until 1965. As this deadline approached, the Commission proposed – as was its duty – a new scheme for funding the CAP, which was an ever growing part of the budget. The Commission's idea was to fund its budget by automatically pooling revenue from the import duties – agreed as part of the CAP – levied on food products, rather than relying on national contributions. This move would make the Commission financially independent from the member states, and according to the EEC Treaty it was scheduled to occur only in 1970. Adding an extra dose of supranationalism, the proposal also called for the Council of Ministers to vote on the annual EEC budget by a simple majority rather than by unanimity, again reducing the control and leverage the member states could exercise over the Commission.

2.5.2   The empty chair crisis

This bold project to shift the delicate balance between intergovernmentalism to supranationalism in favor of the latter also coincided with the programmed move toward the introduction of QMV for other matters in the Council of Ministers. The move to QMV was inscribed in the EEC Treaty as a way to facilitate the creation of a common market. De Gaulle had always been against this plan, but he was not in power when the treaty was signed and so had been unable to prevent it. The worry for the future was that the use of QMV to decide future trade policy could see protectionist policy toward EEC agricultural imports, which favored French interests, overturned by a coalition of free trade states seeking cheaper food prices. De Gaulle thus seized on the Commission's budget plan as the ideal opportunity to take a stand against the supranational logic of integration contained in the EEC Treaty and supported by the Commission (Gillingham 2003, 53–80).

In fact de Gaulle had already sought to implement his vision of French-led Western European integration. In 1961 Great Britain made a dramatic policy reversal and applied to join the EEC. Despite having created the rival EFTA in 1960, British politicians sensed that Franco-German reconciliation under the EEC framework was going to be both a lasting proposition and an engine for economic growth. Under the rules for admitting a candidate country all existing member states needed to approve this change, which is still how EU enlargement functions today. However, de Gaulle was at that time trying to mastermind an intergovernmental plan for integrating the defense and foreign policies of the EEC six. Mistrustful of Britain's instinct to follow America's lead – the French project was aimed at creating an independent European strategy beholden to neither superpower – de Gaulle did not want Britain to join and then derail negotiations over this new aspect of integration. He thus vetoed Britain's application to join the EEC in 1963. This unilateral move was greatly resented by the other EEC member states, particularly the small Benelux countries, which were resistant to such overt French political leadership. In response, the French plan for integrating foreign policy outside the EEC framework came to naught, as other countries were unwilling to submit to French leadership in this vital policy area. The other five EEC members preferred to retain foreign policy independence and work within the supranational EEC framework of economic integration.

In the wake of this failure over European foreign policy coordination, de Gaulle was even more determined to defend intergovernmentalism within the EEC architecture. Affronted by the Commission's budget proposal and the impending introduction of QMV on trade policy, de Gaulle simply stopped high-level French participation in EEC institutions as of June 15, 1965. This was a particularly striking move, as France then held the rotating presidency of the Council of Ministers, which entailed taking the lead for organizing the political business of the EEC. In reference to France's absence at the Council's negotiating table during this period, scholars label this tumultuous time as the "**empty chair crisis.**"

This boycott lasted for six months but was in fact very unpopular in the French farm lobby, which feared that de Gaulle was jeopardizing the very existence of the CAP, which was essential to their long-term interests. The business community also feared that this resurgence of nationalism might kill off the prospect of enacting the common market. Non-participation in the Council of Ministers became a major part of the December 1965 presidential election, which saw de Gaulle re-elected by a much narrower margin than before. In response to this, and thanks to a more conciliatory stance on the part of the Commission, France came back to the negotiating table and settled on an agreement worked out in Luxembourg in January 1966. Known as the "Luxembourg Compromise," this was a gentlemen's agreement whereby the EEC states accepted that, when a vital national interest was at stake in a Council's decision, this body would refrain from using QMV. France thus obtained an informal safeguard against creeping supranationalism, to ensure that policy-making remained consensual.

The resolution of the empty chair crisis clearly showed the sticking power of European integration. If even an ardent nationalist such as de Gaulle was forced to work within the parameters of the EEC, then integration had obviously fundamentally changed the nature of international politics in Western Europe. In particular, the fact that domestic interest groups such as farmers and businesses mobilized against the French president when he blocked cooperation suggests that integration was already having an impact on national politics. Great Britain's sudden enthusiasm for joining the EEC, which de Gaulle again vetoed in 1967, further illustrates the way in which integration reshaped member states' perceived interests. Great Britain preferred to abandon the Commonwealth economic system among its many former colonies in order to pursue cooperation closer to home.

De Gaulle also opposed granting the EEC its own funds, because financial independence would give the Commission more autonomy. Yet, following his withdrawal from French politics, EEC countries were able to negotiate an important financial agreement at the Hague Summit of 1969. This deal allocated to the EEC funds from levies on food imports and the common tariff on industrial goods, as well as a proportion of VAT (valued-added tax, that is, sales tax) receipts. This meant granting the EEC its own funds rather than relying on voluntary national contributions – a very significant supranational development (Dinan 2004, ch. 4). Similarly, with de Gaulle no longer around to wield a veto, Great Britain was eventually allowed to join the EEC in 1973, alongside Denmark and Ireland.

By 1973, therefore, the EEC was voluntarily accepted by West European countries as a set of institutions for pooling state sovereignty for the sake of economic growth. The constraints this process imposed were worthwhile not only because of enhanced trade, but also because the Franco-German reconciliation that the EEC made possible was considered the best guarantee of lasting peace in Western Europe.

2.6   Concluding Summary

Developing an institutional structure to unite the countries of Western Europe was no easy task. They not only had to confront the Soviet threat, which implied some kind of defensive military role for West Germany, but also French wariness (compounded by territorial claims) toward Germany. European countries sought and obtained the involvement of the United States in a mutual defense agreement, NATO. American leaders supported Europe's integration endeavors, which in 1950 saw a breakthrough with Robert Schuman's proposal for a common system of government designed to supervise coal and steel production, the ECSC. The ECSC's hybrid supranational and intergovernmental system reflected a compromise between defenders of national sovereignty and proponents of a supranational project of integration. At the heart of this project was Franco-German reconciliation based on cooperation within shared institutions controlling key resources for war, so as to make conflict "materially unthinkable."

While the creation of NATO provided a framework for European defense, there remained a question mark over what role West Germany would play within it. With American leaders pushing for German rearmament to help deter the Soviet Union, French reluctance led to the consideration of a radical plan for supranational defense integration. This alternative solution envisaged a common European army alongside a plan for a federal political union, but – despite acceptance by other ECSC members – the French parliament refused to ratify it. Consequently, West Germany integrated NATO and European integration focused on the economic dimension.

This less ambitious approach, which dismayed supporters of a federal European state, was reflected in the 1957 EEC Treaty. The guiding goal of the EEC was to stimulate economic growth through the creation of a common market undistorted by national barriers against the free movement of goods, services, capital, and workers. Creating this common market was also intended to build further on Franco-German reconciliation by increasing interdependence and cooperation. Although the EEC fused both intergovernmental and supranational decision-making with an institutional structure like the ECSC, French President Charles de Gaulle attempted to impose his mark on integration. He wanted to strengthen national governments' role and establish a European foreign policy led by France. De Gaulle unilaterally vetoed two UK applications for EEC membership, thinking Britain's Atlantic ties would stymie the development of an independent European foreign policy. His French-dominated, intergovernmental vision of integration failed to take hold though, and the EEC was able to function effectively, creating the CAP and beginning a customs union. By 1973 Great Britain, which had tried to scupper the EEC with the creation of a rival West European free trade bloc, was admitted to join with the blessing of a new French president, helping turn the EEC six into the EEC nine.

Guide to Further Reading

Dinan, D. 2004. *Europe Recast: A History of European Integration*. Boulder: Lynne Rienner.

The most accessible and comprehensive political history of integration.

Moravcsik, A. 1998. *The Choice for Europe: Social Purpose and State Power from Messina to Maastricht*. Ithaca, NY: Cornell University Press.

The standard, highly detailed and sophisticated account of European states' decisions to pursue economic and political integration.

Lundestad, G. 1998. *"Empire" by Integration: The United States and European Integration, 1945–1997*. Oxford: Oxford University Press.

An excellent, thorough survey of the formative role played by the US in helping to create a united Europe.

Discussion Questions

1   What distinguishes the principle of supranational integration from the principle of balance of power?

2   How would you explain the contrast between using NATO to solve Western Europe's security dilemma and pursuing economic integration through a supranational institutional structure?

3   How satisfied do you think advocates of a federal Europe were with the EEC and what kind of institutions they would have preferred?

4   What were de Gaulle's reasons for preventing the United Kingdom from joining the EEC in the 1960s? Was he thinking more of France's interests or Europe's?

5   How would you evaluate what the balance between supranationalism and intergovernmentalism was in EEC decision-making?

Web Resources

This book is supported by a companion website, which can be found at www.wiley.com/go/glencross. There you will find a list of the web links referred to in this chapter wherever you see a "Web" icon in the page margins. In addition, you will find a list of further relevant online resources such as websites for EU institutions, political groups, archives, and think tanks, information on studying abroad, and biographies of key figures. You will also find self-assessment tools in the form of flashcards and independent study questions developed specifically for this chapter.

Glossary

Commissioner's Oath
Oath taken (in front of justices of the CJEU) by the College of European commissioners, who pledge to respect the EU treaties and to be completely independent from national governments.

Common Agricultural Policy (CAP)
A set of agricultural subsidies whereby taxpayers across Europe subsidise farmers' incomes. Designed in the early 1960s to ensure stable and secure food production, it once constituted nearly 90 percent of the EU budget but now represents only 40 percent.

Council of Europe
European international organization created in 1949 to promote human rights. With 47 member states, it has a much larger membership than the EU and functions intergovernmentally, although its court, the European Court of Human Rights, gives binding decisions that signatory states have to obey. Not to be confused with the European Council, the EU's steering body composed of heads of state and government.

Empty chair crisis
1965–1966 political dispute instigated by French President Charles de Gaulle, who refused to send ministers to the Council of Ministers (now Council of the EU). This was a protest against a move toward supranationalism in the form of QMV voting.

It resulted in an informal agreement to retain unanimity in the Council for very important national interests.

European Defence Community (EDC)

A 1952 plan for the creation of a multinational, West European army coming under supranational control. A treaty to this effect was signed by leaders of the six ECSC countries, but the treaty was rejected by a vote in the French parliament in 1954 and thus never implemented.

European Free Trade Association (EFTA)

Founded in 1960 by seven non-EEC states. A looser, intergovernmental arrangement without common policies or even an external tariff, it was championed by Great Britain as a rival to the EEC.

European Political Community (EPC)

A 1953 plan for a federal political union based on a bicameral parliament with executive and legislative functions. It was designed as the political counterpart to the EDC and was rendered redundant when France rejected the EDC.

Franco-German reconciliation

Having fought three wars in less than a century, these two rivals set out to establish peaceful relations after the Second World War. The process was in part bilateral but mostly took place within the context of European integration, both countries pursuing reconciliation via participation in shared institutions and common policies.

Fundamental freedoms

Article 3 of the 1957 EEC Treaty committed member states to "the abolition, as between Member States, of obstacles to freedom of movement of goods, persons, services and capital." These became known as the four fundamental freedoms and are the basis for the single market.

North Atlantic Treaty Organization (NATO)

An intergovernmental military alliance founded in 1949 to protect Western Europe from Soviet aggression. It is a mutual defense pact, whereby an attack on any member state automatically triggers a collective response. It is considered the basis of transatlantic relations because it commits the US to protect Europe.

Qualified Majority Voting (QMV)

Used instead of unanimity, QMV is a supranational voting procedure whereby decisions in the Council of the EU require a certain threshold of countries and population in order to pass. This is controversial because it means that countries can be forced to accept decisions they are against, something that is impossible with unanimity.

Schuman Declaration

1950 speech by the then French Foreign Minister Robert Schuman, calling for the creation of a European Coal and Steel Community. This proposal was intended to provide an institutional context for Franco-German reconciliation by building trust and cooperation.

Treaty of Rome

1957 treaty, signed in Rome, that established the European Economic Community. This treaty, which came into force in 1958, committed member states to respecting the four fundamental freedoms.

References

Bozo, Frédéric. 2001. *Two Strategies for Europe: De Gaulle, the United States and the Atlantic Alliance*. Oxford: Rowman & Littlefield.

Burgess, Michael. 2000. *Federalism and European Union: The Building of Europe, 1950–2000*. London: Routledge.

Dinan, Desmond. 2004. *Europe Recast: A History of European Integration*. Boulder: Lynne Rienner.

Gaddis, John Lewis. 2006. *The Cold War: A New History*. London: Penguin.

George, Stephen. 1998. *An Awkward Partner: Britain in the European Community*. Oxford: Oxford University Press.

Gillingham, John. 2003. *European Integration, 1950–2003: Superstate or New Market Economy*. Cambridge: Cambridge University Press.

Glencross, Andrew R. 2009. "Altiero Spinelli and the Idea of the US Constitution as a Model for Europe: The Promises and Pitfalls of an Analogy." *Journal of Common Market Studies*, 47: 287–307. DOI: 10.1111/j.1468-5965.2009.00805.x

Granieri, Ronald J. 2003. *The Ambivalent Alliance: Konrad Adenauer, the CDU/CSU, and the West, 1949–1966*. New York: Berghahn Books.

Ikenberry, G. John. 2001. *After Victory: Institutions, Strategic Restraint, and the Rebuilding of Order after Major Wars*. Princeton, NJ: Princeton University Press.

Judt, Tony. 2006. *Postwar: A History of Europe since 1945*. London: Random House.

Lundestad, Geir. 1998. *"Empire" by Integration: The United States and European Integration, 1945–1997*. Oxford: Oxford University Press.

Milward, Alan S. 1992. *The European Rescue of the Nation-State*. London: Routledge.

Moravcsik, Andrew. 1998. *The Choice for Europe: Social Purpose and State Power from Messina to Maastricht*. Ithaca, NY: Cornell University Press.

Parsons, Craig. 2003. *A Certain Idea of Europe*. New York: Cornell University Press.

Rathbun, Brian C. 2004. *Partisan Interventions: European Party Politics and Peace Enforcement in the Balkans*. New York: Cornell University Press.

Schain, Martin A., ed. 2001. *The Marshall Plan: Fifty Years After (with an introduction by Tony Judt)*. New York: Palgrave.

Schuman, Robert. 1950. "The Schuman Declaration." Speech given at the Salon de l'Horloge, May 9. Available at http://europa.eu/about-eu/basic-information/symbols/europe-day/schuman-declaration/ (accessed July 23, 2013).

Trachtenberg, Marc. 1999. *A Constructed Peace: The Making of the European Settlement, 1945–1963*. Princeton, NJ: Princeton University Press.

3

The Institutional Development of European Integration, 1973–2010

Contents

Learning Objectives

- to identify the key transformations wrought by treaty reforms between 1973 and 2010;
- to analyze the effects of widening and the relationship between widening and changes in the international order;
- to interpret why state and non-state actors chose to transform the EEC in order to complete the single market;
- to evaluate why political union came onto the agenda in the late 1980s;
- to interpret the successes and failures of the newly launched EU;
- to identify the changes that the Lisbon Treaty brought about and the intentions behind them.

The Politics of European Integration: Political Union or a House Divided?, First Edition. Andrew Glencross.
© 2014 Andrew Glencross. Published 2014 by Blackwell Publishing Ltd.

Timeline of Key Events 3.1: First EEC Enlargement to Lisbon Treaty (1973–2010)

1973 January	Denmark, Ireland, and United Kingdom join the EEC
1978 December	Creation of the European Monetary System
1979 June	First direct elections to the European Parliament
1981 January	Greece joins the EEC
1985 January	Jacques Delors appointed president of the European Commission
1985 March–June	EEC agreement to complete the single market by 1992 and to revise EEC Treaty following the Commission's White Paper on Completing the Internal Market
1986 January	Portugal and Spain join the EEC
1986 February	Single European Act (SEA) signed to complete the single market
1987 April	Turkey starts negotiations for joining the EEC
1989 November	Fall of Berlin Wall
1990 October	Germany officially reunited
1990–1991	Progressive collapse of Soviet Union marking the end of the Cold War
1992 February	Treaty on European Union signed in Maastricht (Netherlands)
1993 January	Abolition of checks on goods and people at internal borders
1993 November	EEC officially becomes the European Union after the Maastricht Treaty is ratified
1995 January	Austria, Finland, and Sweden join the EU
2002 January	European single currency, the euro, replaces national currencies of most member states of that time
2004 May	Republic of Cyprus, Czech Republic, Estonia, Hungary, Latvia, Lithuania, Malta, Poland, Slovakia, and Slovenia join the EU
2004 October	EU member states sign the Treaty Establishing a Constitution for Europe
2005 May-June	Referendums to ratify the Constitutional Treaty fail in France and the Netherlands
2007 January	Bulgaria and Romania join the EU
2007 December	Lisbon Treaty is signed
2009 December	Lisbon Treaty enters into force after ratification by all 27 EU members

3.0   Introduction: The Widening and Deepening of European Integration

By the end of the first decade of the twenty-first century, the European integration project had become a union of 27 member states (Croatia subsequently joined, in July 2013, becoming the 28th member state) with over 500 million citizens. This geographical enlargement was accompanied by a vastly expanded set of policy competences by comparison to those of the EEC. These two phenomena of geographical enlargement and competence expansion are commonly referred to as "widening" and "deepening" respectively. Yet neither widening nor deepening should be considered an inevitable result of internal consensus or external pressure. As this chapter shows, the development of European integration during this period was neither smooth nor inevitable. Rather the institutions and decision-making rules of today's EU are the complex product of (1) pragmatic compromises over political and economic principles; and (2) deals between key national leaders. Supranational integration has appealed to those leaders as a way to solve policy problems in a globally interconnected world.

The complexity of institutional development between 1973 and 2010 reflects the additional complications arising for European policy-making from widening the integration project so as to include new members (Nugent 2004). There were four waves of enlargement during this period: Atlantic enlargement in 1973 (Britain, Denmark, and Ireland); Mediterranean enlargement in 1981/1986 (first Greece, then Spain and Portugal); post Cold-War western enlargement in 1995 (Austria, Finland, and Sweden); and, finally, Central and Eastern European enlargement (Republic of Cyprus, Czech Republic, Estonia, Hungary, Latvia, Lithuania, Malta, Poland, Slovakia and Slovenia in 2004, followed by Bulgaria and Romania in 2007). Rather than presenting each wave in turn, the chapter first examines widening from the perspective of how enlargement came to be associated with consolidating democracy within Europe, as illustrated in the Mediterranean enlargement (Section 3.1). At the same time, this section explores the challenge posed by the **accession** of the United Kingdom: a powerful member state with a complicated relationship with European integration.

Each round of widening has made for a more heterogeneous membership in terms of population size, culture, GDP per capita, or political ideology across the member states. Despite this dramatic change in membership, the principal institutions of the EU remain the same as those created by the EEC Treaty that came into force in 1957: the European Commission, the Council of the EU (formerly the Council of Ministers), the European Parliament, and the Court of Justice. Hence the major developments in deepening integration since 1973 have all involved changes to the rules governing how these institutions interrelate and, perhaps more importantly, to the powers they have over member states, particularly over national law and policy autonomy.

Consequently this chapter analyzes in depth the three most significant treaties behind the deepening of European integration since 1973. These are the Single European Act of 1986, the Maastricht Treaty of 1992, and the Lisbon Treaty of 2009 – which was in fact a largely recycled version of an earlier treaty that was never ratified, the 2004 Constitutional Treaty. A chapter section is devoted to each of these significant treaties and the political debates surrounding them. The Single European Act, discussed in 3.2, was designed to complete the single market by expanding QMV (qualified majority voting) so as to make it easier to pass legislation making the four fundamental freedoms a reality. Both the Maastricht Treaty and the Lisbon Treaty, examined in 3.3 and 3.4 respectively, were specifically designed with an enlarged membership in mind. These treaty revisions were thus adopted in order to expand the EU's competences as well as its capacity to function more efficiently with an ever greater number of member states. The analysis of these treaties demonstrates how Europe's leaders increasingly feel that greater cooperation is the best solution to a variety of policy problems facing the modern state. In this context, member states have voluntarily agreed to significant limitations on their autonomy in exchange for collective solutions geared to delivering better outcomes than would be possible otherwise. Developments since the Lisbon Treaty, namely the economic and political turmoil within the Eurozone beginning in 2010, are so significant as to merit separate treatment in Chapter 12.

3.1   Living with the First Enlargement Round and Preparing for the Next, 1973–1986

The first expansion of the EEC was intended to secure greater economic benefits for all member states by enlarging the single market so as to include Denmark, Ireland, and the United Kingdom. Obviously the defection of these three countries greatly undermined the EFTA (see Chapter 2, Glossary) as a rival, less supranational trade bloc. This initial wave of widening EEC membership coincided with a severe external economic shock: the 1973 oil crisis. Middle Eastern oil-producing countries raised petrol prices to punish western support for Israel during the Arab–Israeli war of that year. Up to that point, continental West European economies had enjoyed a period of uninterrupted economic growth since the end of the Second World War. Post-war growth not only provided a major rise in living standards and low unemployment but also financed an expansion in government welfare programs.

The abrupt end of cheap oil, which had helped underwrite Western Europe's economic growth, was accompanied by a major disruption in the global financial system. The **Bretton Woods system** of fixed exchange rates pegged to the US dollar, which was ultimately convertible to gold – a system designed to protect free trade from speculation and sudden currency fluctuations – collapsed. This was caused by the fact that the US government was unable to balance its budget, thereby undermining its balance of payments (the net difference between imports and exports). US deficits during the Vietnam War forced down the US dollar, making its legal convertibility to a fixed amount of gold unaffordable. Abandoning dollar convertibility led to floating global currency exchange rates by early 1973. Amid the global economic uncertainty, the leaders of Western Europe turned to the EEC to try to resolve this new problem of managing exchange rates and associated monetary policy (Gillingham 2003, 84–104).

Addressing these economic issues did not result in major developments for the EEC, but throughout the period there was pressure to enhance supranational policy-making. Often it was a new member, the United Kingdom, that sought to frustrate efforts to enhance supranationalism (George 1998). This awkward attitude had in fact been foreseen by the original six. That is why, prior to the 1973 enlargement, the EEC six had settled the unfinished business of devising a system for financing the CAP (Common Agricultural Policy; see Section 2.5). Of course, not all policy disputes can be solved prior to widening, which is one reason (among others) why member states are often split over the pros and cons of enlargement (see Box 3.1).

On the EEC policy agenda after the first enlargement was the possibility of a common monetary policy. The 1957 EEC Treaty referred to this objective, which had been reiterated at the 1969 Hague Summit. There was also a pledge to re-examine the question of foreign policy coordination, a proposal that had been derailed during the 1960s by Charles de Gaulle's plans for a French-dominated European foreign policy (see Section 2.5). Yet to these demanding policy priorities the EEC soon had to add an unanticipated new development: the possibility of widening once again.

Box 3.1   Key Debate: The Pros and Cons of Enlargement

Despite repeated enlargement and the enthusiasm of candidate countries, EU widening remains very controversial (O'Brennan 2006). On the pro side, enlargement is considered a means of stabilizing neighboring countries by spreading prosperity and democracy. Enlargement is also pursued in order to enhance economic growth by creating a wider market for goods and services from existing members and by encouraging dynamism and diversity through the movement of labor from new to old member states. Those wary about enlargement worry that EU expansion, which tends to mean bringing in countries with a lower average GDP per capita, is expensive for existing members, who have to fund agricultural subsidies and financial transfers to poorer regions. There are also concerns that adding members inevitably makes joint decision-making harder, possibly leading to lower standards of social and environmental regulation. Finally, EU efforts at stabilizing its periphery can only go so far in countries with weak states and deep economic inequalities. Naturally, the debate over EU widening also takes place within countries seeking EU accession. Citizens in certain wealthy countries, notably Switzerland and Norway, have rejected EU membership, believing they already benefit sufficiently from access to the EU single market under special bilateral treaties. This was also the case in Iceland until the 2008 financial crisis crippled its economy, leading to a swift policy reverse and official application for EU membership. At the same time Turkey, an official EU candidate country, is torn between the desire to be accepted as a full member of the West (it is already a member of NATO and the Council of Europe) and that of becoming a regional power in the Near East. Lastly, enlargement also raises geopolitical questions about EU foreign policy. Blocking Turkish accession could hurt EU interests in the Middle East. Moreover, what the EU sees as helping democracy and economic reform when it discusses the possible membership of the Ukraine, Georgia, or Moldova is considered by Russia as interference within its own sphere of influence.

3.1.1   Mediterranean enlargement and strengthening democracy

Externally, the political environment in which European integration took place changed significantly as the remaining authoritarian regimes in Europe (outside the **Iron Curtain**) collapsed during the 1970s. In 1962 the EEC had signed an Association Treaty with Greece, establishing a customs union that meant Greece would eventually be considered for admission, economic progress permitting. However, this agreement was put on hold after a military junta seized power in 1967. The fall of this undemocratic regime in 1974 was followed by changes elsewhere in the Mediterranean. Spain's long-ruling dictator, General Franco, died in November 1975, paving the way for free elections and a new constitution; Portugal held its first legislative elections under a new democratic constitution in April 1976. Given these three countries' undemocratic political systems, none of them had been a serious candidate for EEC accession; but the situation changed radically, as democratization in each country was accompanied by a desire to join the EEC.

In the Mediterranean countries EEC membership was seen as a means toward economic and political stabilization – a perspective shared by most candidates for EU membership today. Moreover, this wave of democratization encouraged the EEC to emphasize the role that supranationalism could play in protecting and enhancing democracy within European states. Of course, ending balance of power politics (see Box 1.2) was from the outset motivated by a desire to create the right conditions for democracy to flourish in Western Europe. But with this wave of regime change the EEC increasingly had to live up to the claim, found in the preamble to the Treaty of Rome, that member states were committed to "strengthen[ing] the safeguards of peace and liberty" by pooling sovereignty.

French and German leaders chose to fast-track Greece's EEC application, allowing it to join in 1981, five years ahead of Spain and Portugal. Their intention was to strengthen democracy in its historical birthplace at the same time as the EEC itself was increasing its democratic credentials by holding direct elections for the European Parliament, starting in June 1979. Whereas members of the European Parliament had previously been selected by national parliamentarians, direct election meant that this legislature now represented the European people as a whole. Ever since, this democratic mandate has allowed the European Parliament to argue for having greater decision-making responsibilities. Representation in the Parliament is based on each country having a number of seats allocated according to its population; today this number ranges from 6 for Malta to 99 for Germany (see Table 3.1). This principle results in considerable over-representation for small countries; for instance Germany has 16 times more MEPs than Malta, but its population is over 160 times larger. Although in 2013 the number of MEPs stood at 766, the Lisbon Treaty specifies that there should be a maximum of 751 and that no country should have more than 96 MEPs; the reduction is going to occur in 2014.

3.1.2   The British budget contribution dispute

During the 1970 and early 1980s, plans for fulfilling the Treaty of Rome's ambitions to develop a common monetary policy and foreign policy coordination did not lead to much. National governments remained in control of the integration process and were either unable or unwilling to pool more competences. A major factor behind the stagnation of integration in this period was internal dispute, which was made more complicated by the accession of the United Kingdom. The United Kingdom, whose leaders were originally hostile to European integration and have remained among the ones most suspicious of supranationalism ever since, has been at the heart of many of the fiercest battles over European integration (see Box 3.2). The first of these clashes concerned the

Table 3.1   Number of MEPs per EU country (2013)

Country	Number of MEPs	Approximate Population
Germany	99	82 million
France	74	65 million
Italy, United Kingdom	73	62 million
Spain	52	47 million
Poland	51	39 million
Romania	33	22 million
Netherlands	26	17 million
Belgium, Czech Republic, Greece, Hungary, Portugal	22	11 million
Sweden	20	9 million
Austria	19	8 million
Bulgaria	18	7 million
Denmark, Finland, Slovakia	13	5.5 million
Croatia, Ireland, Lithuania	12	4 million
Latvia	9	2.2 million
Slovenia	8	2 million
Estonia, Cyprus, Luxembourg, Malta	6	1 million (Luxembourg and Malta circa 500,000)
Total	766	500 million

net amount that the United Kingdom would contribute to the EEC budget. British politicians protested that, because the United Kingdom imported a lot of food from outside of the EEC (subject to CAP import levies) and had a small, more efficient farm system that warranted fewer agricultural subsidies, the EEC funding mechanism was inequitable. Such was the political turmoil in the United Kingdom – acutely hit as it was by the recession provoked by the 1973 oil crisis – that, one year after joining the EEC and under a new government, this country tried to renegotiate its budget contributions. This budget dispute hampered EEC institutional reform for a decade.

The 1975 renegotiation of Britain's budget contribution resulted in the creation of the European Regional Development Fund, designed to provide support for improving infrastructure in the EEC's poorer regions, notably in the United Kingdom. Reversing income and employment inequalities among Europe's regions remains a key goal of EU regional policy today (see Section 5.4) – a very popular redistributive policy among poorer member states and candidate countries. However, the amount of regional infrastructure funding that went to the United Kingdom in the late 1970s failed to satisfy British politicians, who argued that their net contribution to the EEC budget was still too great. Margaret Thatcher, the British prime minister elected in 1979, made it her mission to see that the British budget contribution was cut. Thatcher's tactic was to block cooperation on substantive EEC policy-making, especially Mediterranean enlargement, until a budget rebate was secured (George 1998, ch. 5).

This obstructiveness threatened enlargement negotiations with Spain and Portugal – Greek accession negotiations having begun in 1976, before Thatcher came to power. To

Box 3.2   Case Study: The United Kingdom:
An Awkward European Partner?

The United Kingdom has a notoriously complicated relationship with European integration. After the Second World War, the centuries-old British Empire crumbled rapidly, leading to profound soul searching about the country's economic and political standing. Joining the EEC was a reflection of significant relative post-war economic and military decline. Yet national pride and a long-standing doctrine of parliamentary sovereignty have made British politicians and citizens alike uncomfortable with supranationalism, and especially with a European federation (Geddes 2004). In fact the decision to join the EEC was so controversial domestically that in 1975, only two years after joining, the United Kingdom held a **referendum** on whether to withdraw. Two thirds of Britons voted to remain in the EEC, but the question of how far to integrate with Europe remains open. British governments have refused to join the euro, opted out of EU immigration and asylum policies, and blocked discussion of increased competences in social policy. A willingness to ally itself with the US, as during the 2003 Iraq War, is also seen as detrimental to European attempts to coordinate an independent foreign policy. In addition, the United Kingdom's enthusiasm for the 2004 enlargement, as well as for Turkish accession, is considered a tactic to water down ambitions for political unity, as deepening integration becomes harder among a more numerous and diverse set of member states. Nevertheless, the UK has a better track record than most member states in implementing EU legislation, is a major net contributor, and is home to many businesses and professionals who favor integration for economic benefits and ease of mobility. The UK also welcomed large numbers of migrant workers from post-2004 EU countries, when other major countries restricted their right to settle, and since 1998 it has played a crucial role in pooling resources to help establish an effective EU foreign policy. At the same time, defending national interests within the EU is hardly the preserve of the United Kingdom. Many other member states also share the British preference for market rather than political integration and for the maintenance of a security relationship with the US. Yet only in the UK is an exit from the EU openly discussed in mainstream party politics, many politicians arguing that the British public should again have its say on whether to remain in the EU.

ensure the budget dispute did not prevent the accession of Spain and Portugal, in 1984 EEC members agreed to a formula whereby a certain percentage of the United Kingdom's annual budget contributions would be paid back. This increasingly controversial rebate remains in place: returning two thirds of British contributions totalled around €3 billion in 2011. Since EU financing requires unanimous agreement, change is only possible if the United Kingdom agrees to give up its refund.

Overall, despite progress toward Mediterranean enlargement and the introduction of direct elections for the European Parliament, the period 1973–1986 is considered largely one of EEC stagnation. The absence of concrete incremental deepening stands in sharp contrast with the next phase of integration, ushered in by the Single European Act signed in 1986. This treaty revision was designed to fulfill economic integration by expanding EEC policy competences that, in turn, would have profound political ramifications (Dinan 2004, ch. 7).

3.2   Completing the Single Market as a Prelude to Monetary and Political Union, 1986–1992

The Single European Act (SEA) of 1986 is an excellent example of how European integration progresses most when the agenda of supranational actors is supported by member state governments with their own reasons for pooling sovereignty. As representatives of the general European interest, supranational actors such as the European Commission and the European Parliament usually have an ideological preference for greater integration. They also have pragmatic institutional reasons to favor deepening, as this increases their policy power, generating more resources and prestige. In 1986 national governments seeking specific economic benefits for their domestic constituencies – such as access to agricultural subsidies and a bigger market that may offer labor mobility and cheaper wages – shared this preference for increased supranationalism. The result was a new treaty agreement to remove non-tariff barriers within the single market.

In 1968 the EEC had already accomplished, as per the Treaty of Rome, a customs union (see Table 2.2): this meant that all goods entering the Community were subject to a uniform tariff. Tariff barriers for goods circulating within the EEC had also been abolished. Yet there remained cumbersome obstacles to the free circulation of goods, services, capital, and people; these obstacles were physical (border controls and customs), fiscal (different rates of direct and indirect taxation), and technical (health, safety, environmental standards). Moreover, many governments subsidized certain national industries or ran state-owned monopolies in sectors such as energy, telecommunications, and air travel. In other words, the supposed common market was far from being fully integrated, preventing companies, entrepreneurs, workers, or students from taking advantage of pan-European opportunities. The inability of the EEC to address these shortcomings was seen as the product of too much intergovernmentalism and as a failure of incremental integration.

In response Jacques Delors, appointed by the member states in 1985 as the eighth president of the European Commission, made it his mission to complete the integration of the single market through a new treaty. This reform would require member states to accept a significant reduction in their ability to veto decisions in the Council of the EU, which meant that decisions for regulating the single market would align more closely than before to the (supranational) preferences of the Commission and Parliament. Harmonizing regulation was almost impossible under the existing system, as the Luxembourg Compromise (see Section 2.5) could be invoked by a country to block such rule changes. The Commission's policy experts argued that reducing member state veto power in the Council of Ministers was the only way to benefit from the economies of scale and dynamism offered by a better functioning single market.

Supporters of supranationalism believed that a new treaty could also pave the way for even greater integration. Their ideal was a true union with expanded policy competences (such as monetary policy, foreign policy, social policy, and taxation) beyond mere market integration. Political activism in support of a genuine European Union came from within the European Parliament. With its new electoral legitimacy and under the impetus of Italian MEP Altiero Spinelli (see Section 2.1), the Parliament adopted a Draft Treaty establishing the European Union in February 1984. This idea of creating something closer to a federal state rather than an international organization recalled the 1954 project for a European Political Community (see Section 2.3). Many of the Draft Treaty's provisions (notably those concerning competences, supranational voting, and the power of the Parliament) have subsequently become part of the contemporary EU. However, at the time of this proposal – which was a purely symbolic text with no legal status – those were very radical ideas.

3.2.1   French, German, and British perspectives on the SEA

The vast majority of EEC member states, though, were not in favor of such a bold move for relinquishing sovereignty over political as well as economic matters (Gilbert 2003, 173–179). However, France, Germany, and the United Kingdom, the dominant EEC member states, were buffeted at this time by hard economic problems, chiefly unemployment, low growth, and a lack of research and development relative to global competitors. Thus they were amenable to a treaty that could revitalize European big business through economies of scale, spur entrepreneurship by abolishing barriers to market entry, and improve public finances, which might even help maintain high welfare spending.

This connection between European integration and preserving welfare spending was made by the French President François Mitterrand. He was the first socialist president of the French Fifth Republic; he was in power for two terms, from 1981 to 1995, and his tenure coincided with fundamental transformations in European politics. Mitterrand was a dogged defender of French national interests – he has been called the "de Gaulle" of the left – yet he came to see integration as necessary and beneficial to France (Tiersky 2003, 157–214). Historians explain this combination as the result of the failed experiment in socialist economic policy during the first two years of his presidency. This socialist economic blueprint included nationalizing certain big companies, raising taxes, hiring more civil servants, increasing the minimum wage and other social spending, as well as greater workers' rights. It was a bold, counter-cyclical attempt to stimulate the economy at a time when most countries were suffering from the second oil shock and trying to reduce public spending. However, French deficit spending meant increased imports, which, in the context of a global recession that reduced the demand for French exports, triggered a **balance of payments crisis**. This generated a vicious cycle whereby a fall in the value of the franc, the French currency, increased the cost of imports, especially dollar-denominated oil, putting further downward pressure on the franc. There was only one way out of this mess: devaluation, followed by a rapid retrenchment of public spending. This outcome was politically damaging to Mitterrand; and so, beaten by the global markets, he turned toward deepening European integration in order to help balance economic competitiveness and social spending. Deepening market integration was attractive because it meant better export opportunities for French firms and cheaper imports due to increased competition. In addition, Mitterrand supported the Single European Act as a prelude to monetary union, an objective also desired by Delors.

By the end of 1978 EEC members' currencies were tied together in the **European Monetary System (EMS)**, which limited their fluctuations in value in order to stabilize intra-EEC trade in the post-Bretton Woods environment. Maintaining the value of the franc within this system had proven impossible without reducing public spending (public deficits generally cause a currency to fall). It was hard for France to peg its currency to a specified level against the German Deutschmark (as per the EMS), because West Germany's huge exporting success and disciplined, anti-inflationary policies made its currency very strong. Thus full monetary integration, whereby Europe would have a single currency, offered the possibility of a strong currency (essential for stable trade both within and outside Europe) based on Germany's economic strength (Marsh 2009). Such a system would thus shield France from pressure from the currency markets when it ran a budget deficit, thereby giving the country more leeway to pursue its chosen public policies than when it had to maintain its own currency against the strong Deutschmark.

West Germany itself, led by Chancellor Helmut Kohl, stood to benefit greatly from the SEA's plan to remove non-tariff barriers to trade in an EEC of over 300 million citizens. The Federal Republic's enormously productive industries would realize increased profits from new market and investment opportunities and would have access to cheaper labor for subcontracting components. Kohl was also a committed European who sought to re-dynamize Franco-German relations. Kohl's support for the SEA was therefore natural, although the idea of monetary union was far more controversial, given that it meant losing sovereignty over an essential policy tool.

The United Kingdom's position was even clearer. Prime Minister Margaret Thatcher wanted a more integrated EEC market to expand economic opportunities for Britain's post-industrial and post-imperial economy. Hence she saw the SEA as an extension of her domestic economic reforms involving deregulation and privatization, which prepared British companies to profit from increased EEC opportunities. In exchange, more EEC supranationalism (that is, increased use of QMV in the Council) to regulate this better integrated economic community was acceptable; but political or monetary union were not.

Negotiations for the Single European Act (so called because it provided for a single unified reform of the EEC Treaty) took place at an **intergovernmental conference (IGC)** initiated by the pro-European Italian government, which wanted to launch a new phase of integration. An IGC is a diplomatic summit between EU heads of state and government meeting to discuss treaty changes. In December 1985 the IGC reconvened in Luxembourg; representatives from the Commission and observers from the Parliament were also present, to add a supranational element. Foreign ministers and heads of government debated three major sticking points: the proposed radical increase in the use of QMV within the Council; the enhanced legislative power of the European Parliament; and the possible move toward monetary union (Dinan 2004, chs 6 and 7).

Expanding the use of QMV was accepted as the only means to complete market integration; the Commission had earlier identified 279 legislative measures necessary for this, in a 1985 White Paper called "Completing the Internal Market." The ambition was to use the SEA reforms to pass this raft of measures abolishing non-tariff barriers by 1992. In order to prevent a minority of countries from blocking the SEA (treaties require unanimous acceptance), the EEC budget was increased so as to allow for greater infrastructure funding for poorer member states, whose firms might initially suffer from enhanced competition. The European Parliament saw its powers increased thanks to the introduction of a "cooperation procedure" whereby it could amend legislation adopted by the Council of Ministers. This meant the Council would increasingly have to take account of the political preferences of the Parliament, adding a further supranational twist to the EEC system. Monetary union, strongly advocated by France while West Germany was unenthusiastic and the United Kingdom downright hostile, was not included in the SEA, but there was a reference to convoking an IGC in the future to decide on this next potential step in integration. Indeed the preamble to the treaty contained a commitment to "transform relations as a whole among their States into a European Union."

By the end of 1992, the SEA had worked – as intended – to create a far more integrated economic community without internal borders, where not only goods and capital but also people could circulate freely. Companies were quick to take advantage, as reflected by a large increase in inter-European mergers. The EEC's political system became more supranational than ever, a change accepted by all member states in return for expected economic benefits and improved EEC decision-making. The Commission, which had originally proposed introducing more QMV to complete the single market, was in charge of proposing a swathe of legislation for harmonizing economic regulations that no one country could veto.

The move to formal political union, in the shape of the Treaty on European Union signed in February 1992, launched the next logical step in integration: monetary union and greater competences, including in foreign policy. However, this new departure was made possible less by the inevitable consequences of the SEA than by the tremendous geopolitical change that suddenly reconfigured the international system (Gilbert 2003, 187–224).

3.3   Designing European Unity for the Post-Cold War Era, 1992–2004

On November 9, 1989, people power in communist-controlled East Berlin brought down the Berlin Wall. This physical barrier, erected in 1961 to prevent citizens from fleeing the oppressive East German regime, symbolized the division of the European continent into a NATO and a Soviet bloc. The fall of this wall triggered the collapse of Soviet control over the communist governments established in East European countries that had been overrun by the Red Army at the end of the Second World War. The demise of the Iron Curtain dividing Europe brought the German question to the fore again, as West and East Germans made clear their desire to form one country, whose population and economic power would be unmatched in Europe (Sarotte 2009).

Germany's place in the continent's balance of power had been a central preoccupation of nineteenth- and early twentieth-century politics, because France and Britain did not want this country to exercise hegemony (in other words, political dominance). The threat of German hegemony had disappeared during the Cold War, through the division of Germany and NATO's defensive alliance. But, with the fall of communism, western leaders worried about how to maintain a stable European order in the future. The 1992 project for creating a European Union was thus designed to ensure that this question was solved for good, and to the satisfaction of anxious foreign powers. In addition, the project was a blueprint for a more efficient, more democratic supranational political system, which would soon have its own currency and embrace many new member states.

France in particular was concerned that German reunification might lead to a rapid expansion of German economic and political power across the continent, relegating France to a dreaded secondary role. The crumbling Soviet Union feared that the end of the Cold War would render Germany's NATO commitments redundant, opening up the possibility of a more aggressive, even nuclear-armed near neighbor. Margaret Thatcher considered German reunification premature and sought, unsuccessfully, to find a way to block it. These anxieties by no means reflected German leaders' intentions for their country's role in post-Cold War Europe. However, Chancellor Helmut Kohl recognized that reuniting his country and returning to the forefront of European diplomacy would require making special multilateral institutional arrangements, just as Adenauer had done when negotiating the creation of a sovereign West Germany in the late 1940s (see Sections 2.1 and 2.2). The shared post-Cold War goal was thus a European Germany instead of a Germanized Europe; thereby a further development of supranationalism was favored. To assuage its neighbors' fears, newly reunited Germany was willing to pool sovereignty in two crucial policy areas: monetary policy – which meant abandoning its currency, the Deutschmark, the emblem of its post-war economic miracle – and foreign policy (Moravcsik 1998, 379–471).

3.3.1   Negotiating the Maastricht Treaty, 1992

The official decision to design a new treaty to reform the EEC was taken by the European Council, the EU's steering institution (see Figure 0.2), as it met in the Dutch city of Maastricht. Heads of state and government signed the 1992 Maastricht Treaty that created the EU (legally this document is called "the Treaty on European Union"). Thus, although the Commission and the European Parliament both expressed a preference for a European Union, it was the member states that took the decision to embark on the EU project for "an ever closer union among the peoples of Europe," as stated in the preamble of the Maastricht Treaty.

The Maastricht Treaty incorporated two long-standing ambitions of enthusiasts of European integration: monetary union (leading ultimately to a single currency) and a common foreign policy. Federalists in particular believed that both of these would help Europe develop a distinct identity, which would loosen citizens' national loyalties. Identifying with the new EU would also become easier thanks to the creation of EU citizenship supplementing national citizenship. The new treaty specified the following rights associated with EU citizenship: the right to move and reside within EU territory; the right to vote and stand for local and European elections in any member state; the right to protection from the diplomatic authorities of any member state when travelling outside the EU; and the right to petition the European Parliament. In another supranational move, the Court of Justice was given the power to impose financial penalties on member states found to have failed to comply with European legislation.

Yet this treaty also contained safeguards designed to prevent the EU from resembling a sovereign federal state, even if it had far greater powers than the EEC. This was a condition imposed by the United Kingdom, which refused to countenance any mention of the word "federal" in the final treaty. More concretely, the treaty ensured that the new Common Foreign and Security Policy (CFSP), as well as the other sensitive policy area, justice and home affairs, would be subject to unanimous, intergovernmental decision-making. This meant excluding the supranational institutions (Commission, Parliament, and Court) from having a say in these matters. In addition, certain countries negotiated **opt-outs** allowing them not to participate in a common policy. For instance, the UK opted out of the commitment to join monetary union, a move followed by Denmark, which also opted out of certain features of the new EU foreign policy involving civilian or military missions (Adler-Nissen 2011). Nevertheless, the new treaty granted more decision-making power to the European Parliament and further cemented QMV as the standard, supranational method for all policy-making, excluding foreign policy or judicial and police matters.

Running to more than 230 articles, the Maastricht Treaty is a very complex legal document the size of a book, not a succinct constitutional blueprint. This size was necessary in order for the treaty to include very precise details not only about the decision-making rules – the basic component of constitutions – covering EU institutions, but also about specific policy objectives and practices. For instance, a lengthy part of the Maastricht Treaty is devoted to the provisions for monetary union, explaining that the European Central Bank set up in Frankfurt to oversee the single currency will have as its goal price stability (under 2 percent inflation in the medium term). Similarly, the treaty covers the minutiae of how the CFSP will function under a different legal system, which allows for greater intergovernmental control. The overall treaty complexity thus illustrates how member states seek to tie themselves to very precise policy procedures and objectives, not allowing much latitude for controversial policies to emerge from the ordinary supranational political system. This level of detail serves to diminish the likelihood that supranational decision-making could result in inconvenient outcomes for member states (Sbragia 2000).

The EU plan for monetary union comprised a three-part timeline, beginning with the abolition of controls on the circulation of capital, followed by a gradual convergence of member states' macroeconomic policies from 1994 to 1999. This second stage involved governments pledging to meet a set of **convergence criteria**, notably to keep budget deficits under 3 percent of GDP and total public debt under 60 percent of GDP. These strict rules were enacted under pressure from the German Central Bank (the Bundesbank). It argued that a stable single European currency – the third stage of monetary integration, culminating in the 2002 launch of the euro – could only survive market pressures if they all obeyed the same fiscal discipline. Establishing fiscal conservatism across the Eurozone was also necessary in order to ensure that the zone could function with a single interest rate. Crucially, EU monetary union did not correspond with full political union: fiscal powers, that is, tax and spending, remain the preserve of national sovereignty within the boundaries set by the convergence criteria. Moreover, under the euro system, member states are still responsible for paying their own national debt (the details are discussed in Section 5.2).

The euro was not the only major new initiative launched by the Maastricht Treaty. The other important objectives for the new EU were to reap the benefits of foreign policy coordination and to prepare the way for enlargement into post-Soviet Central and Eastern Europe. However, even before the signing of the Maastricht Treaty, European leaders faced a major international crisis on their doorstep: the violent break-up of Yugoslavia. The constituent units of this former multinational federation went to war with one another in 1991, unleashing a brutal ethnic conflict with indiscriminate atrocities that raged until 1995. During this period, despite the launch of the CFSP, an institutional mechanism for coordinating foreign policy, the EU was unable to coordinate a diplomatic response robust enough to bring the warring parties to a negotiated settlement (Rathbun 2004). Instead US diplomacy, combined with the use of military force against the Bosnian Serbs by US troops under NATO command, persuaded the belligerents to accept peace terms known as the Dayton Agreement. Simmering tensions in this region erupted again in 1999, in a conflict between Serbian forces and ethnic Albanians in the former Yugoslav province of Kosovo. An end to this violence was only possible when US President Bill Clinton convinced NATO partners to authorize a bombing campaign against Serbia. While the EU was paralyzed, many of its member states preferred to operate under the American-led NATO system (see Box 1.2). These two crises thus revealed inherent limitations on the EU's ability to pursue a fully coordinated and independent foreign policy, despite the creation of a formal institutional process for such cooperation.

3.3.2   Preparing for a new enlargement

Nevertheless, in the 1990s Central and Eastern European countries from behind the former Iron Curtain sought to join the EU – which already welcomed wealthy and stable Austria, Finland, and Sweden as new members in 1995. Preparing for Central and Eastern European enlargement was a headache for the now 15 EU member states, although for the first time they developed official rules for this process (see Box 3.3). Ideologically they were committed to the aim of reuniting the European continent; but West European countries, and particularly their electorates, were very sensitive to various costs of offering EU membership to these poorer economies (Schimmelfennig and Sedelmeier 2005). The recipients of most EU regional and agricultural funds, Ireland, Portugal, Greece, and Spain, worried that enlargement to Eastern and Central

---

Box 3.3   Key Concept: The Enlargement Process

Since 1993, joining the EU is conditional upon having a free market economy and meeting four political conditions known as the **Copenhagen criteria**: democracy, rule of law, respect for human rights, and protection of minorities. Applicant states must also conform to the existing body of EU legislation, known by the French phrase of **_acquis communautaire_**. Applications for membership are addressed to the Council of the EU, which makes its decision by unanimity, having solicited the opinion of both the Commission and the European Parliament. However, the Commission prepares a formal opinion for the Council of the EU about whether the applicant country conforms to the Copenhagen criteria. A country that passes this test and has the support of all EU countries then becomes an "official candidate"; this marks the beginning of an accession procedure that can take many years before membership is achieved. Official candidate status gives access to special EU funds designed to help countries implement the _acquis_ – usually a lengthy procedure. The main task of the Commission thereafter is to monitor the way the candidate country is integrating and applying EU legislation across all EU policy domains. This results in periodic reports prepared for the European Council and the European Parliament. During this phase, the Commission can suspend the accession negotiations as a tool to induce policy reform. This happened with Turkey, with negotiations on the implementation of certain EU policies suspended in 2006. This occurred because Turkey does not recognize the Republic of Cyprus – an EU country – making it impossible to cooperate over a common external tariff and free movement of people. A country that has successfully implemented EU law to the satisfaction of the Commission still needs to sign an accession treaty requiring majority approval by the European Parliament, and this in turn must be ratified by all EU countries.

Europe would mean losing access to these funds, as they would be redirected to poorer states. Nordic member states attached to high environmental protection standards were concerned that the entry of countries with relics of Soviet-era heavy industry would result in a diluted EU commitment to the environment. Similarly, France and Germany were apprehensive that new member states would lead a race to the bottom in wages or worker protection.

Another preoccupation in the prelude to the 2004 enlargement was how EU institutions would function with up to a dozen potential new member states. Here proponents of supranationalism argued for a streamlining of decision-making procedures. A particularly thorny issue was the recalibration of voting weights granted to each country in the Council of the EU, depending on its population. These voting weights are hugely significant, as they determine how many countries are needed to pass a law under QMV. The Commission pushed for reform of the rules surrounding QMV, to make it easier to get a winning majority. At the same time there was pressure to reduce the number of commissioners, as laws proposed by the Commission first need majority support within the College of commissioners. So the fear was that moving from 15 to 25 or more commissioners – each country traditionally having its own – would hamper the Commission's ability to propose policies.

Uncertainty over how exactly to proceed with enlargement after the end of the Cold War was thus the reason why, at the beginning of the twenty-first century, EU leaders decided to link the biggest ever round of widening with a more symbolic form of deepening: a Constitutional Treaty. The timing seemed propitious, as it came after the successful launch of the euro, which became a circulating currency in 2002. The proposed constitution – in reality, a document with the same legal status as an ordinary international treaty – aimed to inspire a new faith in the European integration project. It would clarify to citizens what the EU did for them as well as contain a set of reforms for making policy-making more effective and democratic.

These grand ambitions faced more than the usual difficulty of finding consensus among member states divided over their political and economic preferences. The extra complication was EU citizens' wariness toward repeated widening and deepening that did not necessarily have obvious trickle-down economic benefits for the majority. Consequently, until the 2009 Lisbon Treaty, EU leaders struggled to implement the changes first intended by the 2004 Constitutional Treaty; reform ultimately succeeded, but not in the manner EU elites had hoped.

3.4   From Constitutional Failure to the Lisbon Treaty, 2004–2010

Throughout the 1990s it was not clear whether Central and Eastern European enlargement would happen all in one go or, like a regatta, in a staggered order, rewarding top performing countries in their transition to democracy and the free market. Hence the enlargement question concerned not just what the addition of new member states would mean for the EU system but also how far candidate countries were making progress toward meeting the conditions for membership (O'Brennan 2006). The matter was settled by 2002, as the EU countries decided to make the uniting of Europe the priority. This meant accepting a dramatic round of widening (Republic of Cyprus, Czech Republic, Estonia, Hungary, Latvia, Lithuania, Malta, Poland, Slovakia, Slovenia – all at once) rather than having the staggered entry of a handful of best candidates. Nevertheless, Bulgaria's accession and Romania's accession were delayed until 2007, as the EU wanted to see these two countries pursue further internal reforms.

Two caveats were imposed on the 2004 enlargement. The first was restricted freedom of movement for citizens of new member states (existing EU countries could choose to limit migration from new member states until 2011). The second was a budget settlement – less generous than in past enlargements – minimizing how much existing EU states would pay in agricultural subsidies and regional funds. The total cost of the 2004 enlargement round in the period 2004–2006 was thus a relatively modest 10 percent of the EU's €100 billion annual budget, with an informal rule that half the budget would continue to be spent in the EU-15. Hence the ideal of European unity did not imply huge financial solidarity between Old and New Europe. Nevertheless, the fact that a deal had been reached generated optimism about the future. This set the tone for a radical reflection on the future of integration.

3.4.1   The Constitutional Treaty, 2004

To develop a clearer institutional identity for an expanded EU, a novel approach to revising the existing treaties was used. Member states accepted to send representatives, alongside delegates from the Commission and the European Parliament as well as from 13 official candidate countries, to a Convention on the Future of Europe that met in 2002–2003. The remit of this Convention, presided over by former French President Valéry Giscard d'Estaing, was to devise institutional arrangements to make the expanded EU more efficient and democratic. With this goal in mind, the Convention produced a document called "Treaty Establishing a Constitution for Europe," which would replace the existing treaties with a single legal document. The idea of a convention as well as the Constitutional Treaty it produced demonstrated a European desire to mimic the illustrious Philadelphia Convention (1777–1778), where the Founding Fathers drew up the US Constitution (Magnette 2006).

Yet this European experiment in constitution-making did not exactly have the same results as in the US. For a start, an IGC was convened in Rome to pore over the text of the Constitutional Treaty and amend it in line with member state exigencies. Additionally, the final treaty signed by the now 25 member states in October 2004 was a book-length legal treatise: not something that could be understood by an ordinary citizen, let alone fit into one's back pocket. Thus, although the Constitutional Treaty provided a unified legal basis for the EU, it replicated the hugely intricate legal web of competences, decision-making procedures, and policy specifics. More importantly, ever since the revolutionary jurisprudence of the Court of Justice in the 1960s (discussed in Section 4.4), EU treaties and legislation already had the status of "higher" quasi-constitutional law that trumped member state law.

Overall, therefore, the Constitutional Treaty was a symbolic reform of the EU system rather than a constitutional transformation. There were some institutional modifications though, including the creation of a president of the European Council, a so-called EU foreign minister, and a simplified procedure for extending the EU's policy competences without formal treaty renegotiation. True to the prevailing spirit of compromise, the new treaty disappointed hopes across the political spectrum because it did not opt for streamlining the EU according to a single federal or confederal blueprint (a debate discussed in Chapter 9). Hence federalists bemoaned this new failure to adopt a true federal model. European socialists were dismayed that economic freedoms were not counterbalanced by the creation of new EU social policies. Finally, opponents of integration interpreted the new treaty as a further surrender of national sovereignty for no meaningful gain in policy effectiveness.

The rhetoric of a constitutional foundation for the EU implied a fundamental new departure: a move away from a contract between states to a contract between the EU and its citizens. Having adopted this rhetoric, EU leaders in many countries thus came under pressure to let their citizens have a say on the Constitutional Treaty by holding referendums rather than relying purely on parliamentary ratification. These referendums are important instruments (a topic addressed in Section 11.3) for allowing citizens of a particular country to vote "yes" or "no" to an important EU integration question (Hobolt 2009). They are often used to determine whether citizens agree with their leaders in wanting their country to join the EU; Norwegian citizens, for instance, have rejected EU membership in this way, whereas in 1975 UK citizens voted by referendum to remain in the EEC. Denmark and Sweden have also held referendums on whether to join the euro, which citizens in both instances refused. Holding a referendum on an EU treaty, which is a prerogative of each member state, is risky because a rejection prevents a treaty from coming into force for all member states. By contrast, parliamentary ratification of an international treaty signed by a government with a parliamentary majority is far less likely to fail.

Governments in France, Luxembourg, Spain, and the Netherlands each decided that it was appropriate for the Constitutional Treaty to win the approval of their citizens by referendum. Of course, these four governments, which had already signed the Constitutional Treaty, expected their voters to approve it. The real uncertainty was thought to lie in the United Kingdom, where Prime Minister Tony Blair pledged to hold a referendum in a country traditionally lukewarm about European integration. Thus it was a shock when, in late May 2005, 55 percent of French citizens voted against the Constitutional Treaty and, a few days later, a 62 percent majority in the Netherlands also rejected the constitution.

This was not the first time that a country had failed to ratify an EU treaty by referendum. Such a scenario occurred in Denmark, whose voters rejected the Maastricht Treaty in 1992, and also in Ireland, whose citizens voted against the 2001 Nice Treaty that had recalibrated countries' voting weights in the Council of the EU. In both earlier cases the countries in question quickly resorted to follow-up referendums, asking their citizens to change their mind on the same treaty – a tactic that had worked. But, given the emphasis on democratic legitimacy that surrounded the very idea of the Constitutional Treaty, EU leaders wanted to avoid being seen to contradict the will of French and Dutch citizens by asking them to vote again on the same text. Consequently, the brief period of euro-euphoria that had accompanied the dramatic new EU widening and the European Convention dissipated as national governments and EU institutions returned to the drawing board. The prevailing mood was introspective, querying not only why citizens had turned against the Constitutional Treaty. There was also the underlying question of whether referendums were a good idea for ratifying complex international treaties (Moravcsik 2006). After all, no EU country asks its people to vote on other kinds of international treaties but each country leaves the matter to its parliament to decide – just as, in the USA, the US Senate, not the American people, is responsible for ratifying treaties.

3.4.2   The Lisbon Treaty, 2009

This critical and introspective mood was not helped by the fact that the EU was just emerging from a foreign policy crisis caused by serious divisions among its members over whether to support the US invasion of Iraq in 2003. In addition, EU leaders were concerned about the EU's economic performance, which could not match the dizzying growth rates of emerging powers such as China, South Korea, or Brazil, putting further strain on European welfare state systems. Since institutional reform was supposed to provide the EU with a better coordinated and more responsive foreign policy (through a president and a foreign minister) as well as to help it compete in global markets, EU leaders were determined to pass a new treaty. In order to do so, they retained the most significant institutional innovations of the Constitutional Treaty:

- creation of a president of the European Council appointed by the member state governments for a two-and-a-half-year term to provide leadership on EU policy-making;
- creation of the high representative of the Union for Foreign Affairs and Security Policy appointed by the member state governments for a five-year term to provide leadership for foreign policy;
- formal legal personality for the EU, allowing it to sign international treaties with states and international organizations;
- extending the **co-decision** procedure, giving more legislative power to the European Parliament, especially on the EU budget and international agreements;
- giving force of law to a European Charter of Fundamental Rights when countries implement EU legislation;
- a simplified revision procedure, allowing the European Council to revise treaties without an IGC
- simplified QMV, which will require from 2014 a dual majority of 55 percent of member states representing at least 65 percent of the EU population for legislation to pass.

Stripped of the earlier constitutional language (designating an official anthem and official symbols such as the EU flag, although these continue to be used in practice), these reforms were repackaged as the Lisbon Treaty, signed in the Portuguese capital in December 2007 by what were now 27 member states. The reworked treaty still had to be ratified by each member state, but there was an informal agreement by national governments not to use referendums to prevent another ratification disaster. Some citizens deeply resented being frozen out of the ratification procedure and claimed that this was anti-democratic, since the Lisbon Treaty is essentially based on the Constitutional Treaty that many EU leaders deemed required special democratic legitimacy.

The exception to the controversial no-referendum agreement was Ireland, which is constitutionally obliged to hold a referendum on all EU treaties. A 1987 Irish Supreme Court ruling on the Single European Act – *Crotty v. the Taoiseach* – judged that its provisions for trying to coordinate foreign policies were a restraint on sovereignty. According to the Irish constitution, placing limits on sovereignty can only happen through a constitutional amendment approved by a national referendum. This practice has been followed for every subsequent EU treaty revision. In June 2008 Irish voters rejected the terms of the Lisbon Treaty, but the Irish government immediately came under huge pressure to simply ask its citizens to change their minds in a new referendum. EU institutions and leaders pointed out that since 1973 Ireland had benefited from generous EU financial assistance to develop the Irish economy. Unwilling to be seen as holding up European integration, the Irish government pulled out all the stops for a "yes" vote in a new referendum in October 2009 that was ultimately successful.

The Lisbon Treaty came into effect in December 2009, swiftly followed by the appointment of a president for the European Council and a high representative for Foreign Affairs and Security Policy. This unexpectedly arduous process of institutional reform was supposed to provide the foundation for the next decade of integration. These expectations were quickly blown away by the Eurozone debt crisis that struck after 2010. To deal with this debt problem a new treaty was hastily put together, with particularly important consequences for countries using the euro. These recent legal and institutional changes are explained in Chapter 12.

3.5   Concluding Summary

This chapter has explained the institutional evolution of European integration as the EEC was transformed from an economic project into a supranational political union. A key part of this process consisted in widening: the addition of new member states, in successive rounds of enlargement from 1973 onwards. The deepening of integration has occurred alongside the widening of membership. Notably, the 1986 Single European Act was designed to deliver the economic benefits of a fully integrated market, a necessary precondition on the path to possible monetary and political union. However, national politicians and businesses were more preoccupied with the economic dynamism and enhanced commercial opportunities that this represented than with using the SEA as a platform for radical deepening.

Nevertheless, monetary and political union, the latter in the form of new competences in foreign policy and justice, were realized after the 1992 Treaty on European Union created the EU. This bold departure from limited economic integration came in response to the end of the Cold War. Leaders in Western Europe designed both the single currency and political union in order to strengthen European integration in the wake of German reunification. Political union, however, did not mean that the EU could act as an effective and single actor in foreign policy crises such as the wars in former Yugoslavia. But the euro was successfully launched in 2002, and shortly afterwards member states agreed to a dramatic enlargement in 2004.

It was in this context that EU leaders floated an ambitious proposal to deepen integration still further, notably in foreign policy, under the guise of the Constitutional Treaty. The failure of this project in referendums in France and the Netherlands did not, however, prevent a further move toward supranational integration. This came in the shape of the Lisbon Treaty, which was ratified in 2009. Controversially, this treaty actually reprised many of the changes in decision-making and the new foreign policy instruments contained in the Constitutional Treaty. This was justified on the basis of making the EU more efficient, given an expanded membership. The result is that the EU today is characterized by increased supranational decision-making, a single currency, and a more coordinated foreign policy; but it is still far from being a sovereign federal state.

Guide to Further Reading

Jabko, N. 2006. *Playing the Market: A Political Strategy for Uniting Europe, 1985–2005*. Ithaca, NY: Cornell University Press.

Comprehensive and highly insightful account of how state and non-state actors' interests coalesced to support the creation of a single market despite these actors having contrasting political reasons for it.

Laursen, F., ed. 2012. *The EU's Lisbon Treaty: Institutional Choice and Implementation*. Farnham: Ashgate.

Selection of up-to-date essays on the changes contained in the Lisbon Treaty and on how these changes affect the EU's business across its main policy domains.

Marsh, D. 2009. *The Euro: The Battle for the New Global Currency*. New Haven, CT: Yale University Press.

In-depth account of the politics and personalities involved in the creation of the Euro that also explains the political and economic motivations behind this new currency.

O'Brennan, J. 2006. *The Eastern Enlargement of the European Union*. Abingdon: Routledge.

A lucid historical and empirical guide to the 2004 enlargement of the EU and its institutional as well as geopolitical implications.

Discussion Questions

1   Identify the periods when deepening coincided with widening. Why are the two processes sometimes linked?
2   Analyze the reasons why the United Kingdom is often considered an awkward EU member. Is this interpretation justified?
3   Which economic interests and political leaders supported the SEA? Why did these diverse preferences share the Commission's vision for more supranationalism?
4   Contrast how monetary integration and foreign policy coordination fared after the Maastricht Treaty. Why was it harder to coordinate foreign policy?
5   Is it possible to distinguish the Constitutional Treaty from the Lisbon Treaty? How would you interpret the significance of the failed ratification of the Constitutional Treaty?

Web Resources

This book is supported by a companion website, which can be found at www.wiley.com/go/glencross. There you will find a list of the web links referred to in this chapter wherever you see a "Web" icon in the page margins. In addition, you will find a list of further relevant online resources such as websites for EU institutions, political groups, archives, and think tanks, information on studying abroad, and biographies of key figures. You will also find self-assessment tools in the form of flashcards and independent study questions developed specifically for this chapter.

Glossary

Accession

Name given to the official act whereby a new country joins the EU. Also used when referring to different waves of EU enlargement, hence references to 1973 or 2004 accession countries.

Acquis communautaire

French phrase referring to the body of legislation, jurisprudence, and treaty principles that constitute the sum of legal obligations member states must comply with. Countries seeking to join the EU are required to comply with these obligations prior to accession.

Balance of payments crisis

A crisis whereby a country's currency suddenly falls in value. Usually this is triggered by a deficit between inflows and outflows of trade and investment, with the result that governments resort to borrowing, which further weakens their currency.

Bretton Woods system

Name given to the 1944 agreement to institute a global system of stable exchange rates pegged in value against the dollar, whose value was in turn backed in gold. This system underpinned the spectacular growth of international trade and investment after the Second World War. By the late 1960s inflation and budget deficits in the US made it impossible to maintain dollar convertibility into gold, with the result that the world economy moved to floating exchange rates.

Co-decision

Part of the standard EU legislative procedure. Legislation proposed by the Commission requires joint agreement by both the Council of the EU and the European Parliament in order to become law. Co-decision has made the European Parliament a powerful supranational legislature.

Convergence criteria

Budget, inflation, and overall public debt rules that EU countries had to meet in order to join the euro prior to its launch. These criteria, spelled out formally in the Maastricht Treaty, were designed to make European economies converge and to make the single currency stable.

Copenhagen criteria

A set of political and economic criteria, decided upon at a European Council summit in Copenhagen, that must be met by countries seeking to join the EU. In essence, these criteria provide for a free market and liberal democracy based on human rights.

European Monetary System (EMS)

Policy for regulating the exchange value of West European currencies, set up in 1979 as a response to the collapse of Bretton Woods. The strength of the German Deutschmark made it difficult for some countries to stay in the system, creating pressure for currency union.

Intergovernmental conference (IGC)

A diplomatic summit between EU heads of state and government that meets episodically for high-level negotiations, especially to negotiate treaty revisions.

Iron Curtain

Phrase coined by Winston Churchill, which entered general usage to refer to the totalitarian regimes in Eastern Europe installed and controlled by the Soviet Union after the defeat of Nazi Germany.

Opt-out

Procedure whereby certain member states choose not to participate in common EU policies considered politically unpopular. The United Kingdom has opted out of the euro, Schengen, and the granting of legal status to the Charter of Fundamental Rights, while Sweden and Denmark have opted out of the euro.

Referendum

Procedure whereby citizens are asked to vote yes or no on a specific piece of proposed legislation, usually a matter of extreme importance. National referendums have often been held to decide whether to join the EU, and they are increasingly used by governments to give citizens a say on ratifying new EU treaties.

References

Adler-Nissen, Rebecca. 2011. "Opting out of an Ever Closer Union: The Integration Doxa and the Management of Sovereignty." *West European Politics*, 34: 1092–1113. DOI: 10.1080/01402382.2011.591102

Dinan, Desmond. 2004. *Europe Recast: A History of European Integration*. Boulder, CO: Lynne Rienner.

Geddes, Andrew. 2004. *The European Union and British Politics*. Basingstoke: Palgrave Macmillan.

George, Stephen. 1998. *An Awkward Partner: Britain in the European Community*. Oxford: Oxford University Press.

Gilbert, Mark. 2003. *Surpassing Realism: The Politics of European Integration since 1945*. Oxford: Rowman & Littlefield.

Gillingham, John. 2003. *European Integration, 1950–2003: Superstate or New Market Economy*. Cambridge: Cambridge University Press.

Hobolt, Sara. 2009. *Europe in Question: Referendums on European Integration*. Oxford: Oxford University Press.

Magnette, Paul. 2006. "Comparing Constitutional Change in the United States and the European Union." In Anand Menon and Martin Schain, eds., *Comparative Federalism*, 149–176. Oxford: Oxford University Press.

Marsh, David. 2009. *The Euro: The Politics of the New Global Currency*. New Haven, CT: Yale University Press.

Moravcsik, Andrew. 1998. *The Choice for Europe: Social Purpose and State Power from Messina to Maastricht*. New York: Cornell University Press.

Moravcsik, Andrew. 2006. "What Can We Learn from the Collapse of the European Constitutional Project?" *PolitischeVierteljahresschrift*, 47: 219–241. DOI: 10.1007/s11615-006-0037-7

Nugent, Neill. 2004. *European Union Enlargement*. Basingstoke: Palgrave MacMillan.

O'Brennan, John. 2006. *The Eastern Enlargement of the European Union*. Abingdon: Routledge.

Rathbun, Brian C. 2004. *Partisan Interventions: European Party Politics and Peace Enforcement in the Balkans*. New York: Cornell University Press.

Sarotte, Mary Elise. 2009. *1989: The Struggle to Create Post-Cold War Europe*. Princeton, NJ: Princeton University Press.

Sbragia, Alberta. 2000. "The EU as Coxswain: Governance by Steering." In Jon Pierre, ed., *Debating Governance: Authority, Steering and Democracy*, 219–240. Oxford: Oxford University Press.

Schimmelfennig, Frank, and Ulrich Sedelmeier. 2005. *The Europeanization of Central and Eastern Europe*. New York: Cornell University Press.

Tiersky, Ronald. 2003. *François Mitterrand: A Very French President*. Oxford: Rowman & Littlefield.

Part II
Analyzing Integration

4

The EU's Institutional Dynamics

Contents

Learning Objectives

- to identify the institutional actors involved in EU decision-making;
- to analyze the inputs involved in EU decision-making;
- to distinguish the procedural elements involved in OLP;
- to interpret how important a role different kinds of interest groups play;
- to map and analyze the interactions between national courts and the CJEU;
- to distinguish the different institutional dynamics between OLP and foreign policy;
- to evaluate why foreign policy is organized differently from OLP.

The Politics of European Integration: Political Union or a House Divided?, First Edition. Andrew Glencross.
© 2014 Andrew Glencross. Published 2014 by Blackwell Publishing Ltd.

4.0 Introduction: The Functioning of the EU

Like any political system, the EU consists of a set of institutions representing different actors and interests that are capable of making binding decisions that affect the economy, determine how society is regulated, and set foreign policy. The EU institutions discussed in the previous two chapters are not the only actors in this system. Policy demands can also come from ordinary citizens, through political parties that gain their power from national and European elections, and from private groups such as corporations, NGOs, or specialized interest groups. The interactions between this unwieldy mix of actors shape EU policy-making – that is, the laws and other policies enacted by EU institutions. The dynamic relations that develop between such actors within the formal EU institutional structure and the ways in which they shape what the EU does are the subject of this chapter.

Section 4.1 provides a succinct overview of how EU policy-making is shaped through the interaction of different institutions (Commission, Council, Parliament, Court of Justice) and through political inputs from parties, citizens, and interest groups. With all these inputs into policy-making, it is no surprise that decision-making is complicated and the process of enacting legislation politically fraught. However, as discussed in Section 4.2, the bulk of important policy-making comes in the form of an ordinary legislative procedure (OLP), a consensual process of institutionalized negotiation that links together the Commission, the Council, and the European Parliament.

A key input into OLP comes from the participation of interest groups and experts. EU institutions engaged in complex policy-making decisions require the assistance of these policy specialists to provide information and to legitimize decisions. As explained in Section 4.3, interest groups vary in their resources and ability to mobilize citizens, which results in their having different approaches as to how to influence EU policy-making. The Commission and Parliament are particularly interested in having the input of policy specialists, as they have small administrative resources by comparison with national governments. Moreover, the starting point of OLP is a consultation procedure with the public and experts led by the Commission.

The EU law produced in this fashion either binds member states directly or else provides a framework for them to implement specific policy objectives by transposing these objectives into national law. Failure to implement laws in accordance with EU policy or failure to comply with treaty obligations are grounds for the Commission to bring a non-compliance case to the Court of Justice. Section 4.4 examines how the Commission, as the guardian of the treaties and of EU law, performs this watchdog role of ensuring that member states comply with EU law and treaties. Similarly, the analysis shows how individuals or groups can invoke their EU rights and sue in national courts. These courts are constitutionally obliged to uphold European law when it clashes with national law – a fact that gives them a crucial role in upholding a common EU legal order.

An entirely different procedure for legislation is followed in foreign policy. Instead of the supranational OLP procedure, national governments have preferred to insulate foreign policy-making from too much direct control by the Commission and judicial review by the CJEU. As discussed in Section 4.5, in this extremely sensitive policy area it is the Council that takes the leading role by designing legislation without any need for co-decision, thereby reducing the influence of the Parliament. Nevertheless, supranational actors do have an institutionalized role in EU foreign policy: they help generate consensus and coordinate foreign policy preferences across 28 national governments.

4.1   An Overview of the Dynamics of EU Policy-Making

The first thing to understand about the dynamics of EU policy-making is that member states are far from having complete control over how legislation gets made. As a result of the successive treaty agreements discussed in the first two chapters, national governments have delegated the tasks of proposing and designing policies, in a variety of areas, to EU institutions that they do not control. It is this power over what EU policy is and how it will be conducted that has increasingly been delegated to the supranational branches of the EU: the European Commission and the European Parliament.

The reason for granting this power is to overcome the **collective action problem**: if every country could propose its own laws, or if every law required unanimous agreement from all the member states, then not much would ever get done. In a context where many policy problems – such as pollution, immigration, or crime – are transnational, it makes sense to delegate the power of proposing legislation and of supervising its application to an independent body of experts, detached from national interests and preferences: the Commission. This supranational institution serves the general European interest and can draw on expertise from the highly qualified (and multilingual) staff organized in directorates-general (the equivalent of ministries or departments of state), as well as from national administrations and outside experts.

Equally, to scrutinize policy proposals coming from the Commission and to make sure they are responsive to the needs of Europe's citizens, it is necessary to have democratic political input. The Council of the EU, which represents nationally elected governments, and the directly elected European Parliament provide precisely this input. Why have an extra tier of political representation beyond the Council of the EU? As in many bicameral federal systems (see Chapter 6), one political decision-making body needs to represent the community as a whole, not just the preferences of the separate territorial units. This is the task of the European Parliament: citizens vote for parliamentarians from among political parties with competing political ideologies. The European Parliament's members thus represent an aggregation of preferences and interests not found elsewhere in the EU system. The other political decision-making body, the Council of the EU, represents national interests as articulated by the parties in government in each member state, who send their ministers to sit in the Council.

The CJEU also has a function when it comes to EU policy-making – although this was not a feature that member states originally expected when they signed the Treaty of Rome (Alter 1998). The Court, based in the tiny country of Luxembourg, has the responsibility of interpreting what EU law is and how it constrains the member states. This power of interpretation can have a significant impact on the policy autonomy of member states. On many important matters, such as practices restrictive of intra-EU trade or gender equality, the CJEU has ruled that national law is illegal under the terms of the EU treaties. Consequently this kind of jurisprudence has not only led to the overturning of national legislation but also helped initiate moves to shift policy regulation from the national to the EU level. This means that the CJ contributes indirectly to EU policy-making by outlawing national legislation and thereby encouraging states to find EU-wide solutions (Alter 1998).

Hence the European Commission, the European Parliament, and even the Court of Justice each have an input into policy-making, alongside national governments that act via the Council of the EU and alongside the European Council – the overarching steering body composed of heads of state and of government. The result is a highly complex institutional process of decision-making involving citizens and organized interests, national governments, and the various EU institutions. To make sense of this complexity, the present chapter outlines how policy is formulated as a product of the interactions between all these institutions, which incorporate different actors and interests. However, first it is necessary to highlight the different inputs into policy-making from citizens, organized interests, national governments, and EU institutions.

Citizens provide a variety of policy inputs that potentially shape the policies enacted by the EU. They do so in the following ways:

- by electing national governments, whose preferences are then represented in the intergovernmental EU institutions, the Council of the EU and the European Council;
- by electing MEPs, whose participation in EU legislation is very important thanks to the co-decision procedure;
- by constituting public opinion that influences national governments and parliaments as well as the European Parliament; typically public opinion is channelled through political parties, interest groups, NGOs, and the media;
- by using European law to sue member states (in national courts) for breaching treaty provisions, notably the four fundamental freedoms.

Organized interests, typically lobby groups representing businesses and NGOs campaigning over specific issues, also contribute a variety of inputs:

- by seeking to attract the attention of policy-makers in the Commission, Council, and Parliament, by publicizing certain problems, and by proposing policy responses;
- by mobilizing citizens, union members, NGO members, and so on to make their opinions on certain issues known to EU policy-makers, sometimes through colorful protests in Brussels and at summits held elsewhere;
- by meeting informally with national and EU policy-makers to explain their preferences for how legislation should or should not be drafted.

National governments in turn also provide their own policy inputs in the following ways:

- by negotiating the broad policy goals of the EU in periodic European Council meetings;

- by expressing their preferences and voting in the Council of the EU;
- by proposing policies directly in the specific fields of foreign policy and justice matters;
- by holding the rotating chair of the Council of the EU, which alternates every 6 months, allowing one country to chair and run meetings;
- by sending national officials to expert committees that help prepare the Commission's legislative initiatives and delegates to EU regulatory agencies such as the European Central Bank or the European Food Safety Agency.

EU-level inputs include:

- legislative proposals from the European Commission, the only actor allowed to initiate policy in the vast majority of EU business, notably for regulating the single market;
- reports, resolutions, and proposals of the European Parliament highlighting problems the Commission should address;
- European Council and Council of the EU requests for legislative action to be taken by the Commission, most commonly in justice and home affairs but without specifying technical aspects of legislation;
- CJEU jurisprudence, which settles what the treaties mean, whether member states are in breach of treaty obligations and EU law, and also whether EU law goes beyond the powers conferred in the treaties.

4.2   The Ordinary Legislative Procedure (OLP)

The OLP involves the institutional triangle of Commission, Council of the EU, and European Parliament (see Figure 0.2). It is an inherently supranational process in that national governments are neither in control of the legislative agenda nor able to veto legislation unilaterally. OLP is thus based on member states sharing control over lawmaking with EU institutions where they are not represented. Legislation initiated under this system has to be approved by both the Council of the EU and the European Parliament, through a procedure known as co-decision. This is why the OLP is seen as the fundamental legislative process of a politically integrated Europe (it is also known as "the Union method" – formerly "the Community method").

4.2.1   The role of the Commission

The OLP is set in motion by the European Commission, which is responsible for proposing policy ideas across its many different areas of competence. As a neutral and expert body detached from national interests, the Commission is considered a better judge of what policies the EU should pursue than national governments are. Initially the Commission will proceed by organizing a consultation over the kind of legislation it wishes to propose. Consultation involves getting expertise and advice from national civil servants, interest groups, and MEPs. This also serves to test the waters politically for the opinion of national governments and MEPs, both of which need to be in agreement further down the track if the proposal is to become EU policy. A crucial contact point for the Commission when preparing legislation is the **Committee of Permanent Representatives (COREPER)**, composed of member states' ambassadors to the EU. This body organizes the workload of the Council of the EU and thus serves as a sounding board for how national governments might react to proposed policies. Individual EU citizens can also participate in consultation through an EU web portal, although this involves answering highly specialized questionnaires.

Each commissioner is assigned a particular policy portfolio (see Table 4.1) and makes use of dedicated directorates-general to help organize a consultation and then prepare subsequent legislation. A personal cabinet of six members of staff provides further assistance to each commissioner. The entire College meets every Wednesday morning, deliberating behind closed doors, and decisions on whether to propose a law are taken by consensus (formal votes are rarely taken) – a somewhat unwieldy process, given the 28 members.

Major initiatives in novel policy areas begin with the publication of a "white paper": a lengthy document containing a number of proposals with accompanying justifications about how they help EU objectives such as making the single market function better, protecting the environment, or improving the pan-European transport system. Extensive planning is the hallmark of these white papers, which means that they are launched infrequently. In fact the Commission's monopoly on legislative initiative – for most

Table 4.1 List of Commissioners' policy portfolios (2012)

High Representative for Foreign Affairs and Security	Justice, Fundamental Rights and Citizenship
Competition	Transport
Digital Agenda	Industry and Entrepreneurship
Inter-Institutional Relations and Administration	Environment
Economic and Monetary Affairs	Development
Internal Market and Services	Education, Culture, Multilingualism and Youth
Taxation and Customs Union, Audit, and Anti-Fraud	Trade
Health and Consumer Policy	Research, Innovation and Science
Financial Programming and Budget	Maritime Affairs and Fisheries
International Cooperation, Humanitarian Aid and Crisis Response	Energy
Regional Policy	Climate Action
Enlargement and European Neighborhood Policy	Employment, Social Affairs, and Inclusion
Home Affairs	Agriculture and Rural Development

internal policies, it is the only body that can formally launch a proposal for a new law – does not mean that individual commissioners are fully and solely in control of the policy agenda.

Certain legislative proposals under the OLP are undertaken in order to fulfill international obligations that arise when the EU signs a treaty or an agreement with another state. Hence, after the EU signed the 1997 Kyoto Protocol on Climate Change, the Commission had the responsibility to propose legislation that would enable member states (the EU-15, that is, the countries that were EU members in 1997) to make good on their pledge to reduce carbon emissions by 20 percent from 1990 levels in time for 2020. In addition, the European Parliament has an indirect possibility of initiating legislation by requesting the Commission to initiate a legislative proposal. This is done on the basis of parliamentary committees that can launch an own initiative, which, if accepted by a parliamentary majority, gets passed to the Commission as a request for legislation on a particular subject. However, this parliamentary request does not legally compel the Commission to propose legislation, though the latter has to justify any refusal to do so.

Other legislative proposals stem instead from the political guidelines given by the President of the Commission at the beginning of his or her term of office. These guidelines are a recent move, which reflects the trend to increase political leadership within the Commission in order to generate a more coherent policy program to tackle EU-level problems. Since 2010 Commission President José Manuel Barroso (president from 2004 to 2009, and again from 2009 to 2014) has also given an annual State of the Union speech setting out priorities for the Commission in the coming year. These are reflected in a work program published annually.

The Commission president is appointed by a qualified majority of the European Council for a five-year term, which means that the presidency reflects to some degree the party political composition of national governments at the time of appointment. A center-right president such as Barroso will thus be appointed when, as happened during the late 2000s, center-right parties constitute a majority of national governments, including in important countries such as France and Germany. This by no means implies that the president will automatically pursue the same kind of policies as national governments with a similar party affiliation. As the leader of the College of commissioners, the president not only has to represent the EU interest above national ones but also usually seeks to enhance the Commission's role within the EU system, just as presidents or executives often seek to gain more powers at the expense of parliaments. Nonetheless, the importance of the political leaning of the president has been reinforced by the fact that since 1997 the European Parliament has to grant majority support to the candidate proposed by the European Council. The same rule applies to the College of commissioners (currently numbering 28, with one appointed by each country): the Commission as a whole needs to be approved by a simple majority of the European Parliament. Individual nominees for the College of commissioners are subject to public hearings in the European Parliament, which can exert pressure to remove a nomination they object strongly to. This happened in 2004 when a parliamentary committee objected to the nomination of an Italian Catholic conservative, Rocco Buttiglione, as justice and secu- rity commissioner. Although the European Parliament cannot reject an individual nomination, the fear that MEPs would fail to approve the whole College of commissioners led to the withdrawal of his nomination by the Italian government.

This connection between the Commission and the Parliament means that the former now looks more like a government supported by a parliamentary majority. However, citizens' votes in European elections constitute a rather indirect link to the composition of the Commission because individual commissioners are still nominated by national governments despite the hearing process conducted by Parliament. Yet the European Parliament is tied in another way to the Commission: the former can issue a "motion of **censure**" to compel the College of commissioners to resign as a body. This power is a check against Commission incompetence or political extremism but although 12 such motions have been tabled since 1972 none has been adopted as this requires a very demanding super-majority of two-thirds of votes cast representing a majority of the total number of MEPs. However, there remains an open debate over whether the Commission should be more like a government, hence more political or at least more dependent on the party political make-up of the European Parliament (see Box 4.1).

Box 4.1   Key Debate: A More Political Commission?

The Commission was designed to be a politically independent servant of the European common good. This means not only being free of national biases but also forsaking an explicit political ideology in terms of left or right so as to develop policies based on expertise rather than ideology. Of course, as an institution that depends on the conferral of powers from member states, the Commission has a vested interest in greater integration as this increases its power and prestige – hence it is not neutral in its preference regarding integration per se. Over time, though, the Commission has become more linked to the political composition of the Parliament, the latter having a veto over the president of the Commission as well as over the whole College of commissioners. This linkage is considered a good thing because legislation proposed by the Commission can have important political repercussions at the national level, while the approval of the Parliament gives legitimacy to the unelected commissioners (Hix 2008). The political scientist Simon Hix (2008) has suggested that the democratic connection between citizens and EU policy would be improved further if the European Parliament gained the power to elect the president of the Commission independently of the preferences of the European Council. He argues that this change would make citizens pay more attention to European parliamentary elections and would help improve understanding of the EU political system. However, other experts warn that making the Commission too political would hamper its current ability to promote trust and consensus among national governments from a range of different political parties (Bartolini 2006). In any case, the need for a qualified majority voting (QMV) in the Council in conjunction with a majority in Parliament precludes the appointment of an ideologically radical Commission.

4.2.2 The legislative institutions: The Council of the EU and the European Parliament

Of course, what the Commission can actually propose in terms of legislation is constrained by the powers conferred to it through EU treaties. This means that, in areas such as education and tourism, where the EU only has supporting competences, the Commission cannot propose policies that overrule what national governments do (see the Introduction). Yet, when it comes to shared competences such as regulating the single market, transport, energy, and even certain aspects of immigration and justice, the laws proposed by the Commission will – if accepted by the political decision-making bodies – be binding on member states.

The two institutions that decide whether to accept a legislative proposal from the Commission are the Council of the EU and the European Parliament. These two operate under the co-decision procedure, under which neither can pass a law without the agreement of the other. Co-decision allows the Parliament leeway to introduce amendments (which it usually does) to legislative proposals in a first reading of a Commission proposal, via a simple majority vote on each separate amendment tabled by MEPs. Thereafter, the proposal is read by the Council of the EU, in effect the upper legislative chamber. Although a single institution, the Council has ten "configurations" based on what subject is being discussed, thereby determining which national ministers will attend (see Table 4.2). It also has a six-month "rotating presidency," during which one country is responsible for planning, scheduling, and chairing the Council as well as COREPER. This role is symbolic as well as organizational: the national presidency is a source of prestige and pride for the country holding it.

In the Council of the EU, qualified majority voting is used for the OLP from November 2014; this consists of 55 percent of the countries representing 65 percent of the EU's population. This means that no single country can block a proposal, but a coalition of governments can object to what has been proposed. However, a formal vote is not always necessary when there is broad consensus, and contested voting is rare: only 15 percent of the time do governments actually express a vote against the majority when deciding

Table 4.2   List of Council configurations

General Affairs
Foreign Affairs
Economic and Financial Affairs
Justice and Home Affairs
Employment, Social Policy, Health, and Consumer Affairs
Competitiveness (internal market, industry, research, and space)
Transport, Telecommunications, and Energy
Agriculture and Fisheries
Environment
Education, Youth, Culture, and Sport

upon legislation (Mattila 2009). This unwillingness to express formal dissent is a sign of the strength of the "culture of consensus" operating in the Council (Heisenberg 2005). In fact consensus is facilitated by having the option of taking a formal qualified majority vote. Governments without sufficient support to block legislation have an incentive to reach a compromise rather than be outvoted. Conversely, governments with enough blocking support can resist attempts to push through a law they do not support.

At its first reading of a law, the Council of the EU can pass the proposed legislation if it agrees to the Commission's proposal as amended (or not) by the Parliament. But the Commission plays an active role during the first reading by expressing its opinion on Parliament's amendments. Hence at this stage there is a great deal of negotiation (particularly as there is no time limit for the first reading) between the Commission and the Parliament, which is represented by the specialized committee of MEPs responsible for that particular policy area. In the event that the Commission disagrees with the Parliament's proposed amendments, the Council can pass them, but only by unanimity (that is, only if all countries agree). Thus, depending on the Commission's attitude toward amendments proposed by the Parliament, the Council will need a higher or lower threshold to accept the legislative proposal. Most EU legislation is passed at the first reading, on the basis of coordinating the preferences from all three institutional actors.

However, if the Council of the EU rejects the legislative text received in the first reading, eventually a law can still be passed. A second, and even a third reading are possible; these would begin with the Parliament examining the preferred text of the Council, which is known as a "common position." Second and third readings require a similar back-and-forth exchange between institutions. The rules are different from those of the first reading: they are designed to help engender consensus. For a start, Parliament has three months to respond formally to the Council's common position; if it does not, the latter becomes law. Parliament's amendment possibilities are reduced at this second stage, to prevent tangential elements from being introduced, and the voting threshold for amendments is increased (an absolute majority of MEPs is needed). An absolute majority can also be used to reject the common position and to end the legislative proposal there and then. A third reading takes place only if the Parliament chooses to amend the common position and these modifications are rejected by the Council in its second reading. Here a conciliation committee, bringing together representatives from the two legislative chambers and Commission officials, assembles to produce a compromise text. All in all, there can be up to 28 stages under the co-decision system used for OLP. Throughout the legislative process, the emphasis is therefore on consensual decision-making reached through constant institutional interaction, which is in turn facilitated by discussions behind the scenes and by the coordination provided by interest groups.

Since the passing of the 2009 Lisbon Treaty, the OLP is subject to a new mechanism for ensuring **subsidiarity**, in other words that decisions are made at the level of government most appropriate for achieving the intended results. The principle of subsidiarity is a key demand of governments, worried as they are that the EU has accumulated too many powers over the years, to the detriment of finding national or local policy solutions. Subsidiarity was first enshrined in 1992 in the Maastricht Treaty, but supporters of decentralized decision-making were disappointed by its lack of application. The CJEU had sole responsibility for determining whether EU legislation breached this principle; the result was just over 10 cases in nearly 20 years (Craig 2012).

The Lisbon Treaty gives national parliaments a fundamental role in policing subsidiarity. If, within eight weeks of the Commission announcing a legislative proposal, one third of national parliaments across the EU argue that this policy should be decided at the national level, then the Commission has to review, amend, or withdraw the act. This warning mechanism is known as the **yellow card** and can be applied to all kinds of proposals, including own initiatives from the Parliament and Council measures for foreign policy that come under special provisions (see Section 4.5). The yellow card was first invoked in 2012, when 12 parliaments protested against a Commission proposal limiting workers' right to strike. In this instance the subsidiarity mechanism worked to persuade the Commission to drop the legislative proposal. A stronger version, the **orange card**, applies in the case of OLP when a majority of national parliaments object on the grounds of subsidiarity to a Commission proposal. In this instance, during the first reading of the legislation, the national parliament's objection can be upheld by a 55 percent majority vote in the Council of the EU or by a simple majority in the European Parliament, thereby killing the proposal. At the time of writing, the orange card procedure had not been used yet.

4.3   The Role of Interest Groups and Experts

Like Washington, DC, Brussels is a city full of lawyers and lobbyists. The estimated 15,000 lobbyists (Greenwood 2008) are there to influence the policy-making process by interacting – formally and informally – with representatives of the institutions involved in EU legislation. A multitude of groups aim to have their views on EU legislation taken into account by decision-makers: industry-specific trade federations (e.g. the Committee of Agricultural Organizations in the EU, or the European Insurance Committee), NGOs or public interest groups (e.g. Greenpeace, the European Consumers' Organization), large companies (e.g. car companies such as BMW or Volkswagen, non-EU manufacturers too), national interest groups (e.g. member states' labor unions and business groups; also national groups from non-EU countries such as the EU Committee of the American Chamber of Commerce), regional and local governments from decentralized EU countries (e.g. German Länder, Spanish autonomous communities).

This varied presence is a reflection of the degree of integration that has been achieved in Europe; previously such interests would have tried to influence national legislation only. It is certainly true, then, that where power goes, interest groups follow. Interest groups interact in a complicated fashion with EU institutions, on the basis of the access they have to decision-makers and of the expertise they can provide to those making EU rules – notably Commission bureaucrats, national bureaucrats advising the Council of the EU, and MEPs. Interest groups' influence is a product of this access and expertise but is hard to measure precisely in practice (Greenwood 2008).

Access to decision-makers is a crucial practical issue for interest groups. The ability to discuss in private with those making the rules is also central to contestation over whether organized interests wield too much influence in the EU system, especially well-funded business interests. Some EU countries such as Austria, Belgium, and the Scandinavian countries have a tradition of formally selecting certain interest groups and incorporating them into the policy-making process. This policy of granting privileged access to key business and worker representatives is known as **corporatism**, where the aim is to balance competing interests in order to generate consensus, especially for economic policy. The EU system does not follow this corporatist structure. Rather it operates, like the US political system, as a pluralist order in which interests compete for access amidst a cacophony of different voices and opinions.

Some critics argue that the EU's pluralist structure of interest group representation by definition grants more influence to business groups. There are good theoretical reasons why this critique might be true. **Pluralism** requires open and equal competition in order to achieve positive results: only a multiplicity of interests with equal, unfettered access to decision-makers ensures that no single interest can dominate policy to its own advantage. Yet some interests find it easier to organize and get their message across, thereby overcoming the collective action problem. This is the case with "concentrated interests" – that is, interests where a clearly identifiable group has a lot at stake. A classic instance are farmers, who wish to keep government subsidies for agricultural production in order to maintain their livelihoods and will work together to achieve this. The concentrated interest of farming can thus be contrasted to the **diffuse interest** of consumers: an amorphous majority with nothing in common except a financial interest in not subsidizing farmers' incomes. The possible savings are not sufficient to mobilize the majority of citizens to oppose farm subsidies. Hence in a pluralist system one can expect diffuse interests to lose out because of the mobilization advantages of concentrated interests. Yet the true picture of how interests influence EU legislation is more complex.

4.3.1   Assessing the influence of interest group lobbying

The success of concentrated interests within the EU is borne out by the strength of agricultural lobbies, which traditionally were the most powerful interest actor. A great part of their power comes from their long-standing ties to national farm ministries and to the EU's Agriculture and Rural Affairs Directorate-General. At the same time, farmers' groups are able to mobilize public opinion and put pressure on politicians at the national level. French farmers are particularly adept at organizing visible and disruptive protests – usually with tractors and wagons of rotten produce – in the hope that French politicians will protect their interests in EU policy-making or else will grant financial compensation to mitigate changes in EU rules. However, farmers' groups are also able to coordinate across EU countries – as happened in 1999, when German farmers joined their French counterparts to blockade the European Parliament building, in a protest against cuts in subsidies. This sets farm groups apart, as few organized interests are able to mobilize on EU issues, let alone do something coordinated at the European level in this way. Studies show that instances of mobilizing citizens to protest in the streets against EU policies are rare as compared to protests against national gov-

ernments (Imig and Tarrow 2000). Most lobbying thus takes place within the EU institutional framework.

Within the EU political system access is based on the principle of pluralism; groups
should self-organize to make themselves heard. But there are two bodies that reflect a
different system of interest organization. The Committee of the Regions is based on
bureaucratized interest representation, affording special input to regional actors, while
the European Economic and Social Committee (EESC) is a corporatist body representing business and worker interests as well as civil society. Both are advisory institutions,
which means that they express an opinion on policies initiated through OLP that relate
to their areas of interest. The Committee of the Regions is composed of representatives
of regional and local administrative units from each member state on the basis of the
size of the country. It is consulted on matters relating to EU regional policy – notably
the distribution of funds to poorer EU regions – as well as on those policies that require
implementation by sub-national units, which is the case for transport, energy, and the
environment. The official opinions it delivers are not legally binding (i.e. the OLP does
not need to accommodate their preferences) but they are a way for regional actors to
ensure that the sub-national level is recognized as a key participant in policy-making.

The EESC likewise has only consultative powers, giving opinions on the many EU
policies that have a socio-economic component. Again, membership is proportional to
a country's population, and there are three approximately equal groupings of representatives proposed by national governments from employers (large firms), employees (labor
unions), and other interests (agriculture, small business, professions). In existence since
1957 but having a limited influence on the outcome of decision-making, the EESC has
no binding powers (unlike corporatist structures in certain member states), which is
why both business and worker interests prefer to deal with the real power broker institutions, namely the Commission and the Council.

The weakness of the EESC does not mean that business interests are all-powerful
within the EU's institutional dynamics. Pluralism in the EU allows public interests
(which by definition are diffuse) to articulate their opinions on the basis of providing
much-needed expertise to the Commission and to the MEPs; national governments
have less need here, given their greater resources. With limited time and personnel at
their disposal, the EU's supranational bodies seek out groups that can provide feedback
on the problems associated with existing policies or on the latest scientific findings on
a topic. Indeed, since the 2001 White Paper on European Governance, the EU has
endeavored to consult more closely with civil society groups. This involves non-binding
target-setting and the development of best practices in socio-economic policy, civil
society groups providing inputs that are based on their expert knowledge of the effects
of policy. Here expertise from both scholars and interest groups helps the Commission
by giving legitimacy to proposed policy initiatives (Boswell 2009). Civil society or expert
support can thus help the Commission to persuade other decision-makers that the policies should be adopted. Another part of the Commission's effort to engage with a
broader swathe of interest groups goes to its role in actually funding civil society organizations. By its own counts, the EU spends €1 billion a year subsidizing a variety of NGOs
by financing their projects or commission reports.

Box 4.2   Case Study: Lobbying under the OLP

Under OLP, major pieces of legislation begin with a Commission-led consultation. For instance, when preparing a law for an EU-wide procedure for removing illegal content from websites, the Commission solicits input from businesses (e.g. internet hosts) and from NGOs (e.g. civil rights and copyright organizations). COREPER will also meet to discuss member states' preferences, which are taken very seriously, since the states will not only vote on whether this becomes law but will also have to execute the law if it is passed. Having received this input, the Commission finalizes its proposal, and then co-decision operates to decide whether the proposal becomes law. This first requires the decision of the Parliament, which can add amendments to the law; each amendment, as well as the final text, requires an absolute majority among MEPs. Hence the European Parliament has a key role in shaping legislation under OLP, lobbyists, NGOs and parties being particularly active to influence MEPs at this stage of the process. On a major piece of legislation MEPs are highly active; the 2006 Services Directive, aimed at liberalizing the market for services, saw over 1,000 amendments tabled, of which 151 were adopted as a result of cooperation between the two major party groups (Lindberg 2008). After this "first reading," parliamentary amendments get reviewed by the Commission. The directorate-general in charge of the policy area is then responsible for incorporating the amendments accepted by the Commission. In the case of the 2006 Services Directive, the Commission incorporated most of the amendments, notably the removal of the country of origin principle, which had caused a stir when initially proposed by the Commission (see Section 5.3 for a full discussion). This new text, after Parliament's first reading, is the one presented to the Council for its first reading. If national ministers refuse it, they devise a "common position" with textual changes and send it for review by the Parliament. A common position means a second reading for the Parliament, which, if successful, means that the text becomes law. This is what happened in the Services Directive case, although member states were given three years to implement the legislation, making it legally binding only from 2009 on.

Overall, when it comes to maximizing influence, interest groups will above all seek to provide input on the Commission's first attempts to draft a legislative text. So the biggest advantage for influencing policy is to have direct links with the Commission rather than being on the outside and responding only to already drafted legislative proposals. However, there is the possibility of lobbying the European Parliament when it has its say on the Commission's proposals under OLP (see Box 4.2). In fact, as in the case of a 1998 EU law on biotechnology, such lobbying can be conducted successfully even at the second reading of a text. In this biotechnology example, MEPs were persuaded by an alliance of biotech companies and patient groups to reverse opposition to what, in the unsuccessful first reading, had originally been seen as the Commission's attempt to "patent life."

The previous example reinforces the point that lobbying in the EU is more about relying on influence from within than about exerting pressure from the outside. That is, EU decision-makers are less influenced by media and public opinion than by interest groups and experts. Another important aspect of interest group representation is that lobbying in the EU is not linked directly to financial contributions to electoral campaigns (Mahoney 2007). Hundreds of millions of dollars are spent in the US on "soft money" (money that supports a party or issues rather than a particular candidate); these sums are often raised by political action committees – that is, groups dedicated to advancing an issue or to passing certain legislation. By contrast, interest influence in the EU occurs through access and expertise rather than by virtue of the amount of money raised and from campaign contributions.

4.4   The Commission's Watchdog Role and the Importance of the CJEU

As well as overseeing the expenditure of the EU budget and proposing laws for the legislative branches to vote on, the Commission also has a fundamental watchdog role. It is officially the "guardian of the treaties": in this capacity its task is to ensure that treaty obligations and EU laws are implemented properly by member states. In the absence of a territorial presence to enforce EU rules equivalent to the way the US federal government acts via its district courts, marshals, or even the FBI, the Commission relies on the administrative capacities of each country to actually enforce EU rules in their own judicial system. Hence the Commission, via the different directorates-general, is always monitoring the degree to which member states comply with EU rules covering the gamut of obligations for each policy area where EU legislation supersedes national law (exclusive and shared competences).

Failure to comply with EU treaties and legislation can result in the Commission starting an **infringement procedure** against the offending member state. This procedure, under article 258 TFEU, requires Commission officials to establish proof of infringement that can then ultimately be scrutinized by the justices of the CJEU. The first steps, however, involve the Commission sending a letter of formal notice followed by a reasoned opinion, where the aim is to obtain compliance without a legal ruling, by giving the member state time to adapt to EU law. A referral to the CJEU is thus the last phase of the infringement procedure, where the Court has to determine whether infringement has taken place. It does this on the basis of its evaluation of the material presented by the Commission and counterbalanced by arguments put forward by the country concerned. If the CJEU finds in favor of the Commission, the member state is expected to respect the judgment and to comply actively with the principle of EU law under dispute.

A country can still resist implementation at this stage, because all compliance ultimately depends on the goodwill of the national administrations that enforce the law on their soil. This is why the Commission can initiate a separate legal proceeding, under Article 260 TFEU, to obtain formal recognition from the Court that a member state has failed to comply with an CJEU judgment. If the action is successful, under this mechanism the CJEU can impose fines – these are based on an amount requested by the Commission – on the still recalcitrant member state. For example, in 2005 the French government had to pay a fine of €20 million and a further €57 million for every six month period until it correctly applied EU fisheries conservation rules. Moreover, the Lisbon Treaty added a new mechanism to Article 260. This allows the Court to impose a fine on a member state at the first infringement stage in cases where a country fails to implement a specific EU law within the allotted time (member states often have a number of years to adapt to EU legislation). In these instances, rather than going through the cumbersome article 258 procedure (reasoned opinion, member state response, and so on), the Commission can go straight to the CJEU and ask for a fine at the same time as asking for an infringement ruling.

The CJEU is thus charged with deciding whether the Commission's concerns about a member state's flouting EU rules are valid. Although it is only called upon to adjudicate in disputes as an independent expert, the Court must not be taken to be aloof from the EU's institutional dynamics. Besides the power to determine member state infringements, since 1957 the CJEU has had the legal duty to interpret the meaning of the different EU treaties. It is in this capacity that the Court has had a profound impact on the entire EU legal order.

4.4.1   The development of the Court of Justice's powers

The power to interpret EU (and, before that, EEC) law may not sound terribly important. Yet by using this power the CJEU has produced jurisprudence – that is, rulings that interpret what EU treaties mean for member states – that has transformed the nature of EU law in a way that member states never expected. In doing so, this Court established itself as "the most effective supranational judicial body in the history of the world" (Stone Sweet 2004, 1).

The CJEU was not designed to give legal standing to citizens in order to allow them to contest the compatibility between national and European law; nor were national courts expected to enforce European law against their own governments (Alter 1998). Citizens could use the preliminary ruling system to contest whether the decisions of the Commission or of the Council of the EU failed to respect the terms of the EEC treaty. However, in two major rulings in 1963 and 1964, the Luxembourg-based court declared, first, that the Treaty of Rome created rights for individuals against their state when the latter failed to respect the EEC Treaty and, second, that in a case of conflict of laws, EEC authority must be supreme over national law (Stein 1981). The CJEU was called upon to interpret the treaty in these two cases because Article 177 (now Article 267 TFEU) of the EEC Treaty allowed national courts, when a case involved a European legal issue, to seek a "preliminary ruling" from it on a point of CJEU law where the domestic court was uncertain. In this way national courts used preliminary ruling to allow individuals to contest national law and to have the CJEU adjudicate on the compatibility of EU and national law (Alter 1998).

The preliminary ruling procedure gave rise to the now famous *Van Gend en Loos* (1963) and *Costa v. ENEL* (1964) decisions. The former audaciously established, for the first time, that an international treaty gave individuals the right to redress if an EEC state failed to comply with the treaty. This doctrine of **direct effect** is modeled on the federal principle that law is a direct relationship between government and citizens rather than on the international law principle that treaties are an agreement between states that do not create justiciable rights for citizens. Consequently EU citizens do not have to wait for their governments to adopt legislation enacting treaty rules: all citizens have direct access to these rights from the moment their state ratifies the treaty. The second case was a natural complement, as it established the principle of EEC **supremacy**, whereby, in case of conflict, national law must yield to EEC Treaty provisions or to EEC legislation. The CJEU justified these decisions by saying that the EEC "constitutes a new legal order," akin to the constitutional order of a state.

The CJEU's transformative jurisprudence assisted integration by enabling citizens to sue member states for failing to respect EU law; and this made the Court an active participant in the EU's institutional dynamics. Using the **preliminary reference** procedure (now Article 267 TFEU), individuals and companies can resort to national courts to uphold their EU rights as contained in the actual treaties – notably the free movement of goods, capital, services, and people. Thus, for legal obligations contained in the EU treaties, there is no need to wait for the Commission to begin an infringement proceeding: citizens and legal persons (e.g. companies) can ask national courts to enforce these obligations directly. This right has been taken up with particular enthusiasm by companies seeking to overturn restrictions on their right to sell goods across the single market. Moreover, as the EU treaties have developed to outlaw discrimination on the grounds of nationality, gender, sexual preference or disability (see Section 5.5), a broader range of interests can rely on EU legal principles to fight discrimination in their national law. Figure 4.1 depicts the interactions between the different actors operating in the EU legal system.

The other side to the development of this supranational legal order is the fact that the whole EU legal system relies on the acceptance of CJEU jurisprudence by national courts, which have the responsibility for actually enforcing CJEU decisions by using national administrative and police structures (Weiler 1991). Why would national courts welcome jurisprudence creating direct effect for treaty obligations and the supremacy of European law? The answer is that the preliminary reference mechanism increases the legal power and prestige of national judges, making them welcome participants in the system. By applying the principles of EU treaties in their own rulings, national judges gain the ability to declare national legislation invalid, something that would not otherwise be possible in many EU countries that lack the mechanism of judicial review. Not all national courts are, however, so willing to use this power, and there is variance across countries regarding the eagerness to ask for a preliminary reference, although the annual number of such references has increased consistently since the 1960s.

National constitutional courts have also had to accept the principle that EU treaties and legislation have supremacy over national constitutions. Although there was some resistance – less so, however, than state supreme courts' acceptance of federal legal

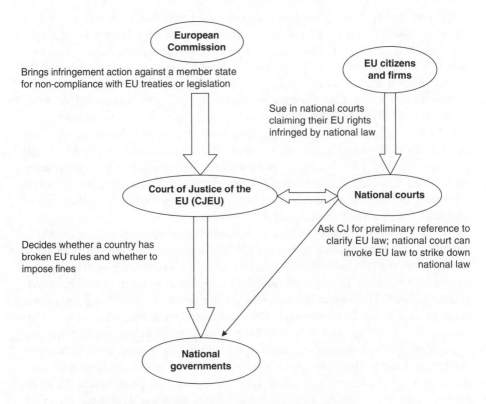

Figure 4.1 Diagram of the EU legal system

sovereignty in the nineteenth-century United States (Goldstein 2001) – all these courts voluntarily accept that EU supremacy is a logical consequence of signing the EU treaties. But this does not preclude the possibility of national courts withdrawing this voluntary acceptance at some future date. The German Constitutional Court hinted at this possibility in rulings on the conformity of the Maastricht and Lisbon Treaties with Germany's constitutional provision guaranteeing democracy to its citizens. The Court, which reviews the constitutionality of any new EU treaty, argued that transferring more competences away from the German parliament at a future date could be unconstitutional, given the problem of having meaningful democratic inputs into EU policy-making. Consequently, it is the jurisprudence of the CJEU, as accepted by national courts, that allows the EU to function as a unified, binding legal entity without a constitution or full political sovereignty. In this way the EU has become a constitutionalized legal order despite not having a formal constitutional document (see Box 4.3).

Yet the CJEU has also been able to shape policy-making by declaring certain national practices illegal under the EU treaties, thereby provoking a European-level policy

Box 4.3 Key Concept: The Constitutionalization of the EU

Constitutionalization refers to the way in which the international treaties regulating European integration have obtained a constitutional status. That is, the treaties are now understood as a form of higher law that binds national governments, and even national constitutions (Stein 1981). As with any national constitution, this means placing limits on what government can do by specifying principles any legislation must conform with – for instance human rights, or human dignity. In the EU context, member state autonomy is constrained by EU treaties specifying all manner of legal principles: gender equality, the four fundamental freedoms, and even the size of public debt for Eurozone countries. Ordinarily, international treaties do not bind national courts directly – it is up to governments to pass laws implementing treaty obligations. Yet the jurisprudence of the Court of Justice interpreted the EEC treaty both as supreme over national legal orders and as creating obligations even in the absence of an implementing law. National courts and national constitutional courts have accepted this interpretation, albeit with some initial resistance, especially in France (Goldstein 2001). The result is that courts throughout the member states routinely strike down national laws or constitutional provisions for breaching EU treaty principles, also allowing individuals to sue governments, and even companies, for failure to comply with EU law. So, even though it is based on international treaties, the EU in effect functions as a constitutional system whereby national governments accept legal parameters on how they can and cannot legislate.

response (Alter 2009). This was the case notably in the *Cassis de Dijon* decision (1979), which ruled that Germany could not restrict the sale of French-made liqueur that did not meet strict German rules for how alcohol must be produced. If the drink was legal in France, the Court argued, it must be available for sale within Germany too, as both countries are part of the same single market. Similarly, the *Nouvelles Frontières* ruling (1986) specified that air travel should be open to competition, thereby prohibiting the existing practice whereby governments set ticket prices for flights. Both these CJEU cases thus outlawed existing national practices and provided the stimulus for common European-level action, helping prompt the move toward, respectively, further market integration in the shape of the Single European Act and Commission legislation for deregulating air travel.

Critics of the CJEU's decision to constitutionalize the treaties and to render decisions with significant policy consequences interpret this jurisprudence as instances of judicial activism: an unelected court using its powers for political reasons, in this case to further integration. This is a powerful critique, given that the CJEU has clearly transformed the nature of the EU legal system without member states and their citizens having a formal say. In this way a question mark is raised over the democratic legitimacy of the CJEU's dynamic role. However, the countries that signed the EU treaties undoubtedly delegated the power to establish the meaning of European law to the CJEU, and their own courts have voluntarily consented to its jurisprudence. Member states eventually realized the implications of delegating the power of legal interpretation to the Court. When granting new competences to the EU over very sensitive issues such as foreign policy, member states have tried to minimize the supervisory role of the CJEU. Indeed, EU foreign policy is an area for which national governments have created a separate legal and political structure, in which the supranational institutions (Commission, Parliament, and Court) play a reduced role by comparison with the OLP. Foreign policy, for the most part, thus follows different institutional dynamics, as explained in the next section.

4.5   Special Provisions for Foreign Policy

Some elements of the EU's foreign relations fall within the OLP. This is the case for the external trade policy and for international development. There the Commission has the monopoly of legislative initiative and can negotiate on behalf of the 28 member states with foreign governments, most notably for trade agreements (under Article 218 TFEU). In these areas of foreign policy national governments accept the benefits that come from having the Commission take the lead and set the agenda, as well as from the efficiency of deciding through qualified majority voting. Moreover, the Lisbon Treaty introduced a consent procedure whereby the European Parliament's consent is necessary for all international agreements the EU makes in policy areas that are covered domestically by the OLP (e.g. trade or climate change).

Yet supranationalism is the exception in foreign policy; matters having to do with defense and security lie outside the institutional dynamics of the OLP and supervision by the CJEU. Instead it is the intergovernmental institutions, the European Council and the Council of the EU, that have formal control over the greater part of EU foreign policy; underscoring the intergovernmental nature of decision-making, qualified majority voting is seldom used when the Council of the EU decides on legislation in this field. These special provisions for foreign policy began after the Maastricht Treaty and are enshrined in the Lisbon Treaty, which means that, in legal and practical terms, the bulk of EU foreign policy is conducted differently from the OLP. As Chapter 8 provides a full discussion of EU foreign policy in theory and practice, this section offers a basic overview of the legal basis and decision-making structure covering foreign policy.

4.5.1   The legal basis and decision-making structure of EU foreign policy

Unlike under the OLP, the Commission does not have a monopoly on legislative initiative in foreign policy. Instead it is the European Council and the Council of the EU that take the lead in proposing legislation in this area. The former, representing the 28 heads of state and government, defines the principles and general guidelines of foreign policy. The Council of the EU is the formal decision-making body responsible for adopting legislation that coordinates foreign policy across 28 countries. The most important legal instrument under this framework is known as a "joint action": a measure agreed by the Council of the EU to coordinate member state resources in pursuit of a common, binding objective. Examples here include implementing an international treaty outlawing biological weapons, or the launching of peace-keeping operations abroad. Another important instrument is the "common position," which specifies the EU's policies toward another country or region. Common positions are again binding on member states, including when they participate in other international organizations.

The Council of the EU also has an executive role to play in foreign policy: it has the responsibility for monitoring member state compliance with the foreign policy legislation it has created. This is different from OLP, where responsibility for compliance monitoring – the watchdog function – lies with the Commission. Foreign policy legislative instruments such as joint actions are thus legally binding on member states, but the task of making sure that all countries adhere to them is not the legal responsibility of the Commission and CJEU. Hence both compliance and decision-making in foreign policy follow the principle of intergovernmentalism, allowing greater respect for national sovereignty. In this sense, foreign policy involves collective self-monitoring by member states rather than delegating this function to supranational bodies.

The same rationale of retaining national sovereignty explains why the CJEU's role is marginal. The Court does not have jurisdiction over the intergovernmental aspects of foreign policy, which means that, unlike under the OLP, it cannot review national policy and declare whether it complies with treaty principles or foreign policy legislation enacted by the Council of the EU. Likewise, EU citizens cannot use their national courts to obtain a preliminary reference to the CJEU on whether national policy is compatible with EU-mandated foreign policy. Of course, it must be pointed out that national constitutional courts generally do not have the power of judicial review over foreign policy, so in this way the EU is not exceptional.

Another significant difference between foreign policy and OLP is the modest role of the European Parliament. A key decision-maker under the co-decision rule applicable to internal EU policies, the Parliament is largely reduced to a consultative role in foreign affairs. This means that MEPs do not get to vote on whether they agree with joint actions; rather they are limited to asking questions of the Council of the EU and to holding an annual debate on the progress of implementing the EU's foreign policy. This contrasts with the European Parliament's authority to veto treaties with third countries covering trade and other economic or socio-cultural cooperation; it also contrasts with its general co-decision power under OLP.

Whereas the Council of the EU is the formal decision-making body for binding legislation, a lot of its work is already done by the time it meets to decide on policy. This is because the agenda for the Council of the EU (which meets in what is known as the Foreign Affairs Council configuration: foreign ministers from the 28 member states) is prepared by the Brussels-based Political and Security Committee (PSC, also known by its catchier French acronym, COPS). The PSC meets twice a week and is composed of national representatives who are national ambassadors to the EU, assisted by officials from each country's permanent representations to the EU. PSC's importance lies in the fact that it is in charge of the day-to-day details of implementing foreign policy as well as preparing how to respond to changing global events. It is also officially in charge of the "political control and strategic direction" of the EU's military and civilian crisis operations. In carrying out this role, PSC tries to find consensus positions over technical issues to do with policy implementation that can reconcile divergent national interests and ideologies on more general points of foreign policy (Bickerton 2011). The preparatory work it conducts thus helps smooth over ideological and political divisions between governments.

The Lisbon Treaty altered the EU foreign policy system by creating the high representative for Foreign Affairs and Security Policy and the European External Action Service (EEAS). The high representative is not only a commissioner but also the chair of the Foreign Affairs Council, thereby adding an element of supranational leadership to foreign policy. The idea behind the EEAS, which is led by the high representative, is to coordinate the diplomatic representation of the 28 EU countries so as to increase further the level of supranational coordination in foreign affairs. These institutional developments and what they mean in practice for achieving EU foreign policy objectives are discussed in Chapter 8.

4.6   Concluding Summary

Member states share the setting of the EU policy agenda and decision-making responsibilities with supranational institutions, notably the Commission and the Parliament. Inputs also come from citizens and interest groups, as well as from CJEU jurisprudence on what the treaties or EU law mean for national autonomy. Under the supranational OLP, the Commission proposes legislation, leaving the Parliament and Council of the EU to co-decide on whether to accept it. Co-decision is intended to add democratic inputs and oversight from national governments and MEPs, thereby bringing together different perspectives. Pressure for consensus is built into the system, so that legislation is passed with overlapping support from all three main institutions.

Interest groups operate under a pluralist opportunity structure, which means that there are no privileged sectors that get a special say in helping shape policy. The partial exception is regional and socio-economic interests, organized in the Committee of the Regions and the EESC; but these have only limited advisory powers. Access to the Commission and to the European Parliament is the key factor in influencing policy. However, concentrated interests, especially business ones, are not necessarily advantaged here, given that diffuse interests are often consulted for their expertise. Indeed the Commission even funds a large number of public interest groups. By comparison with national institutions, EU institutions are seldom subject to public pressure related to the mobilization of citizens by interest groups.

Besides its role in proposing legislation, the Commission also has a watchdog function: it monitors the implementation of EU policies by member states and the conformity of their laws with treaties and EU laws. Failures of compliance can result in the Commission bringing infringement actions against particular countries to the CJEU, which has to adjudicate whether countries fail to meet EU obligations and whether financial penalties for failing to comply with an earlier infringement ruling are to be imposed.

Moreover, national courts are intimately connected to the CJEU through the preliminary reference procedure, which allows individuals to fight, in domestic courts, national legislation that contravenes EU treaty principles or EU laws. This system of voluntary compliance with CJEU jurisprudence is thus a hallmark of the EU legal system, which, thanks to the doctrines of direct effect and supremacy, functions in effect as a constitutional order above national law – at least for policies under OLP.

OLP is complemented by a legally and institutionally very separate intergovernmental system for foreign policy. This framework is designed to allow member states to keep control over the agenda, decision-making, and compliance monitoring of foreign policy. In this field the European Council and the Council of the EU replace the Commission as leading actors by proposing legislation and by scrutinizing member-state compliance. Nevertheless, there are elements of supranational coordination in foreign policy. They include informal coordination via the Political and Security Committee of national ambassadors, who prepare the work of the Foreign Affairs Council in conjunction with input from the Commission. In addition, the creation of a high representative for Foreign Affairs and the creation of the External Action Service add a further supranational dimension to foreign policy.

Guide to Further Reading

Alter, K. 2009. *The European Court's Political Power: Selected Essays*. Oxford: Oxford University Press.

Written by one of the leading scholars of the CJEU in political science, these admittedly challenging essays show exactly how the Court has transformed EU politics and how member states have responded.

Greenwood, J. 2008. *Interest Representation in the European Union* (2nd edn.). Basingstoke: Palgrave.

Covers every aspect of what interest groups do within the EU system and with what consequences.

Hix, S., and B. Høyland. 2011. *The Political System of the European Union*. Basingstoke: Palgrave.

Chapters 1–4 provide the definitive political science explanation of EU institutional dynamics, namely how and why actors matter and what the nature of their interactions is.

Keukeleire, S., and J. MacNaughtan. 2008. *The Foreign Policy of the European Union*. Basingstoke: Palgrave.

Offers a detailed description and explanation of EU foreign policy, covering institutional, policy implementation, and theoretical facets.

Discussion Questions

1   What is the role played by the Commission under the OLP? Why did member states create this institution and what is the rationale behind the powers it has been delegated?

2   How can organized interests and experts influence decision-making and how important is their input in shaping policy?

3   How would you evaluate the contribution the CJEU has made to supranational integration? Which rulings constitutionalized the treaties and how?

4   How and why did national courts assist in the development of the EU legal order and how did member states respond?

5   What distinguishes the decision-making process in foreign policy from the OLP? Explain the reasons for these contrasting legal and institutional frameworks.

Web Resources

This book is supported by a companion website, which can be found at www.wiley.com/go/glencross. There you will find a list of the web links referred to in this chapter wherever you see a "Web" icon in the page margins. In addition, you will find a list of further relevant online resources such as websites for EU institutions, political groups, archives, and think tanks, information on studying abroad, and biographies of key figures. You will also find self-assessment tools in the form of flashcards and independent study questions developed specifically for this chapter.

Glossary

Censure
Name given to a vote of the European Parliament (by a two-thirds majority) that forces the entire College of Commissioners to resign. It has never been used, but this power ensures the Commission is ultimately accountable to EU citizens.

Collective action problem
Concept explaining why policy change that would benefit many individuals is hard to achieve: the personal cost (time, effort, and so on) involved deters participation in mobilization for change.

Committee of Permanent Representatives (COREPER)
This body consists of national ambassadors to the EU and their staff, who prepare the meetings of the European Council and Council of the EU. It is also an important contact when the Commission devises legislative initiatives.

Corporatism
System, common in Northern Europe, for granting certain interest groups privileged access to political decision-making. Corporatism normally privileges business and workers' interest groups, in order to help reconcile these two clashing interests in socio-economic policy.

Diffuse interest
Phrase used to describe an interest shared by a very large group of people who are unlikely to identify and mobilize around an abstract or distant interest such as public

health, clean air, or consumer protection. Hence diffuse interests face a larger collective action problem than concentrated ones, such as those of farmers or industry-specific lobbies.

Direct effect
Fundamental EU legal principle whereby individuals can use national courts to enforce their EU treaty rights before governments pass enacting legislation or when national law contravenes EU legislation. This principle stems from jurisprudence in the *Van Gend en Loos* CJEU case (1963).

Infringement procedure
Process whereby the Commission takes legal action against a member state for not respecting EU law; this can result in a case being brought before the CJEU.

Orange card
Part of the enhanced subsidiarity mechanism introduced by the Lisbon Treaty. If a majority of national parliaments object to a draft law proposed by the Commission, then it is up to the Council of the EU and European Parliament to decide whether to block the draft for breaching subsidiarity.

Pluralism
System of interest group representation based on the principle of open competition between numerous interests for access to political decision-making. It is the prevalent system in both the EU and US federal government.

Preliminary reference
Legal phrase for a preliminary ruling, which happens when a national court asks the CJEU for its official interpretation of EU law. The Court's decision is binding on the national court, and this characteristic makes it an agent for applying EU law through national legal and administrative structures.

Subsidiarity
Principle, enshrined in treaties, stating that EU policy action should occur only when it is more effective than national or local efforts to meet same objective. It is intended to prevent unnecessary accretion of power at EU-level thanks to national parliaments acting as watchdogs of subsidiarity.

Supremacy
Fundamental EU legal principle stating that EU law trumps national legislation and constitutional provisions. Supremacy was first stated as a legal doctrine in the *Costa v. ENEL* CJEU case (1964).

Yellow card
A warning system whereby a third of national parliaments objecting to a draft law proposed by the Commission forces the latter to review, amend, or withdraw the proposal. This is part of the enhanced subsidiarity mechanism introduced by the Lisbon Treaty.

References

Alter, K. 1998. "Who Are the 'Masters of the Treaty'? European Governments and the European Court of Justice." *International Organization*, 52: 121–147. DOI: 10.1162/002081898550572

Alter, K. 2009. *The European Court's Political Power: Selected Essays*. Oxford: Oxford University Press.

Bartolini, Stefano. 2006. "Politics: The Right or the Wrong Sort of Medicine for the EU?" Available at http://personal.lse.ac.uk/hix/Working_Papers/NotreEurope_Hix%20_Bartolini.pdf (accessed July 23, 2013).

Bickerton, Christopher. 2011. *European Union Foreign Policy: From Effectiveness to Functionality*. Basingstoke: Palgrave.

Boswell, Christina. 2009. *The Political Uses of Expert Knowledge: Immigration Policy and Social Research*. Cambridge: Cambridge University Press.

Craig, Paul. 2012. "Subsidiarity: A Political and Legal Analysis." *Journal of Common Market Studies*, 50: 72–87. DOI 10.1111/j.1468-5965.2011.02228.x

Goldstein, Leslie F. 2001. *Constituting Federal Sovereignty: The European Union in Comparative Context*. Baltimore, MD: Johns Hopkins University Press.

Greenwood, Justin. 2008. *Interest Representation in the European Union* (2nd edn.). Basingstoke: Palgrave Macmillan.

Heisenberg, Dorothee. 2005. "The Institution of 'Consensus' in the European Union: Formal versus Informal Decision-Making in the Council." *European Journal of Political Research*, 44: 65–90. DOI: 10.1111/j.1475-6765.2005.00219.x

Hix, Simon. 2008. *What's Wrong with the European Union and How to Fix It*. London: Polity.

Imig, Doug, and Sidney Tarrow. 2000. "Political Contention in a Europeanising Polity." *West European Politics*, 23: 73–93. DOI: 10.1080/01402380008425401

Lindberg, Björn. 2008. "Are Political Parties Controlling Legislative Decision-Making in the European Parliament? The Case of the Services Directive." *Journal of European Public Policy*, 15: 1184–1204. DOI 10.1080/13501760802407706

Mahoney, Christine. 2007. "Lobbying Success in the United States and the European Union." *Journal of Public Policy*, 27: 35–56. DOI 10.1017/S0143814X07000608

Mattila, Mikko. 2009. "Roll Call Analysis of Voting in the European Union Council of Ministers after the 2004 Enlargement." *Journal of European Political Research*, 48: 840–857. DOI: 10.1111/j.1475-6765.2009.01850.x

Stein, Eric. 1981. "Lawyers, Judges, and the Making of a Transnational Constitution." *American Journal of International Law*, 75: 1–27. Available at http://www.jstor.org/stable/2201413 (accessed July 23, 2013).

Stone Sweet, Alec. 2004. *The Judicial Construction of Europe*. Oxford: Oxford University Press.

Weiler, Joseph H. H. 1991. "The Transformation of Europe." *Yale Law Journal*, 100: 2403–2483. Available at http://links.jstor.org/sici?sici=00440094%28199106%29100%3A8%3C2403%3ATTOE%3E2.0.CO%3B2-V (accessed July 20, 2013).

5

EU Policy-Making in Action
Major EU Policies

Contents

Learning Objectives

- to analyze the nature and limitations of the EU budget;
- to evaluate the logic behind Economic and Monetary Union (EMU) and the rules governing it;
- to distinguish between negative and positive integration in single market policy;
- to analyze the functioning of EU regulation in social and environmental policy;
- to identify the different components of EU policy in the field of justice and citizenship;
- to evaluate the importance of conditionality in the enlargement process.

The Politics of European Integration: Political Union or a House Divided?, First Edition. Andrew Glencross.
© 2014 Andrew Glencross. Published 2014 by Blackwell Publishing Ltd.

5.0   Introduction: The EU's Major Policy Areas

This chapter is concerned with the major policies that characterize the EU as a political system capable of producing and executing binding rules across member states. The latter contribute not just by helping decide upon EU policies and by providing the administrative capacity (civil servants, police, courts) for implementing them. In addition, member states supply most of the financial resources that the EU has at its disposal to execute policies that involve spending public money. Hence the overall aim of this chapter is to illustrate, on the basis of the treaty developments and institutional dynamics previously discussed in the abstract, what policies and policy-making look like in practice.

The first move toward understanding this practical side of European integration today is to grasp the nature of the EU budget. Section 5.1 thus examines who contributes what, how this gets decided, and what constitutes the bulk of EU expenditures. As the analysis shows, the EU does not have a budget commensurate with the tax powers and the spending range of national governments. Yet the politics of the EU budget is highly fraught. Another politically sensitive policy area is that of the EU's own currency: the euro. As discussed in Section 5.2, monetary integration entails regulating member states' public finances so as to maintain the strength of the currency. These rules are necessary particularly because the single currency is not based on sharing public debt; they ensure that no government runs up debts that scare off international lenders, leaving other Eurozone members to pick up the bill. Of course, this very scenario actually took place, and its causes and effects are treated separately in Chapter 12.

Given the limited scope of the EU's expenditure policies, most of the EU's legislative output concerns the single market and is designed around making the four fundamental freedoms a reality, which often means overturning national rules that impede them. This process, explained in Section 5.3, is known as deregulation; but the EU also engages in re-regulation – that is, in setting common standards for the entire EU. Social and environmental policy is a classic instance of this kind of re-regulation. Re-regulation is always surrounded by political contestation, given that legislating for things such as maternity pay or air pollution standards imposes costs on companies, as discussed in Section 5.4. But the rationale behind re-regulation is to provide common rules so that every citizen has the same rights (say, clean air, maternity pay) and companies the same obligations; anything short of that would generate unfair competition and unequal living standards. Getting this balance right though is one of the major political debates within the EU (a topic addressed in full in Chapter 7).

A more recent area of EU regulation concerns justice and citizenship, the subject of Section 5.5. Although not directly related to the single market, justice and citizens' rights are an inherent part of living in a common economic space. Over the past decade EU policies in this area have covered new aspects – such as border control, immigration, and police cooperation – raising fundamental political questions about the need for integration in these matters.

The final major policy covered in this chapter straddles the boundary between foreign and domestic affairs: enlargement. Although foreign policy is analyzed in depth in Chapter

8, enlargement is treated here, in Section 5.6, because this policy moulds prospective candidates into member states and is the subject of heated political debate. Enlargement policy thus reveals much about how the EU works and about its self-identity.

5.1   The EU Budget

There is no direct tax paid by citizens to fund the EU budget. The EU also lacks the ability to pay for its budget by issuing public debt. Both these budgetary limitations reflect the fact that the EU is not a state. Nevertheless, the EU does possess a sizeable annual budget: €130 billion in 2012. This money comes from four types of income: agricultural levies (charged on non-EU imports), customs duties (tariffs charged on non-EU imports), a portion of value added tax (a uniform levy on member states' sales taxes), and gross national income (GNI)-based own resource (a uniform levy on member states equivalent to a certain percentage of their GNI). This last category now constitutes over 75 percent of the budget, which means that the richest countries are the ones that pay the most into the budget. These contributions are thus highly contentious and governments wrangle over their net contributions – that is, over the difference between how much member states pay in and what they get out.

Since 1988 the financing of the EU budget has been fixed in advance, for a period of several years. It is the task of the European Council to negotiate the total size of the budget and how countries will contribute. However, the final figure needs to be approved by the European Parliament, which used this veto power in 2013 to reject the European Council's first proposal for the 2014–2020 **multiannual financial framework**. The previous multiannual budget, running from 2007 to 2013, limited the total EU budget to no more than 1.23 percent of the gross national income of the EU. This percentage translated to €860 billion (2004 prices) over the six-year period. An eye-catching sum, larger than the GDP of small EU countries, this figure is, however, small beer in comparison to the level of public spending undertaken by federal states. The maximum possible EU spend of 1.23 percent (in 2013 the proposal for the 2014–2020 period was to bring the total EU budget down to 1 percent of GDP) is dwarfed by the average 20 percent of GDP spent annually by the US federal government in the past four decades, or by the average 15 percent spent by the Canadian federal government in the past decade (Ardy and El-Agraa 2011). Yet the EU budget has risen over time, since in 1960 the EEC budget was only 0.03 percent of the EEC's GDP.

The size of the EU budget is certainly large enough to provoke intense intergovernmental battles. National public opinion is sensitive to budget deals, and so there is close scrutiny over how much countries pay in and what they get out, notably in the form of the Common Agricultural Policy (CAP) agricultural subsidies and so-called cohesion and structural funds. Thanks to these two redistributive policies nearly 90 percent of the EU budget is returned to member states, the rest being spent on EU administration, international aid, and foreign policy expenses. Historically the CAP always represented the biggest part of EU expenditures; but this part fell from 70 percent of the total in 1980 to 40 percent by 2010. Even so, it is still an exceptionally large figure for a sector that represents 5 percent of EU employment and less than 2 percent of GDP.

Agricultural subsidies notably benefit Mediterranean and Eastern European countries with large agricultural sectors. Originally these funds functioned as price support mechanisms (that is, mechanisms for buying farm produce at a minimum price); but price support led to vast overproduction and huge associated costs for storage. Today subsidies take the form of direct payments to farmers; these payments are based on the size of farmed land, giving all farmers greater freedom over how to use their land while they also benefit bigger farmers. Given the sums involved, reform of the CAP is always closely linked to budgetary politics. Hence it is the European Council that has taken responsibility for making the deals that cut the costs of the CAP, although actual detailed proposals for reform come from the commissioner for agriculture and need the final consent of the Council of the EU and of the Parliament. Most notably, in October 2002 it was the Brussels European Council that confirmed the move to direct payments, as part of a plan to limit the future cost of agricultural subsidies after the 2004 enlargement. Capping agricultural subsidies to new member states satisfied net contributors, but net recipients were only placated with increased funding for "cohesion."

Spending on cohesion policy has increased as CAP spending has gone down – in exact proportion to it; now it represents over a third of the EU budget. This involves EU financing for infrastructure (for instance building sites that are financed in this way have to display the EU flag) and for regional development, which is administered by regional authorities across member states. The rationale behind all this funding for road building and air transport infrastructure, all this training for the unemployed, and all this support for small businesses or rural development is the intention to counteract the downsides of market integration. That is, as economic competition increases thanks to the level playing field offered by the single European market, isolated rural areas or regions with inefficient industries often decline, and this process causes long-term unemployment and a low-skills base. EU transfers thus compensate for this decline by equipping poorer regions – including those in richer countries – with the resources to compete in the new economic environment. Richer countries are prepared to pay in more than they receive in return, because of the overall economic benefits of belonging to the single market. The core set of net contributors – Germany, the Netherlands, Belgium, Sweden – are the home of export-oriented companies that benefit greatly from having unfettered access to a wide EU market. In effect, because they benefit from higher employment and tax revenue, these countries are willing to compensate countries whose firms are less competitive under the single market rules (Mattila 2006).

The Commission is in charge of proposing how exactly to spend EU money once the multiannual perspective has been established. Each year it therefore prepares a draft annual budget that is subject to the co-decision procedure. In order to pass, the budget needs a qualified majority voting (QMV) in the Council of the EU and a majority in the European Parliament. Amendments from the two legislative branches are possible

and the final outcome will reflect a compromise position between these two bodies.

As institutional supporters of supranationalism, the Commission and the European Parliament continually argue for increasing the EU budget in order to tackle problems within and beyond the EU. In particular, the Commission has long sought new revenue streams, notably a share of corporation tax, to finance increased spending. Yet taxation policy is one of the few remaining areas where a decision cannot be made unless all member states are unanimously in favor. This rule constrains the growth of the EU budget – an indication of how member states, especially net contributors, wish to retain the final say over EU spending.

5.2   The Euro

Coins and banknotes denominated in euros went into circulation on January 1, 2002, replacing a variety of national currencies. By 2013 the euro was the money used by more than 300 million citizens across 17 EU countries. Introducing a single currency was a long-standing goal of proponents of integration for many reasons, political as well as economic. However, not all countries were convinced of the benefits of having a single currency to go with a single market. Among the pre-2004 member states, Denmark, Sweden, and the United Kingdom have not joined the euro; but all post-2004 accession countries are legally bound by their treaties of accession to adopt the euro eventually.

Economists dispute whether the Eurozone meets the criteria for an **optimum currency area** – in other words whether it is a space where having a single currency and interest rate is economically efficient for all. Low labor mobility and the absence of a common business cycle (some regions can experience a boom when others are stagnant) mean that the EU does not have the level of integration economists would expect of an optimum currency area (de Grauwe 2009). However, for a fully integrated market there are certain clear efficiencies that result from having a single currency. A single currency reduces transaction costs (e.g. bank fees for currency conversion), spurs price competition (helping offset inflation), and eliminates the exchange rate volatility, which harms cross-country trade. A strong European currency with interest rates set by an independent central bank was also expected to bring lower inflation and interest rates, thus helping investment, and to provide greater stability amid the volatility of global financial markets. In a world of floating exchange rates and enormous volumes of daily financial transactions, small European countries otherwise vulnerable to currency speculation and sudden balance of trade problems benefit greatly from being part of a strong currency bloc, with pooled foreign currency reserves (McNamara 1998). However, relinquishing the right to issue a national currency means that governments lose the ability to set interest rates in accord with national economic conditions and cannot devalue their currency as a last resort, in order to regain competitiveness. Interest rates are set for the Eurozone by the politically independent European Central Bank (ECB, located in Frankfurt, Germany), whose primary objective is fighting inflation.

5.2.1   Preparing for European Monetary Union

Despite concerns over whether Europe is an optimum currency area, the euro project was set in motion by the 1992 Maastricht Treaty, which committed EU countries to European Monetary Union (EMU). (For the political background to this decision to abandon national currencies, see Sections 3.2 and 3.3). In order to prepare for the euro, the treaty created binding rules for all member states to observe in the realm of

---

Box 5.1   Key Concept: The Stability and Growth Pact

The SGP is supposed to provide the fiscal discipline necessary to keep the Euro-zone stable. Unlike normal central banks, the ECB does not issue sovereign debt, as governments using the single currency remain responsible for issuing and servicing their own (euro-denominated) national debt. Ordinarily, the global financial markets – the private investors that lend money to finance government debt – punish excessive state borrowing by pushing up the cost of state borrowing and by selling off national currency, thus lowering its value (as happened in France in 1983: see Section 3.2). This external constraint is what normally compels governments to curb excessive borrowing. However, in the Eurozone, countries are shielded from such a constraint, because the overall value of the currency depends not on a single government's borrowing but on how the markets judge the debt burden of the entire zone. Small economies in particular can in theory free-ride on the fiscal responsibility of other countries, at least in the short term, as excess borrowing will not translate into a falling currency price. The SGP (which limits total public debt to 60 percent of GDP, and annual government debt to 3 percent of GDP) was thus intended to be an internal substitute for market discipline, being designed to prevent governments from borrowing recklessly. It was the German government that insisted on the SGP, in order to avoid free-riding on the combined strengths of the euro (Marsh 2009). As Germany had highly successful export industries and its fiscal responsibility was the main source of the euro's stability, other countries acquiesced in the SGP proposal in order to make the single currency a reality.

---

monetary and fiscal policy. These rules required governments to keep annual budget deficits at less than 3 percent of GDP and the accumulated public debt under 60 percent of GDP. This 60 percent figure was difficult for Belgium, Italy, and Greece to meet. The rules were fudged in order to allow these countries to join, and this was permitted on the basis of the fact that they were on the right course for hitting the target figure eventually. To ensure fiscal stability once the euro was in operation, a **Stability and Growth Pact (SGP)** was made part of the Maastricht and subsequent treaties (see Box 5.1). This pact included the **excessive deficit procedure**: a mechanism for sanctioning countries – first through warnings and in the last resort through fines – that broke the same 3 percent and 60 percent rules laid down for joining the euro. Although the Commission plays a role in identifying excessive borrowing and formulates recommendations for how to get government finances back on track, the enforcement mechanism of the SGP requires the approval of the Council, and this feature makes it the subject of intergovernmental control.

Prior to the launch of the euro, governments seeking to join succeeded in improving their fiscal position and in reducing their public debt – even countries like Greece and

Italy, which traditionally have found it difficult to do so. This happened because countries knew that they would not be allowed to join if they did not meet the budget criteria. After 2002, however, France and Germany broke the rules on excess government deficits. The Commission, tasked with monitoring the SGP, sought to take action against these countries, but this required a QMV decision in the Council of the EU sitting in the **ECOFIN** formation. ECOFIN comprises national finance ministers (see Table 4.2 for a list of Council configurations), but only those from the Eurozone get to vote on Eurozone business. To the dismay of many governments, France and Germany were able to use their voting and diplomatic strength to avoid the application of the normal sanctions for breaching EMU rules. A case was brought before the CJEU, in an attempt to enforce the SGP rules, but the judges were reluctant to force Germany and France to play by the original rules. In the end EMU rules were reconfigured so as to allow for greater flexibility: countries could borrow more if they needed to stimulate their economies (Collignon 2004).

A currency without a state, the euro underwent an extremely turbulent time after the 2008 financial crisis, which hurt government finances by reducing tax receipts and by increasing spending on welfare as well as on bank bailouts. The crisis' impact on state finances spooked the markets, which, because Eurozone countries still issue their own sovereign debt, lend at different rates of interest to governments within the single currency. Initially, after the euro's launch, borrowing costs went down for high-debt countries such as Italy and Greece, as markets were reassured by the Eurozone's fiscal rules and by the likelihood of lower inflation. However, as government finances worsened after the 2008 financial crisis and the SGP rules were flouted more openly (see Figure 5.1), investors charged a premium on lending money to countries they deemed less likely to pay back their debts. As a result, the cost of borrowing became much higher for countries

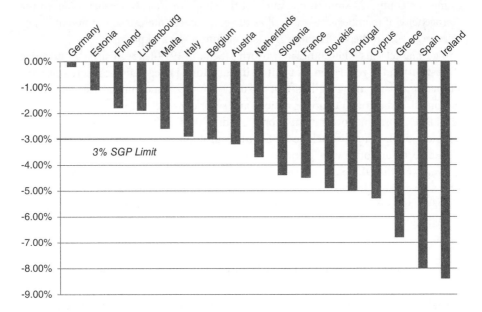

Figure 5.1 Budget deficits (as % of GDP) in Eurozone countries (2012). Source: Data from the European Commission

like Greece than for Germany, making it even more expensive for these countries to finance their existing debt and further damaging their fiscal situation. This spike in borrowing costs sparked huge uncertainty over how these countries could continue to finance themselves, especially since the Lisbon Treaty contains a "no bailout clause" (Article 125). This clause states that spendthrift countries will not have their debts paid by others. Fears that lenders would not be repaid resulted in certain countries, such as Ireland and Greece, no longer being able to borrow from the markets; this put them at risk of a sovereign default (not repaying their debt). Although initially restricted to small economies, this financial shockwave caused political upheaval, given the need to either help finance these Eurozone countries' debts or else allow the countries themselves to abandon the single currency, potentially unraveling the whole project. The Eurozone crisis and its repercussions on integration are the subject of Chapter 12.

5.3   The Single Market

The single market is the culmination of years of legislation and jurisprudence. The process started with the Treaty of Rome, which paved the way for the free movement of goods, people, services, and capital – what is known collectively as "the four fundamental freedoms." Success in creating an integrated market across national borders makes the EU stand out from other regional organizations that have only been able to abolish tariff barriers. Today the single market is an inherently supranational policy field. It relies on the Ordinary Legislative Procedure (OLP) in order to prevent individual member states from blocking agreement on common rules. Additionally, the CJEU's power to strike down national laws that restrict the four fundamental freedoms ensures the continued smooth operation of the single market. Nevertheless, given the heterogeneity of member states as well as the entrenched interests and different policy preferences within them, the single market remains a work in progress.

Single market legislation comes in two forms (Scharpf 1999): deregulation (or **negative integration**) and re-regulation (or **positive integration**). Deregulation concerns dismantling national laws and practices that obstruct the four fundamental freedoms. This is accomplished through treaty provisions and secondary legislation (i.e. laws made via the OLP) that prevent governments from impeding the free flow of goods, people, services, and capital. Examples include the EU treaty prohibition of state subsidies to companies and treaty rules outlawing restrictions on EU nationals owning property. Re-regulation also works via the OLP but concerns the establishment of new EU-wide legislation so as to harmonize regulatory standards across the EU. This happens for instance with EU clean-air standards, water treatment rules or setting a 48-hour maximum working week. Re-regulation at the EU level thus replaces previous, disparate national rules.

5.3.1   Pursuing deregulation or negative integration

Deregulation was necessary for abolishing a complex set of **non-tariff barriers** to the four fundamental freedoms. Historically, European governments owned certain large companies – typically in sectors such as energy, airlines, or telecommunications, where economies of scale encouraged monopolies that hurt consumer interests. It was also common for governments to provide subsidies to big employers faced with financial difficulties. These practices persisted after the EEC Treaty was signed; but a combination of individual legal cases and European Commission legislation, both of which drew explicitly on the pledge to protect the four fundamental freedoms, helped eliminate them (Egan 2001).

An important element of deregulation came in the shape of a Court of Justice ruling that gave birth to the principle of "**mutual recognition**." This is the principle whereby a product legally sold in one member state can be sold in all EU countries, regardless of whether it complies with all national regulatory specifications. Mutual recognition is deregulatory, as it means that governments have to allow competition from other goods produced in the EU. The doctrine comes from the 1979 *Cassis de Dijon* case, which overturned the German government's ban on the import of a French liqueur manufactured from blackcurrants. Nevertheless, according to the treaties, national restrictions on cross-border trade are still permissible for reasons of public health and consumer and environmental protection. These exceptions are often tested in court. In fact consumer protection was the ostensible grounds for the German ban on the liqueur Cassis de Dijon. The German government claimed that restricting the importation of low-alcohol liqueur was necessary in order to avoid confusing customers who expected something stronger. The Court of Justice dismissed this argument as an illegitimate use of the consumer protection exemption and considered the ban an unfair restriction of a fundamental freedom. This and a set of similar cases emboldened the European Commission in the 1980s to legislate against these non-tariff barriers. The results are known as "liberalization" – a description that covers (1) a wave of privatizations in major economic sectors such as civil aviation, finance, telecommunications, and energy; (2) the end of state subsidies; and (3) the opening of government tenders to firms from other EU countries (Egan 2001). The Single European Act contributed to liberalization by increasing the use of QMV, thereby reducing member states' ability to veto liberalizing legislation. Overall, negative integration produces enhanced competition, which translates into better services for consumers and greater innovation, and this also improves EU firms' ability to compete internationally.

5.3.2   Pursuing re-regulation or positive integration

Alongside creating a borderless market space, the EU is also responsible for setting common standards for how goods and services are produced and sold (a process also known as harmonization), thereby replacing an alphabet soup of heterogeneous national rules. Examples here include public health standards for testing medicine, providing greater consumer rights for air passengers, or introducing a common cellphone standard interoperable across the EU. Sometimes very technical rules can seem highly fussy – up until recently the Commission stipulated the maximum amount of bend allowed when selling cucumbers – and an imposition of red tape on small and medium-sized businesses. Such rules thus provide ammunition for anti-EU parties and commentators, who associate European integration with petty law-making and with an insistence on "one size fits all" that ignores local conditions.

However, the purpose of positive integration is fundamental and complementary to deregulation: to ensure that EU businesses, workers, and consumers have the same rights and responsibilities across the EU. In many respects this is a question of fairness: if companies from different countries are subject to different environmental standards, then those operating where standards are lowest can gain a competitive advantage. Similarly, common EU norms and standards prevent national governments from trying to create regulatory loopholes that favor certain national industries. A level playing field thus requires certain common minimum standards. At the same time EU-level re-regulation is a way to deal with policy issues that individual member states are not able to solve individually. Transborder pollution is a good example here, as common rules for factory emissions prevent one country's lax standards from creating acid rain or other airborne pollution problems for another. The politics of introducing these rules covering the production and circulation of goods and services in the single market is explored in depth in Section 7.3.

One major area where the harmonization of national policies is very difficult is taxation. Taxes such as those on labor, on products (e.g. alcohol and tobacco), and on companies affect the operation of the single market. EU competence in tax policy is very limited, because this area is subject to unanimous decision-making, whereas most single market legislation is adopted via QMV. There is limited EU tax harmonization, involving setting minimum rates for value-added (sales) tax in order to prevent cross-border distortions in trade. Member states are, however, free to set their own income and corporate tax rates. In the EU, countries thus compete among themselves to attract investment and skilled workers by offering lower tax burdens. Ireland's low corporation tax, for instance, has prompted complaints about unfair competition from the French and German governments. The latter are concerned that, in the absence of harmonized rates of corporation tax, firms will relocate to low-tax countries, leaving those with higher rates to suffer reduced tax income. In this way integration is often controversial in a context of different tax structures.

5.3.3   The single market as a work in progress

The single market is supposed to allow for the free movement of EU citizens. Yet there remain significant impediments to labor mobility, owing to linguistic diversity and to differences in national employment rules. Worker mobility brings with it language and cultural challenges, as well as administrative hurdles such as changing pension and healthcare schemes, which follow from moving country. As a result, labor mobility – which is much lower than that of inter-state mobility in the US – is more restricted by comparison with the free movement of goods and capital. Attempts have been made to improve labor mobility by introducing EU legislation that compels employers to recognize professional qualifications (such as medical degrees, pharmacy training or engineering skills) obtained in other EU countries. Of course, the enormous benefit of EU integration is that EU citizens now have the right to study and earn qualifications – at the same cost as in-country residents – in whichever country they want. Indeed the EU funds Erasmus, a student exchange scheme that allows for 200,000 students a year to study in another EU country, thereby acquiring language and other skills to help their future mobility.

Nevertheless, a single market for services is far from being complete. The Commission has long sought to deregulate services as fully as goods and capital. In 2004 it proposed that businesses be allowed to operate under the "country of origin principle," meaning that, if they were legally able to provide a service in their home country, they could also do so in another member state. This provision would be analogous to the mutual recognition doctrine, thereby allowing citizens and businesses to buy services from EU suppliers even if these services do not conform to national training standards or national employment law.

Creating a right to bring in cheaper contract workers (notably from Eastern European countries) is very controversial in Western Europe, where this practice is seen – like tax competition – as a threat to hard-won social rights. Given the disparity in wages and the absence of collective bargaining agreements in many Eastern member states, the right to operate under home country rules has been blocked, for fear of creating downward pressure on wages and workers' rights. This clash over whether services should be allowed to operate according to the rules of their home country or else be subject to national employment law is part of an overarching dispute over the nature of the single market. The rival political philosophies of neoliberalism and the social market advocate, respectively, extending liberalization to achieve growth and preserving social rights either by protecting national regulation or through enhanced EU re-regulation (see Box 5.2).

Negative and positive integration are thus controversial measures. Deregulation affects national sovereignty by preventing governments from legislating as they once did or as they would prefer. The ability, for example, to discriminate against citizens or companies from other EU countries or to subsidize national industries is gone forever, to the dissatisfaction of certain politicians, who would like to prohibit immigration from EU countries or to favor national firms in government contracts. Re-regulation also constitutes a challenge to sovereignty, this time by compelling governments to find common ground with other EU countries. In addition, positive integration challenges EU legislators to find a balance between efficiency (making everyone better off) and equity (ensuring market competition does not lead to an unequal distribution of resources) when setting common standards (see Chapter 7).

This trade-off leads to heated political debate under the OLP, since governments as well as MEPs have different preferences on regulatory matters. It is precisely in order to defuse controversies over the varying preferences and national effects of proposed EU single market policy – deregulatory as well as re-regulatory – that legislation is first initiated by the independent European Commission. By delegating this power to an expert body, governments try to ensure that the legislation for the single market promotes open competition and fair rules, which favor no particular country (Majone 2005). Yet critics of this arrangement argue that the Commission concentrates on negative integration – as in the case of the country of origin proposal for services – at the expense of improving fairness through positive integration. A deregulatory bias risks

---

Box 5.2   Key Debate: Neoliberalism versus the Social Market

Neoliberalism is a general term for a set of economic policies first implemented by Margaret Thatcher and Ronald Reagan in the 1980s, as a "trickle down" alternative to stimulating growth through government spending. These policies chiefly consist of privatizing state-owned firms, prioritizing control over inflation rather than fighting unemployment, and deregulating industries and services, especially the financial sector. Similar policies have been pursued by the EU when the single market and the euro were created, and they have elicited accusations that the EU offers national politicians a cover for implementing policies that their own electorates would not approve of. This is because many West European countries have a tradition of government intervention to regulate capitalism through welfare provision and spending so as to protect the weakest in society (Sapir 2006). This reflects the once dominant political ideology of social democracy (see Chapter 1, Glossary), which was based on a regulated or "social market" rather than a purely free market. Many European voters remain attached to this social market model and advocate applying it to the whole EU. This idea is not only controversial in many of the member states that are more inclined to a free market, but also very difficult to put into practice, given the large economic disparities within the EU and the latter's limited capacity for redistributing wealth through the budget. In the past, the clash between these two principles mostly came to the fore in treaty negotiations where national vetoes made it hard for social market principles to be introduced. However, the empowerment of the European Parliament, whose members represent parties organized according to the traditional left/right spectrum of European politics, means that this debate is increasingly played out in the EU's legislature. At stake here is the ability of national governments to provide public services and to protect employees without running foul of EU free movement principles or competition law – a delicate balance, ultimately adjudicated by the CJEU.

---

leading to unfairness in living standards, because liberalization favors the owners of capital and high-skilled labor above less skilled workers and national social rights (Scharpf 2002). Although positive integration is possible in social and environmental policy (which will be discussed below), the lack of tax and spending powers means that the EU has fewer means for ensuring a fair distribution of resources than national governments do.

5.4   Social and Environmental Policy

Beyond the economic aspect of the single market, EU rules have had a concrete impact on member states' social and environmental policies. Two principal areas of social policy where European integration has made a difference are gender equality and, more recently, protection against discrimination on the grounds of disability, age, ethnicity, religion, and sexual preference. The Treaty of Rome (Article 119) stipulated equal pay for equal work regardless of gender, and this became the basis for subsequent EU legislation in the 1970s that ensured equal pay and equal treatment. The CJEU helped enforce these provisions, as in the famous Barber decision (*Barber v. Guardian Royal Exchange Assurance Group*, 1990), where a British man successfully sued his employer for allowing female employees to obtain a company pension at a younger age than men.

The 1997 Amsterdam Treaty extended EU competences to allow for implementing legislation to combat discrimination on "racial or ethnic origin, religion or belief, age, disability and sexual orientation" (Article 13 TEU). This led to a 2000 EU law compelling member states to treat persons equally regardless of their racial or ethnic origin. A 2008 Commission proposal for implementing equal treatment irrespective of religion or belief, age, disability, and sexual orientation is also currently in progress. Once this non-discrimination law is passed via OLP, EU residents will be able to invoke these rights against their government or employers and to seek redress in national courts – since the latter are constitutionally obliged to enforce EU rules even if these contradict national law (Ellis 2005). Hence the extension of EU competences in the field of non-discrimination has enabled considerable expansion in the protection of citizens' rights within member states.

Working conditions are another fundamental area of social policy where EU legislation matters a great deal. Perhaps the most important measure here is the 2003 Working Time Directive, which was adopted through the co-decision procedure. This directive stipulates that all EU workers are entitled to 4 weeks' annual paid leave and minimum daily and weekly rest periods; and, most controversially, it sets a maximum limit on weekly working time of not more than an average of 48 hours. This has impacted shift work, particularly in the hospital sector, where some member states claim that the regulation results in higher costs and harms healthcare provision. However, EU legislation allows member states to grant individuals the right to opt out and work longer – a possibility that the majority of countries have enacted. A guaranteed right to fourteen weeks' paid maternity leave is another significant example of EU employment law.

What characterizes EU social policy is regulation rather than social spending, because, unlike member states, the EU does not have the tax receipts to fund pension, unemployment, or social security schemes. The European Social Fund (ESF) and the European Globalization Adjustment Fund (EGF) are exceptions to this rule. The former, established by the Treaty of Rome, is part of the EU's cohesion spending and focuses on regional spending on social inclusion, training, and education. Whereas the ESF allocated a total of €75 billion for 2007–2013, the EGF has an annual budget of €500 million. Launched in 2006, the EGF provides temporary funding in countries where companies suddenly restructure in the face of international competition.

5.4.1   EU environmental policy

Environmental protection is another fundamental EU policy. Although an unexpected development – environmental protection was not included in the Treaty of Rome (Weale

1999) – regulation in this area is vast and relates to eliminating cross-border pollution, ensuring common minimum standards, and even meeting international environmental treaty obligations. The Commission has been a key promoter of environmental regulation; but it has also been strongly supported by governments from countries with active green movements (e.g. Germany and the Nordic countries) as well as by the European Parliament. The EU's success in creating extensive rules to protect the environment is often used to show the non-economic benefits of European integration as well as to contradict accusations of the Commission's pursuing only neoliberal policies. However, national implementation is far from perfect, especially in poorer member states that lack administrative capacity or in countries where corruption makes officials turn a blind eye.

Originally the Commission used its competence over the single market as the legal platform for introducing environmental legislation. However, specific powers to legislate in this area were introduced as part of the Single European Act (SEA), while the Amsterdam Treaty committed the EU to promoting sustainable development and environmental protection. This wide-ranging ambition translates into different types of policy measures. There are regulations relating to cross-border issues such as river and sea pollution, shipping hazardous waste, or transborder industrial accidents. The EU also determines national pollution control policy, notably by setting air quality standards for cities across the EU. Member states consequently have to monitor air quality and to take measures to reduce pollution, or else they would be liable to infringement proceedings initiated by the European Commission; London was threatened with such proceedings in 2010. In addition, the EU creates legislation that aims to set environmental standards for products made and sold within the single market. For instance, vehicles produced or sold in the EU need to meet certain fuel efficiency and emissions standards. Given the size of the EU market, this regulation has a knock-on effect on car production worldwide, which is why non-EU businesses are present in Brussels, so as to follow and to lobby policy-makers on which environmental standards to adopt.

Firms are not the only entities with a keen interest in influencing EU environmental legislation. The Council of the EU is often split between governments that do not want to impose costly regulations on consumers or producers and governments that want to raise environmental standards across the EU. Under the treaties, member states are allowed to adopt more stringent standards than the EU minimum; but doing so can penalize exporting companies or push consumers to buy goods from countries with lower standards. Hence these countries have an incentive to see standards harmonized upwards. Under QMV, evidence from a range of environmental legislation shows that an activist set of countries (Germany, the Netherlands, and the Nordic countries) have indeed succeeded in raising standards EU-wide rather than accepting a lowest common denominator (McCormick 2001).

Alongside the dedication to internal environmental protection, the EU has a fundamental role in international environmental policy. Article 191 TFEU contains the objective of "promoting measures at international level to deal with regional or worldwide environmental problems, and in particular combating climate change." Most significantly, the EU is a signatory of the 1997 UN **Kyoto Protocol** on climate change. To meet the terms of Kyoto, the EU adopted the "20–20–20" targets, legally committing itself to a 20 percent reduction in carbon emissions from 1990 levels, to generating 20 percent of its energy needs through renewable means by 2020, and to a 20 percent reduction in energy use through energy efficiency. Under this scheme member states have to meet binding national reductions targets, greater demands being made of wealthier EU countries.

However, the EU has little direct control over how countries generate their energy, since decisions relating to energy supply, energy sources, or energy taxes are subject to unanimous voting. In order to help reduce carbon emissions, it thus launched in 2005 the EU Emission Trading Scheme. This scheme, the largest of its kind in the world, provides commercial incentives for reducing and offsetting carbon emissions. It is an instance of "cap and trade," where firms in heavily emitting industries (power plants, cement factories, steelworks, and the like) receive fixed carbon emissions allocations and then have an incentive to reduce their carbon use in order to re-sell unused credits. Yet the process of allocating and pricing carbon credits so as to create incentives for companies to reduce their emissions has proved very difficult to administer.

Overall, the EU self-consciously seeks to serve as a beacon for international efforts to forestall climate change. Alongside its numerous internal policies – and flashier gestures such as banning incandescent light bulbs – the EU is taking the initiative to implement a successor treaty to Kyoto (Delreux 2011). At the 2011 UN Climate Conference in Durban, the EU commissioner for Climate Action proposed a road map for implementing a global legal framework for reducing carbon emissions. This illustrates how the Commission not only seeks to lead by example and to protect the environment but also wants to persuade other countries to adopt this objective.

5.5   Justice and Citizenship

The development of EU policies concerning justice and citizenship is another sign of how European integration has gone beyond the economic sphere. Today justice, freedom, and security form a key policy area, which involves creating a common juridical space for multiple issues such as immigration, police and intelligence cooperation, asylum, personal mobility. and fundamental rights.

These were not policy areas covered by the original EEC Treaty; indeed the first policy measures took place outside the EEC legal framework. A core set of EEC countries – France, West Germany, and the Benelux countries – were frustrated at the inability of the EEC to remove internal border controls and to coordinate rules on external border issues, notably asylum applications and visas for **third country nationals**. In response, these countries signed the 1985 Schengen Agreement (see **Schengen Area**), paving the way for the removal of internal physical controls on all citizens moving across internal borders as well as setting common rules on visas and on the processing of asylum applications. The beneficial impact Schengen had on individual mobility and cross-border trade persuaded the vast majority of EU countries to participate; the UK and Ireland have stayed out, but non-EU members Iceland, Norway, and Switzerland also participated.

Since the 1997 Amsterdam Treaty, Schengen rules have become part of EU law and policy-making rather than being outside the treaty system. Originally asylum policy, visa policy, extradition, and police co-operation were classified as intergovernmental areas of decision-making. This meant not only that member states had veto power over legislation but also that they could propose policies themselves (unlike under the OLP), thereby minimizing the input from the Commission and European Parliament. Today, however, these policy issues are subject to supranational decision-making under the OLP.

National governments have an obvious incentive to coordinate in the field of justice, given the amount of cross-border mobility generated by the four fundamental freedoms and by the removal of physical border controls under Schengen. To address various problems that this increased mobility gives rise to, the EU has implemented a common Schengen visa for third country nationals, has introduced a European arrest warrant (see Box 5.3), and has coordinated procedures for non-EU individuals seeking asylum – procedures whereby their request is processed in the first EU country they arrived in. There has also been a gradual process of harmonizing criminal offenses and even of sentencing, as mandated by Article 31 TEU. This is especially the case for transnational crimes. Thus member states now all have statutes against human trafficking, cyber-crime, money laundering, and terrorism. This harmonization ensures that criminals cannot escape punishment on account of differences in what EU countries consider a crime. This could happen prior to EU coordination, for instance when not all states had specific anti-terrorism laws because only a few had experienced this problem.

At the moment, criminal justice is a national competence. This means that national governments have sole responsibility for administering the law and for prosecuting individuals, even if they are bound to respect EU minimum sentences. The Lisbon Treaty could alter this arrangement, as it contains (in Article 86 TFEU) a provision for the Council of the EU to create a European public prosecutor. The European Commission argues that this position is necessary for enforcing EU rules that are not always properly respected in certain member states, notably fraud related to EU spending. Many member states are, however, reluctant to allow an EU official to prosecute individuals directly.

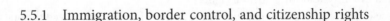

5.5.1   Immigration, border control, and citizenship rights

EU cooperation has also developed significantly in the field of immigration policy. This is a very sensitive topic, as European countries experience a decline in the native birth-rate and significant migration from abroad. National governments are caught between public pressure to control migration flows from outside the EU and coordinating immigration and asylum rules to meet the realities of an integrated and open market based on free movement. Consequently, and because the removal of physical checks on internal mobility also applies to third country nationals, member states are increasingly trying to work together to secure the EU's external borders. This explains the creation of FRONTEX, an EU agency responsible for external border security. Its mission includes training border guards, developing joint patrols to assist countries facing a sudden influx of irregular immigrants, and coordinating sea patrols by using pooled

Box 5.3   Case Study: The European Arrest Warrant

Prior to the European Arrest Warrant (EAW), an EU citizen wanted for a crime committed in another member state went through a lengthy process of extradition. This lasted on average over 9 months, as national courts did not have a common set of rules for accepting extradition requests. There was great interest in speeding up the process, especially as the free movement of people led to more and more cross-border criminal activity. Launched in 2003, the EAW has reduced the time taken for an EU citizen to be brought before a court in another member state to an average of 43 days. An EAW can only be issued (1) for prosecutions concerning a crime that carries a minimum penalty of over one year of prison; or (2) for the enforcement of a custodial sentence of over four months (that is, for sending to prison a person already found guilty and sentenced to four months of incarceration or more). Like the single market, the EAW works on the principle of mutual recognition: a warrant issued by another EU country is as valid as one issued within the same country. That said, an EAW requested by Slovakia, for example, for a crime committed there could only lead to the arrest of a Briton in, say, Belgium, provided that a Belgian court first approved the grounds for the warrant according to legal criteria specified by the EU. Thus the active involvement of national courts is a prerequisite for the police arresting a suspect and sending him or her back to the country where the alleged crime took place. Despite this domestic legal safeguard, the EAW is not without its critics, who argue that different judicial cultures and levels of police competence mean that EU citizens are potentially exposed to arbitrary arrest. Indeed, in 2007 the Council of the EU issued a request for judges examining EAWs to apply the principle of proportionality – a principle stating that the means should not exceed the ends. This was because EAWs that met the official criteria for severity of offense or length of custodial sentence had been executed for crimes such as the theft of two car tyres, or that of a pig. Thus integration in this area has led to significant efficiency gains and has helped the cause of justice, but at the same time it has raised issues of accountability and fairness across rather diverse jurisdictions.

resources of member states to intercept migrants who attempt to cross the Mediterranean. Here the EU provides some funds to develop national capacity, but above all the personnel and equipment come from member states, while FRONTEX provides coordination. In addition, the EU is seeking to negotiate bilateral agreements with other countries, especially in North Africa, for processing incoming legal migrants and for returning illegal ones (Boswell 2003).

Measures to prevent illegal immigration into the EU have often been criticized as contradicting the EU's commitment to human rights and as creating a "fortress Europe," based on discrimination against migrants (Geddes 2000). These policies are also criticized for being short-sighted from a demographic perspective. However, the launch of a common EU work permit (or "blue card") for skilled foreign workers shows that EU policy-makers also seek to harness cooperation in attracting certain immigrants. The plan behind this is (1) to avoid a situation where member states may compete with one another to remedy skill shortages; and (2) to make the internal market function better by allowing skilled non-EU workers to circulate according to demand. However, the EU legislation for this initiative, voted in 2009 (when Denmark, the United Kingdom, and Ireland chose not to participate), does not secure full freedom of movement. Notably, member states can determine how many blue cards they will issue and can reject applications from blue-card holders who switch countries of work.

A final aspect of the EU's area of justice, freedom, and security concerns citizenship rights. The 1992 Maastricht Treaty created the category of EU citizenship, which is complementary to national citizenship: any person who is a citizen of a member state is thus automatically an EU citizen. EU citizenship allows individuals to study, work, and reside wherever they choose. EU citizens can also vote and stand for election, at the municipal level as well as in European parliamentary elections, in whichever EU country they reside. Outside the EU, citizens have the right to diplomatic or consular assistance from another member state if their own country has no diplomatic presence. The European Commission monitors also national practices to ensure that states do not engage in discrimination, as enshrined in the treaties. For instance, France's attempt in 2010 to dismantle illegal Bulgarian and Romanian Roma (gypsy) camps and deport these EU citizens resulted in the European Commission initiating legal action for breach of EU legislation that prohibits ethnic profiling and collective expulsions.

5.6   Enlargement

The formal boundaries of Europe, and thus the countries that are potential EU members, are unclear (see Box 1.1). Nevertheless, enlargement has been a fundamental feature of European integration since the creation of the EEC attracted the interest of the United Kingdom and other states on the outside. This external demand for widening is a sign of the success of integration. Other countries want to join this club because of the opportunities that accessing the single market can bring to their citizens and firms. This is a very attractive package for European countries outside the EU, which tend to be poorer than the existing member states. For prospective member states, integration means labor mobility, as it would allow visa-free travel and residency to citizens seeking opportunities in wealthier EU countries. Businesses in new member states also profit from easier access to capital and investment from foreign companies seeking lower wage costs. On top of this, there are prestige benefits – participation in EU institutions, hosting summits, and so on – and access to the CAP as well as structural funding for poorer regions. Hence seeking EU membership is a vote-winning strategy for politicians in these countries, which helps explain the long list of candidates for accession (see Table 5.1).

Table 5.1   Candidates for EU membership (correct as of July 2013)

Country	Application Status	Negotiation Status
Albania	Pending EU recognition as viable candidate	Application submitted April 2009
Bosnia and Herzegovina	Not yet applied	Formal application likely
Iceland	Official candidate (since 2010)	Implementing EU rules to meet entry criteria
Kosovo	Not yet applied	Formal application likely
Former Yugoslav Republic of Macedonia	Official candidate (since 2005)	Implementing EU rules to meet entry criteria
Montenegro	Official candidate (since 2010)	Implementing EU rules to meet entry criteria
Serbia	Official candidate (since 2012)	Implementing EU rules to meet entry criteria
Turkey	Official candidate (since 2005)	Implementing EU rules to meet entry criteria

5.6.1   Conditions placed on admitting new members

Given the Copenhagen Criteria regulating eligibility for membership (see Box 3.3), joining the EU constitutes official recognition of a country's democratic stability as well as of its readiness to participate in deciding upon and implementing EU policies. However, in most cases this is only possible after an arduous process of adaptation, which is based on countries' ability to implement reforms. This process of meeting the requirements for EU membership is known as **conditionality,** from the conditions that first have to be satisfied (Grabbe 2006). Conditionality was developed following the end of the Cold War, to ensure that widening did not undermine the functioning of the EU and the ability to integrate further. As member states are responsible for executing EU policies, it is imperative that all of them have the administrative capacity to put EU policies into practice. This presupposes not only the rule of law and a democratic process for exercising power, but also having civil servants and judges knowledgeable about EU rules. Meeting these conditions was no problem for wealthy, democratically stable countries such as Austria, Sweden, and Finland, which joined in 1995 – barely two years after the beginning of formal negotiations.

Conditionality was therefore designed with Eastern and Central European countries in mind. Back in the 1990s, these countries were fledgling democracies transitioning to a market-based economy. Moreover, 10 percent of their working population was linked to agriculture. In this context enlargement would prove expensive in terms of CAP and structural spending and would complicate decision-making processes, given the entry of a large number of new states. Thus, beyond setting conditions for adapting to EU rules, leaders of the then EU 15 responded in two ways: they devised a way to minimize the costs of enlargement; and they proceeded to streamline decision-making procedures (Schneider 2007).

The 2004 enlargement deal functioned by phasing in CAP payments to farmers in new member states. The assumption (which proved correct) behind this move was that the agricultural labor force would dwindle as these countries integrated the single market, which provides other career opportunities and stimulates consolidation in farm holdings. So, after the 10-year transition period, the EU budget is not being consumed by payments to new member states' farmers. Another key economic aspect of enlargement was the introduction of transitional limits on free movement for citizens of post-2004 countries. Governments of existing member states had the option to limit immigration from these countries for up to 8 years, which many states such as Germany and France did.

In 2007 Bulgaria and Romania joined the EU and, because of concerns with their political and judicial systems, they became subject to post-accession conditionality. Here the novelty was that the Commission reserved the right to monitor progress in complying with EU rules. This monitoring came with the possibility of activating a "safeguard clause" that could deprive these countries of EU funds – or even ban them from exporting food products – until they comply. The reasoning behind permitting accession while retaining conditionality was in fact generated by fear – namely the fear that blocking accession would actually undo the progress already made, especially in reforming the legal order (Trauner 2009). Hence the Commission was given responsibility for a Cooperation and Verification Mechanism designed to monitor Bulgaria's and Romania's efforts to implement judicial reform and to fight corruption and organized crime.

Consequently the process of widening the EU has been explicitly designed to minimize the negative impact that enlargement could have on deepening. Institutional changes via treaty reform have been negotiated prior to, or alongside, widening – for example the SEA accompanied Spanish and Portuguese accession, while the Constitutional Treaty deliberately coincided with the 2004 wave. Furthermore, conditionality, before and even after accession, is designed to provide unity for the EU space despite economic disparities and cultural heterogeneity. Encouragingly, academic studies of countries that joined in 2004 show a better track record of implementing EU law in those countries than in older member states (Sedelmeier 2008). Indeed, in the five years before the ratification of the Lisbon Treaty, the EU system continued to function well even without the changes intended by the Constitutional Treaty. This demonstrates that new member states were well prepared for participation in common decision-making institutions.

Nevertheless, enlargement raises important questions apart from the constant concern of how to finance poorer member states. After 2004, experts warned of "enlargement fatigue" within older EU countries, where citizens would grow wary of the merits of further EU expansion (see Box 3.1). This is particularly true about attitudes toward negotiations with Turkey: EU citizens and politicians are worried about the capacity to absorb such a large new member state that would become a key player in all EU decision-making. Leaders in France and Germany have also questioned whether Turkish citizens and politicians share enough EU values to integrate both common decision-making processes and a single market with free movement of labor. Consequently there is talk of offering associate membership to Turkey rather than full EU membership, in recognition of the fact that, with this candidate, differential integration might be preferable (this topic of differentiation is discussed in Section 9.4).

The 2004 enlargement has also been criticized in terms of the effects it had on new member states that were just returning to democracy and full political sovereignty. In particular, Bickerton (2009) has argued that this round of EU enlargement meant imposing limitations on sovereignty that never applied to countries in Western Europe. There are even accusations that the EU has expanded in an imperialistic fashion, at the cost of local autonomy and preferences (Zielonka 2006). Yet a look at the list of candidate countries shows the continuing demand for joining the EU. Moreover, enlargement is in the interests of existing member states, which want to use widening to stabilize the European neighborhood and to inject greater economic dynamism into the single market. These factors, combined with the success of previous enlargements in expanding the rule of law and democratic stability, suggest that widening will continue to be on the EU policy agenda in the foreseeable future.

5.7   Concluding Summary

This chapter surveyed the EU's major policies. Although many of these relate to coordinating national regulations and resources for meeting shared objectives, the EU nonetheless has significant expenditure policies. Its budget is very large compared to that of other regional organizations or international organizations, even if it seems insubstantial by comparison with government spending by federal states. This budget is funded by the member states and 80 percent of it is spent on two major redistributive policies: CAP (subsidies to farmers) and structural funds (development grants for poorer regions).

The regulatory output of the EU, which does not involve spending large sums of money, can be seen particularly in single market policy-making. Creating a shared space where the four fundamental freedoms are a reality is a central policy concern, which lies at the heart of using integration to stimulate economic growth. However, this aim requires difficult and politically sensitive decisions over deregulating national practices that impede the single market and over setting common standards for producing and selling goods, services, and so on. This process of setting common standards is an example of re-regulation, something that is particularly evident in social and environmental policy, where policy-makers weigh up the costs of imposing EU-level regulation to replace different national ones.

Politically sensitive regulation is also a characteristic of justice and citizenship, where the EU is increasingly involved in tasks such as border control and coordinating police and judicial agents across member states. These moves are, notably, a response to the creation of a borderless travel area, Schengen, which requires member states to share rules, to participate together in controlling those who enter it from the outside, and to track criminal activity among those within it. At the same time the EU wants to balance such measures with a concern for the rights of EU citizens and third country nationals.

Finally, enlargement – the process of widening EU membership – is a major and highly successful policy, where foreign and domestic policies overlap. Widening is conducted according to a set of criteria that are strictly monitored; this process is known as conditionality, which in the case of Bulgaria and Romania has continued to be applied even after accession to the EU. To mitigate the possible costs and disruptions of widening, the EU has typically made efforts to deepen before or alongside widening. Hence widening has prompted important reforms within the EU, alongside having a considerable impact on new member states' economies and politics.

Guide to Further Reading

Grabbe, H. 2006. *The EU's Transformative Power: Europeanization through Conditionality in Central and Eastern Europe*. Basingstoke: Palgrave.

Major empirical study of EU conditionality, notably of how it was designed and how it worked in the 2004 enlargement countries.

Majone, G. 2005. *Dilemmas of European Integration: The Ambiguities and Pitfalls of Integration by Stealth*. Oxford: Oxford University Press.

A provocative, insightful, and clearly argued examination of how the EU's consensus-oriented institutional design can result in imperfect policy-making.

Meunier, S., and W. Jacoby. 2010. *Europe and the Management of Globalization*. Abingdon: Routledge.

A collection of informative and theoretically sophisticated essays covering the EU's attempts to manage globalization through legislation and participation in global governance institutions.

Richardson, J., ed. 2006. *European Union: Power and Policy Making*. Abingdon: Routledge.

Comprehensive yet in-depth overview of the gamut of EU policy-making activity covering both inputs and outputs. Written in an accessible fashion by leading experts in each policy area.

Discussion Questions

1   Identify the major spending proprieties within the EU budget and evaluate how the size of this budget affects what the EU can and cannot do.
2   What were the reasons for supporting the creation of the euro? What made some countries decide against joining the single currency?
3   "The single market remains the core of economic and political integration." Evaluate whether this remains true, given the continued expansion of EU competences.
4   What explains the expansion of EU competences in justice and citizenship? Analyze the impact that policies in this area have on those living in the EU.
5   Analyze the resources that member states contribute to the Common Foreign and Security Policy. How effectively are these coordinated through EU institutions?

Web Resources

This book is supported by a companion website, which can be found at www.wiley.com/ go/glencross. There you will find a list of the web links referred to in this chapter wherever you see a "Web" icon in the page margins. In addition, you will find a list of further relevant online resources such as websites for EU institutions, political groups, archives, and think tanks, information on studying abroad, and biographies of key figures. You will also find self-assessment tools in the form of flashcards and independent study questions developed specifically for this chapter.

Glossary

Conditionality
Process whereby conditions need to be met by prospective member states before joining the EU. The states' incentive to meet these demanding conditions is access to the single market and structural funds, as well as the prestige of being admitted to EU membership.

ECOFIN
Name given to the finance ministers' configuration of the Council of the EU. ECOFIN is distinctive in that it has two configurations: in votes on Eurozone issues, only finance ministers from countries using the euro can vote.

Excessive deficit procedure
This mechanism is part of the Stability and Growth Pact, whereby the Commission monitors government debt levels to determine if they break the deficit-to-GDP ratio of 3 percent and the debt-to-GDP ratio of 60 percent. Under this procedure the Council formally requests member states to correct their deficits, and it can decide to impose financial penalties for continued excessive debt.

Kyoto Protocol
A 1997 UN agreement that obliges industrialized countries to reduce carbon emissions by 5 percent from 1991 levels. It is legally binding in theory but has a weak enforcement mechanism for punishing compliance failure.

Multiannual financial framework
Name given to the money allocated in advance by member states to finance the EU budget for a period of several years. The European Council negotiates the final figure subject to approval by the European Parliament.

Mutual recognition
Phrase describing the legal principle that goods produced in one member state are entitled to be sold unhindered throughout the single market. This move makes the single market more efficient and reduces the need for the EU to harmonize certain regulatory standards.

Negative integration

Phrase describing EU treaty principles and legislation that eliminate non-tariff barriers and prevent governments from restricting the four fundamental freedoms. Integration is said to be negative, or deregulatory, because it involves removing national policies harmful to the single market.

Non-tariff barriers

National rules or policies that impede the operation of the single market other than through tariffs or quota restrictions. For example, state-owned, state-controlled, or state-subsidized companies constitute unfair competition vis-à-vis other EU firms.

Optimum currency area

Economic concept describing an area where the use of a single currency and thus of a single interest rate is economically most efficient. There is a lively debate over whether the Eurozone fits the criteria, given its low labor mobility and the absence of fiscal transfers, both of which contribute to the efficiency of a currency area.

Positive integration

Phrase describing EU legislation that creates common standards for goods and services within the single market, as well as the harmonization of employment, environmental, and even criminal law. Integration is positive, or re-regulatory, because it involves replacing national rules with EU ones.

Schengen area

A set of EU and associated countries that have agreed to abolish internal border controls and to coordinate asylum and visa procedures. This area was established by a sub-set of member states, via intergovernmental cooperation outside the EEC framework; but it has subsequently become part of supranational EU policy-making.

Stability and Growth Pact (SGP)

An agreement between EU countries to maintain healthy public finances to keep the euro stable. Governments that breach the rules are liable to fines but political disagreement between member states has created problems in the application of these sanctions.

Third country nationals

Citizens of countries outside the EU. This category includes temporary visitors, permanent residents, as well as potentially irregular migrants. EU policies such as visa and asylum rules or border control increasingly affect third country nationals.

References

Ardy, Brian, and Ali El-Agraa. 2011. "The Economics of the Single Market." In Ali El-Agraa, ed., *The European Union: Economics and Policies*, 102–111. Cambridge: Cambridge University Press.

Bickerton, Christopher. 2009. "From Brezhnev to Brussels: Transformations of Sovereignty in Eastern Europe." *International Politics*, 46: 732–752. DOI: 10.1057/ip.2009.20

Boswell, Christina. 2003. *European Migration Policies in Flux: Changing Patterns of Inclusion and Exclusion.* Oxford: Blackwell.

Collignon, Stefan. 2004. "The End of the Stability and Growth Pact?" *International Economics and Economic Policy,* 1: 15–19. DOI: 10.1007/s10368-004-0009-6

De Grauwe, Paul. 2009. "The Fragility of the Eurozone's Institutions." *Open Economies Review,* 21: 167–174. DOI: 10.1007/s11079-009-9152-6

Delreux, Tom. 2011. *The EU as International Environmental Negotiator.* Farnham: Ashgate.

Egan, Michelle. 2001. *Constructing a European Market: Standards, Regulation, and Governance.* Oxford: Oxford University Press.

Ellis, Evelyn. 2005. *EU Anti-discrimination Law.* Oxford: Oxford University Press.

Geddes, Andrew. 2000. *Immigration and European Integration: Towards Fortress Europe.* Manchester: Manchester University Press.

Grabbe, Heather. 2006. *The EU's Transformative Power: Europeanization through Conditionality in Central and Eastern Europe.* Basingstoke: Palgrave.

Majone, Giandomenico. 2005. *Dilemmas of European Integration: The Ambiguities and Pitfalls of Integration by Stealth.* Oxford: Oxford University Press.

Marsh, David. 2009. *The Euro: The Politics of the New Global Currency.* New Haven, CT: Yale University Press.

Mattila, Mikko. 2006. "Fiscal Transfers and Redistribution in the European Union: Do Smaller Member States Get More than Their Share?" *Journal of European Public Policy,* 13: 34–51. DOI: 10.1080/13501760500380726

McCormick, John. 2001. *Environmental Policy in the European Union.* New York: Palgrave.

McNamara, Kathleen. 1998. *The Currency of Ideas: Monetary Politics in the European Union.* Ithaca, NY: Cornell University Press.

Sapir, André. 2006. "Globalization and the Reform of European Social Models." *Journal of Common Market Studies,* 44: 369–390. DOI: 10.1111/j.1468-5965.2006.00627.x

Scharpf, Fritz W. 1999. *Governing in Europe: Effective and Democratic?* Oxford: Oxford University Press.

Scharpf, Fritz W. 2002. "The European Social Model: Coping with the Challenges of Diversity."*Journal of Common Market Studies,* 40: 645–670. DOI: 10.1111/1468-5965.00392

Schneider, Christina J. 2007. "Enlargement Processes and Distributional Conflicts: The Politics of Discriminatory Membership in the European Union." *Public Choice,* 132: 85–102. DOI: 10.1007/s11127-006-9135-8

Sedelmeier, Ulrich. 2008. "After Conditionality: Post-Accession Compliance with EU Law in East Central Europe." *Journal of European Public Policy,* 15: 806–825. DOI: 10.1080/13501760802196549

Trauner, Florian. 2009. "Post-Accession Compliance with EU Law in Bulgaria and Romania: A Comparative Perspective." *European Integration online Papers (EIoP),* vol. 13, special issue 2: Art. 21. DOI: 10.1695/2009021

Weale, Albert. 1999. "European Environmental Policy by Stealth: The Dysfunctionality of Functionalism?" *Environment and Planning C,* 17: 37–51. DOI: 10.1068/c170037

Zielonka, Jan. 2006. *Europe as Empire: The Nature of the Enlarged European Union.* Oxford: Oxford University Press.

6

The EU in Comparative Perspective

Contents

Learning Objectives

- to identify similarities and differences between the EU and federal states as well as international organizations;
- to identify ways in which the EU can be considered a unique political system;
- to analyze the EU system using the concepts of federalism and separation of powers;
- to interpret why the EU is more supranational in its decision-making than international organizations;
- to distinguish between theoretical explanations for different elements of the EU's uniqueness;
- to evaluate how far the EU can truly be considered a unique political system.

The Politics of European Integration: Political Union or a House Divided?, First Edition. Andrew Glencross.
© 2014 Andrew Glencross. Published 2014 by Blackwell Publishing Ltd.

6.0   Introduction: Why Compare?

Former President of the Commission Jacques Delors famously claimed that European integration had created a "UPO": an unidentified political object. This quip tries to capture the fact that the EU does not quite resemble other political systems, notably federations or international organizations. What these differences actually consist of is something that can only become apparent through comparison. Comparing systems yields insights into the EU's specificity through the process of describing what makes it different. At the same time, comparative perspectives can also reveal similarities that allow explanatory theories from the study of federalism and international organizations to be used to understand politics and policies within the EU. The EU is not so unique then as to require a completely different theoretical apparatus for explaining decision-making (Hix 1994).

Hence the purpose of this chapter is both descriptive and explanatory. Unlike federations, as explained in Section 6.1, the EU is not a sovereign state (notably, it does not have a UN seat) and lacks sovereign powers in essential areas such as taxation and foreign policy. However, the EU's divided system of government matches one of the key principles of federalism: the separation of powers between different territorial levels of government. Even without a formal federal constitution it is thus possible to analyze the EU's political and policy dynamics by applying theories used to explain similar processes in federal states.

Yet the binding contracts signed between member states – the treaties on which the EU is founded – have the same legal basis as those of other international organizations. Unlike in other regional organizations such as the North American Free Trade Association (NAFTA), the African Union, or Association of Southeast Asian Nations (ASEAN), however, the EU treaties have morphed into a constitutionalized system where national courts enforce treaty rules and EU legislation. Another fundamental difference from existing international organizations, to be discussed in Section 6.2, concerns the absence of the **reciprocity principle** operating in the EU system. The World Trade Organization, NAFTA, or Mercosur allow member states to retaliate – in other words to take countermeasures – if another state fails to uphold its treaty commitments. Explaining why the EU member states rely on trust in the enforcement capacity of the EU institutions is thus a key objective of this section.

Finally, in Section 6.3 the chapter also examines the argument that the EU is something *sui generis* (the Latin expression for something unique, or one of a kind). Exploring this claim about uniqueness is important, because many analysts and politicians interpret the EU as being different from other political systems, especially the nation-state. There already are three seemingly unique aspects of integration: the way it reconfigures political authority and identity; the way the EU tries to be a force for the good in international politics; and the way it brings together different peoples under a common democratic system. These three features are described in turn, before we turn to historical and theoretical explanations as to why these unique characteristics occurred.

Overall, examining whether and why the EU is truly unique – and can stay that way even as its competences expand – means testing the uses and limits of comparison itself.

Comparison allows much to be learnt about how the EU functions, but it does not provide easy answers about how it will evolve or how its institutions can be made more effective or legitimate.

6.1   The EU Compared with Federal States

Scholars were initially reluctant to compare European integration with the political dynamics present in federal states. Regional integration, where groups of neighboring states sign treaties in order to open up trade and to grant certain reciprocal rights to businesses and citizens, was on the rise globally after 1945. The EEC was thus first studied in comparison with other attempts at creating regional organizations. With the constitutionalization of its legal system (see Box 4.3) and with the steady growth of its competences, the EU is far more integrated than other regional blocs, which are solely focused on free trade. Hence the EU is now deemed a sufficiently consolidated political system to be examined alongside other federal states.

Federal states are distinguished by virtue of having vertically divided institutions of government, some powers being exercised at the center for the entire state (notably foreign policy and major economic tasks) and others being exercised by autonomous territorial units. Typically, these autonomous units – such as the 50 states in the USA, or the 16 Länder in Germany – not only control their own affairs but also play a role in decisions affecting the entire country. In particular, federal constitutions normally allow territorial units to have a say in constitutional change. This is in order to prevent the federal center from encroaching on the prerogatives of the units. However, to avoid blocking reform and to prevent territorial secession, federations neither give individual units veto power over constitutional change nor allow them to leave the federation unilaterally. Moreover, while territorial units are independent in domestic policy, they are forbidden from conducting their own foreign relations.

Federalism, as the political philosophy behind this **vertical separation of powers** in government, can be understood both as an outcome and as a process. In terms of outcome, federalism entails creating legally separate spheres of government. This is, above all, a barrier to unnecessary centralization; a heterogeneous population requires local autonomy if it is to render policy-making responsive to the needs of citizens in different communities. As a process, federalism is considered a means of policy experimentation and consensus building between political communities. It functions this way thanks to the ability of territorial units to implement their own policies and to have a say in federal matters, especially to protect their citizens' rights and customs. Consequently federalism is seen as a political system for reconciling important differences in a democratic fashion, which is why it is used in large and very diverse countries such as the USA and India.

6.1.1   Why depict the EU as a federation?

When scholars compare the EU with other federal systems, they contrast both the outcome and the processes of European integration. The USA is a common object in comparing federal outcomes, because of its lengthy history of constitutional development and jurisprudence, which cover the shifting boundaries between state and federal authority (Fabbrini 2007). Pertinent contrasts can be made between legal developments in both systems. For instance, one study shows, surprisingly, that national courts in Europe were more willing to yield to EU supremacy than were state courts in the US willing to acquiesce to federal sovereignty during the pre-Civil War period (Goldstein 2001). Another useful descriptive comparison can be made between the methods by which the constitutional system was established in each case. Whereas the US Constitution was drafted by a constitutional convention and ratified by specially elected state conventions, the constitutionalization of the treaties took place through CJEU jurisprudence, as applied by national courts (see Section 4.4). The absence of a founding constitutional moment has opened up a debate as to whether such a foundation is necessary for federalism and whether it is needed to create a bond between EU citizens (see Box 6.1).

Box 6.1 Key Debate: Does the EU Require a "Constitutional Moment"?

The EU is often said to lack a "constitutional moment," where citizens debate and decide upon the legal and political structure of integration, endowing it with popular legitimacy. This absence is the result of the EU's constitutional and federal-like structure having emerged over time, through a set of complex treaties and jurisprudence rather than via a founding document. The lack of a constitutional moment for enacting a new political system also makes the EU different from countries where the federal constitution signals a new political era (e.g. Germany and Canada) or a dramatic break from past oppression (e.g. India and Malaysia). The Convention on the Future of Europe (2002–2003; see Section 3.4) was designed to rectify this situation and to produce a single constitutional document: the Constitutional Treaty. This meant assembling a collegial body of EU officials, national delegates, and NGO representatives deliberately seeking to mimic the Philadelphia Convention of 1787–1788, which drafted the US constitution and which is treated as the quintessential constitutional moment (Ackerman 1991). Yet the Constitutional Treaty did not greatly alter the institutional and competence structure of the EU. Instead, the idea behind calling a constitutional convention to draft an EU constitution was to signal the transformation of national sovereignty that had already taken place and to develop citizens' attachment to these changes (Walker 2004). However, only four countries held referendums on the Constitutional Treaty, and citizens in two of these rejected a document drafted by European elites and subsequently reworded by national governments. The lack of enthusiasm for this constitution was consequently interpreted as a sign that citizens prefer it when integration focuses on pragmatic policy questions rather than on abstract questions of how to generate a European political identity (Moravcsik 2006).

In a federation, the vertical separation of powers between the federal center and the territorial units can also be accompanied by a **horizontal separation of powers** – that is, between the institutions that decide and those that execute federal policies. This allows systems with a dual separation of powers (USA and Switzerland) to be distinguished from parliamentary federations (Germany, Canada, Australia). In the latter, the executive and legislative functions are fused, as parliament furnishes the members of the government and provides a legislative majority to enact its proposals; in the former, the executive and the legislature are functionally independent, competing to determine which laws exactly are passed. The horizontal separation of powers within the EU means that the European Parliament is an extremely powerful legislature, which resembles the US Congress more than national parliaments (Kreppel 2006). Although it does not have the power to initiate legislation – a prerogative of the Commission under the Ordinary Legislative Procedure (OLP) – co-decision gives the European Parliament an independent voice to shape and contest proposals from the Commission (see Section 4.2). In contrast, national parliaments are controlled by the party or party coalition in government, a situation that makes them far more compliant institutions for passing the laws proposed by the executive.

Moreover, the EU system displays an internal diversity and decentralization of political parties similar to that present in the USA (Kreppel 2006). That is, the political groups in the European Parliament are organized nationally, and beneath the surface of ideological unity they can contain diverse policy preferences. Of course, the US functions as a two-party system, while the European Parliament is multi-party. However, the two biggest party groups in the latter, the European People's Party and the Progressive Alliance of Socialists and Democrats (controlling roughly 70 percent of seats), display more bipartisanship than can be found in national parliaments within the EU. This is because the need for inter-institutional agreement in order to pass legislation compels a greater level of cross-party consensus than when the executive and the parliament are fused, as in parliamentary federations.

Unlike other dual separation of powers federations, however, the EU lacks a direct electoral mechanism for aggregating the preferences of individual citizens on EU policy choices. The European Parliament certainly aggregates votes from citizens across member states, but candidates stand for national parties and are selected according to electoral lists chosen by national party cadres. This means that MEPs do not really have a collective electoral mandate to push certain issues on the EU agenda.

Switzerland and the USA have referendums and the presidency, respectively, precisely in order to allow citizens a more direct say on what happens at the federal level than would otherwise be possible through their elected representatives in the legislature. Referendums in Switzerland allow voters to express a preference on new laws or on amending the constitution, whereas the US presidential election serves to give a popular mandate for the executive's policy proposals. These mechanisms furnish a democratic connection between the people and the federal center. The absence of such a mechanism in the EU has thus given rise both to calls for a direct, EU-wide election of the president of the Commission and to proposals for EU-wide referendums on treaty change (options discussed in Section 10.3). Consequently the EU remains a highly decentralized political system, with little opportunity for cross-national citizen mobilization over EU-level decision-making.

6.1.2   Explaining EU politics using federalism

From an explanatory perspective, many scholars argue that the EU's political and policy dynamics are best understood by applying theories used to explain similar processes in federal states. One significant theory for explaining policy outcomes under federalism, which has also been applied to the EU, is the "joint-decision trap" (Scharpf 1988). This theory treats the EU as a federal-like "compulsory negotiation system" where devising policy or new treaties automatically requires not a simple majority preference in a parliament but a high degree of consensus, if not unanimity, among member states. In these conditions, a single national government or a small group of member states can block reform of the status quo. The result of this joint-decision trap is a tendency toward lowest common denominator solutions, which can generate consensus across all countries but are ineffective when it comes to solving policy problems. Alternatively, the threat of a national veto to necessary policy reform can be mitigated by **side payments**, as happened with the creation of the structural funds to compensate for greater integration of the single market (Moravcsik 1998). The national veto over treaty reform allows member states to hold out for the best side payment deal they can get, something no longer possible under the supranational OLP. Hence this theory about the veto obstacles to consensus suggests that EU policy effectiveness requires getting closer to a decision-making system based on a simple majority, as QMV (qualified majority voting) tries to achieve, or else to sufficient funding of side payments from national governments expecting to benefit from integration (Scharpf 2006).

Despite the insights it offers, the joint-decision trap model overlooks certain institutional features that can mitigate lowest common denominator decision-making or the recourse to side payments. For a start, the purpose of the European Commission is to set the policy agenda by explaining why EU action is necessary and to craft legislative initiatives – which are based on extensive consultation – that curry favor across a broad section of member states. In addition, the constant institutional interaction between national representatives, Commission officials and MEPs helps create a level of understanding and mutual learning that in turn helps generate policy consensus, overcoming conflicts of interests and ideas (Hayes-Renshaw and Wallace 2006).

Another explanatory approach to understanding the EU by comparison with other federal systems consists of studying the dynamics that allow federalism to succeed in maintaining two different levels of government. This is a delicate balancing act, given the aggrandizing instincts of the federal center and the desire for as much autonomy as possible at the lower level. To protect against excessive centralization, the EU has strong structural safeguards (Kelemen 2010). These safeguards are the product of the EU's institutional design, which gives member states a say in deciding policy, via the Council of the EU and the European Council, and ultimate control over policy implementation, since the EU relies on member states to follow EU rules voluntarily. At the same time, the CJEU provides a robust judicial mechanism for preventing member states from shirking their responsibilities under EU law (see Section 4.4). This enforcement system thus prevents member states from abusing their autonomy. However, like other federal courts, the CJEU has proved more effective in ensuring member state compliance than in checking the expansion of pooled competences, as is possible under the subsidiarity rule. The CJEU is well disposed toward expanded EU competences because this increases its power. In addition, member states have no credible threat to reverse jurisprudence, since only a treaty revision could do so – an immense collective action problem (Alter 1998). Hence the institutional structure of the EU favors territorial autonomy and decentralization, while its legal structure is integrative.

The way political parties are organized in federations is another feature used to explain centralizing and decentralizing tendencies. Integrated party systems, where party financing and organization are linked across territorial levels of government, support centralization, whereas decentralized party organization, with separate parties contesting elections at different levels, favors territorial autonomy (Bednar 2011). Here the EU displays contradictory features. Increased cohesion among party groups within the European Parliament exists alongside continued financial and ideological autonomy among national parties that both form national governments and sit in the European Parliament as party groups (Kelemen 2010). Historically, party systems in federations become more integrated as federal competences increase, especially fiscal powers (Chhibber and Kollman 2004). As the EU has seen only limited expansion in its control over taxation, this could explain the attenuated integration of its party system despite significant expansion of its other competences.

6.2   The EU Compared with International Organizations

In addition to treating the EU as comparable to federal systems, we can also contrast the EU with international organizations (IOs) such as the UN, the World Trade Organization (WTO), NAFTA, or the African Union. These are not political systems based on a division of competences between different levels of government over a single territory. Rather, IOs are the product of international treaties between sovereign states; these treaties create institutions and rules that allow the states in question to cooperate toward solving certain policy problems while they retain their sovereignty. Contrasting the EU with IOs entails scrutinizing the similarities and differences in the legal and political practices related to the terms and application of the treaties that established these organizations. There is also a set of explanatory theories that account for the behavior of actors within such systems, which can also be applied to certain EU dynamics, especially treaty reform and inter-institutional relations.

Descriptively, a contrast with IOs remains useful even though, as shown in the previous section, the level of EU integration today makes for pertinent comparisons with federal systems. Traditionally, only states were recognized as subjects, arbitrators, and enforcers of international law. This meant, for instance, that international treaties could only bind national courts to apply treaty principles if the government passed subsequent legislation incorporating those treaty provisions into domestic law. Moreover, the enforcement of international law – for instance when a government violated a treaty or failed to repay its debt – would take place either through unilateral or through collective action by sovereign states. In the twenty-first century, though, it is not uncommon for states to sign "self-executing" treaties that empower domestic courts to enforce treaty law directly, without further national legislation. Equally, it is commonplace today to see international courts and IOs, rather than states, determining the content of international law as well as enforcing it.

These developments mean that the EU's legal principles of direct effect and supremacy are not as unusual as they once were. For instance, the dispute settlement mechanism of the WTO, an IO responsible for liberalizing international trade, can issue binding decisions that governments have to comply with, which is akin to the supremacy of CJEU jurisprudence. Likewise, domestic courts and police authorities in countries that have ratified the treaty establishing the International Criminal Court (a court for prosecuting war crimes and genocide) are compelled to arrest individuals wanted by that court. Consequently, national courts are more empowered than ever before to enforce international law directly – as happened with the constitutionalization of the EU treaties. Hence the increased domestic enforcement of international law and the growing effectiveness of international courts suggest that EU integration has been at the forefront of a broader legalization of international relations (Goldstein, Kahler, Keohane, and Slaughter 2001).

6.2.1   The absence of reciprocity or the *quid pro quo* principle in the EU

One notable difference, however, between the EU and IOs concerns the role of reciprocity in determining states' treaty obligations. Under traditional public international law, states were the judge and jury of their treaty obligations, which meant that they could take countermeasures if they decided that another state failed to uphold its treaty commitments. Treaty obligations were thus based on the *quid pro quo* principle. It was legitimate not to respect a treaty that other states failed to comply with because this non-compliance invalidated the terms of the agreement. This reciprocity principle remains central to international agreements to liberalize trade – such as the WTO, Mercosur, or NAFTA. Yet, significantly, the EU system is not based on reciprocity or countermeasures (Phelan 2012).

The WTO treaty allows a member state to take retaliatory countermeasure if it has suffered trade disadvantages as a result of the failure of another country to fulfill its obligations to ease restrictions on imports. Countermeasures take the form of trade sanctions intended not only to punish the other country in proportion to the loss suffered but also to compel conformity with WTO rules. Hence, when the EU banned the import of hormone-treated beef, the US and Canada (large exporters of such beef) were allowed, in 1998, to adopt retaliatory trade sanctions after the EU ban was judged contrary to WTO rules on risk assessment. In practice, this meant that the US imposed retaliatory tariffs on goods worth $116 million per year, which by 2009 prompted the EU to overhaul its ban.

Unlike the WTO or regional free trade agreements such as Mercosur (which covers much of South America) or NAFTA, the EU system specifically prohibits countermeasures. Indeed, the CJEU has made it clear that the reciprocity principle is not part of EU law. In the 1981 Essevi case, the CJEU made it clear "that in no circumstances may the Member State rely on similar infringements by other Member States in order to escape their own obligations under the provisions of the Treaty." In other words, the French decision to ban British beef after the BSE or "mad cow disease" crisis in 1999 did not give the British government the right to impose retaliatory measures on French imports. Instead of taking countermeasures to persuade other countries to meet their treaty obligations, member states have to respect all EU treaty rules and EU laws, regardless of the behavior of any one of them. Thus a government's failure to implement EU rules properly does not give other EU countries the right to do the same (Weiler 1981). The alternative to reciprocity is that member states place their trust both in the Commission's ability to uncover rule breaking by national governments and in the CJEU's ability to sanction rule breaking.

Of course, should trust in the EU's enforcement system break down, member states are free to withdraw completely. This right, which holds for all the countries that belong to treaty-based IOs, is formally enshrined in Article 50 (TEU). Just as state sovereignty allows states to join an IO – a principle that complicates the EU's ability, as a non-state, to sign international treaties (see Box 6.2) – states have a corresponding sovereign right to leave. The EU's **withdrawal clause** states that "any member state may decide to withdraw from the Union in accordance with its own constitutional requirements" (Art. 50 TEU).

A final descriptive contrast worth making between the EU and IOs concerns – again – the consequences stemming from the EU's treaty foundation. As a union of sovereign states, all member states have to give their consent if there is to be a revision of the treaties. This unanimity requirement follows the accepted principle of international law. Notably, Article 40.4 of the Vienna Convention on the Law of Treaties (1969) specifies that states cannot be forced to become parties to amended multilateral treaties to which they have not consented (de Witte 2004). The unanimity requirement explains not only why treaty renegotiation is such a thorny problem, but also why some countries have been offered an opt-out (see Chapter 3, Glossary) in relation to certain legal obligations they did not wish to fulfill (e.g. the British and Irish opt-out from Schengen). At various moments of treaty renegotiation, opt-outs (like side payments) that allowed treaty reform to pass by unanimity were preferable to sticking with an ineffective status quo. In addition, the treaties specifically provide legal scope for "enhanced cooperation" as a means of sidestepping the unanimity requirement. This mechanism (discussed in detail in Section 9.4) allows a core group of countries to use EU institutions and procedures in order to pursue new policy initiatives that other member states do not want to commit themselves to. Such a legal option is unnecessary in a federation, where constitutional reform might require more than a normal legislative majority but not the unanimous approval of all territorial units.

6.2.2   Explaining why the EU has integrated more

From an explanatory perspective, a comparison between the EU and IOs can especially illuminate the reasons why the EU has developed differently from other regional trade organizations. Here the puzzle is why EU countries have accepted a far higher degree of supranationalism than exists in NAFTA or Mercosur, even though all three organizations

Box 6.2   Case Study: The EU and Membership of
International Organizations

As the EU is a non-state entity, its external relations with other IOs are a complex matter under international law. The EU's eagerness to participate in multilateral international institutions and agreements clashes with many IOs' membership criteria, which permit only states to join. Hence the EU only has observer status at the UN and is a full member of only one UN specialized agency out of 17: the Food and Agriculture Organization. Moreover, as befits their sovereign status, EU member states are in essence free to vote as they wish in the General Assembly and Security Council. Studies show increased convergence since the 1990s in how EU countries vote in the EU, but this still does not constitute an automatic, common EU position (Laatikainen and Smith 2006). The EU has no seat in the UN Security Council, in the World Bank, and in the International Monetary Fund, thereby being prevented from participating in these institutions of global governance. This exclusion shows the limitations that result from the EU's lack of external sovereignty. However, the European Community (the legal person created by the EEC's Common Commercial Policy covering external trade) is a founding member of the WTO. This is because the Commission has sole competence over negotiating external trade. So, although EU member states are also WTO members, they all share a common external tariff set by the EU, and only the Commission represents member states in disputes with other WTO members. In an attempt to enable further EU participation in IOs, international conferences, and treaties, the Lisbon Treaty confers legal personality on the EU itself. The hope is that this will facilitate the Common Foreign and Security Policy (CFSP) by allowing the EU to take on more tasks in tandem with IOs, as already evidenced by the more than 50 UN multilateral agreements where the EU is the only non-state participant. Yet such progress depends on consensus within the EU as well as on acquiescence from its partners.

seek to increase prosperity by freeing trade. One theoretical explanation of this puzzle focuses on the nature of the EU treaties as incomplete contracts, which do not specify fully how pooled sovereignty will function in every possible situation (Cooley and Spruyt 2009). The EEC Treaty delegated the important tasks of proposing legislation and resolving legal disputes to supranational institutions precisely in order to provide solutions for working out the details of economic integration and to respond to unforeseen situations. This contrasts markedly with a complete contract, such as the NAFTA agreement, which outlines in full exactly what sovereign powers have been transferred or abandoned, without relying on problem solving by supranational institutions. Under a complete contract there can be no surprises equivalent to the CJEU's direct effect or supremacy decisions.

The reason why states accept to live with an incomplete contract and delegate responsibilities to institutions they do not fully control is said to lie in their respective power and ability to establish trust (Cooley and Spruyt 2009). The signatories of the EEC treaty were relatively matched in terms of population and economic power. Equally, they all needed one another as trade partners, since there was no ready alternative market for their exports. In these circumstances, even the most economically powerful states, France and Germany, were willing to bind themselves through an incomplete contract creating supranational institutions. Without such a commitment weaker countries would have no incentive to join, as there would be no improvement on the existing status quo. Conversely, the NAFTA agreement has one much stronger economic partner, the USA, which has significant trade relations beyond Canada and Mexico. As the stronger partner with other trade options, the US thus had no incentive to agree to an incomplete contract and to cede more sovereignty to supranational institutions. A complete contract that prevents the US from acting unilaterally over certain trade issues is still a good deal for the weaker partners, as it gives them preferential access to a huge market. So, in a situation of asymmetrical economic power, only a complete contract is possible, whereas with a symmetry of economic power an incomplete contract can be signed.

Another way of explaining this difference between the EU's institutional design system and how IOs normally function is through delegation theory. Delegation theory explains how and why a "principal" creates an "agent" in order to perform a task that the principal cannot or should not perform directly (so this is also known as a principal–agent theory). In the EU example, member states are the principals and have created agents in the form of supranational institutions, notably the Commission and the CJEU. Why, though, would states be interested in creating institutions they do not control directly?

In some circumstances, delegation is intended to make policy-making more efficient and consistent. For instance, the Interstate Commerce Commission was created by the US government in the late nineteenth century to regulate railways with more expertise and impartiality than direct congressional regulation could achieve. This specialized agency existed to implement the wishes of the principal – the US government – at arm's length. The logic of delegation behind the EU's supranational institutions is, however, different. The Commission and the CJEU were not created to follow blindly the wishes of the principals that created them. Rather they were created as a way to enhance the credibility of their commitment to the fundamental freedoms. This is necessary because member states often have a short-term economic or political incentive not to play by the rules, for example when they are faced with complying with a costly or unpopular EU law.

Hence the EU's supranational institutions are perhaps better described not as agents doing the bidding of member states, but as independent trustees (or fiduciary institutions) responsible for making sure that the principals stick to their treaty commitments (Majone 2002). They are thus required to be independent and are entrusted with the power to take decisions that do not please their principals, for instance by suggesting new laws for liberalizing services or by fining a government that does not apply EU law. Without these delegated competences, the Commission and CJEU would be unable to make the EU treaties credible – in other words, to make all member states certain that the terms of the treaty will be enforced. Yet it is rare for countries to join together to create such **trustee institutions** to monitor and enforce treaty obligations. For instance, the UN Secretariat is far less powerful than the Commission, given that it has no legislative power, which is also the case for the WTO Secretariat. Intergovernmentalism in decision-making remains the norm in contemporary IOs, thus making the increasingly supranational EU highly distinctive in comparison.

Pooling sovereignty to create supranational institutions is helped by the fact that each EU member state is a democracy that respects the rule of law. Democratic states find it easier to cooperate than non-democracies, given that their leaders know that their democratic partners have powerful domestic institutional restraints preventing them from shirking treaty responsibilities (Lipson 2003). In addition, the fact that national courts help implement CJEU rulings (see Section 4.4) reinforces trust between EU countries beyond the confidence engendered by the operation of supranational decision-making. However, Mercosur and NAFTA also constitute regional trade agreements between democracies and yet have not followed the same path of ever increasing supranational integration. Since this aspect of EU integration has not been replicated elsewhere, there remains a need to explore what exactly might be unique about this phenomenon.

6.3   The *sui generis* Interpretation

The previous two sections described and explained what can be learnt by comparing the EU to both federal states and IOs. This analysis demonstrated that the EU does not resemble perfectly either a federal system or a classic intergovernmental IO. Instead its institutional design, legal system, and political processes have elements of both. Given this mixture or hybridity, it is very tempting to describe the EU as unique, especially since other regional organizations, sharing the basic commitment to removing trade barriers, have not followed the same supranational logic. As a hybrid political system, the EU also constitutes a challenge for certain theoretical predictions about integration. Most notably, it has defied predictions that incremental integration inevitably leads to full political union and that a single currency requires full economic coordination. Consequently the EU challenges the conventional assumption that only the sovereign state has a place in international politics. Hence scholars have tried to explain this unique, *sui generis* character of integration by referring to historical and institutional specificities at play in Europe.

Different conceptual terms have been devised to try to describe what makes the EU stand out from other political systems. Scholars use new terms to make sense of how the EU differs when it comes to sovereignty, relations with other states, and how democracy is organized. The present section looks in turn at these various descriptions of the EU's uniqueness, before examining the explanatory claims used to analyze why these differences exist.

6.3.1 Three facets of EU uniqueness

The EU has been called a "postmodern state" because it has only a weak political core and its authority is fragmented both spatially and functionally (Caporaso 1996). This postmodern interpretation refers to the fact that, unlike in the classic sovereign state, in the EU there is no authoritative central government responsible for making binding decisions over the entire territory. Rather, different political institutions (EU, national, and even local) have a say, depending on the type of decision involved (function) and on the territory concerned (space). Decision-making rules differ according to function, CFSP being separate from OLP, and the same rules do not always apply across the 28 member states, given some countries' opt-outs from certain policies such as the euro.

The intellectual and cultural movement of postmodernism is used as a label to capture the EU's novelty precisely because the postmodern condition involves challenging fixed assumptions about categories (like the state) and identities (like nationality). Puzzling institutional complexity and a dearth of reliable knowledge (see Box 6.3) are not the

---

Box 6.3   Key Concept: The Knowledge Deficit about the EU

It is not easy for EU citizens to understand how and why EU rules and policies affect their lives. The legal and institutional complexity of the treaties contrasts unfavorably with the succinct principles and neater institutional design of, say, the US constitution. However, the problem is not just one of comprehension. Citizens complain of a knowledge or information deficit stemming from the difficulty of obtaining reliable information on what the EU does and on how exactly it constrains member states' autonomy. The Commission runs its own public opinion surveys, Eurobarometer, which show that in spring 2011 49 percent of citizens say they are unfamiliar with how the EU works. In addition, polling data show that those with a good understanding of the EU are wealthier and more educated, as well as more likely to support integration as something good for their country. The reasons behind this lack of information are manifold. Brussels has a large cohort of accredited journalists, but the media prefer to cover extraordinary events, such as emergency summits and treaty talks, not the everyday business of the OLP and CJEU jurisprudence. Equally, national political parties have proved poor at relaying how they participate in EU decision-making through their MEPs and ministers sitting in the Council of the EU. When in government, national politicians prefer to blame the EU for unpopular rules and, when in opposition, they claim they would get a better deal for their country. This attitude creates a climate where biased and erroneous claims about the EU flourish. In many countries the presence of populist anti-EU parties – from both the extreme left and the extreme right – further undermine citizens' ability to stay reliably informed about the EU. (See Chapter 11 for a discussion of the role integration plays in national politics.)

only postmodern headaches facing citizens. EU citizens are free to choose their own allegiances and identity. There is no enforced and overlapping EU political identity, so citizens can decide to identify with their region, with their country, with the EU, or with some combination thereof (Fligstein 2008). This choice contrasts with the traditional practice whereby nation-states – including federal ones – cultivate a national identity that creates a sense of belonging to a broader political or "imagined community" with a shared heritage (Anderson 1983). With 23 official working languages and mass media segmented into different linguistic communities, it is not surprising that the EU's official motto is the rather postmodern phrase "united in diversity."

The EU's unconventional role in international politics has also been interpreted as one of its most distinctive features. Enlargement policy, the use of CFSP and of humanitarian aid to stabilize problems in neighboring countries, and the promotion of a rule-based, multilateral international order are seen as a fundamental break with the power politics normally pursued by global players. The EU neither threatens countries that fail to respect international law or that jeopardize its interests nor has developed military alliances to counter hostile threats. Instead, the EU's foreign policy is designed to strengthen international law and global governance (see Section 8.1). Additionally, the EU does not turn its back on its neighbors, offering instead the promise of membership or development assistance to spread democracy and prosperity. Hence the EU has been called a "metrosexual superpower" (Khanna 2004) or a "normative power" (Manners 2002) – that is, one whose influence on other countries is based on the power of attraction of its own way of conducting foreign affairs (see Section 8.3).

A third and final descriptive observation about the EU's uniqueness concerns how it functions as a democratic system. Since this is a union of both states and peoples, democratic channels of accountability exist at the national as well as at the EU-level. Governments are elected by citizens across member states, legitimizing their decision-making role in the Council of the EU, while MEPs in turn provide a democratic check on legislation approved by the Council of the EU. Moreover, national politicians sitting in both councils wear two hats: elected nationally, they also make important decisions affecting the EU as a whole, although only their own citizens can vote them out of office. The result of these direct and indirect linkages between EU citizens and EU decision-making is far greater citizen participation and elected representation than in IOs, none of which has an elected legislature – let alone one with such responsibilities as the European Parliament. However, as discussed in Section 6.1, the EU has fewer mechanisms for transmitting directly the policy preferences of an EU majority as compared with other dual separation of powers federations such as the USA or Switzerland. In the absence of this majoritarian element, it is hard to say that EU government is of the people, for the people, and by the people.

Consequently, many scholars view the EU as a different kind of democratic system altogether. This is perhaps best captured in the argument that the EU is a "*demoicracy*" rather than a plain democracy (Nicolaïdis 2004). That is, instead of having a single political community or "demos," the EU consists of multiple democratic communities or peoples (*dēmos* means "people" in ancient Greek, and its plural is *dēmoi*). This multiplicity renders impossible the creation of a purely representative democracy, that is, a popularly elected government representing a majority of Europeans taken as a single people. The separate peoples do form, to a degree, a single, Europe-wide democracy through representation in the European Parliament. However, this democracy coexists with distinct national democratic practices such as elections to establish governments, and sometimes referendums on EU matters. The result is a messy hybrid, which can produce friction, since EU-level decisions (e.g. restrictions on budget deficits within the Eurozone) require implementation by governments that may encounter significant domestic opposition in doing so. In a *demoicracy*, therefore, political decisions are negotiated not only through EU institutions but also within member states. For such a system to work successfully, the different peoples of Europe need to accept EU decision-making and its outcomes – something that is far from being always a given (Schmidt 2005).

Explaining these different facets of uniqueness is not simple. An essential explanatory starting point is the question of why sovereign states would accept the creation of a postmodern arrangement of authority. Ordinarily, states are extremely jealous of their sovereignty and unwilling to lose autonomy except in return for concrete benefits, and not just in absolute terms. States have an eye on winning out in relation to the position of other countries because this increases their power and security in relation to their neighbors and rivals. European integration, however, does not follow this kind of logic. Member states pool sovereignty and transfer competences to supranational institutions in a way that primarily allows citizens and companies to benefit from unfettered cross-border interactions. The negative integration (see Section 5.3) at the core of the single market means that states have also lost certain competences that their citizens used to expect, for example subsidizing firms or protecting industries from foreign competition. Hence the principal beneficiaries of integration appear to have been private actors rather than the states themselves.

6.3.2   Explaining why European integration looks unique

Explanations for this unusual situation invariably resort to historical factors, pointing out the extraordinary circumstances facing a devastated Western Europe after 1945. One important argument is that states needed to rebuild not just their countries but also the trust of their citizens. Economic integration occurred because, by enhancing growth and prosperity through trade, government could more easily provide what citizens wanted: housing, infrastructure, and welfare. Consequently, the historian Alan Milward (1992) refers to integration as the "rescue of the nation-state" in Europe (see Section 1.5).

Another historically based theory for this choice concerns the importance of ideas about how inter-state relations should be organized to enable the coexistence of peace, prosperity, and liberal democracy. The post-1945 battle of ideas concerned how to overcome the pernicious effects of the balance of power system, in existence since the emergence of sovereign states (see Box 1.2). There was a realization that European democracies had been undermined by both economic protectionism, which made all countries poorer, and reliance on expensive military spending to deter threats. Proponents of the two opposite models of federation and confederation lost out, in the first decade or so after 1945, to a middle-ground position of supranationalism mixed with intergovernmentalism (Parsons 2003). This choice, enshrined in the Treaty of Rome, has constrained the direction of integration ever since because supranationalism became self-reinforcing. On the one hand, supranational institutions exercised their autonomy under the treaties in order to make decisions (such as the CJEU's direct effect doctrine) or propose policies (such as the Common Agricultural Policy, CAP) that committed the member states to a hybrid system. On the other hand, the cost to governments of reforming the status quo – which involved re-negotiating with partners – increased over time, as did the cost of withdrawal, given the citizens' and the firms' adaptation to the new system. This overall self-reinforcing effect is termed "**path dependency**": the theory that past decisions – in the EU case, over institutional and policy design – constrain political outcomes, limiting institutional change (Pierson 1996).

This historical and institutional perspective on EU uniqueness is not shared by all scholars trying to explain what makes this system distinct. One school of thought, known as **realism** in international relations, claims that the explanation for EU exceptionalism is not internal to the member states but lies outwith them. This perspective builds on the premise that states' most important concern is their own security: without it they cannot fully exercise their sovereignty (Waltz 1979). So what is considered distinctive about economic and political integration in Western Europe is that it has developed under the shadow of a security guarantee provided by the US-led NATO (see Section 2.1). During the Cold War in particular, states could afford to bind themselves to common economic regulations and decision-making rules, even though they risked not benefiting from them equally. They did not have to worry about who benefited most, because this would not jeopardize their security – security worries were resolved by the US commitment to NATO (Joffe 1984). Members of other regional organizations have not had such an external security guarantee to facilitate mutual trust and self-binding. This left Europe supposedly uniquely positioned for supranational integration.

The other side of the realist argument is that it explains why member states have avoided pooling sovereignty in the most sensitive policy areas, notably foreign policy. Here the reasoning is that member states will be more jealous about keeping this element of sovereignty as compared to economic competences. This follows precisely from the assumption that providing security is the ultimate responsibility – and indeed justification – of the state. So the competence to determine security is not something that can be bargained away as easily as economic competences. Thus realists have long argued that only the need to respond independently to an external threat can engender genuine security cooperation and the pooling of military and diplomatic resources (Hoffmann 1966). Furthermore, the enthusiasm for pooling sovereignty, while continuing to have an external security guarantee, is seen by realists as free riding on a US-led NATO (Kagan 2003). These interpretations of the EU's foreign policy role are open to debate and discussed in detail in Chapter 8.

Less contested, however, is the fact that, by comparison, accountability works rather differently in the EU *demoicracy* and in member states. What this entails for the quality of democracy – a subject of great controversy – is explored in Chapter 10. The preoccupation here is rather with explaining why the EU, a democratic system bringing together many peoples, looks like a different kind of democratic system. This is because the EU system is, unlike a representative democracy, not based on a popularly elected government or president. So it is less responsive to majority preferences. One explanation is that this reflects the very fact that there is no single EU people, or demos, to represent (Weiler 1999). The lack of an overarching political community makes the selection of representatives to govern in the name of a majority of Europeans impossible. Hence the consensus-based decision-making and continued reliance on national politicians (via both councils) is necessary if one wants to accommodate the preferences of different peoples.

A final explanation for the same institutional architecture of accountability is that economic integration was never intended to lead to full political integration; this means that a democratically elected government is unnecessary (Majone 1998). The task of regulating the single market by enforcing negative integration and by devising standards for positive integration can be accomplished by unelected expert institutions – a topic explored in Section 7.1. The Commission and the CJEU, from this perspective, are entrusted – on the basis of mandates from member states in the form of treaties – with powers best exercised independently of the preferences of the EU majority. This kind of government is thus designed to produce the best regulatory decisions and the most unbiased enforcement of EU law. Of course, there is a role for national governments. Since they have the final say over how to tax their citizens, how to spend this revenue, and how much to allot to the EU, they require an influential presence in EU decision-making. However, because the EU has no independent tax-raising power and is fiscally constrained by the member states, majoritarian democratic control over actual legislation is redundant (Moravcsik 2002). In other words, some scholars see no real need for political representation when there is no taxation.

6.4   Concluding Summary

This chapter situated the EU in relation to federal states and to IOs. The aim was to describe and explain similarities and differences with these other political systems. This showed how the EU has a dual separation of powers that makes it unlike a parliamentary federation. The powerful European Parliament is more like the US Congress than like national parliaments. However, the EU lacks supplementary mechanisms, like the presidency and the referendums used in the USA and Switzerland, for connecting citizens to policy outcomes. Nevertheless, theories of decision-making and institutional dynamics used to study federalism can explain key political processes, such as the difficulty of joint decision-making and the stability of EU–member state relations. In this way it is possible to say that European integration has produced a brand of federalism without a federation.

Yet the applicability of comparisons with federal systems does not mean that a contrast with international organizations is redundant. As a treaty-based system, the EU retains important features of an IO, notably the unanimity requirement for treaty reform. This explains the need to devise opt-outs and enhanced cooperation for cases where not all member states agree on delegating new competences. However, the EU's legal system explicitly rejects the reciprocity principle, found in the WTO or NAFTA, in favor of trust in EU supranationalism. This can be explained in terms of the need to delegate competences to trustee institutions capable of more effective policy-making and of more credible legal enforcement. Equally, member states accepted these treaties constraints because they needed one another as trade partners.

Finally, the EU can also be described as having unique features when it comes to its postmodern configuration of spatially and functionally differentiated authority, its rejection of power politics in foreign affairs, and its *demoicracy*. The last term conveys the fact that the EU is a democracy of multiple peoples, not just one political community. Explaining these unique elements often requires a deep understanding of historical factors, notably states' need, after 1945, to regain legitimacy by promoting economic growth, and leaders' desire to find an alternative to the balance of power. The initial supranational design constrained future institutional evolution: it made this evolution "path dependent" by establishing a hybrid intergovernmental and supranational structure to which private and public interests adapted. Likewise, the EU's distinctive foreign policy stance can be read as a compromise position, whereby member states want to work together to have an influence on global affairs without actually creating a new super-state. Finally, there are competing theories as to why EU democracy is different. Some attribute its distinctive democratic practices to the lack of a single people whose majority preferences can be represented; others think the EU administers many tasks that can be performed more efficiently without responding to electoral preferences.

Guide to Further Reading

Goldstein, J., M. Kahler, R. O. Keohane, and A.-M. Slaughter. 2001. *Legalization and World Politics*. Cambridge, MA: MIT Press.

Theoretically complex and empirically rich account of international law as an increasingly important constraint on state behavior in international politics.

Magnette, P. 2005. *What Is the European Union? Nature and Prospects*. Basingstoke: Palgrave.

Succinct and detailed survey of the EU's institutional dynamics, which places them in the context of the evolving balance between supranationalism and intergovernmentalism.

Menon, A., and M. Schain, eds. 2006. *Comparative Federalism: The European Union and the United States in Comparative Perspective*. Oxford: Oxford University Press.

A thought-provoking collection of essays contrasting EU integration with the constitutional and political processes of federalism in the USA.

Discussion Questions

1 How do the EU's institutional design and its political processes resemble those of federal states? What are the reasons for this similarity?
2 Why is reciprocity not part of the EU legal system? What compensates for its absence?

3 How would you interpret the importance of the EU's having a treaty foundation? Would having a constitution make a difference?

4 What are considered the distinguishing characteristics of EU uniqueness? What is the EU being compared to when it is described as unique?

5 Evaluate the theories seeking to explain the EU's uniqueness. Are these theories convincing enough to preclude comparative analysis?

Web Resources

This book is supported by a companion website, which can be found at www.wiley.com/go/glencross. There you will find a list of the web links referred to in this chapter wherever you see a "Web" icon in the page margins. In addition, you will find a list of further relevant online resources such as websites for EU institutions, political groups, archives, and think tanks, information on studying abroad, and biographies of key figures. You will also find self-assessment tools in the form of flashcards and independent study questions developed specifically for this chapter.

Glossary

Demoicracy
Concept used to describe the EU's democratic system as one consisting of multiple political communities. Given the multiplicity of "peoples" (*demoi*), national democratic practices coexist alongside EU-level democratic practices, notably democratic representation in the European Parliament.

Horizontal separation of powers
A political system whereby the institutions of government (the executive, legislative, and judicial branches) function independently of one another. This independence prevents any one branch from becoming too powerful, allowing for the mutual accountability necessary to protect the rule of law.

Path dependency
As applied to political institutions, the theory that institutional change is constrained by past decisions regarding institutional and policy design. This constraint exists because political and private actors adapt to existing conditions, which makes change more difficult to implement.

Realism
Theory of international relations that assumes that states seek first and foremost to guarantee their own security and hence will try to gain power and prosperity in relation to their rivals. Scholars who follow this line of reasoning are known as realists.

Reciprocity principle
Principle in international law whereby states agree to meet their obligations on condition that other states do the same. Like behavior will be returned, negatively as well as positively: other states' not playing by the rules justifies one in doing the same.

Side payments

Phrase describing financial inducements used during bargaining in order to get parties to agree to a deal. In the EU system, side payments have been used to help secure treaty reform, given that each state has a veto and can use it to negotiate the best deal for its country.

Sui generis

Latin expression meaning "unique, of its own kind." In the context of European integration it refers to the EU's uniqueness as a political system that is neither a federal state nor an international organization.

Trustee institutions

Also known as fiduciaries. In delegation theory, a trustee is empowered with the autonomy to interpret the best interests of the principals and to act accordingly. In this respect a trustee differs from an agent designated to act according to the instructions of the principals.

Vertical separation of powers

A political system in which powers are split between two (or more) levels of government. Some competences are exercised for the entire territory, while territorial units administer other competences autonomously.

Withdrawal clause

Article in the Lisbon Treaty that allows a country to withdraw fully from EU institutions and to renegotiate its political and legal relationship with the EU.

References

Ackerman, Bruce. 1991. *We The People: Foundations*. Cambridge, MA: Harvard University Press.

Alter, Karen. 1998. "Who Are the 'Masters of the Treaty'? European Governments and the European Court of Justice." *International Organization*, 52: 121–147. DOI: 10.1162/002081898550572

Amministrazione delle Finanze dello Stato v. Essevi SpA and Carlo Salengo [1981] ECR 1413.

Anderson, Benedict. 1983. *Imagined Communities: Reflections on the Origins and Spread of Nationalism*. London: Verso.

Bednar, Jenna. 2011. "The Political Science of Federalism." *Annual Review of Law and Social Science*, 7: 269–288. DOI: 10.1146/annurev-lawsocsci-102510-105522

Caporaso, James. 1996. "The European Union and Forms of State: Westphalian, Regulatory or Post-Modern?" *Journal of Common Market Studies*, 34: 29–52. DOI: 10.1111/j.1468-5965.1996.tb00559.x

Chhibber, Pradeep K., and Ken Kollman. 2004. *The Formation of National Party Systems: Federalism and Party Competition in Canada, Great Britain, India, and the United States*. Princeton, NJ: Princeton University Press.

Cooley, Alexander, and Hendrik Spruyt. 2009. *Contracting States: Sovereign Transfers in International Relations*. Princeton, NJ: Princeton University Press.

de Witte, Bruno. 2004. "Treaty Revision in the European Union: Constitutional Change through International Law." *Netherlands Yearbook of International Law*, 35: 51–84. DOI: 10.1017/S0167676804000510

Fabbrini, Sergio. 2007. *Compound Democracies: Why the United States and Europe are Becoming Similar.* Oxford: Oxford University Press.

Fligstein, Neil. 2008. *Euroclash: The EU, European Identity, and the Future of Europe.* Oxford: Oxford University Press.

Goldstein, Judith, Miles Kahler, Robert O. Keohane, and Anne-Marie Slaughter. 2001. *Legalization and World Politics.* Cambridge, MA: MIT Press.

Goldstein, Leslie F. 2001. *Constituting Federal Sovereignty: The European Union in Comparative Context.* Baltimore, MD: Johns Hopkins University Press.

Hayes-Renshaw, Fiona, and Helen Wallace. 2006. *The Council of Ministers.* Basingstoke: Palgrave Macmillan.

Hix, Simon. 1994. "The Study of the European Community: The Challenge to Comparative Politics." *West European Politics,* 17: 1–30. DOI: 10.1080/01402389408424999

Hoffmann, Stanley. 1966. "Obstinate or Obsolete? The Fate of the Nation-State and the Case of Western Europe." *Daedalus,* 95: 892–908.

Joffe, Josef. 1984. "Europe's American Pacifier." *Survival,* 26: 174–181. DOI: 10.1080/00396338408442183

Kagan, Robert. 2003. *Of Paradise and Power: America and Europe in the New World Order.* New York: Knopf.

Kelemen, R. Daniel. 2010. "The Durability of EU Federalism." Paper presented at the conference *The Constitutionalization of the European Union,* University of Florida, March 20, 2010. Available at http://www.ces.ufl.edu/files/pdf/JMCE/workshops/2010/DurabilityOfEUFederalism_032010.pdf (accessed July 15, 2013).

Khanna, Parag. 2004. "The Metrosexual Superpower." *Foreign Policy,* 143 (July/August): 66–68. Available at http://www.foreignpolicy.com/articles/2004/07/01/the_metrosexual_superpower (accessed July 15, 2013).

Kreppel, Amie. 2006. "Understanding the European Parliament from a Federalist Perspective: The Legislatures of the USA and EU Compared." In Martin Schain and Anand Menon, eds., *Comparative Federalism: The European Union and the United States,* 245–274. Oxford: Oxford University Press.

Laatikainen, Katie V., and Karen E. Smith. 2006. *Intersecting Multilateralisms: The EU and the United Nations.* Basingstoke: Palgrave.

Lipson, Charles. 2003. *Reliable Partners: How Democracies Have Made a Separate Peace.* Princeton, NJ: Princeton University Press.

Majone, Giandomenico. 1998. "Europe's 'Democratic Deficit': The Question of Standards." *European Law Journal,* 4: 5–28. DOI: 10.1111/1468-0386.00040

Majone, Giandomenico. 2002. "The European Commission: The Limits of Centralization and the Perils of Parliamentarization." *Governance,* 15: 375–392.

Manners, Ian. 2002. "Normative Power Europe: A Contradiction in Terms?" *Journal of Common Market Studies,* 40: 235–258. DOI: 10.1111/1468-5965.00353

Milward, Alan S. 1992. *The European Rescue of the Nation-State.* London: Routledge.

Moravcsik, Andrew. 1998. *The Choice for Europe: Social Purpose and State Power from Messina to Maastricht.* New York: Cornell University Press.

Moravcsik, Andrew. 2002. "Reassessing Legitimacy in the European Union." *Journal of Common Market Studies,* 40: 603–624. DOI: 10.1111/1468-5965.00390

Moravcsik, Andrew. 2006. "What Can We Learn from the Collapse of the European Constitutional Project?" *Politische Vierteljahresschrift,* 47: 219–241. DOI: 10.1007/s11615-006-0037-7

Nicolaïdis, Kalypso. 2004. "We the Peoples of Europe . . ." *Foreign Affairs,* 83: 97–119.

Parsons, Craig. 2003. *A Certain Idea of Europe.* New York: Cornell University Press.

Phelan, William. 2012. "What Is *sui generis* about the European Union? Costly International Co-operation in a Self-Contained Regime." *International Studies Review*, 14: 367–385. DOI: 10.1111/j.1468-2486.2012.01136.x

Pierson, Paul. 1996. "The Path to European Integration: A Historical Institutionalist Analysis." *Comparative Political Studies*, 29: 123–163. DOI: 10.1177/0010414096029002001

Scharpf, Fritz W. 1988. "The Joint-Decision Trap: Lessons from German Federalism and European Integration." *Public Administration*, 66: 239–278. DOI: 10.1111/j.1467-9299.1988.tb00694.x

Scharpf, Fritz W. 2006. "The Joint-Decision Trap Revisited." *Journal of Common Market Studies*, 44: 845–864. DOI: 10.1111/j.1468-5965.2006.00665.x

Schmidt, Vivien A. 2005. "Democracy in Europe: The Impact of European Integration." *Perspectives on Politics*, 3: 761–779. DOI: 10.1017/S1537592705050437

Walker, Neil. 2004. "The Legacy of Europe's Constitutional Moment." *Constellations*, 11: 368–392. DOI: 10.1111/j.1351-0487.2004.00383.x

Waltz, Kenneth. 1979. *Theory of International Politics*. New York: McGraw-Hill.

Weiler, Joseph H. H. 1981. "The Community System: The Dual Character of Supranationalism." *Yearbook of European Law*, 1: 267–306. DOI: 10.1093/yel/1.1.267

Weiler, Joseph H. H. 1999. *The Constitution of Europe*. Cambridge: Cambridge University Press.

Part III

Debating the EU System and Its Policy Outputs

7

EU Internal Policies
The Theory, Practice, and Politics of Regulation

Contents

Learning Objectives

- to distinguish between the different objectives of regulation;
- to analyze the relationship between regulatory theory and European integration;
- to evaluate why EU regulation in practice engenders political contestation and is surrounded by effectiveness issues;
- to identify how and why political considerations influence EU regulatory outputs;
- to explain why the EU can be seen as more than just a regulatory state;
- to distinguish between the different theories explaining the growth of EU regulatory competences;
- to evaluate critical perspectives on the consequences of regulation on national politics.

7.0 Introduction: Regulatory Outputs and EU Politics

At the core of European integration is the objective of creating a single market. This goal rests on two pillars: ensuring that member states respect the four fundamental freedoms, and crafting EU-wide regulation when common rules are needed. These regulatory outputs – a category that also includes the supranational enforcement mechanism overseen by the Commission and by the CJEU – are a function of the competences conferred by member states in successive treaties. These competences have increased significantly over time, allowing the EU to do more to break down national barriers to the four fundamental freedoms (see Section 5.3 on negative integration). Likewise, the EU now has extensive scope to create binding regulation for the entire single market (positive integration or re-regulation). Consequently, two of the most debated aspects of the EU's internal policies relate to its ability to dismantle (liberalize) national regulations for the sake of fundamental freedoms and to its power to substitute EU-wide regulations for national ones.

To understand the terms of these debates it is first necessary to explore regulatory theory, that is, the principles and assumptions behind regulating a market, understood as an arena of economic interactions linking supply and demand. Regulatory theory is a guide for understanding the problems associated with government regulation of markets, which is the EU's principal task. As explained in Section 7.1, European integration has used supranational institutions to overcome national regulatory barriers that, for domestic political reasons, obstructed the four fundamental freedoms. The use of supranationalism here points to the way in which political considerations can hamper effective regulation. To remedy this problem, the EU system relies extensively upon **non-majoritarian institutions**, such as the Commission and the CJEU, that are isolated from politics.

The functioning of the EU model of regulation in practice is the subject of Section 7.2. Using specific examples, this section examines the practical aspects of both deregulation and re-regulation, as well as the political controversies they engender. Particularly sensitive is the deregulation of services, which is pursued for the sake of **market efficiency** but raises concerns about a race to the bottom in social regulation. Nevertheless, the example of environmental regulation shows that EU rules can raise the average regulatory standard across the EU. Yet enforcing such standards – despite the EU's supranational enforcement mechanism – can be problematic. These effectiveness issues in turn can prompt attempts to expand the scope of EU competences.

The practical issues to do with dismantling obstacles to free movement and with setting new EU-wide regulatory standards are not free from political considerations and consequences. As explained in Section 7.3, the EU's regulatory outputs are therefore inherently political, which is why member states, MEPs, and interest groups all seek to influence regulatory policies. Again, this section uses examples to examine the clash between politics and efficiency in regulatory policy. Particularly important here are the preferences of different actors (both state and private) and how the EU system allows them to influence regulatory outputs. In addition, the analysis reveals the political objectives contained in the treaties, demonstrating that, although the EU is sometimes characterized as a regulatory state focused on market efficiency, its regulatory outputs can also be used to achieve equity.

Finally, Section 7.4 takes a step back to explore both the theories explaining this growth in regulatory outputs and those analyzing its consequences on member states. Explanations for why integration has developed from limited economic regulation to a host of important policy competences differ in terms of causal argument and the key actors they identify in this process. In particular, there is disagreement over how far national governments remain in control and how far supranational actors can profit from a shift in the preferences of interest groups and political actors for more EU-level policy-making. Scholars agree, though, on the importance of the consequences of integration. Yet here there is tension between a neutral interpretation of these developments and a more critical perspective, which suggests that regulatory outputs privilege the winners from market competition at the expense of others. For better or worse, EU regulation is thus an inherently political affair.

7.1 Regulatory Theory and European Integration

The bulk of the EU's internal legislation (policies directly affecting only EU member states, as well as citizens and businesses established there) involves regulatory issues relating to the single market. In principle, regulation entails making policies as a result of which – as far as possible – everyone is better off. Examples include environmental standards for clean water and air, hygiene rules for selling food, or clinical testing procedures for new medicines. Having such standards improves the well-being of all citizens, but regulations like these do not appear spontaneously. Regulation is thus intimately connected to two other concepts: a market, understood as an arena of economic interactions linking supply and demand; and government – that is, an authoritative agent with the ability to intervene to alter how a market works. This section aims to show how regulatory theory explains the need for government regulation and how the EU has been designed to both establish and regulate a single market.

Regulatory theory assumes that a free market (one where there is plentiful competition, customers are well informed, and new suppliers can easily offer products) is inherently good because it matches supply with demand in an efficient way. This is the principle known as the "invisible hand," whereby citizens pursuing their self-interest in a free market actually ensure the best possible allocation of goods at the optimal price: in other words they ensure a mutually beneficial outcome (Marris and Mueller 1980). Efficient markets will also stimulate economic growth, as they encourage competition and maximize an economy's productive potential. Yet regulation is premised on the fact that markets do not always function well, preventing an efficient outcome (den Hertog 2000). Regulatory policies thus require the government to decide upon and apply rules to regulate how actors (for example consumers and producers) behave in certain market interactions. Government is, from this perspective, intended to make markets work more efficiently, but not to become a substitute for them.

7.1.1   Regulating against market failure

This notion of making a market more efficient can best be understood by using an example. In the case of air quality, regulation means setting emissions standards – as the EU does – for the manufacture of cars or buses and for the operation of power stations. Why regulate against air pollution caused by the market for cars, transport, or energy? Obviously, there is likely to be a political demand for such standards from green political parties and environmental groups. However, regulation for the sake of efficiency is different from intervening in markets on the basis of political or ideological preferences such as to protect the environment or to stop global warming. Rather, intervention for the sake of efficiency becomes necessary when certain socio-economic interactions constituting a market have failed in some way: a condition known as **market failure** (Bator 1958).

In the air quality example mentioned above, an unregulated market for cars, buses, and producing power is a failure because of the high levels of pollution it causes. Regulatory theory interprets this as a problem of **negative externality**, whereby the production or use of a good, for example a car, involves a cost passed on to a third party, for example citizens in an urban environment who then suffer from respiratory diseases (Meade 1973). The cost is external to the market operating between buyer and seller, hence its designation as a negative externality. In response, regulation is necessary in order to ensure that the hidden cost (health and other damaging effects of air pollution) does not fall on third parties. The market for vehicles that pollute, therefore, cannot be considered efficient if some of the costs of these vehicles (say, treating respiratory diseases caused by air pollution) are not factored into the price.

Remedying this particular negative externality, air pollution, thus entails intervening in the market to set regulatory standards that compel producers of harmful goods to spend money designing and manufacturing less polluting vehicles or power plants. Negative externalities can also be remedied by incentivizing better practices, as in the case of the EU Emission Trading Scheme (see Section 5.4), which makes it financially beneficial for firms to reduce carbon emissions. In all cases, the intention is to alter the market by changing what is offered or by changing the demand in order to account for hidden costs suffered by people not actually participating in those commercial exchanges. The aim is to make sure that the regulated market takes account of negative externalities such as pollution so as to minimize or even eradicate costs hitherto borne by third parties (Mitnick 1980).

Alongside negative externalities, there are other forms of market failure thought to require regulation from a government: monopoly power and asymmetric information (Majone 1997). Again, regulating against these entails making the market more efficient than it otherwise is. Monopoly power is inefficient because the absence of competition limits choice and innovation while increasing prices for consumers. Governments thus enact strict laws to prevent a single firm (or a group, acting together in what is called a cartel) from dominating a market. EU law can require a company (EU-based or foreign) with a dominant market share to be broken up, and it can prohibit a merger between two companies that would create such dominance. The latter was the reason why in

2001 the European Commission vetoed the proposed merger between US firms General Electric and Honeywell.

Asymmetric information is another reason why a market might function inefficiently and hence require regulation. Consumers need to know what a good will actually cost, what its quality is, or what exactly is provided in a contract for services, in order to make an informed purchasing decision. For instance, in the case of air travel, consumers using so-called low-cost airlines often face confusing charges for services such as paying by credit card. This opacity makes it hard to identify the final ticket price, so customers may not be in a position to compare prices and get the best deal. Information is asymmetric in this case because the airline knows more about the product it is selling than the consumer. Regulation is necessary in order to prevent such practices by obliging companies to provide full and clear information about their products. The EU has thus passed consumer protection legislation that empowers the Commission to monitor airlines' websites and to pursue legal action against companies that do not provide full information on ticket prices.

7.1.2   The debate over how to regulate

Regulatory theory is concerned with how governments should regulate as well as with what they should regulate. In particular, there is a lively debate over whether regulation should be in the hands of independent experts or whether elected legislatures should determine exactly how to regulate markets (Majone 2000). This debate exists because almost all regulation is politically charged and involves opposing interests. For instance, regulating the market for cars by requiring greater fuel efficiency affects a range of actors: car firms and their shareholders concerned about profits, workers concerned about employment, and politicians concerned about winning elections. These interested parties will be worried about the costs of regulating a market – for example reduced profits, job losses, and fewer votes if companies lay off workers and make less profit. Such concerns will, in a political decision-making context, have to be balanced by consideration for the ideological goal of protecting the environment and citizens' health, causes supported by numerous organized interests such as NGOs. In fact European political parties are traditionally organized along ideological lines – this is known as the left–right divide – on the basis of the kind of government regulation they favor (see Box 7.1).

In a politically charged context, there are good reasons to believe that deciding upon, and implementing regulation for the sake of market efficiency should be done with as little political influence as possible. For Majone (1996), this means that non-majoritarian institutions should be responsible for setting regulatory standards and enforcing them. This is because regulation functions best when impartial experts make and apply rules under the supervision of an impartial legal authority. Non-majoritarian means "non-elected, politically independent bodies" (Majone 2006, 613), for instance courts like the CJEU, but also a body such as the Commission. Closely associated with the notion of a trustee institution (see Section 6.2), this argument sees the Commission and the Court as entrusted with certain vital responsibilities that require impartiality, and thus independence from electoral politics.

Box 7.1   Key Concept: The Left–Right Divide in
European Politics

For many decades European political parties have defined themselves according to the kind of government intervention in the market that they support. Center-right parties are traditionally in favor of loosely regulated markets focusing primarily on efficiency, whereas center-left parties favor greater regulation in order to achieve equity or social justice (Hix 2008). Equity here means not just equal opportunity but also equality of outcomes, so that market efficiency does not come at the expense of workers' rights, affordable healthcare, basic living standards, and the like. Center-left parties thus support regulating markets for political ends beyond efficiency (for example helping workers at the expense of owners of capital) in order to create a social market (see Box 5.2). By contrast, their center-right opponents fear that the focus on equity will come at the expense of efficiency, jeopardizing growth and hence, in the long run, living standards. This dispute illustrates the fundamental **equity/efficiency trade-off** between efficiency and equity that results when governments regulate markets; Okun (1975) represents this process as drawing the boundary line between the "domain of dollars" and the "domain of rights." Historically, therefore, the boundary between these two domains has been set on the basis of the respective strength of parties on each side of the left–right divide.

As appointed experts unconcerned about being re-elected, decision-makers in a non-majoritarian regulatory institution and the courts supervising them can, in theory, just concentrate on making markets more efficient. This is why Majone claims that they will do a better job when it comes to regulating against market failure. Indeed the institutional design of the EU in large part reflects this assumption. As it is not elected, the Commission is insulated not only from national biases (as evidenced in the Commissioner's oath), but also from electoral politics itself. Moreover, the Commission has the monopoly of legislative initiative under the Ordinary Legislative Procedure (OLP), as well as the responsibility for checking member state enforcement of EU law (see Section 4.4). These powers, as well as the general oversight of EU rules provided by the CJEU, mean that the initiation and monitoring of EU regulation are detached from overt political considerations that could interfere with the primary task of regulating against market failure.

In fact the task of creating a single EU-wide market via deregulation (or negative integration: see Section 5.3) pitted the Commission's focus on market efficiency against the tendency of member states to regulate national markets under the influence of political and ideological factors. Even after signing up to the EEC Treaty, which committed them to the four fundamental freedoms, member states retained practices that impeded the mobility of labor, capital, goods, and services (Egan 2001). Notable examples here are state subsidies granted to companies in order to protect employment, the preferential treatment of state-owned companies in competition law, or technical standards designed to protect domestic industries against competition from other member states. These practices distort the single market by hampering competition from other EU firms. Rules and regulations that distorted competition existed because national politicians were heavily influenced by political factors when they intervened in national markets, chiefly to protect vested interests such as domestic firms or labor unions. Consequently, countries with a treaty commitment to upholding the four fundamental freedoms nevertheless practised regulation that prevented efficient market competition. The EU's non-elected supranational institutions, acting for the sake of market efficiency, which in turn stimulates economic growth, were – and remain – key to dismantling these inefficient anti-competitive practices. Some of these national biases remain, though, as discussed in Section 7.2.

A final issue with regulation via non-majoritarian institutions is precisely that of legitimacy and accountability. Elected politicians are accountable to voters via the ballot box and, as elected representatives, have a legitimate mandate to make regulatory decisions – deciding how to settle the equity/efficiency trade-off at the heart of the left–right political divide (see Box 7.1). In the EU case, however, national politicians have conferred upon the unelected Commission certain regulatory competences to propose and oversee regulatory policies that create an efficient EU-wide market. In this context, citizens and elected politicians worry that the EU system is not responsive enough to public preferences; it can appear to be a government *for* the people but not *by* the people. More specifically, unelected officials such as commissioners or judges in the CJEU have a large say in deciding how to make the trade-off between efficiency and equity when regulating the single market. This goes against the European tradition of using political inputs (expressed via public opinion or elections) to determine regulatory policies. This anxiety over the democratic legitimacy of EU policy-making is discussed in detail in Chapter 10; right now it is important to examine how regulating the single market works in practice.

7.2   EU Regulation in Practice

This section illustrates how exactly the EU regulates the single market in terms of both negative and positive integration (see Chapter 5, Glossary). The aim is to show, by drawing on examples from the OLP and the treaties, the reasoning behind regulation in practice and to clarify the political debates this engenders. In addition, it is important to examine issues to do with the effectiveness of implementing EU rules (regulating for common standards as well as deregulating national markets), which in the decentralized EU is mostly undertaken by member states.

7.2.1   Deregulation in practice

The main task of European integration, as per the treaties ratified by member states, is to create a single market where capital, labor, services, and goods are mobile. This is necessary for making the EU market efficient, so that goods and services are produced more cheaply and consumers have more choice, which leads to an optimal allocation of goods and services. Physical barriers on the movement of goods and people were already abolished by the end of 1992. That is, the member states agreed on legislation that meant dismantling border controls and associated paperwork for goods circulating between EU countries, a task made much easier by the extension of QMV (qualified majority voting) after the Single European Act. Schengen achieved a similar goal of border-free travel for all citizens within the countries participating in this border-free zone (see Section 5.5). The free movement of goods was also helped by the doctrine of mutual recognition developed by the CJEU.

The EU also played a key role in liberalizing important service sectors such as telecommunications, air travel, and postal services. In these cases the Commission proposed legislation in order to deregulate certain markets (although sometimes countries have independently chosen to deregulate prior to EU legislation). The extension of QMV made it much easier to pass this legislation, which for instance compels governments to open up telecoms infrastructure to multiple firms or to allow competition in postal services. In all these cases the aim is to introduce new players from across the EU to invest in, own, and offer services in different countries, thereby dismantling existing regulation that privileges big national telecom companies or postal monopolies. This deregulation remains a work in progress, with the Commission continuing to seek to deregulate certain markets. In the case of railways, for instance, the Commission has proposed legislation that will make for a completely deregulated market by 2019. Whereas today most EU countries have a national train operator with a monopoly over domestic travel, deregulation would allow foreign companies to operate rail services within any EU country, not just cross-border services. As in all deregulation, the shake-up of EU railways is intended to introduce competition by preventing the dominance of big national players and discrimination against new entrants. Of course, this kind of move entails political contestation, as it clashes with vested interests and national political preferences (a topic to be discussed in Section 7.3).

The area where deregulation remains most difficult to implement, however, concerns more locally based services. National governments have an extensive set of rules for who is entitled to work in a pharmacy, operate a hairdresser's, offer plumbing services, and so on. Many of these rules relate to qualifications, implemented to ensure that customers get good service; but they do so at the cost of making it very hard for citizens from other countries to set up such businesses. In 2006 the EU passed legislation (the Directive on Services in the Internal Market) to enable citizens from other EU countries to offer such services when moving to another country. Most importantly, this compelled governments to establish a webportal explaining what qualifications, licenses, and other formalities are required if one wants to establish a services business. This is an important step in establishing an integrated market, as it clarifies exactly how to offer services – something traditionally very difficult to understand by someone not educated or trained in that particular country.

However, this legislation stops well short of deregulating the provision of such services. That is what the original version of the law, drafted in 2004, intended to achieve: market efficiency through the "country of origin" principle. This principle would have

---

Box 7.2   Key Debate: Does Integration Lead to
Social Dumping and a Race to the Bottom?

Both "social dumping" and "race to the bottom" refer to the process whereby competition between states with different regulatory standards is thought to lead to a lowering of those standards. The fear is that, when firms can relocate to a more advantageous jurisdiction – one offering for instance lower taxes or looser employment law – governments will be obliged to lower standards to prevent firms from relocating. In the EU single market, firms are free to relocate and take advantage of regulatory competition in the shape of low corporation tax in Ireland or less strict employment rules on hiring and firing in the UK and Eastern Europe. In this context, politicians and employees are worried about governments being forced to dilute national standards in order to compete on equal terms – that is, about their being forced into a race to the bottom. Yet, although there is some regulatory competition among EU countries, there is also a large amount of legislation establishing common EU standards across key policy fields, such as the health and safety of workers and of the environment. Empirical studies show that the EU's regulatory output in environmental policy and labor standards does not undermine national rules in these areas. On the contrary, there are many instances where EU regulation aims for a higher standard than the existing national norms, notably in environmental policy (McCormick 2001). Moreover, there are limits to how far EU-led deregulation affects national policies in social policy and elsewhere. For instance, governments are entitled to fund "services of general interest" such as a universal postal service or a regional train service in a rural area; they can also pursue higher environmental standards than those the EU imposes.

---

allowed citizens to offer services abroad on the basis of the labor law of the country where they were incorporated, not that in which they did business. So a Latvian welder could be employed on a Danish building site on (much cheaper) Latvian terms, not Danish ones, obviously increasing competition – but at the expense of local workers. The Commission's proposal for making the cross-border services industry more efficient caused uproar. Unionized services staff as well as politicians denounced this law as ushering in unfair competition, which would erode national wage bargaining and would lower employment rights (Nicolaïdis and Schmidt 2007). Particularly powerful was the accusation that this policy was tantamount to **social dumping** or to a "race to the bottom" that would erode European social policy norms (see Box 7.2). The controversy this aroused led to a split in the Council, allowing the European Parliament to succeed in brokering the watered-down version that passed in 2006. In this case, therefore, the EU's political institutions succeeded in stymieing the Commission's primary emphasis on market efficiency.

7.2.2   Regulating for common standards and its effectiveness

Alongside deregulating national impediments to the four fundamental freedoms, the EU has established certain common regulatory standards across member states so as to make markets more efficient. The Commission is thus heavily involved in proposing legislation that sets minimum technical, safety, environmental, and social standards across the EU. Given the involvement of political actors and interest groups, this kind of regulation is often a highly politicized affair, where market efficiency is not the sole consideration. In this way EU legislation reflects political inputs that make regulation more than just a technical affair of rendering markets more efficient.

Especially in environmental policy, the EU has taken an activist stance, promoting respect for the environment above simple market efficiency. By treaty law, the EU is committed to promoting a "high level of protection and improvement of the quality of the environment" (Art. 3.3 TEU). To achieve this, the EU has passed extensive legislation regulating all manner of environmental concerns, including water quality, waste disposal, eco-labeling, and carbon emissions. With this treaty objective, the Commission has gone beyond its usual concern for market efficiency (for instance in regulating against negative externalities such as pollution) when proposing regulation. The activism of national governments from countries with high levels of environmental protection and active green movements, such as Austria, Germany, and the Nordic countries, also contributed greatly by creating a supporting coalition in the Council (Liefferink and Andersen 1998). The result has been an impressive increase in the average standard of environmental protection across member states, particularly in Mediterranean countries (Schreurs 2004). Hence this is a policy area where European integration can lift average regulatory standards upwards.

At the same time member states are entitled to adopt higher environmental standards, providing these are not disguised measures to support national businesses. Ultimately it is up to the CJEU to determine whether environmental protection rules are legitimate measures for protecting human health, or also flora and fauna. The legality of these measures is often tested in courts, as meeting environmental requirements for making or selling goods imposes costs on firms and can favor domestic producers over foreign ones. A notable case concerns the German government's law obliging electricity retailers to purchase a proportion of their supply from German wind farms. This measure was part of a move to reduce Germany's carbon emissions, something that could not be achieved by simply subsidizing the building of wind farms, as that would be illegal state aid under EU competition law. Yet the obligation to buy from German wind farms discriminates against electricity retailers whose supply comes from other EU sources. The Court of Justice, in its decision – PreussenElektra 2001 – accepted that this was a legitimate way to achieve a desirable environmental goal, thereby justifying a possible distortion of competition in the single market (Armenteros and Lefevere 2002).

Environmental regulation is also a good example for highlighting the importance of national implementation of EU rules. It is the responsibility of national governments, as well as of local or municipal authorities where they have such competences, to implement environmental and other regulations. This means that protecting the environment according to common EU standards depends on national administrative capacity, and even willingness to act. Consequently, there are problems making EU regulation a reality in jurisdictions where administrators and politicians are reluctant to conform fully to EU law. Given differences in wealth across the EU, not all countries and localities have the means to inspect sites regularly and to conduct tests, while levels of environmental activism also differ. The EU system is designed to help overcome some of these limitations, as the Commission, in its watchdog role (see Section 4.4), can bring infringement proceedings against a member state and can also ask the CJEU to impose fines on that country. For instance, in 1997 the Court backed the Commission and imposed a daily fine of €20,000 on Greece until it shut down an illegal landfill site.

Of course, fining a government – after lengthy judicial proceedings – can be a limited method of ensuring compliance when those actually responsible for breaking the law (for instance firms dumping waste illegally) are not actually punished. Implementing EU law effectively in a context where not all states criminalize actions that harm the environment is thus a headache. This is why in 2010 the EU, using its competence in justice policy, passed legislation obliging member states to attach minimum criminal sanctions to breaches of existing EU environmental regulations. For the sake of effective regulation, therefore, EU policy-making in the environment also entails regulating national criminal law. The same logic of not always trusting member state enforcement lies behind the Commission's desire to create a European public prosecutor to try individuals who break EU law (see Section 5.5). This increase in the EU's regulatory activity for the sake of ensuring effectiveness reflects the way in which regulating a huge, complex single market requires a steady accumulation of competences at the EU level (Börzel 2005).

7.3   Not Just a Regulatory State: The Politics of EU Regulatory Outputs

After surveying the goals, controversies, and effectiveness issues that surround EU regulation in practice, it is important to explore what this means in terms of how far European integration actually manages to separate regulation from politics. The purpose of this section is thus to examine the different factors involved in EU regulation, notably how political preferences and objectives still play a role. Despite the importance of non-majoritarian institutions, political actors – including national governments, MEPs, citizens, firms, and interest groups – are active in the politics surrounding EU regulatory outputs. While the EU has features of a regulatory state, where efficiency and expertise are privileged over market intervention for political ends (see Box 7.3), politics is still an essential part of EU regulation. Overall, the aim is to show that, in addition to EU's focus on market efficiency, its regulatory outputs have inherent political implications and in fact include certain political objectives.

7.3.1   The politics of deregulation

On the surface, deregulation appears to be a technical measure that is purely designed to improve market efficiency by removing distortions imposed by national governments for political reasons. Impartial, unelected institutions such as the Commission and the

Box 7.3   Case Study: The Rise of the Regulatory State

After 1945 Western European states converged to a large degree on a model of government that involved extensive intervention in the economy, where government spending accounted for 50 percent of total GDP. This interventionism occurred via public ownership of companies, income redistribution through taxation, and monetary policy (controlling interest rates and currency prices). The goal of this kind of state was inherently political: to achieve full employment and to create a social market (see Box 5.2). Starting in the late 1970s, this model was called into question because it distorted markets – often for electoral reasons such as protecting domestic jobs – preventing them from being efficient. In a time of increased global competition, this hampered growth, created unemployment, and reduced the tax receipts necessary to sustain welfare spending. Consequently, governments moved toward making markets efficient via regulation rather than intervening for political goals. The policy shift toward market regulation entailed privatization, liberalization, and handing control of monetary policy to an independent central bank (Majone 1997). The regulatory state, as Majone calls it, thus represents a move away from controlling the economy through tax and spend policies and through monetary policy, in favor of regulation for market efficiency. Associated with this shift from economic interventionism to making markets efficient is the rise of government by administration: independent agencies regulate economic sectors through decisions overseen by courts. Compared with the interventionist state, the regulatory state provides governments with fewer means to control the economy apart from through regulation. The EU itself, although not a sovereign state, has many of the characteristics of a regulatory state, namely the use of regulation to achieve market efficiency and an independent central bank for the Eurozone.

CJEU are well placed to implement deregulation as, unlike national governments, they do not seek to protect jobs or privilege firms in a particular country. However, there is a great deal of politics behind deregulating certain markets, as there are interest groups both for and against it. For instance, in the railways example mentioned in Section 7.2, private investors and big transport companies support EU-wide deregulation, as this opens up new opportunities for their businesses. Indeed European airlines have shown a great interest in rail deregulation, as this could allow for profitable link-ups to ferry passengers short distances between airports, replacing expensive short-haul flights. Interest groups associated with these businesses thus lobby member states' governments to mobilize a political coalition that can secure passage of deregulatory legislation in the Council.

As in the case of the initial Services Directive of 2004, opposition to deregulation tends to come from labor unions. They fear the effects of increased competition on employment conditions and on the number of jobs available in the sectors they represent. In particular, employees in large companies previously shielded from inter-European competition worry about their future pay and conditions after deregulation. This is especially the case when governments use EU deregulation as an opportunity to privatize state-owned firms, although EU deregulation formally requires only non-discrimination against new entrants, and no state subsidies. Hence in 2011, when the European Parliament was about to vote on measures for liberalizing the rail sector, European railway workers from 13 member states coordinated a variety of protest actions, including strikes and rallies. The European Parliament, for its part, was sensitive to some of their demands, notably using its power of amendment to remove a legislative provision that would have forced railway companies to run a minimum service in the event of strikes.

The previous example illustrates the difference in the tactics of organized interests. Business groups privilege an insider strategy targeting government policy-makers, while professional associations and NGOs target public mobilization in order to influence the Parliament – an outsider strategy (Dür and Mateo González 2012). At the same time, railway liberalization highlights why governments can be interested in EU deregulation for reasons that go beyond market efficiency. The proposal (removed by the Parliament) to ensure minimum railway service provision in the event of a strike was favored by certain governments. Notably, the French center-right government of the time saw this measure as a way to restrict the use of industrial action, which railway unions use in order to secure pay and other concessions. Likewise, deregulation provides an opportunity for a national government to introduce further policy reform such as privatization.

What EU deregulation can therefore provide is an opportunity to facilitate national policy change that ordinarily would be very unpopular. In this context, EU-level decision-making offers a convenient mechanism for blame-avoidance, thereby minimizing negative electoral consequences (Pierson 1996). Thanks to the knowledge deficit surrounding the EU (see Box 6.3) and to the pressure for consensus positions within the Council, it is perfectly possible for a government that voted in favor of an EU law to tell its electorate that this legislation has been imposed on it. National governments can thus potentially benefit from a "European screen" when implementing unpopular measures (Grossman 2007).

Of course, governments have a clear set of political preferences when it comes to EU-mandated deregulation. Deregulation typically pits governments that support free market competition against more protectionist ones, which seek to restrict both intra- and extra-EU competition in certain sectors. The free market camp, normally involving the governments of countries such as Ireland, the United Kingdom, and the Netherlands, favors the introduction of greater competition for the sake of market efficiency and growth. To overcome the fears and possible blockages of more protectionist governments, EU deregulation is often done progressively. This gives governments and firms time to adapt. This is what happened in the case of electricity liberalization, where the French government used this adjustment period to reorganize the electricity industry and to prepare it for foreign competition, notably by seeking to develop national champions (Bauby and Varone 2007). These measures reflect the fact that finding a consensus over how to deregulate markets is rarely easy.

In addition, despite EU legislation and supranational enforcement mechanisms, member states can still get away with practices that call into question how deregulated and competitive the single market really is. A good example is when governments seek to discourage foreign takeovers of big companies against the spirit of the four fundamental freedoms. In 2007 for instance, the French government succeeded in merging two big French energy companies, in response to a proposed takeover by an Italian energy firm. This was done out of a fear that a takeover would mean job cuts or would threaten French industrial policy, notably the promotion of nuclear energy. Similar moves have occurred in Italy, where the government resisted the takeover of the national airline in 2008, and in Spain, where a German company was outmaneuvered in an energy takeover bid. These are instances where governments have sought either to protect or to establish "national champions" in sensitive or strategic policy sectors. In such instances the European Commission has proved either powerless or unwilling to challenge practices that go against single market deregulation – that is, open competition undistorted by national politics (Menon 2008).

7.3.2 Balancing winning and losing sides in regulatory outputs

As a consensus-based political system, the EU is concerned with trying to balance out winners and losers in both deregulation and re-regulation, so that all countries can benefit. This is a challenge, as deregulation pits stronger, dynamic firms against others, less able to compete in a bigger, open market. To compensate for the adjusting costs that follow increased competition born in a deregulated EU-wide market, the EU has a set of structural funds. These represent 40 percent of the EU budget and are designed to even out the ability of Europe's regions to compete in the single market by financing infrastructure and training projects in poorer regions (see Section 5.1). The ultimate aim is the convergence of regional economies (Anderson 1995); this means that this is in effect a **redistributive policy**, in which the regions that do best from integration compensate those that find it difficult to compete. Like nation-level redistribution (for example welfare spending), this entails a transfer from winners to losers in market competition, but in theory structural funding is supposed to be temporary (until a particular region converges with the EU average). Nevertheless, this concern for the losers from integration is a preoccupation that takes EU policy beyond considerations of mere market efficiency.

Similar concerns about winners and losers from competition in an open economy arise in the context of wrangling over positive integration, that is, EU re-regulation. This is because implementing new regulation on the environment, worker safety, factory emissions, and so on is costly both for governments, tasked as they are with administering and enforcing new rules, and for firms, who will have to change how they operate. Consequently governments favor regulatory standards that match those they already adhere to, which leads to a competition between governments to "upload" their regulatory standards to become the EU norm (Börzel 2002). In environmental policy, for example, the most economically advanced countries succeeded in uploading their regulatory preferences over the desire of Mediterranean countries to have less onerous standards. Governments in Spain and Greece thus faced greater costs implementing these standards, although this is partly offset by payments from structural funds for things such as water treatment plants (Börzel 2002).

The outcome of struggles over these kinds of regulatory standards matters greatly for the competitiveness of firms across jurisdictions. Companies operating in a regulatory environment that then becomes the EU norm will have an edge over firms that need to adjust to new rules. However, firms operating across the single market also tend to have a preference for a single set of rules rather than a jumble of norms in different jurisdictions. Common standards not only lower costs for companies operating in multiple EU countries but can also, given the global importance of the EU market, provide the basis for global norms, giving EU firms a competitive edge. A notable example is the GSM standard for cellular telecommunications, which was first adopted in Europe and became the global standard enabling EU firms to capture global market share. Consequently big firms support Commission proposals for common standards in preference to a patch-work of national rules.

By contrast, EU firms, large and small, are anxious to prevent regulation imposing costs for the sake of benefiting certain groups for political or ideological reasons. This kind of market intervention is most closely associated with the EU's competences in social policy, especially regarding the health and safety of workers. For instance, since 1992 EU rules entitle all women to benefit from a minimum of 14 weeks' maternity leave paid at least at the level of the nation's sick pay. In 2008 the Commission proposed to increase this leave to a minimum of 18 weeks, paid at 100 percent pay (up to a fixed amount set by governments). Since this proposal places the costs of promoting the rights of pregnant women on to firms, the latter have lobbied governments to oppose this measure in the Council. Opposition came from a number of governments, including those of the United Kingdom, Denmark, Estonia, and the Czech Republic, which objected to placing these costs on business. At the same time, MEPs voting on the first reading of this legislative proposal actually amended it to increase minimum paid leave by a further two weeks. Given the absence of a qualified majority in favor of the proposal in the Council, the legislation remains blocked (at the time of writing), as neither legislature is so far willing to compromise.

7.3.3   How political preferences influence regulatory outputs

Divisions between the positions of the Council and those of the Parliament over social regulation have become common following the consolidation of ideological voting in the Parliament. That is, MEPs are increasingly likely to vote on party lines, on the basis of the left–right divide. So center-left parties favor regulatory higher standards and market intervention for the sake of equity, by comparison with center-right parties' preference for lower common standards and emphasis on market efficiency rather than equity of outcomes (Hix 1999). Political groups in the Parliament have become more tight-knit as the powers of this legislature have increased (Hix, Noury, and Roland 2007). The result is that MEPs are now less likely to vote on the basis of national interest (although this can happen). This tendency contrasts with the situation in the Council, where governments tend to vote on EU regulations from the perspective of national interest (costs of implementation, effects on the competitiveness of national industry), not from that of the left–right political dimension.

The stakes in the political bargaining over EU regulation are high because of the volume of this legislation and of the constraints it imposes on governments and businesses. The precise percentage of national legislation passed to implement EU rules is hard to discern, owing to the different implementation methods available to governments. This situation has become a source of controversy, as anti-EU parties are claiming that national parliaments have become rubber-stamping institutions for EU rules. One such party, the United Kingdom Independence Party, notably claims that 75 percent of British laws are the result of EU decisions, while a report for the British government estimates that approximately 7 percent of primary laws passed by the British parliament relate to an EU decision (Miller, 2010). However, that same report states that 50 percent of laws with a significant economic impact are the result of implementing EU legislation.

The economic repercussions of EU regulatory outputs such as environmental standards, maternity rules, or the 48-hour maximum working week are significant. Of course, all these were passed with the approval, via co-decision, of both the Council (where the informal norm is to build a wide consensus rather than rely on a formal QMV) and the Parliament. The need for consensus between the two political decision-making bodies thus reduces the ability to introduce radical regulatory outputs at the EU level. Extreme free market deregulation or extensive social justice regulation will not succeed in generating a consensus to pass the co-decision threshold. Hence the European Parliament's power of amendment is not a way to implement a radical regulatory agenda. For instance, in environmental policy, co-decision has resulted in increasing the number of parliamentary amendments accepted by the Council; but these tend not to have a significant impact on the actual outcome the law seeks to achieve (Burns and Carter 2010).

The origin of all this regulation, of course, is the Commission. So why is this non-majoritarian body proposing such politically sensitive legislation as the maximum working week or the time and conditions awarded for maternity, or even mooting mandatory quotas for female participation in boards of directors? The answer is that the treaties entrust the Commission with policy competences while also endowing them with certain political objectives. Alongside the treaty commitment to high environmental protection, there is a pledge to create a "highly competitive social market economy aiming at full employment and social progress," to "combat social exclusion and discrimination," and to "promote . . . equality between women and men, solidarity between generations, and protection of the rights of the child" (Art. 3.3 TEU). As a result, the Commission not only ensures the efficiency of the market but can also propose legislation to meet these political objectives. So, although it is not a government formally representing political opinions and party ideologies, the Commission does have a certain political mandate based on the text of the treaties. Unlike a national government, however, the EU cannot spend money on social security – a national competence – or use the tax system – a field where member states can simply veto proposals – to implement these political objectives.

Hence the EU system has not abandoned politics; it is not a purely apolitical, regulatory state that relies solely on non-majoritarian institutions. Rather, European integration has placed regulation at the center of a consensual political system that seeks to marry market efficiency with a set of political objectives enshrined in the EU treaties. Eventual regulatory outputs are determined by the political interplay of preferences between the Council and the Parliament – an exchange that determines the boundary between equity and market efficiency. The overall result is, therefore, less a separation between politics and market intervention than the placing of constitutional limits both to what national governments can do to interfere with market efficiency and to what exactly the EU can do to create a social market economy. What remains to be seen, then, is how the development and consequences of this regulatory system can be theorized and its policy outcomes explained.

7.4 Theorizing EU Regulation and Explaining Its Effects

From the early moments of European integration scholars have sought to analyze and theorize this process. In particular, a set of theories have been developed that explain why exactly certain regulatory competences have been pooled and common regulations established. These theories also seek to predict the conditions under which such integration can and cannot take place, namely by identifying the actors and interests involved in facilitating integration. As well as examining major theories of integration – neo-functionalism, liberal intergovernmentalism, and supranational governance – this section looks at the theoretical analysis of the consequences of integration. This involves surveying **Europeanization** – a term used to refer to the way integration changes national political processes and structures – as well as critical perspectives on integration, which question what integration means for upholding social market principles.

7.4.1   Explaining the growth of EU regulation

The first theory developed to explain the success of incremental integration, first in economic regulation and then in related domains, was neo-functionalism. Associated with the work of Ernst Haas (1958), neo-functionalism claimed, on the basis of evidence from the European Coal and Steel Community, that delegating competences created an inherent pressure for further integration. Granting policy competences to supranational institutions, Haas argued, created new political and economic incentives among important policy actors for expanding the realm of cooperation. The key to this process was the **spillover** effect, which takes two forms.

First there is functional spillover, whereby sectoral integration of one part of the economy has repercussions for other interconnected policy functions that also need to be integrated. For instance, making the free movement of workers a reality is not just about integrating health and safety conditions for workers (so they can move without sacrificing employment conditions). In addition, there needs to be recognition of qualifications (so workers can be hired for an equivalent job), non-discrimination (so national citizens are not privileged over other EU workers), and even a common arrest warrant (as mobility cannot lead to criminal impunity). In this fashion, a single sectoral goal has manifold components relating to other policy areas. Interest groups (businesses and labor unions) and political actors (parties, parliamentarians) would, neo-functionalism suggests, recognize this logic and respond to these developments by shifting their focus from the nation-state to supranational institutions. This shift in allegiance and political mobilization from the national to the transnational level was what Haas called political spillover – political pressure from within member states to address policy problems at the European level. On this understanding, states cannot expect to remain in control of integration, and so, logically, economic integration must proceed to cover more and more politically sensitive areas.

Empirical evidence seemed to call Haas' assumptions into question when, in the 1970s and early 1980s, there was little further progress in integration and the single market was far from a reality. In this context, political scientists considered it important to explain how national sovereignty limited incremental integration, reducing spillover. The best developed theory explaining how governments retain control over the pace and scope of integration is called *liberal intergovernmentalism* (Moravcsik 1993). This theory rejects the notion of rampant supranational spillover and looks instead at how member states seek to determine the course of integration to meet the interests of domestic constituencies. On this basis, national governments are the key actors, responding to the preferences of domestic interest groups – notably economic ones – then bargaining with other countries in treaty negotiations to obtain policies and decision-making structures that most suit their domestic preferences (Moravcsik 1998). So the move to QMV enshrined in the Single European Act, which made extensive deregulatory legislation possible, was the result of national interest groups pushing for deregulation in an EU framework where side payments (the structural funds) were established for countries that would lose out. Hence liberal intergovernmentalism sees supranational institutions as executors of regulatory competences that member states bargained over, not as autonomous policy actors or as vectors for transnational political mobilization.

Treaty negotiation, with the concomitant national veto, allows governments to negotiate major policies (especially economic ones) according to preferences organized through national politics. However, most internal policies proceed via the supranational OLP and, as shown throughout this chapter, involve regulatory outputs affecting a host of national interests. Meanwhile interest groups are increasingly organized at the EU-level, while the powerful European Parliament votes on ideological rather than national lines. This evolving context, where governments coexist alongside other important policy-making actors, led theorists to explore the connections between transnational economic interests and supranational institutions. Stone Sweet and Sandholz (1997) call this process "supranational governance," whereby regulatory policies migrate from the national to the supranational level on the basis of a demand for EU-wide regulations from economic and political interests that support Commission single market legislation. Moreover, single market regulation will be supported by governments of countries with firms that are most actively engaged in cross-national business. This forms the basis for a coalition that helps drive integration, notably regulatory outputs, independently from inter-governmental bargaining.

7.4.2   Theorizing the consequences of EU regulation

These explanatory theories, privileging as they do different causal factors, remain of value in identifying why integration proceeds, even if none can give an exhaustive account of how and why the EU's regulatory output has developed as it has. Yet theoretical explanations need to be complemented by an analysis of the political consequences arising from the growth of EU policy-making. An important theoretical description of this process is "Europeanization." This concept is part of an argument – with echoes of spillover and supranational governance – that EU policy-making is taking place in a broader context of pervasive national adaptation to European rules, norms, and exchange of ideas (Featherstone and Radaelli 2003). In part this adaptation is due to the need to implement EU rules at the national level. Yet Europeanization is intended to describe the fact that EU regulation is not necessarily a top-down affair but the voluntary product of domestic actors recasting their preferences, ideologies, or strategies within an accepted EU institutional framework. As a result, key actors such as political parties, interest groups, and expert bodies have become Europeanized: they think and act within an integration context rather than in separate national spheres.

Here, though, it is important to recognize the existence of a critical perspective on integration and its regulatory effects on European states. In that sense Europeanization is not necessarily a politically neutral phenomenon. For a start, there is a concern that one of the chief results of creating an integrated single market, free of national distortions, is to weaken national governments' ability to sustain social market conditions (van der Pijl 2006). That is, the acceptance of deregulation and the logic of pursuing an efficient EU-wide market have significantly narrowed the range of tools available to governments to intervene in the economy for the purpose of equity. Interest rates are set by the ECB (for Eurozone countries), state aid and favoring national businesses are prohibited, while deficit spending designed to help the economy in a recession is prohibited by the Stability and Growth Pact (see Box 5.1). The net result is that member state governments can do less to shield workers or businesses from increased intra-EU competition, and also from greater global competition, since the EU pursues free trade externally. Deregulation concerns all four fundamental freedoms, including the free movement of labor. This is important, because workers from countries with low-average wages tend to move to richer countries, potentially increasing competition for low-skilled jobs. Such a situation is said to have arisen in Britain, which welcomed a million immigrants from new member states after the 2004 enlargement. Additionally, the free movement of capital allows firms to relocate their business to countries with lower taxation or regions with lower wage costs. Hence there is an imbalance in who gains most from integration: firms (and owners of capital generally) benefit greatly by having access to more favorable tax jurisdictions and to a supply of cheaper labor. By contrast, ordinary workers are exposed to a more competitive environment, in which firms can relocate or potentially hire cheaper employees, thereby squeezing wages (van der Pijl

2006). Critical accounts of the effects of single market integration thus see integration as serving the interests of capitalism against the interests of workers (Bonefeld 2001). This kind of complaint fuels demands for a genuine "social Europe," one that places social justice (equity) above market efficiency and free trade.

7.5   Concluding Summary

This chapter examined EU regulatory outputs: both deregulation and the ability to substitute EU-wide regulation for national rules. Regulating markets is related to achieving efficiency – that is, the best possible allocation of goods at the optimal price. Efficiency leaves everyone better off, but markets do not always achieve this because of monopoly, asymmetric information, and negative externalities. The EU system is designed to allow the Commission to remedy these instances of market failure. Moreover, EU competences allow supranational institutions to overturn national impediments enacted for political reasons, preventing competition (that is, efficiency) in the single market. The EU system is considered a better source of market regulation because non-majoritarian institutions such as the Commission and the CJEU can pursue efficiency even when they are politically unpopular.

In practice, however, EU regulation is not separated from politics. Proposals to deregulate markets are controversial, with opposition notably from firms and workers in sectors opened to competition. Creating EU-wide regulatory standards also has important political repercussions, as governments and firms face costs when implementing them. Hence all regulatory outputs are surrounded by interest group lobbying, as business groups pursue an insider strategy and NGOs are more reliant on outsider strategy such as political mobilization. Political wrangling continues after legislation is agreed upon, because of the possible use of transitory measures that negotiate side payments such as the structural funds and implementation issues. In certain cases effectiveness issues even create pressure for further integration, a process known as spillover.

As well as regulating for market efficiency, the treaties contain political objectives such as high environmental standards of protection, gender equality, and high levels of health and safety for workers. These are areas where the EU is most likely to raise average standards and to go beyond just making the market more efficient. Social regulation is thus possible, although this does not involve decisions over tax and spending, as in national redistributive policies.

Explanations for how this process has occurred focus on different key actors: member states, domestic interests, and supranational institutions. Neo-functionalism, liberal intergovernmentalism, and supranational governance are theories identifying different causal factors that influence how these support integration and whether they are successful. Scholars also analyze the consequences of EU regulation on member states, the concept of Europeanization suggesting a neutral phenomenon of adaptation – top-down as well as bottom-up – to EU rules and procedures. Yet there are critics of the current EU regulatory system, which is said to be biased toward capital and capitalists at the expense of social justice.

Guide to Further Reading

Egan, M. 2001. *Constructing a European Market: Standards, Regulation, and Governance*. Oxford: Oxford University Press.

Detailed empirical account that uses political economy and governance theory to explain the development of both deregulation and re-regulation.

Majone, G. 1996. *Regulating Europe*. New York: Routledge.

Classic text examining EU integration from a regulatory perspective and linking practical examples to theoretical debates, notably the quality and legitimacy of regulation.

Menon, A. 2008. *Europe: The State of the Union*. London: *Atlantic*.

A very readable, topical survey of the EU's policy outputs that provides a host of insights on the design as well as on the effectiveness of regulation in different sectors.

Wiener, A., and T. Diez. 2009. *European Integration Theory*. Oxford: Oxford University Press.

The best introduction to theoretical debates over European integration, covering all major perspectives and written by leading experts.

Discussion Questions

1   How do the regulatory competences of the EU relate to regulatory theory, and what does the Commission do to ensure market efficiency?
2   What is contentious about market deregulation? Which interest groups support and which ones oppose this policy?
3   How do EU regulatory outputs affect member states, and how do national governments respond to this new policy-making environment?
4   How exactly can the EU regulate markets for political objectives, and what are the results of such regulation?
5   Why is there a critical perspective on the consequences of EU regulation, and is this position justified?

Web Resources

This book is supported by a companion website, which can be found at www.wiley.com/go/glencross. There you will find a list of the web links referred to in this chapter wherever you see a "Web" icon in the page margins. In addition, you will find a list of further relevant online resources such as websites for EU institutions, political groups, archives, and think tanks, information on studying abroad, and biographies of key figures. You will also find self-assessment tools in the form of flashcards and independent study questions developed specifically for this chapter.

Glossary

Equity/efficiency trade-off

Tension running through the heart of government intervention in markets, caused by the conflict between creating efficiency and achieving equity. The trade-off manifests itself in European party politics: parties on the left advocate intervention for the sake of equity and social justice, parties on the right prefer regulation for market efficiency and place less emphasis on equity.

Europeanization

Conceptual term referring to the way integration changes national politics and political actors as a result of national adaptation to EU rules, norms, and exchange of ideas. Not merely a top-down process, because Europeanized national actors voluntarily seek to use the EU level for policy change.

Market efficiency

Situation in which a market for a good or a service functions efficiently to provide the best possible allocation of goods at the optimal price. This is a mutually beneficial outcome, which is not possible when there is market failure. The motive behind deregulation is to bring competition to a market so as to make it efficient.

Market failure

Phrase from regulatory theory used to describe an inefficient market. This situation can arise from monopoly, incomplete information, negative externalities, or inadequate provision of public goods. Some form of government intervention is the solution to market failure.

Negative externality

Type of market failure whereby the price mechanism fails to reflect costs borne by individuals external to that particular market; factories polluting local residents' air or water supplies would be an example of negative externality. Regulating against this phenomenon is based on making market price reflect real costs or else incentivizing alternative goods with fewer negative externalities.

Non-majoritarian institutions

Decision-making bodies not made up of elected politicians representing a party ideology or public preferences. Instead these are expert bodies such as courts or regulatory agencies, which are designed to take decisions on the basis of their knowledge rather than to follow the political or ideological preferences of a majority.

Redistributive policy

Government intervention in the economy that redistributes a financial benefit from one group to another, for political reasons. European countries have traditionally used taxation and social spending to redistribute from winners to losers, in a competitive market environment.

Social dumping

Phrase used in relation to the competition between jurisdictions with different regulatory standards. Companies' ability to take advantage of lower wage and tax costs, or of looser employment law, are said to profit from social dumping, which encourages governments to lower their regulatory standards so as to remain competitive.

Spillover

Incremental process whereby a particular policy competence conferred to the EU requires in turn the conferral of more competences in order to ensure effectiveness. For example, environmental regulatory standards have been succeeded by the harmonization of the criminal sanctions for breaking those rules.

References

Anderson, Christopher J. 1995. "When in Doubt, Use Proxies: Attitudes toward Domestic Politics and Support for European Integration." *Comparative Political Studies*, 31: 569–601. DOI: 10.1177/0010414098031005002

Armenteros, Mercedes, and Jürgen Lefevere. 2002. "European Court of Justice, 13 March 2001,Case C-379/98, PreussenElektra Aktiengesellschaft v. Schleswag Aktiengesellschaft." *Review of European Community and International Environmental Law*, 10: 344–347.DOI: 10.1111/1467-9388.00294

Bator, Francis M. 1958. "The Anatomy of Market Failure." *Quarterly Journal of Economics*, 72: 351–379. DOI: 10.2307/1882231

Bauby, Pierre, and Frédéric Varone. 2007. "Europeanization of the French Electricity Policy: Four Paradoxes." *Journal of European Public Policy*, 14: 1048–1060. DOI: 10.1080/13501760701576536

Börzel, Tanja. 2002. "Member-State Responses to Europeanization." *Journal of Common Market Studies*, 40: 193–214. DOI: 10.1111/1468-5965.00351

Börzel, Tanja. 2005. "Mind the Gap! European Integration between Level and Scope." *Journal of European Public Policy*, 12: 217–223. DOI: 10.1080/13501760500043860

Bonefeld, Werner. 2001. "European Monetary Union: Ideology and Class." In Werner Bonefeld, ed., *The Politics of Europe: Monetary Union and Class*, 64–106. Basingstoke: Palgrave.

Burns, Charlotte, and Neil Carter. 2010. "Is Co-decision Good for the Environment? An Analysis of the European Parliament's Green Credentials." *Political Studies*, 58: 123–142. DOI: 10.1111/j.1467-9248.2009.00782.x

den Hertog, Jan. 2000."General Theories of Regulation." In Boudewijn Bouckaert and Gerrit De Geest, eds., *Encyclopedia of Law and Economics*, volume 3: *The Regulation of Contracts*, 223–270. Cheltenham: Edward Elgar.

Dür, Andreas, and Gemma Mateo González. 2012. "Gaining Access or Going Public? Interest Group Strategies in Five European Countries." Available at SSRN: http://ssrn.com/abstract=2125812

Egan, Michelle. 2001. *Constructing a European Market: Standards, Regulation, and Governance*. Oxford: Oxford University Press.

Featherstone, Kevin, and Claudio Radaelli, eds. 2003. *The Politics of Europeanisation*. Oxford: Oxford University Press.

Grossman, Emiliano. 2007. "Introduction: France and the EU: From Opportunity to Constraint." *Journal of European Public Policy*, 14: 983–991. DOI: 10.1080/13501760701576478

Haas, Ernst B. 1958. *The Uniting of Europe*. Stanford: Stanford University Press.

Hix, Simon. 1999. "Dimensions and Alignments in European Union Politics: Cognitive Constraints and Partisan Responses."*European Journal of Political Research*, 35: 69–106. DOI: 10.1111/1475-6765.00442

Hix, Simon. 2008. *What's Wrong with the European Union and How to Fix It.* London: Polity.

Hix, Simon, Abdul Noury, and Gérard Roland. 2007. *Democratic Politics in the European Parliament.* Cambridge: Cambridge University Press.

Liefferink, Duncan, and Mikael S. Andersen. 1998. "Strategies of the 'Green' Member States in EU Environmental Policy-Making." *Journal of European Public Policy,* 5: 254–270. DOI: 10.1080/135017698343974

Majone, Giandomenico. 1996. *Regulating Europe.* New York: Routledge.

Majone, Giandomenico. 1997. "From the Positive to the Regulatory State: Causes and Consequences of Changes in the Mode of Governance." *Journal of Public Policy,* 17: 139–167. DOI: 10.1017/S0143814X00003524

Majone, Giandomenico. 2000. "The Credibility Crisis of Community Regulation." *Journal of Common Market Studies,* 38: 273–302. DOI: 10.1111/1468-5965.00220

Majone, Giandomenico. 2006. "The Common Sense of European Integration." *Journal of European Public Policy,* 13: 607–620. DOI: 10.1080/13501760600808212

Marris, Robin, and Dennis Mueller. 1980. "The Corporation, Competition, and the Invisible Hand." *Journal of Economic Literature,* 18: 32–63.

McCormick, John. 2001. *Environmental Policy in the European Union.* New York: Palgrave.

Meade, James A. 1973. *The Theory of Economic Externalities.* Leiden: Sijthoff.

Menon, Anand. 2008. *Europe: The State of the Union.* London: Atlantic.

Miller, Vaughne. 2010. "How Much Legislation Comes from Europe?" House of Commons Library Research Papers, 10/62 (October 13). London: House of Commons Library. Available at www.parliament.uk/briefing-papers/RP10-62.pdf (accessed July 15, 2013).

Mitnick, Barry M. 1980. *The Political Economy of Regulation.* New York: Columbia University Press.

Moravcsik, Andrew. 1993. "Preferences and Power in the European Community: A Liberal Intergovernmentalist Approach." *Journal of Common Market Studies,* 31: 473–524. DOI: 10.1111/j.1468-5965.1993.tb00477.x

Moravcsik, Andrew. 1998. *The Choice for Europe: Social Purpose and State Power from Messina to Maastricht.* New York: Cornell University Press.

Nicolaïdis, Kalypso, and Susanne K. Schmidt. 2007. "Mutual Recognition 'on Trial': The Long Road to Services Liberalization." *Journal of European Public Policy,* 14: 717–734. DOI: 10.1080/13501760701427904

Okun, Arthu O. 1975. *Equality and Efficiency: The Big Tradeoff.* Washington, DC: Brookings Institution Press.

Pierson, Paul. 1996. "The Path to European Integration: A Historical Institutionalist Analysis." *Comparative Political Studies,* 29: 123–163. DOI: 10.1177/001041409602900200

Schreurs, Miranda. 2004. "Environmental Protection in an Expanding European Community: Lessons from Past Accessions." *Environmental Politics,* 13: 27–51. DOI: 10.1080/09644010410001685128

Stone Sweet, Alec, and Wayne Sandholz. 1997. "European Integration and Supranational Governance." *Journal of European Public Policy,* 4: 297–317. DOI: 10.1080/13501769780000011

van der Pijl, Kees. 2006. "A Lockean Europe?" *New Left Review,* 37: 9–37.

8

The Institutionalization of EU Foreign Policy and Debates over the EU's International Role

Contents

Learning Objectives

- to analyze the institutional development of EU foreign policy and its consequences for member states;
- to distinguish between Common Foreign and Security Policy (CFSP) and Common Security and Defence Policy (CSDP);
- to identify issues of effectiveness surrounding EU foreign policy;
- to analyze how the institutionalization of foreign policy has sought to remedy problems of capacity and consensus;
- to interpret why the EU is defined as a normative power and why this is contested;
- to distinguish between different causal factors used to explain the development of CFSP;
- to evaluate similarities and differences between competing explanations of CFSP.

The Politics of European Integration: Political Union or a House Divided?, First Edition. Andrew Glencross.
© 2014 Andrew Glencross. Published 2014 by Blackwell Publishing Ltd.

8.0   Introduction: What Is at Stake in Understanding EU Foreign Relations?

EU foreign relations matter a great deal, as integration has developed significantly in this area over the past decades (EU enlargement is treated as a separate issue of foreign relations; see Section 5.6). The EU is a growing presence in international politics, undertaking civilian and military operations, promoting values such as human rights and democracy, as well as being the world's largest aid donor. Such actions have attracted a lot of attention, as politicians and scholars debate the effectiveness of EU foreign policy and scrutinize the ideology or aims behind it while also seeking to explain why integration has taken place in this domain.

Before entering these debates, though, we need to explore the institutional organization of foreign policy. Coordinating foreign policy via the EU by using specific institutions, established outside the Ordinary Legislative Procedure (OLP), has significant repercussions on national sovereignty. Traditionally, foreign policy is an area in which states have sought to retain as much independence as possible in order to pursue their own interests and to provide for their own security. As a result, EU cooperation in this policy field requires a delicate balancing act. Member states want to act, as much as possible, in unison, to maximize the EU's foreign policy clout; yet they also desire to retain autonomy over extremely sensitive decisions, such as how to organize their armed forces and when to commit to a humanitarian mission. Departing from the OLP system, EU foreign policy has nevertheless become highly institutionalized and this, as explained in Section 8.1, has led to a "Brusselization" of national foreign policies whereby EU coordination becomes the norm.

Designing this institutional framework and endowing it with the proper resources and objectives leaves open the question of how this system works in practice. As the EU is a non-state without independent tax-raising powers or an army of its own, there are many question marks over what it can actually accomplish in international politics. The hope is that the correct institutional mechanism for cooperation allows the EU to have a multiplier effect – in other words it enables member states to pool their resources in order to have maximum impact on the global stage. How effectively EU foreign policy institutionalization works, especially when member states remain torn (notably in crisis situations) over how far to follow US foreign policy preferences is discussed in Section 8.2.

Beyond the effectiveness question, there is also an ideological or normative debate surrounding the question whether the EU is indeed a different kind of foreign policy actor by comparison with other leading states. In this debate (to be explored in Section 8.3), scholars argue over how far the CFSP commitment to **multilateralism**, international law, and human rights marks a departure from the pursuit of power or national interests. Most importantly, the EU has explicitly rejected what Thomas Schelling called the "diplomacy of violence" – the use of force and threats to change other states' behavior. This has led to controversy over whether the EU really is putting ideology ahead of interests and to what degree these normative objectives can be achieved through peaceful diplomacy alone. Here there is a debate over whether it is right for the EU to tell other states how to behave in international politics and whether CFSP's emphasis on multilateralism is a veiled way of challenging US primacy.

Finally, besides pondering all these issues involving institutions, effectiveness, and ideology, scholars spend a great deal of time discussing why integration has taken place in this sensitive policy area. Foreign policy is often seen as a hard case for testing theories about why states agree to limit their autonomy, because this is a sensitive policy area with great consequences for sovereignty. There are many competing explanations as to why CFSP has developed and why it contains normative objectives. As highlighted in Section 8.4, to make sense of these developments, different explanatory models privilege power, national interests, and notions of identity.

8.1   The Institutions and Institutionalization of EU Foreign Policy

Foreign and security policy are key components of statehood, and hence coordinating them is a challenge to national sovereignty and member states' autonomy in foreign policy. Traditionally, integration in this area lagged behind supranational developments in economic coordination. Nevertheless, after the Maastricht Treaty (1992), the EU acquired formal legal instruments for unifying member states' foreign and security policy. Since that time, there have been major developments both in creating institutions to deliver a coordinated EU foreign policy and in using these instruments to enact an increasingly ambitious policy agenda. This process of institutionalizing foreign policy coordination was necessary because member states wanted integration in this policy field, in order to function differently. Institutionalization – illustrated by the crea-tion of the high representative for Foreign Affairs and Security, the External Action Service, and the Political and Security Committee (PSC) (see Section 4.5) – is a tool to make EU foreign policy a reality while minimizing supranationalism (Smith 2004). The policy-making role of the Commission and of the Parliament is thus minimized in this policy area, allowing member states to control the pace and direction of foreign policy integration.

This process of institutionalizing foreign policy coordination takes place alongside existing EU competences, in what was traditionally labeled "**external relations**," notably trade policy and development. These are strictly limited areas of foreign affairs where the Commission is the leading actor, for instance in negotiating a bilateral trade deal with South Korea, or in managing the €22 billion (2008–2013) European Development Fund. External trade policy was a corollary of removing internal tariffs after the EEC Treaty of 1957. With the abolition of these tariffs, the EEC countries had to agree upon a common external tariff for goods from beyond the EEC. Article 133 of the EEC Treaty specified a "common commercial policy" giving the EEC the power to set tariffs, con- clude trade agreements with other countries, and pursue trade liberalization.

These are important powers that constrain national autonomy. For instance, upon joining the EEC, the UK had to abolish the preferential tariff agreements it had with Commonwealth countries, while successive French governments have had to accept the trade liberalization agenda preferred by the majority of EU countries (Meunier and

Nicolaïdis 2006). However, setting the agenda in external relations does not make the Commission omnipotent. The Commission negotiates free trade agreements with a third country and represents member states in multilateral negotiations within the World Trade Organization, but it does so on the basis of a policy mandate granted by the Council. In addition, free trade agreements concluded by the EU still require national ratification by each country, which is why the Commission needs to follow the Council's mandate closely. Nevertheless, external relations is the most integrated aspect of foreign policy in that negotiations are conducted by the Commission on behalf of the 28 member states.

8.1.1   The Common Foreign and Security Policy and the Common Security and Defence Policy

Institutionally, the rest of foreign policy beyond trade and development involves more complicated decision-making processes and a multiplicity of leading actors speaking on behalf of the EU (see Section 4.5). What is perhaps most confusing in this area of EU competence is the fact that there are two designated "policies": the Common Foreign and Security Policy – CFSP – and the Common Security and Defence Policy – CSDP (formerly European Security and Defence Policy, ESDP). In reality, these are phrases and acronyms used to describe "institutions that make [policies] but are not proper policies" in themselves (Jørgensen 2006, 509). In other words, the labels "CFSP" and "CSDP" refer to institutional decision-making processes used to articulate and execute EU foreign policy. Moreover, CSDP is a mechanism designed to provide the EU with pooled assets to conduct civilian and military missions. So the CSDP is a specific set of policies within the broader set of policy ambitions and institutions that constitute CFSP.

Both the CFSP and the CSDP have at their core legally binding objectives and specify procedures not only for how member states make decisions but also for how they can contribute their resources. Article 21 (TEU) sets out the overarching ambition behind the CFSP, which is to establish "a high degree of cooperation in all fields of international relations" so as to

- safeguard the EU's values, fundamental interests, security, independence, and integrity;
- consolidate and support democracy, the rule of law, human rights, and the principles of international law;
- preserve peace, prevent conflicts and strengthen international security, in accordance with the purposes and principles of the United Nations Charter;
- promote an international system based on stronger multilateral cooperation and good global governance.

In order to make this happen, Article 24 (TEU) specifies that member states

> shall support the Union's external and security policy actively and unreservedly in a spirit of loyalty and mutual solidarity and shall comply with the Union's action in this area . . .

They shall refrain from any action which is contrary to the interests of the Union or likely to impair its effectiveness as a cohesive force in international relations. The Council and the High Representative shall ensure compliance with these principles.

This holds especially for "coordinat[ing] their action in international organizations and at international conferences. They shall uphold the Union's positions in such forums. The High Representative of the Union for Foreign Affairs and Security Policy shall organise this coordination" (Article 34 TEU).

The CSDP is also part of the treaties. The rationale behind it is to

provide the Union with an operational capacity drawing on civilian and military assets. The Union may use them on missions outside the Union for peace-keeping, conflict prevention and strengthening international security in accordance with the principles of the United Nations Charter. The performance of these tasks shall be undertaken using capabilities provided by the Member States. (Article 42 TEU)

These CSDP tasks were originally formulated in 1992. They are known in the integration jargon as the **Petersberg tasks** and relate more concretely to "joint disarmament operations, humanitarian and rescue tasks, military advice and assistance tasks, conflict prevention and peace-keeping tasks, tasks of combat forces in crisis management, including peace-making and post-conflict stabilisation" (Article 43 TEU).

Foreign policy is thus integral to the EU, even though this whole area lies outside the OLP (see Section 4.5). In line with these principles of providing peace-keeping and stabilization, the EU has conducted small-scale interventions both near to and far from its borders, as shown in Table 8.1. The most significant military operation to date is its mission in Bosnia-Herzegovina, which at its peak saw the deployment of 7,000 troops to stabilize this fractious part of former Yugoslavia. With the exception of the brief operation in the former Yugoslav Republic of Macedonia (which requested assistance), military operations have been conducted on the basis of a UN Security Council mandate. This is because, under the terms of the CFSP, any use of EU troops would have to be consistent with the principles of the UN Charter and in accordance with international law. In another sign of the EU's commitment to multilateralism in world politics, civilian missions also tend to take place under the auspices of the UN. These involve mostly the deployment of experts in law, policing, and public administration, who provide state-building assistance to local authorities. This is the kind of niche operation the EU has been conducting in Iraq since 2005, where 60 experts offer legal and human rights training to local judges and prosecutors. In other words, EU interventions under CSDP are neither unilateral acts nor instances of force projection.

8.1.2   Building capacity

To meet the continuing demand from the UN for peace-keeping and civilian operations, the EU is committed to developing its capacities in this field by pooling national military resources. In 1999 the European Council announced a plan to create, by 2003,

Table 8.1   EU CSDP civilian missions and military operations (2003–2013)

Civilian Missions	Function	Military Operations	Function	Personnel
Aceh, Indonesia (2005–2006)	Monitoring peace agreement	Bosnia-Herzegovina (2004–)	Stabilization after ethnic conflict	7000 (peak)
Afghanistan (2007–)	Police assistance	Chad/Central African Republic (2008–2009)	Civilian protection and aid delivery	3700
Bosnia-Herzegovina (2003–2012)	Police assistance	Democratic Republic of Congo (2003, 2006)	Providing security for elections	2000 (2003) 2500 (2006)
Democratic Republic of Congo (2005–)	Police assistance	Former Yugoslav Republic of Macedonia (2003)	Stabilization after ethnic conflict	300
Former Yugoslav Republic of Macedonia (2004–2006)	Police assistance	Mali (2013–)	Training Malian army	500
Georgia (2004–2005)	Assistance with rule of law	Somalia (2008–)	Anti-piracy naval operation	1100
Georgia (2008–)	Monitoring peace agreement	Sudan (2005–2007)	Logistical support for African Union	100
Guinea–Bissau (2008–2010)	Security sector reform			
Iraq (2005–)	Assistance with rule of law			
Kosovo (2008–)	Assistance with rule of law			
Palestinian Territories (2005–)	Police assistance			
Sudan (2005–2007)	Police assistance			

Source: Data from EU Consilium Website http://www.consilium.europa.eu/eeas/security-defence/eu-operations?amp;lang=en

a 60,000-strong "rapid reaction force" capable of deploying at short notice and at a distance, for a year-long mission. Problems in achieving this goal led to a 2004 European Council decision to prioritize establishing EU battlegroups, battalions of 1,500 troops able to deploy at 10 days' notice. A set of 17 battlegroups (some of them contributed by larger member states, others multinational, made up of forces pooled from several countries) has been available since 2007; two are on standby for potential deployment.

Table 8.2 National contributions to the EU Anti-Piracy Mission (July 2009)

Country	Ships	Aircraft
France	2 frigates, 1 corvette, 1 patrol boat	1 maritime patrol plane
Germany	2 frigates, 1 oil tanker	1 maritime patrol plane
Greece	1 frigate	
Italy	1 frigate	
Spain	1 frigate, 1 oil tanker	1 maritime patrol plane
Sweden	3 corvettes	

Source: Data from Council of the EU, http://www.consilium.europa.eu/uedocs/cmsUpload/naviresjuin.pdf

The cost of establishing these battlegroups was borne by member states, and their actual deployment abroad is largely the financial responsibility of national governments. Only a fraction of the overall EU budget goes to pay for the costs of civilian CSDP missions. Certain costs of military operations are financed through a special mechanism (not part of the overall EU budget) called Athena, which for instance contributes €23 million toward the cost of the military force in Bosnia (EUFOR). Member state contributions to CSDP missions thus vary: they reflect governments' ability to bear the political and financial costs associated with deploying military assets. For instance only a select group of countries participate in the EU's Anti-Piracy Mission (see Table 8.2).

Given the EU's reliance on member states to bear the costs of acquiring and deploying military assets, new measures for streamlining military capacity across the EU have been adopted. This is necessary because of inefficiencies in the way national governments equip and train their armed forces – an area where single market legislation prohibiting practices such as state subsidies does not apply. The combined military spending of EU countries is impressive: €195 billion in 2010, which was nearly a third of the USA's spending. But the whole, which corresponds roughly to 2 million forces in personnel, is less than the sum of the parts. This is problematic for the future, given the steady decrease in European defense budgets since the end of the Cold War. Inefficiencies are characterized by duplication and incompatibilities. For instance, EU countries use four competing battle tanks, are designing over 20 different armored fighting vehicles, and operate three different combat aircraft programs. Such fragmented procurement of equipment leads to higher costs and poses issues of interoperability. Large military bureaucracies – a hangover from the days of conscription – reduce the amount of combat-ready troops, so that a maximum of 15 percent of combined national personnel forces are considered deployable (Biscop 2008).

One important CFSP goal is therefore to move toward a more integrated EU-wide market for defense research and procurement, a sector that member states have shielded from single market competition rules for reasons of national interest and job protection. The European Defence Agency (EDA) was established to achieve savings in this area through economies of scale. It thus promotes armaments cooperation and joint research and development across member states and has succeeded in creating a voluntary code of conduct whereby member states agree to accept foreign bids for all contracts above

€1 million. It should also be noted that there is increased willingness among states to engage in intra-European military cooperation, even independently of the EU. This trend toward "pooling and sharing" can be seen in the Airbus A400M cargo transporter project and in the 2010 Anglo-French Treaty to establish a joint expeditionary force using an integrated aircraft carrier strike group.

Returning to CFSP decision-making, it is clear that member states are in the driving seat – and not just because they ultimately control civilian and military assets. It is the European Council that, according to the treaties, defines the "principles and general guidelines" of the CFSP. The actual legal instruments of CFSP are joint actions and common positions (see Section 4.5), which are the province of the Council, decisions being normally made by unanimity. However, the CSDP operates slightly differently because Denmark has formally opted out of this mechanism and thus does not contribute assets. In addition, any member state is entitled not to be bound by a CFSP decision. This possibility of non-participation comes under a seldom used procedure known as **constructive abstention**, as when Cyprus decided in 2008 to abstain from a CSDP police mission in Kosovo because there was no specific UN Security Council mandate for it. Constructive abstention is a way to pursue a CFSP even when there is no unanimity. However, if countries representing a third of the votes in the Council of the EU abstain, then a joint action or common policy cannot pass. The CFSP also has a procedure for allowing further integration among a core group of states wishing to go beyond what can be agreed under the CFSP and the CSDP. This procedure is called **permanent structured cooperation** but has not been used yet, although one proposal examined by certain countries is a plan for EU military headquarters.

Although the actual results delivered through all this institutionalization are open to debate (see Section 8.2), there is no question that CFSP and CSDP have had a major impact by making member states collaborate on building capacities and on coordinating civilian and military deployments. Despite the fact that the EU is not a sovereign entity with a single foreign policy, national foreign policies are increasingly coordinated, while significant progress has also been made in integrating defense procurement and planning. All member states wear two hats – one European and one national – in foreign policy; hence they take into consideration the use of EU instruments and the opinion of their partners when executing foreign policy. Scholars thus speak of the "Brusselization" of national foreign policies, which, although formally independent, more often than not are formulated within an EU context (Allen 1998). In many ways, this is the equivalent to the Europeanization seen in the context of EU regulatory outputs (see Section 7.4).

8.2   The Debate over EU Foreign Policy Effectiveness

The traditional quip used to query the effectiveness of EU foreign policy is former US Secretary of State Henry Kissinger's remark: "Whom do I call if I want to call Europe?" A more advanced version suggests that there is now an answering machine able to take the call, with an automated message announcing: "Press one for British foreign policy, two for German foreign policy, three for French foreign policy" (and so on). As a non-state entity, the EU cannot always speak with a single voice or find agreement over foreign policy in crisis situations. Yet the caricature of the EU as a disjointed foreign policy actor is unfair, given the institutionalization and the amount of legislation actually passed in this area.

A genuine source of complication, however, is the fact that the EU has multiple actors charged with foreign policy responsibilities. Since the Lisbon Treaty entered into force, the president of the European Council, who has the authority to call extraordinary meetings of the European Council in a situation of crisis, coexists alongside the high representative for Foreign Affairs and Security Policy. The latter chairs the Council of the EU in its foreign policy configuration (the Foreign Affairs Council) and is authorized to speak on behalf of the EU at the UN. In addition, in the past, the country holding the EU's rotating six-month presidency traditionally sought to take the initiative in foreign policy (Smith 2004). For instance, it was in this capacity that France tried to broker a ceasefire in 2008 during the conflict between Russia and Georgia; but this role has been superseded by the Lisbon changes creating the two new figureheads for the EU. There also remains an important foreign affairs role for the president of the Commission, whose institution is in charge of foreign trade and development policy.

The creation of the European External Action Service (EEAS), eventually supposed to have 7,000 personnel and a €3 billion budget, is the latest element in this complex institutional development (see Section 4.5). Indeed the establishment of the EEAS highlights the desire to increase coordination across EU foreign policy actors (Carta 2011). The EEAS is thus intended not just to provide personnel to carry out EU foreign policy on the ground, but also to link together previously separated external relations and CFSP actions. This goal of linking together the Commission-led aspect of foreign policy (external relations) and the Council-led CFSP is why the high representative is both vice-president of the Commission and a participant in CFSP decision-making.

Member state preferences – despite the Brusselization of national foreign policy – still matter a great deal in foreign policy, and acute divisions appear at times in moments of crisis. These divisions are more serious for foreign policy effectiveness than the gap between external relations and CFSP. Notable examples of such discord include splits over how to deal with ethnic conflict in the former Yugoslavia in the 1990s; divisions over whether to support the US invasion of Iraq in 2003; or the question of intervening in Libya in 2011. In all three instances the EU was bypassed as a key foreign policy actor because certain member states either preferred to work via NATO (in the case of the former Yugoslavia and Libya) or else opted to join a US-led coalition (for Iraq). These examples highlight the importance of the Transatlantic dimension when national governments in the EU think about foreign policy.

8.2.1   The Transatlantic dimension

Transatlantic relations, by which is meant how European governments relate to the US administration, are a looming presence in EU foreign policy. This is because most EU countries (22 out of 28) are NATO members, which entails military coordination and participation in missions outside the EU framework. NATO is a Transatlantic security community based on a mutual defense pact (see Section 2.1 and Box 2.1), but its role since the end of the Cold War has evolved to include peace-keeping and humanitarian missions (Sperling and Webber 2009). Consequently, EU member states not only have an alternative vehicle for military operations, but also have to balance US and European preferences in security and in foreign policy. Many see this tension between developing an EU foreign policy and accommodating US preferences either via NATO or through mission-specific coalitions as a threat to the coherence of CFSP (Calleo 2003). Indeed it is common to distinguish between "Atlanticist" member states favoring a Transatlantic approach to security (Britain, Denmark, the Netherlands, and Eastern European countries) and supporters of an independent European foreign policy led by France (Calleo 2003).

In principle, however, the development of EU security policy since 1992 has been deliberately complementary to the NATO mutual defense pact. NATO's 2010 New Strategic Concept policy document refers to the "strategic partnership" with the EU, meaning that both NATO and the EU "should play complementary and mutually reinforcing roles in supporting international peace and security." For its part, the Lisbon Treaty states that the development of CSDP "shall respect the obligations of certain Member States, which see their common defence realized in NATO . . . and be compatible with the common security and defence policy established within that framework" (Art. 42.2). Behind this formal rhetoric, though, there has been Transatlantic tension. Since 1998 in fact, and in response to putative EU moves toward a more independent security strategy, the US government has articulated three redlines that must not be breached in the context of EU–NATO relations. These are: no "decoupling from NATO," no "duplication" of NATO command structures or alliance-wide resources, and no "discrimination" against NATO members that are not EU members (Gallis and Archick 2005).

The 2003 proposal advanced by France, Germany, Belgium, and Luxembourg, to create a European military headquarters, a planning staff, and an armaments agency in Belgium was interpreted on the other side of the Atlantic as a breach of these redlines. This led Washington to lobby hard for the insertion, in the EU Constitutional Treaty (and thus also in the subsequent Lisbon Treaty), of a formal recognition of "compatibility" between EU ambitions and NATO, which resulted in Article I-41.2. In fact the wording of this treaty article changed substantially from the first draft. Originally it specified compatibility only until such time as the EU had fully established its own common security and defense policy – which led to accusations that the Constitutional Treaty would violate the NATO charter itself (Cimbalo 2004). More recently, US policy has been supportive of the CSDP in order to encourage "burden sharing" from EU allies, which corresponds with the USA's growing operational shift toward the Pacific theatre at the expense of Europe.

Transatlantic disputes and internal discord over whether to follow US preferences are more the exception than the rule. In practice there is close cooperation between the US and the EU, for instance over fighting terrorism, applying sanctions to dissuade Iran from acquiring the nuclear bomb, and restricting arms to China. Relations are also tight between NATO and the EU, as was evidenced when the latter took over responsibilities for stabilizing Bosnia and Herzegovina from NATO in 2004. Under the 2002 "Berlin-

Plus" agreement the EU has also been able to use NATO military assets and command structures for CSDP missions. Since the launch of the CSDP, these missions have been far more numerous than NATO's humanitarian or peace-keeping operations. Yet NATO remains an important framework for European security precisely because of worries about EU effectiveness in terms of the EU having the capabilities and will to act. These fears go to the heart of a fundamental debate over missing elements in EU effectiveness: the "capability–expectations gap" (Hill 1993).

Christopher Hill identified this gap as one between what the EU is expected to do in foreign policy and what it actually can deliver on the basis of its resources and its legal instruments for achieving consensus and for acting upon it. Over the past two decades, institutionalization has specifically sought to address all three elements, as discussed in Section 8.1. The results are still contested, though, given that CSDP missions are small in scale (the largest, in Bosnia, involved 7,000 personnel, while many involve less than a 100) and that riskier deployments, where EU personnel could become embroiled in a conflict situation, have been rejected (Menon 2009, 231). Some see this as evidence of the EU being "risk averse" in CSDP (Dobbins 2008).

In this risk-averse context, one advantage of NATO is its ability to draw on US resources, for instance by supplying precision-guided munitions, as became necessary during the 2011 NATO intervention in Libya. Having US backing is thus still considered essential for the riskiest kinds of missions – such as intervening in Bosnia, Kosovo, or Libya, operations that require air power and involve the greatest likelihood of escalation. Indeed, as a US-sponsored security pact, NATO is seen as vital by many Eastern European countries wanting a credible deterrent from outside aggression. These countries sought EU accession for its economic benefits, while they also joined NATO in response to fears about Russian designs to maintain a sphere of influence in places that used to be part of, or controlled by, the Soviet Union. Hence there is no majority among member states in favor of abandoning the US-led alliance for the sake of a purely EU-led security policy.

One way of separating EU and NATO operations, therefore, is to see the former as based on "**soft power**" (see Box 8.1), while hard power is wielded through the latter. Although there is some truth in this characterization, it fails to account for the efforts the EU has undertaken to promote capacity building for military assets and their deployment in CSDP, as exemplified in the EU's Anti-Piracy Mission off the Somalian coast (Germond and Smith 2009). Nevertheless, even as EU operational and institutional capacities have grown, concerns remain about the ability to reach a consensus position within the Council of the EU that can authorize action.

8.2.2   Finding consensus

To capture the lingering decision-making issues confronting the EU, Toje (2008) talks of a "consensus–expectations" gap. This is a "gap between what the member-states are expected to agree on and what they are actually able to consent to" (Toje 2008, 122). Beyond thorny Transatlantic questions, there are other sources of friction within foreign policy decision-making that complicate the search for consensus. These include

Box 8.1   Key Concept: The EU and Soft Power

The phrase "soft power" was coined by Joseph Nye (2004, x) to refer to "the ability to get what you want through attraction rather than coercion." In other words, it is a way to influence another state's behavior, but not through threats of force or the use of sanctions. Instead soft power relies on having values, culture, and institutions that are admired, thereby serving as a basis for cooperation and emulation. This approach is therefore distinguished from hard power, which relies on having the military capacity to threaten other states. The EU is very much associated with soft power, notably because enlargement has proceeded on the basis of countries voluntarily agreeing to transform their societies and economies in order to join the club. This EU way of encouraging change and of actively helping its neighbors to go down this route via trade agreements, CSDP missions, and development aid has been described as the best means of establishing international order in the twenty-first century (Leonard 2005). However, there is a question mark over how far enlargement meets the proper definition of soft power, given the economic inducements offered to the EU's neighbors to make them conform to its rules and values. After all, not only does the EU provide significant funds to prepare countries for membership, but most candidate countries are poorer than the EU average and so can expect to be net beneficiaries from the budget. Where the economic incentives are not so great (that is, where full EU membership is not an option and the power of attraction is all there is), the EU has met with limited success, as when dealing with North Africa or Russia. In addition, EU countries remain bearers of hard power, yet they often prefer to exercise this through NATO, as in the operations in Libya or Afghanistan.

concerns that CSDP missions in sub-Saharan Africa implicitly uphold French foreign policy ambitions in the region (Menon 2009, 240). In the mid-1990s there was also a distinct lack of European solidarity over how to reform the Security Council, as Italy actively lobbied to prevent a permanent seat being given to Germany (Hill 2006). Finally, over a crucial European issue such as the future status of Kosovo, EU member states continue to respond differently, five countries opposing the unilateral declaration of independence of this former province of Serbia.

Nevertheless, consensus is very much a reality of EU CFSP, as exemplified by the fact that voting cohesion among EU countries at the UN has risen markedly since the 1980s, despite an expanded membership (Hosli, van Kampen, Meijerink, and Tennis 2010). Depending on the measurement tool used, cohesion among EU countries is between 80 and 90 percent. In fact much of the dissent is accounted for by the different voting behavior of the UK and France, permanent Security Council members with contrasting preferences on issues such as nuclear disarmament (Laatikainen and Smith 2006). This level of cohesion reflects shared values as well as the Brusselization of foreign policy. Of course, this consensus takes place within the legal and decision-making parameters member states have designed for the CFSP, which give them room to disagree if necessary.

Consensus building in EU foreign policy invariably involves the three largest countries: France, Germany, and the United Kingdom. Among the EU-28, these three countries have unmatched diplomatic, military, and economic resources and thus play a central role in decision-making, especially in considerations over launching a CSDP mission. This power disparity is exemplified by the fact these three states form the so-called EU-3, representing the EU in multiparty international talks on Iran's nuclear program. This special role played by the EU's major powers, in charge as they are of formulating EU policy toward Iran, can cause friction, as when other member states complained about not having access to negotiation documents (Sauer 2007). Moreover, the creation of the president of the European Council – which reduces the agenda-setting role of the rotating national presidency of the Council – reinforced fears that smaller countries might have a reduced say in CFSP.

Overall, therefore, the CFSP has a mixed effectiveness record. Coordination via legal instruments and capacity building measures has developed considerably, despite occasional crises that make consensus impossible. This illustrates how the CFSP is not designed to enforce consensus, but rather to make it more likely and to maximize its effectiveness when it exists. Meeting foreign policy expectations remains problematic, however, given the ambitious tasks the EU has set itself in this area. These tasks include a commitment to upholding a multilateral international order as well as to promoting democracy, and even something as specific as helping resolve the Israeli–Palestinian problem. Exploring the CFSP from the perspective of effectiveness gives only a partial picture, as it does not shed light on where these ambitious aims come from and why they were adopted. Consequently, it is necessary to enquire into the ideological or normative aims of EU foreign policy (see Section 8.3) and into the explanatory debates outlining why EU foreign policy developed in this fashion (see Section 8.4).

8.3   The Ideological Debate over the Aims of EU Foreign Policy

Another fundamental debate over EU foreign policy concerns the ideology or norms behind CFSP objectives. This overlaps with the debate over the EU's uniqueness (Section 6.3) and relates to the fact that the EU is not a state, which makes it a different kind of foreign policy actor. More precisely, the EU has foreign policy goals and means of achieving them that seem unconventional compared with those of normal states. For a start, security understood in terms of defending a specific territory does not seem a major preoccupation. The CSDP is more concerned with stabilizing the neighborhood, with promoting human rights, and with protecting individuals beyond the EU than with developing the force to minimize threats to EU territory and interests. These goals, combined with an emphasis on multilateralism and international law, represent a desire to transform the international order into a more just and rule-governed one. Such objectives, combined with the absence of a unified military force, explain why the EU was often described as a "civilian power" rather than as a military power (Smith 2000). This entails a contrast between concern for civilian matters, namely justice and rights, and focus on military power.

Yet the increased focus on developing military capabilities and missions has not turned the EU into a state or diluted the ambitions of the CFSP to achieve justice and human security in international politics. To make sense of these enduring commitments, the EU has thus been described as a "**normative power**" (Manners 2002), one based on promoting ideas such as human rights and justice. The origin of this EU approach is said to lie in the EU's own institutional identity as an alternative to balance of power, built on ideals of cooperation and placing law above power. In this way the EU's foreign policy ideals are an outward expression of its internal goals. Indeed this is a long-standing aspect of European integration; Jean Monnet (1963, 26) explained decades ago that "unity in Europe does not create a new kind of great power."

8.3.1   The EU as a normative power?

Manners' own example of the EU's normative foreign policy is the successful pressure the EU placed on applicant countries such as Poland and Cyprus and on potential applicants to abolish the death penalty in the 1990s. This is in fact a formal condition for EU accession, representing a concern for the just and humane treatment of all individuals. Hence the ideological aspect of EU foreign policy involves trying to diffuse this norm, as well as others, such as multilateralism, and rejecting the use of force to settle disputes. The emphasis on these norms often corresponds with the preferences of EU citizens in the matter of how the international order should be regulated. Polling from 2011 shows that only 33 percent of EU citizens feel that war is sometimes necessary, by comparison with 74 percent in the US (German Marshall Fund 2011). Similarly, 69 percent of EU citizens feel that the EU should be involved in establishing democracy in other countries, something supported by only 37 percent of Americans.

This mixture of aversion to war and a commitment to spreading certain values through persuasion has been described by Robert Kagan (2003) as Kantian pacifism, after the philosophy of perpetual peace espoused by Kant (see Section 1.2). Kagan contrasts this attitude toward international politics with the US attitude, which he characterizes as Hobbesian – in other words based on understanding the need for force where there is disorder, as the English philosopher Thomas Hobbes understood it. In this sense Europeans are said to be from Venus (the goddess of love) and Americans from Mars (the god of war), the former pursuing normative goals and the latter equipping themselves to survive disorder. Another way of capturing this difference is offered by Robert Cooper (2000). He sees European governments as operating in a postmodern security environment in which nationalism has been tamed and aggression is dismissed as a means to protect national interests. This contrasts with governments in the US as well as in China or Russia, which refuse to place universal values above national interests, reserving the right to use force in order to secure them.

Detached from pursuing national interests, the EU thus "sees itself as a potential superpower for civilian crisis management" (Smith 2011, 159). This puts it in a unique situation to deal with challenges emerging from failed states that other major powers, preoccupied as they are with national interest, are reluctant to engage with. Of course, this ambition is part of the reason why the EU has developed military capabilities, as persuasion alone will not fix problems associated with state failure – such as refugee crises and ethnic conflict. The military component of this ideological aspect of EU foreign policy was laid out in a 2003 document entitled the European Security Strategy. This document specified that the CSDP should involve "active policies . . . to counter the new dynamic threats. We need to develop a strategic culture that fosters early, rapid, and when necessary, robust intervention." This move has been criticized as marking the beginning of a "militarization" of EU foreign policy: the latter would be associated with "martial primacy" rather than norm promotion (Manners 2006). However, this critique acknowledges the existence of a crucial safeguard for the normative element of EU foreign policy: the commitment to launch CSDP missions that conform with international law, and typically with a UN Security Council mandate. Despite the multilateral emphasis of the CFSP, some scholars nevertheless consider the EU's attempts to spread norms in international politics to be of an imperial character (Merlingen 2007). For such scholars, norm promotion is always dangerous, as it conceals power relationships – for instance when a CSDP rule of law mission limits the agency of local stakeholders by relying on appointed European experts rather than on locally accountable officials (Merlingen 2007).

There is an alternative perspective on this principled commitment to multilateralism: working via international organizations to uphold international law and to give legitimacy to civilian or military interventions. Robert Pape (2005) identifies the EU's upholding of the norm of multilateralism as a means of **soft balancing** – that is, as an indirect way to challenge USA's primacy in international politics. This is how Pape interprets European states' pressure on the USA to act against Iraq in 2003 only with a new UN Security Council mandate. The emphasis on diplomatic niceties, procedural rules, and the need to build legitimacy through consensus with other states is thus not merely an expression of EU preferences, but also a cloak for frustrating US ambitions.

One important foreign policy tool the EU often deploys on the basis of values is that of economic sanctions. As a key part of the CFSP, these are put in place by a decision of the Council of the EU (see Box 8.2) and can target particular individuals, goods, or a regime. In many cases sanctions are implemented in response to a UN Security Council resolution; such are the restrictions on oil imports imposed as punishment for Iran's uranium enrichment program, or the freezing of assets of terrorist-sponsoring organizations. The rationale behind EU sanctions is thus to punish a state, a regime, or even an individual for specific violations of international law or human rights. The hope is, at least for states and political regimes, that economic losses caused by sanctions will eventually help change behavior or at least support domestic reform. Enforcing sanctions is a matter of principle, and it can have negative economic repercussions for member EU states. As a significant importer of Iranian oil, EU countries had to make alternative and more costly energy arrangements after banning all oil imports from Iran in 2012. Similarly, since the repression of the Tiananmen Square protests in 1989, the EU has maintained a ban on arms exports to China, which defense industry lobbies and certain member states would like to loosen in order to profit from this trade.

Box 8.2   Case Study: EU Sanctions

Sanctions are an important aspect of EU foreign policy. They are applied in line with CFSP objectives set out in Article 21 TEU, which commits the EU to upholding the UN Charter, promoting human rights and international cooperation. In line with this commitment, many sanctions stem from UN Security Council resolutions aimed at upholding peace and stability through measures such as arms or commodity embargoes (say, on "blood diamonds") in conflict situations. Others are autonomously enacted by the EU, allowing it to act even when the UN Security Council is deadlocked, for instance by restricting trade with Burma and Zimbabwe and by preventing government figures from travelling to the EU. This also happened in 2010–2011, when the EU imposed sanctions on institutions financially supporting the former president of the Côte d'Ivoire, who refused to step down after losing an election. As part of its aid policy toward African, Caribbean, and Pacific countries, the EU can withhold development cooperation where good governance is contravened, as in Zimbabwe under the government of Robert Mugabe. Sanctions have to be approved by unanimity in the Council, and the PSC (see Section 4.5) plays an important role. The PSC meets in Brussels, often more than once a week, one of its tasks being to prepare and review cases for imposing or lifting sanctions. Thus in April 2012, when the Council voted to lift sanctions targeting the Burmese regime for suspending democratic elections, this decision rubber-stamped a consensus position already negotiated by national representatives working within the PSC. The effectiveness of EU sanctions is open to question in terms of their ability to change state behavior, because applying as well as lifting sanctions requires unanimity, which is not always possible (Portela 2010). However, EU sanctions can prod the wider international community into responding to a crisis situation and can give momentum to domestic opposition, both of which occurred in Côte d'Ivoire in 2010–2011.

However, supporters of a normative power Europe worry about whether the EU has the wherewithal and the outward focus to conduct a foreign policy that is based on upholding international law and justice. Here the major worry is that a loss of European global influence will turn the EU into a large Switzerland: prosperous and secure but internationally insignificant (Vennesson 2010). Issues of EU effectiveness and capabilities are intimately bound up in the normative power debate, as it would be hypocritical to promote certain norms and yet not to assume the costs of upholding them (Smith 2011). Hence it is necessary to examine the different explanations behind the emergence of CFSP and its ideological component.

8.4   The Explanatory Debate over EU Foreign Policy

There are many different aspects of CFSP argued over by scholars. Traditionally, what needed to be explained was why foreign policy took a back seat to economic integration and why the former continues to be run on largely intergovernmental lines. Explanations of these phenomena vary, as they also do for another much debated facet of foreign policy integration: why the CFSP has been endowed with the normative ends stated in the treaties. Moreover, as the CFSP has developed substantially over the past decade, there is great interest in explaining how the consensus necessary to conduct EU foreign policy has been rendered possible.

Competing explanations for all these aspects of the CFSP can be distinguished on the basis of three key explanatory factors: power, interests, and identity. That is, some see the development of CFSP as a response to the changing distribution of power among European states and other international actors. A second explanation relates to the fact that major governments within the EU saw it to be in their national interest to pursue this kind of foreign policy integration. Thirdly, there is the argument that foreign policy integration both serves the goal of creating a European identity and draws on existing cultural similarities between EU member states.

8.4.1   Power and interests as explanatory factors

The initial lack of foreign policy integration was most commonly explained through the low salience of economic regulation, which allows governments to pool sovereignty in this area with few constraints or complaints. This is in contrast to public sensitivity regarding the "high politics" of diplomacy and military alliances, where integration becomes hotly contested within member states (Hoffmann 1966). In other words, power matters most to states and their citizens, so integration in areas that directly affect their power – notably the power to conduct an independent foreign policy – will be much harder to achieve. The basis for this assumed divide between high and low politics is the international relations theory of realism, which posits that states are above all concerned with being secure. From this realist perspective, foreign policy is considered the residual element of sovereignty, which states will try not to relinquish. Only in extremely grave circumstances, when sovereignty has to be exchanged for security, do realists expect full political union (Parent 2011).

A corollary to this realist take on integration is that the international situation facing European states after 1945 – which alone could prompt sovereign states to unite as a federation –was not threatening enough to justify foreign policy integration (Parent 2011). Indeed the founding father of neorealism, Kenneth Waltz (1979), argued that the very absence of a serious security threat explained why economic integration could proceed without foreign policy coordination. Economic integration, which involves absolute gains (everyone becomes wealthier) between states, thereby potentially allowing others to become more powerful in relative terms, is ordinarily difficult to accomplish.

Yet Western European states were comfortable with economic integration because an outside power, the USA via NATO, provided security against an external threat and stabilized intra-European relations (Waltz 1979). In this way power considerations among European countries could be set aside, allowing for cooperation on economic issues.

By extension, one explanation for the rise of EU foreign policy integration after the end of the Cold War is the need to find a new mechanism for stabilizing intra-European relations. As Jones (2007) argues, the reunification of Germany, the demise of the Soviet Union, and resulting question marks over the US commitment to Europe constituted a new security environment. In this context, other EU member states feared potential German regional hegemony as Germany was the most powerful economy in Europe, thus marking a return to the preoccupation with power. The response was to devise a system for binding European states' foreign policy via the CFSP, thereby providing a safety mechanism to control Germany's potential hegemonic ambitions.

Jones and others also link the development of the CSDP to another concern related to power: the desire to demonstrate European military effectiveness so as to regain relevance within the Transatlantic relationship. The 1990s had proved troubling from this perspective, as US-led interventions in Bosnia and Kosovo exposed not only European divisions, but also a lack of operational capacity for deploying hard power. Given the absence of an existential security threat, there was no need to develop a common army – unlike during the early Cold War plan for a European Defence Community (see Section 2.3). Instead, all that the EU requires is "an instrument for coalitional coercive diplomacy" (Hyde-Price 2007, 230), which explains the limited means and goals of the CSDP. This is enough to stabilize crises, especially when active participation by the USA can no longer be taken for granted.

8.4.2   Identity as an explanatory factor

Realism, however, does not capture the identity or symbolic aspect of foreign policy for European integration. That is, the construction of EU foreign policy has been closely linked to the desire to construct a European identity. In this sense the EU's foreign policy serves not merely an external purpose, but also an internal one: it is a means toward affirming the EU as an actor with its own identity (Bickerton 2011). EU elites thus want foreign policy to play a part in legitimizing European integration, especially because European citizens consistently support the idea that the EU should play a more prominent international role (Krotz 2009, 559–560). This attitude helps explains why, once the Constitutional Treaty was derailed by national referendums, concerted efforts were made to pass a new treaty expanding EU foreign policy institutionalization.

Taking this identity explanation for CFSP integration even further, there is an argument that integration here reflects a shared strategic culture (Meyer 2007). What this means is that EU countries share a similar perception of security threats and the legitimate way to use force (or not) to deal with them. This fits with the constructivist theory of international relations, which sees inter-state behavior as the product of ideas and constructed identities rather than power or material interests (Checkel 2007). In the EU

Box 8.3   Key Debate: Multilateralism as the Preference of the Weak?

Robert Kagan (2003) has put forward a strong critique of the claim that the EU has adopted normative and multilateral ends out of choice. Instead, he argues that these are the product of weakness and explain why the EU has chosen a different strategic path from the far more powerful US. Multilateralism is understood by Kagan as the strategy of the weak because, unlike the US, the EU does not have the hard power resources to act unilaterally and to use coercion to get its way. Moving toward a rule-governed international order is considered to be in the interest of the weaker international players, as it places law above power, thereby weakening the advantages of those who possess hard power. Obviously, the success of European integration and the end of the Cold War reduced the need for retaining hard power capacities. However, Kagan also claims that this has lulled EU countries into a false sense of security, where they believe that their happily peaceful Kantian situation can be extended globally. This entails not only adopting normative foreign policy ends, but also delegating hard power responsibilities to the United States, which remains conscious of the Hobbesian nature of international politics. Many scholars have criticized this depiction of a Transatlantic divide based on a power differential for being too crude and for failing to acknowledge how genuine the EU's normative and multilateral preferences are (Menon, Nicolaïdis, and Walsh 2004).

---

context – a geographical space detached from the balance of power considerations that still preoccupy many other regions – there has been a "normative convergence" in favor of humanitarianism and multilateralism (Meyer 2007). This can be explained as an outward reflection of Europe's supranational integration, but also as a conscious choice to deprioritize territorial defense and to forsake power projection. Nevertheless, labeling this a choice has been disputed, given member states' dwindling power projection capacities (see Box 8.3).

Smaller countries with fewer capacities for an independent foreign policy already tend to have political elites that favor integration in this area; this reflects their self-identification as small powers (Koenig-Archibugi 2004). Large countries such as France and Germany have played a key role in determining the scope and direction of foreign policy integration, something that can also be linked to identity factors. From a German perspective, the CFSP and the CSDP are associated with the "normalization" of that country's foreign policy after reunification (Katzenstein 1997). German politicians welcomed the normative agenda of the CFSP as a way to demonstrate Germany's commitment to integration and as a means for becoming a more normal actor in international politics. This meant participating in humanitarian and peace-keeping operations rather than staying on the sidelines in order to avoid uncomfortable associations with German militarism. Normalization is also associated with seeking to accept external responsibilities in a way that could help Germany's case for a permanent UN Security Council seat. The turning point in German foreign policy preferences was its participation in NATO's Kosovo campaign, which was authorized by a Socialist–Green government coalition and opened the way for the development of the CSDP (Rathbun 2004).

France's attitude toward foreign policy integration, unlike that of Germany, was never diffident. French governments since de Gaulle have been associated with the project of creating a *Europe puissance* – a Europe as a global power (Gordon 1993). This reflects the idea that foreign policy integration would naturally come under French leadership given Germany's self-limiting role in international politics. During the Cold War, de Gaulle's idea was to turn Europe into a "third force" capable of pursuing a foreign policy independently from the rival superpowers. The attraction of an independent European foreign policy remained after 1989, as illustrated by a former French foreign minister who, in 2003, denounced the "hyper power" of the United States as something that required a European counterweight. A necessary component of French ambitions to integrate foreign policy, though, was intergovernmentalism. This was because French governments remained committed to sovereignty in this area, especially on matters such as nuclear weapons and relations with former colonies, notably in Africa (Irondelle 2008). Hence French support for an integrated European foreign policy is not intended to infringe upon the state having freedom of action to defend vital strategic interests.

However, there is also a pragmatic angle to French participation in the development of the CSDP. France pushed for a "militarized" EU foreign policy as a means of developing hard power capacities that would allow for a more ambitious set of policy objectives (Irondelle 2008). This is based on a recognition that French assets alone are insufficient for sustaining the kind of foreign policy integration it favors. Similar pragmatic motives underlie the United Kingdom's relationship to the CSDP. Former British Prime Minister Tony Blair played a key role in launching it by signaling Britain's intention to commit to endowing the EU with "the capacity for autonomous action" on the international stage. This was done in the form of the Saint-Malo declaration, the product of a joint Franco-British summit in that French city. British politicians had long been hesitant about foreign policy integration, owing to their preference for NATO and for nurturing a so-called special relationship with the United States. From the British perspective, the CSDP was intended not as a rival security organization but as an additional option for taking action, especially when NATO could not otherwise act (Longhurst and Miskimmon 2007). As with France, this was a reflection of the fact that playing a leading international role would require working via the EU.

There are thus many different explanatory theories focusing on different causal factors. None can explain in entirety the CFSP: its origins, its limitations, and its functioning. All three causal factors (power, interests, and identity) play a part in explaining different aspects of the CFSP, which is too complex to be explained by a single factor. However, there is a consensus among these competing explanations that the chances of the EU becoming a unitary, or fully supranational, foreign policy actor are very slim (Krotz 2009). By extension, most analysts also acknowledge that the current limited ambitions of the CSDP are not the first step in developing a power projection capacity designed to challenge the global distribution of power (Howorth and Menon 2009).

8.5   Concluding Summary

The institutional development of EU foreign policy took hold following the Maastricht Treaty. There already was an external dimension to European integration, with trade and development coming under the aegis of the Commission in the domain known as "external relations." Maastricht created legal mechanisms, based on intergovernmentalism, for the EU to act more widely on the global stage. The success of this institutionalization, whereby member states remain formally sovereign and independent in foreign policy, has led to the Brusselization of national foreign policy. This is due to the CFSP and the CSDP, which increasingly make member states coordinate their foreign policies. The former constitutes a set of policy objectives enshrined in the treaties, while the latter is the mechanism for pooling and developing the resources needed for civilian and military operations abroad.

Institutionalization of foreign policy continued with the Lisbon Treaty, which sought to coordinate Commission-led external relations and CFSP better. However, it is still the case that many different leaders – the Commission president, the president of the European Council, the high representative, alongside national leaders – speak on behalf of the EU for foreign policy. The continuing importance of NATO after the Cold War means that Transatlantic relations can impinge on EU foreign policy, especially in crisis moments when there is a question of deploying hard power. Nevertheless, the CFSP and NATO are formally intended to be compatible, the former being generally based on soft power while hard power is used only for humanitarian or peace-keeping missions. Limiting the ends of foreign policy in this way has helped generate consensus while the CSDP has developed EU capacities.

Given the ideological goals for foreign policy, which include promoting democracy and international law, the EU has been labeled a normative power. This suggests putting values ahead of interests, which can be seen in sanctions against nefarious regimes and in the CSDP missions outside of Europe. Yet the desire to develop hard power assets can be considered contradictory to normative ends and has even been interpreted as a prelude to balancing against US hegemony. In addition to these debates, there are many competing explanations of why EU foreign policy has become integrated and why this has happened in an intergovernmental fashion. Power, national interests, and identity, all play a role in explaining why foreign policy follows a different path from economic integration. There is disagreement over the motivating factors leading states to pursue foreign policy integration, but scholars agree that there is no pressing security need or national interest to develop a common army or a fully integrated foreign policy.

Guide to Further Reading

Bickerton, C. 2011. *European Union Foreign Policy: From Effectiveness to Functionality*. Basingstoke: Palgrave.

    Succinct and well-made argument for considering the development of foreign policy as a means of legitimizing integration, and not just as a way for the EU to act externally.

Hill, C., and M. Smith. 2011. *International Relations and the European Union*. Cambridge: Cambridge University Press.

Rich and sophisticated collection of essays by leading experts covering every angle of EU foreign policy and drawing on up-to-date empirical analysis and on major theories of international relations.

Keukeleire, S., and J. MacNaughtan. 2008. *The Foreign Policy of the European Union*. Basingstoke: Palgrave.

Textbook offering comprehensive coverage of all the different aspects of EU foreign policy, including the debates over effectiveness, norms, and explanatory factors.

Smith, M. 2004. *Europe's Foreign and Security Policy: The Institutionalization of Cooperation*. Cambridge: Cambridge University Press.

The most rigorous empirical and theoretical account of how the institutionalization of foreign policy has impacted member states by changing their behavior and policy preferences.

Discussion Questions

1   How have the CFSP and the CSDP been institutionalized and what legal constraints do they place on member states' foreign policy?
2   What has the CSDP achieved, and how does its work relate to NATO?
3   Why is the effectiveness of EU foreign policy disputed, and what role do Transatlantic relations play in this issue?
4   Why has the EU been called a "normative power"? Is this label justified?
5   How would realism explain the EU's reliance on soft power? Is this a convincing explanation?

Web Resources

This book is supported by a companion website, which can be found at www.wiley.com/go/glencross. There you will find a list of the web links referred to in this chapter wherever you see a "Web" icon in the page margins. In addition, you will find a list of further relevant online resources such as websites for EU institutions, political groups, archives, and think tanks, information on studying abroad, and biographies of key figures. You will also find self-assessment tools in the form of flashcards and independent study questions developed specifically for this chapter.

Glossary

Constructive abstention
   Decision-making rule in CFSP that allows a member state to abstain from pursuing a certain policy or from participating in a CSDP mission. However, there is a legal obligation not to impede the conduct of an EU policy that a member state does not participate in.

External relations

Phrase formerly used to describe trade and development policies, which were under the Commission's authority. Since the Lisbon Treaty the EU has tried to link together all EU external action via the High Representative and the External Action Service, although the CFSP still has a different legal basis.

Multilateralism

Term used to describe countries working together to solve problems in international relations. Closely associated with upholding international law in order to find peaceful ways of settling disputes, notably via the UN system.

Normative power

An actor in international politics, a state, or also an international organization, which forsakes power or self-interest to promote instead normative ends such as individual rights and justice. In the case of the EU, these norms are seen as an external projection of what the EU does internally.

Permanent structured cooperation

Legal expression for enhanced cooperation procedure when applied to the CFSP. Allows a core group of member states to go further in CFSP or CSDP.

Petersberg tasks

Name given to the tasks for which the EU can undertake a CSDP mission: joint disarmament operations, humanitarian and rescue tasks, military advice and assistance tasks, conflict prevention and peace-keeping tasks, crisis management, including peace-making and post-conflict stabilization. Named after a Berlin hotel where these aims were formulated.

Soft balancing

Concept associated with neorealist international relations theory. It suggests there are indirect or "soft" means for weaker powers to frustrate stronger states without explicitly working against their interests, that is, without hard balancing. Soft balancing is associated with the EU's insistence on using multilateral procedures and international legitimacy, to the detriment of US unilateralism.

Soft power

Conceptual phrase coined by Joseph Nye to describe the ability of a state to influence another country via attraction, not coercion. The concept suggests that states seek to cooperate with countries that have created a positive image and role. It is this "soft power" that acts as a magnet for cooperation, or even for emulation.

References

Allen, Dave. 1998. "Who Speaks for Europe? The Search for an Effective and Coherent Foreign Policy." In John Peterson and Helene Sjursen, eds., A Common Foreign Policy for Europe? Competing Visions of CFSP, 44–58. London: Routledge.

Bickerton, Christopher. 2011. European Union Foreign Policy: From Effectiveness to Functionality. Basingstoke: Palgrave.

Biscop, Sven. 2008. "Permanent Structured Cooperation and the Future of ESDP." Egmont Papers, No. 20 (April). Brussels: Academia Press. Available at www.egmontinstitute.be/papers/08/sec-gov/080918-Biscop-Helsinki-paper.pdf (accessed July 20, 2013).

Calleo, David. 2003. "Transatlantic Folly: NATO vs the EU." World Policy Journal, 20: 17–24.

Carta, Caterina. 2011. The European Union Diplomatic Service: Ideas, Preferences, and Identities. London: Routledge.

Checkel, Jeffrey T., ed. 2007. International Institutions and Socialization in Europe. Cambridge: Cambridge University Press.

Cimbalo, Jeffrey L. 2004. "Saving NATO from Europe." Foreign Affairs, 83: 111–120.

Cooper, Robert. 2000. The Postmodern State and World Order. London: Demos.

Dobbins, James. 2008. "Europe's Role in Nation-Building." Survival, 50: 83–110. DOI: 10.1080/00396330802173115

Gallis, Paul, and Kristin Archick. 2005. NATO and the European Union. Congressional Research Service Report. Washington, DC: Library of Congress.

German Marshall Fund. 2011. Transatlantic Trends. Berlin: Marshall Fund.

Germond, Basil, and Michael E. Smith. 2009. "Interest Definition and Threat Perception in the European Union: Explaining the First ESDP Anti-Piracy Naval Operation." Contemporary Security Policy, 30: 573–593. DOI: 10.1080/13523260903327741

Gordon, Philip H. 1993. A Certain Idea of France: French Security Policy and the Gaullist Legacy. Princeton, NJ: Princeton University Press.

Hill, Christopher. 1993. "The Capability–Expectations Gap, or Conceptualizing Europe's Role." Journal of Common Market Studies, 31: 305–328. DOI: 10.1111/j.1468-5965.1993.tb00466.x

Hill, Christopher. 2006. "The European Powers in the Security Council: Differing Interests, Differing Arenas." In Katie

Verlin Laatikainen and Karen E. Smith, eds., Intersecting Multilateralisms: The European Union at the United Nations, 49–69. Basingstoke: Palgrave.

Hoffmann, Stanley. 1966. "Obstinate or Obsolete? The Fate of the Nation-State and the Case of Western Europe." Daedalus, 95: 892–908.

Hosli, Madeleine, Evelyn van Kampen, Frits Meijerink, and Katherine Tennis. 2010. "Voting Cohesion in the United Nations' General Assembly: The Case of the European Union." Paper presented at the ECPR Fifth Pan-European Conference, 24–26 June 2010, Porto. Available at http://www.jhubc.it/ecpr-porto/virtualpaperroom/082.pdf (accessed July 20, 2013).

Howorth, Jolyon, and Anand Menon. 2009. "Still Not Pushing Back: Why the European Union Is Not Balancing the United States." Journal of Conflict Resolution, 53: 727–744. DOI: 10.1177/0022002709339362

Hyde-Price, Adrian. 2007. European Security in the Twenty-First Century. Abingdon: Routledge.

Irondelle, Bastien. 2008. "European Foreign Policy: The End of French Europe." Journal of European Integration, 30: 153–168. DOI: 10.1080/07036330801959556

Jones, Seth G. 2007. The Rise of European Security Cooperation. Cambridge: Cambridge University Press.

Jørgensen, Knud E. 2006. "Overview: The European Union and the World." In Knud E. Jørgensen, Mark Pollack, and Ben Rosamond, eds., Handbook of European Union Politics, 507–525. London: Sage.

Kagan, Robert. 2003. Of Paradise and Power: America and Europe in the New World Order. New York: Knopf.

Katzenstein, Peter J. 1997. "United Germany in an Integrating Europe." In Peter J. Katzenstein, ed., Tamed Power: Germany in Europe, 1–48. Ithaca, NY: Cornell University Press.

Koenig-Archibugi, Mathias. 2004. "International Governance as New raison d'état?

The Case of the EU Common Foreign and Security Policy." *European Journal of International Relations*, 10: 147–188. DOI: 10.1177/1354066104042933

Krotz, Ulrich. 2009. "Momentum and Impediments: Why Europe Won't Emerge as a Full Political Actor on the World Stage Soon." *Journal of Common Market Studies*, 47: 555–578. DOI: 10.1111/j.1468-5965.2009.01815.x

Laatikainen, Katie V., and Karen E. Smith. 2006. *Intersecting Multilateralisms: The EU and the United Nations*. Basingstoke: Palgrave.

Leonard, Mark. 2005. *Why Europe Will Run the Twenty-First Century*. London: Fourth Estate.

Longhurst, Kerry, and Alister Miskimmon. 2007. "Same Challenges, Diverging Responses: Germany, the UK and European Security." *German Politics*, 16: 79–94. DOI: 10.1080/09644000601157442

Manners, Ian. 2002. "Normative Power Europe: A Contradiction in Terms?" *Journal of Common Market Studies*, 40: 235–258. DOI: 10.1111/1468-5965.00353

Manners, Ian. 2006. "Normative Power Europe Reconsidered: Beyond the Crossroads." *Journal of European Public Policy*, 13: 182–199. DOI: 10.1080/13501760500451600

Menon, Anand. 2009. "Empowering Paradise? The ESDP at Ten." *International Affairs*, 85: 227–246. DOI: 10.1111/j.1468-2346.2009.00791.x

Menon, Anand, Kalypso Nicolaïdis, and Jennifer Walsh. 2004. "In Defence of Europe: A Response to Kagan." *Journal of European Affairs*, 2: 5–14.

Merlingen, Michael. 2007. "Everything Is Dangerous: A Critique of 'Normative Power Europe.'" *Security Dialogue*, 38: 435–453. DOI: 10.1177/0967010607084995

Meunier, Sophie, and Kalypso Nicolaïdis. 2006. "The European Union as a Conflicted Trade Power." *Journal of European Public Policy*, 13: 906–925. DOI: 10.1080/13501760600838623

Meyer, Christoph O. 2007. *The Quest for a European Strategic Culture: Changing Norms on Security and Defence in the EU*. Basingstoke: Palgrave.

Monnet, Jean. 1963. "A Ferment of Change." *Journal of Common Market Studies*, 1: 203–211. DOI: 10.1111/j.1468-5965.1963.tb01060.x

Nye, Joseph. 2004. *Soft Power: The Means to Success in World Politics*. Cambridge, MA: Perseus Books.

Pape, Robert A. 2005. "Soft Balancing against the United States." *International Security*, 30: 7–45. DOI: 10.1162/0162288054894607

Parent, Joseph. 2011. *Uniting States: Voluntary Union in World Politics*. Oxford: Oxford University Press.

Portela, Clara. 2010. *European Union Sanctions and Foreign Policy: When and Why Do They Work?* Abingdon: Routledge.

Rathbun, Brian C. 2004. *Partisan Interventions: European Party Politics and Peace Enforcement in the Balkans*. New York: Cornell University Press.

Sauer, Tom. 2007. "Coercive Diplomacy by the EU: The Case of Iran." Discussion Papers in Diplomacy, No. 106. The Hague: Clingendael. Available at http://www.clingendael.nl/publications/2007/20070100_cdsp_diplomacy_sauer.pdf (accessed July 20, 2013).

Smith, Karen E. 2000. "The End of Civilian Power EU: A Welcome Demise or Cause for Concern?" *International Spectator*, 35: 11–28. DOI: 10.1080/03932720008458123

Smith, Michael. 2004. *Europe's Foreign and Security Policy: The Institutionalization of Cooperation*. Cambridge: Cambridge University Press.

Smith, Michael. 2011. "A Liberal Grand Strategy in a Realist World? Power, Purpose, and the EU's Changing Global Role." *Journal of European Public Policy*, 18: 144–163. DOI: 10.1080/13501763.2011.544487

Sperling, James, and Mark Webber. 2009. "NATO: From Kosovo to Kabul."

International Affairs, 85: 491–511. DOI: 10.1111/j.1468-2346.2009.00810.x

Toje, Asle. 2008. "The Consensus–Expectations Gap: Explaining Europe's Ineffective Foreign Policy." *Security Dialogue*, 39: 121–141. DOI: 10.1177/0967010607086826

Vennesson, Pascal. 2010. "Competing Visions for the European Union Grand Strategy." *European Foreign Affairs Review*, 15: 57–75.

Waltz, Kenneth. 1979. *Theory of International Politics*. New York: McGraw-Hill.

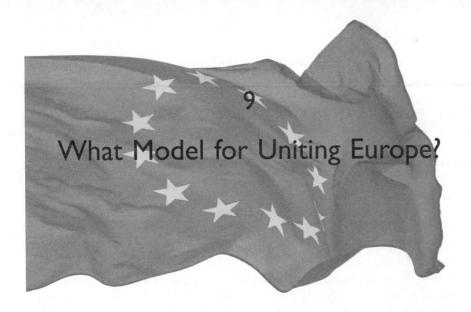

9

What Model for Uniting Europe?

Contents

Learning Objectives

- to identify the pros and cons of having a more federal EU;
- to analyze the factors that limit the introduction of more confederalism into the EU;
- to evaluate the balance between federal and confederal elements in today's EU;
- to identify the features of networked governance and analyze the arguments in favor of this model;
- to evaluate the nature of and reasons for the existing elements of differentiated integration;
- to evaluate the significance of the absence of political finality in the EU.

The Politics of European Integration: Political Union or a House Divided?, First Edition. Andrew Glencross.
© 2014 Andrew Glencross. Published 2014 by Blackwell Publishing Ltd.

9.0   Introduction: Competing Models of European Integration

The politics of European integration concerns not just what the EU does (that is, its actual and proposed policies) but also how it is organized (in other words, its legal and institutional framework). In comparison to political systems such as today's US federal system, or the UN, the EU continues to undergo frequent institutional reform. It is thus an ongoing institutional project, which means that supporters and critics of the EU argue constantly over competing models for how the EU should be organized. The purpose of this chapter is to analyze the arguments surrounding four rival models for integration. These represent four different institutional and legal models based on competing visions of the objectives behind integration.

The reason why there is so much disagreement over the institutional organization of the EU is that European integration lacks what is termed **political finality** (Fischer 2000). That is, there is no accepted endpoint of how integration will develop; the Maastricht Treaty's Preamble commits member states to "lay[ing] the foundations of an ever closer union among the peoples of Europe" – an ambiguous and open-ended goal. Consequently there are many attempts to specify what this ever closer union should look like, and there are also questions over whether further integration is always better.

Perhaps the most significant issue surrounding the debate over political finality is that of whether the EU needs to be organized in a particular way in order to be more effective and more legitimate. Supporters of a federal endpoint to integration believe this form of government to be most appropriate on both counts, as explained in Section 9.1. This is because federalism, at least in theory, could overcome the high consensus threshold and the unanimity blockages that hamper EU policy-making today. By extension, this could make its policies be more in tune with citizens' preferences. Conversely, those who are against abandoning national sovereignty wholesale advocate a more intergovernmental, or confederal, system as a better means of effective and accountable cooperation. The confederal model of integration is discussed in Section 9.2; it explains why some associate policy effectiveness with a more limited EU, focusing solely on the single market. Another important argument in favor of confederalism is that it enhances democratic accountability by making elected national governments responsible for all major EU policy decisions. Confederalists consider this preferable to having supranational institutions shape policy, be they unelected (the Commission and Court) or not (the Parliament).

As well as discussing these opposing federal and confederal models, the chapter examines whether European integration actually requires political finality. This is because there is an argument – relating to both effectiveness and democratic accountability – for keeping the current ambiguous institutional mixture. Some scholars and politicians thus claim that neither federalism nor confederalism is the correct organizational model for the EU. They point out that the EU's unique strength is its ability to function through **networked governance**, by linking decision-makers, judges, and stakeholders. The principles behind this perspective are examined in Section 9.3. Another alternative, that of **differentiated integration** – which allows EU countries to integrate on a selective basis, not on a "one size fits all" model of EU membership – is treated in Section 9.4. As well as forsaking the finality question, these institutional models share a belief that integration functions best by enabling policy-making beyond the nation-state. Networked governance and differentiated integration do not aim to turn the EU into a copy of the nation-state. Hence in these alternative models the absence of political finality, in line with the *sui generis* vision of the EU (see Section 6.3), can be seen as vital for making the EU work.

All four competing models – federalism, confederalism, government networks, and differentiated integration – are thus analyzed in turn in this chapter. The aim is to understand their respective strengths and weaknesses as templates for an effective and legitimate EU system. Of course, since institutional reform is premised on unanimous treaty agreement that requires compromise between different national preferences, it is hard to imagine that the EU will ever fully conform to one ideal institutional template.

9.1 Federalism

There are two poles on the spectrum of what EU political finality should ultimately look like. At one extreme there is the federal model. This suggests that the EU needs to have all the important competences of government (notably taxation and foreign policy), as advocated already in the 1940s and 1950s by Altiero Spinelli and others (Burgess 2000). The polar opposite to federalism is confederalism, which argues for the need to revert to more intergovernmentalism (see Section 9.2). By contrast, the federal model favors supranationalism for all policy-making, democratic control being provided by a more powerful European Parliament so as to enhance the link between citizens' preferences and policy outcomes.

From a federalist perspective, more supranational competences and decision-making are essential for making the EU more effective. Removing national vetoes would notably allow all policy options, such as harmonizing tax rates or replacing nuclear power with renewable energy sources, to be on the table. By extension, expanded supranationalism could make the EU more legitimate by enabling it to meet citizens' policy expectations better. For instance, if it had full tax powers, the EU could engage in more redistribution between rich and poor regions, or it could prohibit countries from competing for investment through low corporation tax. Currently the need to find compromises between member state preferences in policy areas where states still hold a veto limits such moves.

Transforming the EU into a fully federal system would require three fundamental institutional changes. For a start, federation implies external sovereignty, that is, foreign and diplomatic relations with other countries, conducted only through the EU. This would leave no room for member states to conduct an independent foreign policy. The implication that, through such a change, the EU would always find it easier to establish a consensus on important issues is not correct – citizens and their elected representatives across Europe will continue to have rather different preferences. However, with a UN seat, a unitary system of diplomatic representation, and the sole ability to make binding international treaties, an EU federation means that, once decided upon, EU foreign policy could not be undermined by member states going it alone or refusing to participate.

A second institutional reform necessitated by federalism is the recalibration of the relationship between the Council of the EU and the European Parliament. Building on the current system of co-decision, federalists argue that the Council of the EU should become an upper house of parliament (Fischer 2000). Most federal systems, for instance those of the US, Germany, or India, are **bicameral**, containing a lower chamber directly elected by the people alongside an upper legislative chamber that represents territorial units. A federal upper house exists to monitor the work of the lower chamber, ensuring that the interests and rights of territorial units are respected, notably for constitutional reform or changes in the attribution of competences. In theory, reducing the importance of the Council of the EU (by removing vetoes and the Council's special legislative and executive functions in foreign policy) should enable the party-based preferences of MEPs to matter even more than they do in the current Ordinary Legislative Procedure (OLP). Introducing federal bicameralism in the EU is thus designed to lessen the importance of national interests in favor of citizens' policy preferences, as these are represented by the party affiliation of their elected MEPs.

In turn, this change in the legislature implies a third element in this mooted federal overhaul: some form of elected government. While the College of commissioners is currently subject to approval by the European Parliament, as is the choice of the Commission president, the composition and portfolios of the unelected commissioners are not tied directly to the preferences of the European Parliament. Parliamentary federations, for example Germany or Australia, are based on a stronger connection between the legislative and executive. In these systems the executive is constituted by – and dependent upon – political parties with a majority of parliamentary seats. This connection between the executive and the legislative is the essence of a directly elected government. At the moment the Commission, which has a monopoly of legislative initiative under OLP, lacks such a close connection with the parliament. The European Parliament, in Vernon Bogdanor's (2003, 56) phrase, "is not at present a government-choosing body, divided between a government and an opposition." With full tax-raising powers, the parliament of a federal EU is bound to want to have more say in who gets to propose legislation and who is in charge of executing EU policies. This could take the form of making the composition of the Commission reflect directly the party majority of the elected MEPs (see Box 4.1) by having them elect the Commission's president, who would then select a college on the basis of his party affiliation (Fischer 2000).

9.1.1   Problems with the federal vision

Federalism can therefore result in increasing policy options, minimizing the need to accommodate national interests, and providing a closer electoral connection to citizens. That is why this model is proposed as a way to improve accountability as well as the effectiveness of policy-making. Yet there are grounds for questioning both these assumptions.

In the current EU system, legislation is first formulated by the unelected, politically neutral European Commission, which acts in the general European interest. This political independence makes it (in principle) an honest broker for finding consensus policy positions and an impartial agent for identifying whether member states have broken EU rules. Conversely, what can be called a *politicized* Commission – one closely tied to, if not directed by, the partisan composition of the European Parliament – could pursue party interests over European ones (see Box 4.1). For instance, decisions whether to prosecute member states for breaching EU rules might be influenced by whether or not the government of the country was a member of the same party or coalition as that controlling the Commission. A blind eye could also be turned to infractions in countries run by political allies, something not possible with the independent Commission in place today. Likewise, with the European Parliament in control of the legislative agenda, this could translate into a set of partisan policies that favor some regions or interests over others. As a result, the federal model of government is considered suspect as a means of delivering effective regulation for a single market – a shared commercial space with common rules for all in the interest of all (Majone 2005).

Another problem with the assumed benefits of creating a parliamentary-style federation is the appropriateness of this model of accountability in such a heterogeneous political community. Some of the most diverse federations, such as Switzerland and the USA, deliberately do not follow the classic parliamentary model. The latter is based on an inherently majoritarian principle, which offers fewer safeguards to unit autonomy when this clashes with the preferences of the majority of citizens. The horizontal separation of powers, which divides the legislative from the executive, as in the current separation between the Commission and the legislative institutions, can thus be considered a more appropriate system of accountability for the EU (Fabbrini 2005).

Over time, though, successive treaty reforms have introduced many supranational innovations that bring the EU closer to a federal model. Indeed most of the proposals contained in the 1984 Spinelli Draft Treaty on European Union, a constitutional blueprint for a federal Europe passed by the European Parliament, have actually been realized. These changes, notably the use of qualified majority voting (QMV) as the standard decision-making procedure in the Council and the development of co-decision with the Parliament, have been introduced in order to overcome decision-making blockages caused by vetoes and to enhance democratic control over EU policy outputs (Ponzano 2010). In addition, the constitutionalized status of EU law further contributes to the EU's federal features (see Section 4.4). However, the political impetus behind creating a federal Europe remains very limited despite all the academic interest in this subject. Hence it is questionable whether conditions in Europe are propitious for full federal integration (see Box 9.1).

The absence of mainstream mass party support for a federal vision of integration is evident: none of the European Parliament's party groups self-identifies as federalist or makes this form of constitutional change a policy priority. Active promotion of a European-level federation is the preserve of lobby groups such as the Union of European Federalists or the Spinelli Group. Of course, there has never been mass support for such a dramatic dismantling of national sovereignty, which is why in the 1950s

Box 9.1   Key Debate: Is Europe Ready for Federalism?

Accompanying the process of European integration is the question of whether Europe is ready to be transformed into a federation. Historically, one of the most powerful motives behind this process is what scholars call "coming together" federalism (Stepan 1999), whereby independent states join forces for a common goal such as security, otherwise not realizable alone. This is greatly facilitated by having a common language, ethnicity, or religion, as in most of the former colonies that became the US, although no such homogeneity was present in the coming together federation that is Switzerland (Kriesi and Trechsel 2008, 1–17). Supporters of EU federalism thus claim that language and other cultural divisions are not insurmountable obstacles to a European federation – what matters is creating a political system with the right institutions and decision-making structures. These are said to have the ability to establish shared commitments and perhaps even forge a common political identity, just as nation-states managed to turn "peasants into Frenchmen" in the nineteenth century (Weber 1976). Particularly important in this respect are political parties, which from the mid-nineteenth century on were responsible for mobilizing citizens and for creating social as well as political bonds within regionally divided European nation-states (Caramani 2004). However, the institutionalization of integration has had limited unifying effects. Expanding the European Parliament's competences has notably failed to increase turnout or produce a merger of national parties into EU-wide parties. Attempts to propound an EU identity in the form of a flag and anthem are yet to produce a serious rival to national patriotism with only 10 percent of EU citizens identifying themselves primarily as European (Fligstein 2008). In this context, the debate about Europe's readiness for federalism appears blocked between naysayers and those who argue that a bold leap forward in integration could ultimately create a new political bond not yet present.

integration first proceeded along economic lines rather than as full political union. Nonetheless, successive treaty reforms have continued to advance the supranational element, which takes the EU closer to federalism.

9.2   Confederalism

Given the uncertainty over what an EU federation might actually look like and the lack of popular support for such a radical transformation, it is not surprising that the confederal model is sometimes seen as a better template for integration. Applying this model to the EU is a question of how far supranationalism should be rolled back and replaced with intergovernmentalism. The principal assumption behind the confederal model is that national politicians are more accountable and that integration needs to respect the wishes of majorities within the member states. The institutional debate about applying this model is thus about how to reconfigure decision-making within the EU so as to give more voice to national democratic structures and protect national policy autonomy. Ultimately, supporters of this model – which Charles de Gaulle used to refer to as a **Europe of nations** – wish to ensure that integration does not lead to the replacement of national identity and national politics.

A confederation is a union of equal, sovereign states (each already recognized by other states) that have formed a common government for limited purposes, namely to achieve what cannot be undertaken alone (Forsyth 1981). Thus a confederation is a treaty-based union that concedes few powers to the center for the sake of the liberty of the constituent units, which are in principle free to secede. Historically, the chief reason for establishing a confederation is defensive: different units uniting for the sake of better securing their territorial authority. However, this is a rare form of political organization, and one accompanied by an important structural weakness (see Box 9.2).

Box 9.2   Key Concept: The Structural Weakness of Confederation

The most notable examples of confederation are associations of states for the purpose of self-defense. Such associations include the United Provinces of the Netherlands (1579–1795), the Swiss Confederation (1291–1848), and the US under the Articles of Confederation (1781–1789). A crucial difference between a confederation and a federation is that, even though both require a central political authority, in a confederation this authority binds the states only as collective actors. That is, confederalism consists of a union of states, whereas federalism is both a union of states and a community of individuals. So in the former compliance with the authority of the confederation is the responsibility of the territorial unit; conversely, a federation has direct authority over the citizens, for instance to guarantee certain individual rights through its own courts or to collect taxes through its own agents. This contrast was captured by Alexander Hamilton, one of the authors of the *Federalist*, a set of pamphlets used to support the replacement of the US Articles of Confederation by the Federal Constitution drafted in Philadelphia in 1787–1788. In *Federalist*, 15, Hamilton argued that the "characteristic difference between a league [confederation] and a [federal] government" is the fact that "the authority of the Union [must extend] to the persons of the citizens" (Hamilton, Jay, and Madison 2003, 68). A confederation is thus less constraining on unit sovereignty, since it has no direct means of enforcing compliance with its rules and decisions. This is a huge structural problem: confederations are dependent on the goodwill of the territorial units to execute policies and to raise money. As a result, there are few lasting examples of confederalism (Forsyth 1981).

Returning to the EU, it is important to note its existing confederal characteristics before examining why some argue that these need to be extended. As the EU is a treaty-based system, its member states remain sovereign – they notably have their own diplomatic relations with other states – and are free to leave the EU at any time. This right is encapsulated in the withdrawal clause (see Chapter 6, Glossary) contained in the Lisbon Treaty. Moreover, the voluntary compliance of member states is essential on matters such as raising revenue or sticking to the EU's common foreign policy stance; the EU has no coercive authority – no army or federal marshals – to oblige member states to meet such commitments. Intergovernmental decision-making policy areas like taxation, enlargement, treaty reform, and foreign policy are also in keeping with a confederal model, as they require unanimous agreement. This prevents countries from being obliged to agree to a policy they are against, and in this way they protect their sovereignty and freedom of action.

Unanimity is thus a key part of the debate over EU confederalism. National vetoes are associated not only with the preservation of sovereignty but also with accountability to citizens. This is because, in theory, vetoes empower national governments to respect the preferences of citizens when they oppose a certain EU policy, for instance an increase in EU financial contributions. At the same time the unanimity rule establishes clear lines of political responsibility when governments fail to follow their citizens' preferences: they can be voted out of office, thereby warning the following government not to stray from what citizens desire on this policy issue.

But under the OLP, which is based on QMV in the Council and on co-decision with the Parliament, national governments find it hard to control the content of legislation when the Commission and the Parliament agree on legislation (Tsebelis and Garrett 2000). In this case governments can rightly claim that it is not their fault that legislation passes against their initial preferences. Here sanctioning a national government because it deviates from voters' preferences becomes a weak mechanism for preventing unwelcome EU legislation. This is because a different government would face exactly the same institutionalized mechanism for generating a consensus position; under the OLP a single government cannot formally block legislation or reject amendments proposed by the Parliament. Hence a change of national government will not help citizens see their preferences met. From a confederal perspective the OLP is therefore problematic for accountability. It encourages cooperation between governments across the EU – which is necessary for effective decision-making – but comes at the expense of decreasing national governments' responsiveness to their citizens' preferences.

The OLP mechanism thus dilutes national influence over legislative outcomes. This helps explain why the extension of QMV has always been strongly criticized by defenders of national sovereignty. De Gaulle's actions in the 1965 empty chair crisis, where he withdrew French participation in the Council (see Section 2.5), were precisely a protest against the introduction of QMV. Indeed in this period, prior to QMV becoming the norm for decision-making, confederalism was a genuine rival model for integration (Parsons 2003). In 1961 de Gaulle proposed a plan for a "Union of the European Peoples" without supranational institutions. Known as the Fouchet Plan, this proposal for a purely intergovernmental approach to integration was rejected by the other EEC member states. It foundered because small states wished to retain a supranational element, notably the Commission, in order to monitor treaty compliance. This watchdog role is essential to preventing large states from breaking the rules with impunity (see Section 4.4).

However, even under QMV there is an informal tendency within the Council to actually rely on unanimous decision-making rather than to have divisive votes. This tendency is known as the "culture of consensus" (Heisenberg 2005), which seeks to find a common position acceptable to all national governments. Between 2009 and 2012, for example, 65 percent of the Council decisions taken in areas where QMV applies (not taxation or foreign policy) were adopted unanimously (Votewatch Europe 2012). Nevertheless, many governments remain reluctant to move completely to QMV for all Council decision-making. This is demonstrated by the retention of unanimity for taxation and foreign policy in treaty negotiations. For instance, for British Prime Minister Tony Blair, retention of the national veto in these two policy areas constituted "red lines" not to be crossed during negotiations for the Lisbon Treaty in 2007.

But, although QMV is the mainstay of the OLP, the Lisbon Treaty did introduce a more confederal element: the yellow and orange card procedures for monitoring subsidiarity (see Section 4.2). The latter provision allows a majority of national parliaments (the so-called orange card warning procedure) to force a review of a policy proposed by the European Commission. This is confederal in inspiration, because it provides national legislatures, which have a direct connection with national electorates, and these have the ability to challenge the decisions taken under the OLP. Although not the equivalent of a national veto, the orange card does enable national political mobilization across member states in order to challenge a law enacted via supranational decision-making. In practice, however, it is hard for parliaments to mobilize together to trigger this warning procedure, as there are few formal links between national parliaments and parliamentarians.

9.2.1 Proposals for more confederalism in the EU

While these existing confederal features give some reassurance to opponents of federalism, there are proposals for more radical change, designed to protect national sovereignty and the accountability it can bring. Particularly potent is the suggestion to return the European Parliament to its original unelected, consultative role. This idea is intended to repatriate power back to the national governments acting in the Council, thereby minimizing the supranational role of the European Parliament (Gillingham 2006). Reducing the powers of the Parliament would prevent it from moving legislation away from the initial preferences of national governments, as it currently does under co-decision (Tsebelis and Garrett 2000). This could thus enhance the accountability bond between citizens and policy-making, on the assumption that the majority opinion in the European Parliament is more likely than that in the Council to diverge from the preferences of a national electorate. Of course, MEPs are expressing the wishes of their electorate and can be voted out of office for their performance, but confederal-minded opponents of the European Parliament argue that this is too tenuous a link. They point to low voter turnout in European elections (a topic discussed in detail in Section 10.2) as an indicator that the Parliament cannot be trusted to protect what citizens really wish. In this context, the confederalist argument is that governments, which remain more sensitive to citizens' preferences, should be solely responsible for EU legislation (Gillingham 2006).

Another confederal proposal is to reduce the scale of the EU by reducing its competences, especially in agricultural, justice, social policy, and foreign affairs. This is in line with the traditional understanding of a confederation as a union of states dedicated only to limited purposes, all other powers being reserved for the territorial units. Majone (2005), for instance, argues that the growth in EU competences distracts from the EU's major task: economic regulation for the single market. The latter constitutes the *raison d'être* of confederally based integration, because it is something that all member states can agree on and that requires the delegation of certain powers to common institutions.

However, a purely confederal model of integration is difficult to reconcile with the EU's principal supranational institutions: the Commission and the Court of Justice. Confederalism is largely incompatible with these institutions because they are not designed to be subject to direct control by member states. Instead they are trustee institutions with certain competences entrusted to them – competences to act in the general interest (see Section 6.2). So, without the Commission, it is hard to imagine where policy inputs could come from. After all, the Council of the EU is a political decision-making body without the capacity or neutrality for administering policies or for investigating member state compliance.

Voluntary compliance of member states with EU legislation is highly dependent on member states' knowing that the Commission has the ability to identify and act upon infringements of EU law. By extension, the Court of Justice's ability not only to give authoritative interpretations of EU law but also to enforce it via national courts is the ultimate guarantee that treaty commitments will be respected. This allows the EU system to work even in the absence of reciprocity or enforcement via tit-for-tat punishments between member states (see Section 6.2). In the absence of a supranational watchdog and enforcement mechanism, the legal architecture underpinning the successful operation of the single market would rest on good faith alone. Consequently, an EU based purely on confederalism would be very different from the supranational architecture in place today. Yet, alongside providing a competing model of integration, confederalist arguments continue to serve as justification for keeping national governments and parliaments at the heart of EU decision-making.

9.3   The Networked Governance Model

Federalism and confederalism both presuppose the need for political finality, which represents the desire for an institutional endpoint to integration in place of a constant evolution of rules and institutions. For federalism, the endpoint is complete political union, while confederalism implies keeping national sovereignty as something that integration must never abolish. By contrast, the networked governance model for uniting Europe suggests that adopting the EU system of bringing together national and supranational actors is preferable to choosing one over the other. Although generally supportive of greater integration, this model concludes that transforming the EU into a fully federal state would actually negate some of the benefits of mixing and distributing cooperation among different kinds of actors.

From the perspective of networked governance, state sovereignty – whether in the form of federalism or confederalism – is too hierarchical and inappropriate for a post-sovereign era. This post-sovereign condition is characterized by the disaggregation of power across multiple actors with overlapping authority (Slaughter 2004). For instance, a policy issue such as financial regulation in Europe cannot be addressed by a single country; a combination of national and EU law-makers – as well as regulatory agencies at both levels, input from central bank governors, and private sector actors – are required to make sound financial regulation. This context calls for a more fluid system of governance, which cannot be reduced to an institutional model based on state sovereignty.

Hence the logic behind government networks is that, compared to sticking with purely national institutions, transnational networks of lawyers, bureaucrats, and politicians can provide better policy-making and accountability when addressing complex policy issues. In fact the EU's ability to create such linkages is considered a template for how global governance should function to solve problems that no single state can address (Slaughter 2004). From this perspective, the correct model for the EU is not one based on the nation-state (federalism or confederalism), but rather one that recognizes the success of the EU in coordinating different actors across jurisdictions. Political finality is thus a misplaced priority, since both federalism and confederalism seek to prioritize one level of government over the other. This goes against the primary objective of networked governance, which is to bring together different decision-making actors, public and private. Another phrase to describe this system is **multilevel governance**: such governance is based on connecting, at the local, national, and supranational level, political authority that is fragmented across multiple private and public actors (Hooghe and Marks 2001).

As integration has progressed, the EU has brought together national and supranational judges, bureaucrats, and politicians on the basis of permanent, institutionalized dialogue and exchange (Alter 1998). Supranational judges in the CJEU are in constant dialogue with national judges over the interpretation of EU law. This is because national courts not only have the power to refer cases to the CJEU but also have to apply EU law whenever it clashes with national legislation. Similarly, bureaucrats in the European Commission charged with preparing and administering EU policies and with monitoring national compliance with EU rules are reliant on cooperation with national administrations for data, policy implementation, and even policy ideas. Finally, national politicians now have to debate and coordinate policies in most areas alongside their EU counterparts while also accepting the scrutiny of the Commission and of MEPs. Overall, therefore, networked governance in the EU provides numerous interactions between actors, which in turn ensures checks and balances. As a result, countries are prevented from taking unilateral decisions that hurt their fellow member states, with the result that member states are guided toward consensual policy-making.

Equally importantly, these networks allow for a non-hierarchical structure of governance, which allows for policy to be made by consent rather than command. As defined by a leading scholar, networked governance means that decision-makers are "dependent upon the cooperation and joint resource mobilization of policy actors outside their hierarchical control" (Börzel 1998, 260). Devoid of dominant centralized political actors, networked governance can thus make room for respecting local differences and can create a better environment for policy learning (Jordan and Schout 2006). A case in point is the EU's **Lisbon Strategy**, which was based on the idea of learning policy by exchanging information on best practices – a system labeled "the open method of coordination" (see Box 9.3). This system relies on **soft law** – non-binding benchmarks for policy objectives – and not on hard law – binding rules. Here the advantage is that soft law respects the autonomy of local decision-makers, empowering them to find the most appropriate solutions and to implement them at their own pace, without being confronted with top-down orders.

Box 9.3   Case Study: Open Method of Coordination

The open method of coordination (OMC) was officially announced at the Lisbon Summit in 2000. The idea behind OMC is to generate policy change in areas where member states are reluctant to pass binding legislation overseen by supranational institutions. Thus OMC is used in employment, social inclusion, and pensions policy as part of the Lisbon Strategy for improving growth and employment in the EU. It involves using what is known as "soft law" – that is, non-binding targets and recommendations about best practices – rather than the traditional EU method of hard law – which goes through legislation proposed by the Commission and then negotiated with the Council and the Parliament. Targets such as higher employment rates for seniors, or pensions reforms designed to encourage more individual savings, are set by the Council alone, and the member states' performance is reviewed by this same body. There is thus no formal legal obligation to meet these targets and the Commission's role is minimized, unlike under OLP. National politicians and officials exchange policy information and review different national practices to encourage the transfer of best practices. Instead of the normal EU compliance mechanism, it is peer pressure to match the best performing countries' practices that is intended to stimulate policy change. This model has allowed countries to retain certain policy competences, but its results have been questioned, especially the grandiose aim of making the EU the "most competitive knowledge economy in the world" (Lisbon European Council 2000). Critics claim that OMC networks have created new bureaucratic procedures, have produced more meetings than results, and have not caused policy change in politically sensitive areas such as pensions policy (Featherstone 2005). Indeed some economists suggest that policy change is more likely to occur simply through competition for outside investment between countries and regions rather than through complex bureaucratic procedures.

In addition, the networked governance model appears to have certain robust safeguards in order to ensure democratic accountability. For a start, the entire network of EU governance as constructed under OLP is subject to a strict rule of law apparatus. The CJEU not only oversees member state compliance but also determines whether EU institutions overstep their authority. Regulatory networks centered on the Commission's single market legislation are legally obliged to consult with the affected parties, to provide impact assessments, and to obtain expert advice. Hence this model can provide for better policy deliberation and experimentation by comparison with ordinary legislation enacted through a parliament made up of political representatives (Cohen and Sabel 1997). The other benefit is that, when regulation is delegated to the Commission, policy-making is protected from the drawbacks of democracy: fickle voters and the politicians' short-term horizons. Institutionalized networks of governance actors in key areas such as monetary policy, banking, or competition regulation can thus be freed from short-term political pressures (for instance pandering to groups or lobbies for the sake of re-election), so as to provide the long-term planning necessary for economic growth (Majone 2001). Consequently, it has been argued that participating in these networks of international law and policy experts can enhance the protection of individual rights as well as the quality of policy-making (Keohane, Macedo, and Moravcsik 2009). In this sense government networks established by the EU can be said to constitute "democracy-enhancing multilateralism" (Keohane et al. 2009).

9.3.1   Concerns about legitimacy and effectiveness

However, the networked governance principle is based on an administrative rather than political model of decision-making. This means that it is more concerned with decision-making rules and legal procedures for coordinating policy actors than with sovereignty (that is, with who enforces the rules) and with political legitimacy (that is, with who has the right to make decisions). Traditionally, the principle of state sovereignty secures clarity as to how the rules will be enforced – via the state's ability to use coercion or the threat thereof to execute the law. Sovereignty also ensures clarity as to the legitimacy of decision-making, since sovereignty is exercised in the name of a specific people via its elected representatives. Networked governance does not replicate this model. A state's enforcement capacities and its elected representatives are considered incapable of solving complex contemporary policy problems alone, which means that sovereignty is outdated. Questions can thus be asked of this model regarding policy effectiveness in the absence of sovereign powers of enforcement. Additionally, there is an issue of how far policy outputs produced in this way can remain responsive to citizens' preferences as articulated in elections and party government.

In terms of effectiveness, the non-hierarchical foundation of networked governance can affect both binding (hard law) and non-binding (soft law) policies. The dispute over applying the Stability and Growth Pact (SGP) sanctions to Germany and France in 2004 (see Section 5.2) illustrates even the limitations of hard law under networked governance. In this case the formal rules, enforceable through fines set by the Court of Justice, were set aside as two powerful states simply refused to be bound by the terms of the

SGP. This scuppered the enforcement of the mechanism designed to keep government debts from undermining the euro, which is why this episode is seen as a key factor in the subsequent sovereign debt crisis (see Chapter 12). Yet, as a non-state lacking sovereignty and subject to the voluntary consent of participating national governments, the EU had to accommodate this change of heart from two of the EU's most powerful countries. In this context networked governance can, in extreme cases, be trumped by national sovereignty.

Similarly, the Lisbon Strategy, relying on OMC (see Box 9.3), has not proved very successful in transforming member states' economies (Hix and Høyland 2011, 202). This non-binding system of policy learning by exchanging information on best practices lacks a supranational enforcement mechanism, which means that it cannot compel structural reform in policy areas such as employment law or social security. Consequently, the networked governance model is dependent on the goodwill of national governments for hard law implementation, while soft law initiatives have a limited ability to promote far-reaching policy change among reluctant governments.

These two examples also point to the legitimacy problem bedeviling networked governance. To legitimize policy outputs, this system relies on the rule of law and on policy deliberation among interested parties – not on elections (Keohane et al. 2009). In this context national governments can use their status as elected representatives to challenge particularly unwelcome hard law, just as France and Germany did regarding the SGP in 2004. Lacking electoral legitimacy, institutions such as the Commission, or global governance actors such as the World Trade Organization or the International Monetary Fund are labeled "technocratic," in other words policy experts removed from political pressures. Rule by these technocrats – **technocracy** – is contested by governments, opposition parties, and NGOs when technocratic decisions clash with national public opinion (see Chapter 10 for how this relates to the question of how democratic the EU is). Consequently, networked governance is a model for integration that works best as long as national governments comply with their commitments and citizens accept the decisions taken on their behalf.

9.4   The Differentiated Integration Model

The fourth and final model for how the EU should be organized is one based on member states voluntarily choosing their own level of involvement in the EU system. This model is sometimes referred to as Europe *à la carte* because it implies countries choosing from a menu of options for how far to integrate. Overall, differentiated integration is seen as a way of reconciling the need to find policy solutions with the need for democracy as practised through national structures. This model assumes that national politics is the best forum for deciding whether and how to participate in EU policies. Here the reasoning is that the democratic connection between citizens and EU policy outputs is largely indirect and that public participation is less active at the EU level than at the national level. Consequently, differentiated integration rests on allowing national governments the freedom to choose on what terms to integrate, taking account of the democratically expressed preferences of their voters. This stands in contrast to accepting the culture of consensus, whereby member states are prodded into greater integration thanks to supranational decision-making structures.

Another name for this model of integration is **variable geometry**, which indicates the existence of different levels of participation in EU policies. In many ways, this model is actually a description of the EU today. Some countries have refused to participate in the euro (Denmark, Sweden, the United Kingdom); others have not joined Schengen (Ireland and the United Kingdom); some have also opted out of the legal application of the Charter of Fundamental Rights (the United Kingdom, the Czech Republic), while Denmark has opted out of the Common Security and Defence Policy, which means that it does not participate in the European Defence Agency (see Section 8.1). There are also certain legal exemptions inserted into the treaties in order to protect national autonomy in particularly sensitive matters. These exemptions include the Maastricht Treaty amendment, which protects Ireland's right to legislate against abortion, the Danish accession treaty's provision prohibiting non-Danish residents from purchasing second homes, and Sweden's retention of a state-run monopoly for selling alcohol.

Indeed it is even possible to argue that countries closely associated with the EU, namely Norway and Switzerland, have in fact chosen a differentiated level of EU membership, which makes them quasi-members of the EU. The compromise of quasi-membership has been adopted because a majority of citizens in both countries were unconvinced about the need to integrate fully into the EU. These citizens' preference has been for limited integration, with preservation of national autonomy – especially in foreign and monetary policy. Norwegian voters rejected the chance to join the EEC in a 1972 referendum, and in 1994 a referendum on joining the EU also failed; Swiss citizens have never been asked to vote on EU membership because already in 1992 they rejected a move to join the looser European Economic Area (EEA), aimed at creating a single market area beyond the EU. Norway, however, has joined the EEA and has adopted all the single market legislation passed by the EU, including the working time directive – despite not participating in the decision-making behind these rules. It has also joined Schengen and even participates on an *ad hoc* basis in the EU's Common Foreign and Security Policy (Eliassen and Sitter 2004). For its part, Switzerland has used a series of bilateral treaties to introduce single market legislation, thereby adopting the EU's four fundamental freedoms. Switzerland is also a member of Schengen and even gave €635 million to help post-2004 accession countries (Kriesi and Trechsel 2008). The net result is that the free movement of goods, services, capital, and trade extends to both Switzerland and Norway, while their citizens and firms have the same reciprocal privileges throughout the EU.

Existing differentiated integration, or variable geometry, has developed in a piecemeal fashion, sometimes on the basis of resorting to national referendums when governments were uncertain about the preferences of their citizens for greater integration. Swedish and Danish citizens, for instance, voted in a referendum against joining the euro, while British politicians have promised not to join the single currency without a national referendum. In some instances, however, policy opt-outs that seemingly indicate differentiated integration are in reality symbolic acts rather than acts of substance. For example, the Danish currency (Danish *krone*) is pegged to the euro, which means that the central bank intervenes to follow the movement of the euro: an implicit mimicry of

EU monetary policy. Similarly, the United Kingdom's opt-out from the Charter of Fundamental Rights in the application of EU legislation has not been tested in the CJEU, which will have the final word on whether this provision can stand – since the CJEU is the interpreter of the treaties. As a result, it is not clear how far *ad hoc* opt-outs preserve national autonomy, especially since governments and their officials pursue compensatory diplomatic engagement to retain influence in policy areas where they have formally opted out (Adler-Nissen 2011).

9.4.1   Differentiation to allow some countries to integrate more

Regardless of the sometimes symbolic element of differentiation, this model is not necessarily about setting limits to integration. Rather it also opens a way for a core set of EU countries to develop new policies together, while allowing other member states to remain part of the single market system. Differentiation can thus facilitate further integration, beyond what consensus among the whole 28 member states otherwise permits, generating policy experimentation that may eventually become the EU norm. The best example of such an initiative is the way in which Schengen started outside the EEC framework before becoming incorporated in the normal EU legal system (see Section 5.5).

The Lisbon Treaty contains legal provisions that make more differentiation possible by allowing certain countries to experiment with more shared policy-making. This process is known as **enhanced cooperation**: a policy initiative proposed by a third of member states in an area that is not part of exclusive EU competences and that does not represent an extension of the EU's overall legal powers. Enhanced cooperation can be used in cases where legislation cannot pass under OLP for lack of a qualified majority, or when Council members are reluctant to force a formal vote and break with the culture of consensus.

Except in foreign policy, the process of enhanced cooperation begins with a proposal from the Commission, which then requires adoption by one third of the member states. Non-participating member states are free to join at a later stage, while the decision to use this procedure requires the consent of the European Parliament. A notable example of enhanced cooperation is the 2013 proposal for a Financial Transaction Tax. Originally the Commission intended that this plan – which aims to tax equity and debt transactions in order to raise revenue and to curb speculation – apply to the entire EU. However, given the strong objections of certain governments, it soon became obvious that there was no way of reaching a qualified majority in the Council. In response, 11 countries requested the Commission to draw up plans to use enhanced cooperation to create a tax such as it would apply only to those 11 participating countries.

Traditionally the European Commission has been wary about differentiated integration, for fear of losing its role as the overseer and initiator of EU policies. The Commission wants to ensure a common legal space, so that policies are made in citizens' best interests. This is why, everywhere except in foreign policy, the Commission has to give its green light to the process. Another legal hurdle for extending differentiation within the EU is the fact that groups of member states may not make policies that discriminate against other EU citizens (Piris 2011). Most importantly, then, enhanced cooperation cannot occur at the expense of the four fundamental freedoms. So a core set of countries cannot use enhanced cooperation to prevent the free movement of labor from other member states or to penalize firms from other EU countries. Nevertheless, differentiated integration could be used for significant supranational economic integration, for instance by coordinating personal and corporate tax rates across a set of countries.

One proposal to make differentiated integration more widespread consists of having citizens across member states vote in a national referendum to indicate a preference for a limited system of integration, or else for a federal system (Schmitter 2000, 120–123). Through this choice, member states could position themselves either as participants in full supranational integration or as members of a looser system, one based only on economic integration. In this way there would be a formal legal and political division between two parallel degrees of integration.

Integration at two or even several speeds is something that has also been proposed as a solution to the quandary of further EU enlargement. Leaders such as the then French President Nicolas Sarkozy and the German Chancellor Angela Merkel proposed offering some form of associate membership to Turkey rather than full EU member-ship. Associate status is designed to limit the possible impact of Turkish accession on EU decision-making, notably by excluding Turkey – on course to have a larger popula-tion than Germany – from playing a leading role in EU decision-making. The idea is highly controversial, because enlargement has hitherto been based on equal mem-bership rights, a promise that helps incentivize candidate countries to implement far-reaching policy change in order to meet the conditions for accession. Formally differentiating types of EU membership would thus constitute crossing a Rubicon, although this would be in keeping with citizens' preferences, as only 34 percent of EU citizens support accepting Turkey as a full EU member state (Gerhards and Hans 2011; see Section 5.6).

Within the set of existing EU policies, further differentiation besides enhanced coop-eration is very difficult to achieve, as countries cannot simply refuse to accept legislation after it has been formulated. Negotiating an opt-out is only possible during treaty reform, not after the passage of legislation. Thus it is not feasible to expect that compe-tences can be returned to the national level, for the sake of differentiation, in the course of ordinary EU policy-making. One possible exception is the option, created by the Lisbon Treaty's formal procedure, for a country to leave the EU. In this instance, exiting the EU could pave the way for renegotiated quasi-membership for a country willing to take this very bold decision – something that none has ever tried to do. However, in 2013 British Prime Minister Cameron announced his intention of re-negotiating the UK's relationship with the EU if he were to be re-elected in the 2015 national parlia-mentary election – and then of subjecting this deal to an "in or out" referendum on staying in the EU. This proposal owes much to domestic party politics in a member state with a long-standing ambivalence toward integration (see Box 3.2). Nevertheless, more differentiation could occur as a result of a skeptical national political attitude to the current functioning of integration.

9.5 Concluding Summary

This chapter has examined four possible models for how the EU should be organized. These models constitute different visions of how to render policy-making beyond the nation-state efficient and democratic. Treaty reform, dealing with both institutional change and proposed transfers of competences from member states, takes place against this background of different visions for uniting Europe. The very possibility of taking the EU in a new direction exists because of the lack of political finality – that is, the absence of a fixed endpoint to integration. Two contrasting models of integration seek to establish political finality by moving integration toward either full federation or a looser confederal system. Conversely, two other models, networked governance and differentiated integration, seek in separate ways to build on the perceived strengths that come from the absence of political finality.

The ever changing treaty architecture contains elements of both federalism and confederalism. Supranationalism, which entails federal features, is a necessary condition of economic integration, and it is also institutionally too entrenched to be replaced by a purely confederal or intergovernmental system. Yet there are good arguments for keeping certain national prerogatives, especially because national governments remain more connected to citizens' inputs than to EU-level decision-making. At the same time, federalists are right to suggest that only full federalism can allow the EU to tackle the gamut of policy issues that matter to citizens, such as social regulation or a more effective foreign policy. However, member states are not only too jealous of their sovereignty – especially over tax and foreign relations – but also too vital as administrative actors to become territorial sub-units in a fully federal and sovereign EU.

The two models not preoccupied with political finality, networked governance and differentiated integration, reflect the messy reality of the EU's mixture of supranationalism and intergovernmentalism. They also seek to highlight positive features of this system from a democratic and efficiency perspective that is based, respectively, on the ability to coordinate policies without hierarchy and on the ability to integrate only as far as national electorates desire. Neither model is, however, fully satisfactory in terms of delivering democratic and efficient decision-making. Networked governance faces issues of policy effectiveness in the absence of sovereignty and does not allocate a significant role for citizen inputs. Differentiated integration is an *ad hoc* procedure, as already reflected in the way the EU system incorporates opt-outs and other guarantees of national autonomy that perhaps cannot be extended much further. The absence of a perfect model for integration thus means that citizens and politicians will continue to argue about how the EU system should be organized.

Guide to Further Reading

Gillingham, John. 2006. *Design for a New Europe*. Cambridge: Cambridge University Press.
A controversial critique of the existing EU system, which claims that the system needs fundamental institutional reform in order to be effective and democratic.

Glencross, A., and A. Trechsel, eds. 2010. *EU Federalism and Constitutionalism: The Legacy of Altiero Spinelli*. Lanham, MD: Lexington Books.

Comprehensive and critical survey of how the EU's constitutional system has developed and of the role played by federalism in this process.

Piris, J.-C. 2011. *The Future of Europe: Towards a Two-Speed EU?* Cambridge: Cambridge University Press.

A powerful argument for why differentiated integration, with a core of pioneer countries pooling more sovereignty, is the best model for the EU's future.

Slaughter, A.-M. 2004. *A New World Order*. Princeton, NJ: Princeton University Press.

A study of how agents of the state can be coordinated across national borders in a non-hierarchical fashion; has many examples based on EU practices.

Discussion Questions

1 What are the strengths of the federal model of integration and what are its weaknesses?
2 What are the remaining confederal features of the EU, and what do they mean for accountability and policy effectiveness?
3 What practices exemplify networked governance in the EU? Is this model of non-hierarchical policy coordination better than one based on political finality?
4 Which political actors favor enhanced cooperation? What are the downsides of using this procedure?
5 Is the EU's lack of political finality a good or a bad thing?

Web Resources

This book is supported by a companion website, which can be found at www.wiley.com/go/glencross. There you will find a list of the web links referred to in this chapter wherever you see a "Web" icon in the page margins. In addition, you will find a list of further relevant online resources such as websites for EU institutions, political groups, archives, and think tanks, information on studying abroad, and biographies of key figures. You will also find self-assessment tools in the form of flashcards and independent study questions developed specifically for this chapter.

Glossary

Bicameral
"With two chambers" or (more literally) "double-chambered," with reference to the principle of having two legislative chambers checking each other. Federal bicameralism entails having one chamber directly elected by citizens and another made up of representatives of the territorial units.

Differentiated integration

Expression describing the process whereby the EU allows for different levels of member state participation across policy areas. It implies that different degrees of European integration are available to countries depending on national preferences.

Enhanced cooperation

Legal phrase contained in the Lisbon Treaty, where it designates a core group of member states developing together policies that do not become the law for all the other member states. Such policies require approval from a third of the member states as well as from the Parliament, and they should not harm the fundamental freedoms of other EU citizens.

Europe of nations

This is how French President Charles de Gaulle referred to a confederal model of integration based on respect for national identity and sovereignty. This model stands in opposition to supranationalism or federalism.

Networked governance

Theory of how the EU and other international organizations function by bringing together different levels of government as well as other actors – such as experts and private firms. Some consider it to have accountability and effectiveness benefits, although these advantages are contested by others.

Lisbon Strategy

Policy initiative to use the open method of coordination to achieve socio-economic reform for the sake of making the EU economy more competitive internationally. Named after a 2000 European Council summit in Lisbon.

Multilevel governance

Concept used to describe the EU system as the outcome of a collaboration between political actors at different levels of government. It captures the fact the EU's mode of governing is based on multiple forms of political authority rather than on the hierarchical concept of sovereignty.

Open method of coordination (OMC)

Soft law mechanism for stimulating policy change at the national level without conferring binding competences upon the EU. Used since 2000 to develop the Lisbon Strategy.

Political finality

Phrase used to refer to what the EU will or should eventually become as a political system. Repeated treaty reform suggests that the EU system is yet to reach political finality, although sometimes this is considered a good thing.

Soft law

A procedure for inducing policy change through best practices, expert advice, and benchmarking; none of these are legally binding – unlike hard law, which is enforced through courts. The EU's open method of coordination, used in certain policy areas where member states are reluctant to transfer competences, relies on soft law.

Technocracy

Rule by technocrats – that is, unelected experts who make policy decisions in the best interest of others. Used sometimes as a pejorative label for the Commission, to distinguish it from an elected government.

Variable geometry

Another way of referring to differentiated integration.

References

Adler-Nissen, Rebecca. 2011. "Opting out of an Ever Closer Union: The Integration Doxa and the Management of Sovereignty." *West European Politics*, 34: 1092–1113. DOI: 10.1080/01402382.2011.591102

Alter, Karen. 1998. "Who Are the 'Masters of the Treaty'? European Governments and the European Court of Justice." *International Organization*, 52: 121–147. DOI: 10.1162/002081898550572

Börzel, Tanja. 1998. "Organising Babylon: On the Different Conceptions of Policy Networks." *Public Administration*, 76: 253–273. DOI: 10.1111/1467-9299.00100

Bogdanor, Vernon. 2003. "Federalism and the Nature of the European Union." In Kalypso Nicolaïdis and Stephen Weatherill, eds., *Whose Europe? National Models and the Constitution of the EU*, 49–61. Papers of a Multi-Disciplinary Conference held at Oxford University. Available at http://denning.law.ox.ac.uk/iecl/pdfs/whoseeurope.pdf (accessed August 31, 2012).

Burgess, Michael. 2000. *Federalism and European Union: The Building of Europe, 1950–2000*. London: Routledge.

Caramani, Daniele. 2004. *The Nationalization of Politics: The Formation of National Electorates and Party Systems in Western Europe*. Cambridge: Cambridge University Press.

Cohen, Joshua, and Charles Sabel. 1997. "Directly Deliberative Polyarchy." *European Law Journal*, 3: 313–342. DOI: 10.1111/1468-0386.00034

Eliassen, Kjell, and Nick Sitter. 2003. "Ever Closer Cooperation? The Limits of the 'Norwegian Method' of European Integration." *Scandinavian Political Studies*, 26: 125–144. DOI: 10.1111/1467-9477.00082

Fabbrini, Sergio. 2005. "Madison in Brussels: The EU and the USA as Compound Democracies." *European Political Science*, 4: 188–198. DOI: 10.1057/palgrave.eps.2210023

Featherstone, Kevin. 2005. "Soft Co-ordination Meets 'Hard' Politics: The EU and Pension Reform in Greece." *Journal of European Public Policy*, 12: 733–750. DOI: 10.1080/13501760500160631

Fischer, Joschka. 2000. "From Confederacy to Federation: Thoughts on the Finality of European Integration." In Christian Joerges, Yves Mény, and Joseph H. H. Weiler, eds., *What Kind of Constitution for What Kind of Policy: Responses to Joschka Fischer*, 19–30. Florence: European University Institute.

Fligstein, Neil. 2008. *Euroclash: The EU, European Identity, and the Future of Europe*. Oxford: Oxford University Press.

Forsyth, Murray. 1981. *Unions of States: The Theory and Practice of Confederation*. Leicester: Leicester University Press.

Gerhards, Jürgen, and Silke Hans. 2011. "Why Not Turkey? Attitudes towards Turkish Membership in the EU among Citizens in 27 European Countries." *Journal of Common Market Studies*, 49: 741–766. DOI: 10.1111/j.1468-5965.2010.02155.x

Gillingham, John. 2006. *Design for a New Europe*. Cambridge: Cambridge University Press.

Hamilton, Alexander, John Jay, and James Madison. 2003. *The Federalist with Letters of Brutus*. Cambridge: Cambridge University Press.

Heisenberg, Dorothee. 2005. "The Institution of 'Consensus' in the European Union: Formal versus Informal Decision-Making in the Council." *European Journal of Political Research*, 44: 65–90. DOI: 10.1111/j.1475-6765.2005.00219.x

Hix, Simon, and Bjørn Høyland. 2011. *The Political System of the European Union*. Basingstoke: Palgrave.

Hooghe, Liesbet, and Gary Marks. 2001. *Multi-Level Governance and European Integration*. Oxford: Rowman & Littlefield.

Jordan, Andrew, and Adriaan Schout. 2006. *The Coordination of the European Union: Exploring the Capacities for Networked Governance*. Oxford: Oxford University Press.

Keohane, Robert, Stephen Macedo, and Andrew Moravcsik. 2009. "Democracy-Enhancing Multilateralism." *International Organization*, 63: 1–31. DOI:10.1017/S0020818309090018

Kriesi, Hanspeter, and Alexander H. Trechsel. 2008. *The Politics of Switzerland: Continuity and Change in a Consensus Democracy*. Cambridge: Cambridge University Press.

Lisbon European Council. 2000. "Presidency Conclusions." 23rd and 24th March. Available at http://www.europarl.europa.eu/summits/lis1_en.htm (accessed July 20, 2013).

Majone, Giandomenico. 2001. "Two Logics of Delegation: Agency and Fiduciary Relations in EU Governance." *European Union Politics*, 2: 103–121. DOI: 10.1177/1465116501002001005

Majone, Giandomenico. 2005. *Dilemmas of European Integration: The Ambiguities and Pitfalls of Integration by Stealth*. Oxford: Oxford University Press.

Parsons, Craig. 2003. *A Certain Idea of Europe*. New York: Cornell University Press.

Piris, Jean-Claude. 2011. *The Future of Europe: Towards a Two-Speed EU?* Cambridge: Cambridge University Press.

Ponzano, Paolo. 2010. "The 'Spinelli Treaty' of February 1984: The Start of the Process of Constitutionalizing the EU." In Andrew Glencross and Alexander H. Trechsel, eds., *EU Federalism and Constitutionalism: The Legacy of Altiero Spinelli*, 3–10. Lanham, MD: Lexington Books.

Schmitter, Philippe. 2000. *How to Democratize the European Union – And Why Bother?* Lanham, MD: Rowman & Littlefield.

Slaughter, Anne-Marie. 2004. *A New World Order*. Princeton, NJ: Princeton University Press.

Stepan, Alfred. 1999. "Federalism and Democracy: Beyond the US Model." *Journal of Democracy*, 10: 19–34. DOI: 10.1353/jod.1999.0072

Tsebelis, George, and Geoffrey Garrett. 2000. "Legislative Politics in the European Union." *European Union Politics*, 1: 9–36. DOI: 10.1177/1465116500001001002

Votewatch Europe. 2012. "Agreeing to Disagree: The Voting Records of Member States in the Council since 2009." Votewatch Europe Annual Report. Available at http://www.votewatch.eu/blog/wp-content/uploads/2012/07/votewatch-annual-report-july-2012-final-7-july.pdf (accessed July 15, 2013).

Weber, Eugene. 1976. *Peasants into Frenchmen: The Modernization of Rural France, 1870-1914*. Stanford, CA: Stanford University Press.

Part IV

Democracy and Integration

10

Democracy in the European Union

Contents

Learning Objectives

- to identify the differences between majoritarian and non-majoritarian forms of democracy;
- to analyze what the EU's non-majoritarian democracy consists of and what role indirect accountability plays within it;
- to distinguish between arguments for and against the claim that there is a democratic deficit in the EU;
- to analyze the grounds on which the EU is said not to be responsive to its citizens and to assess the validity of this criticism;
- to identify suggestions for how to improve EU democracy and evaluate how feasible they are;
- to evaluate the risks associated with changing democratic accountability in the EU and what this means for whether it will happen.

The Politics of European Integration: Political Union or a House Divided?, First Edition. Andrew Glencross.
© 2014 Andrew Glencross. Published 2014 by Blackwell Publishing Ltd.

10.0   Introduction: More Integration, More Democracy?

The institutional developments surveyed in Part I of this book showed the growth of EU competences, while Parts II and III examined its institutions and debates over its policy outputs respectively. Part IV is all about how democracy fits into the picture. This is vital, because the most controversial aspect of European integration concerns whether its institutions and decision-making are sufficiently democratic. After all, the EU is committed by the treaties to uphold democratic principles at home and abroad. Yet, as the scope of integration has increased over time, there has been a very real worry that democratic accountability has not kept pace with this process.

In principle, the development of EU institutions and the conferring of further competences should be accompanied by the development of new means for making democracy function beyond member states. As Commission President José Manuel Barroso declared in 2012, "more integration demands more democracy" (Barroso 2012). However, the way accountability works in the current EU system differs somewhat from the way democracy functions in most member states. Accountability involves making those who exercise power responsive to the preferences and concerns of those affected by the decisions of the powerful. Democratic accountability is usually associated with majoritarianism, that is, with a government elected by, and responsive to, the majority of people in a certain community. As Section 10.1 explains, this model does not correspond well to the way accountability functions in the EU. The result is that the EU relies on a less majoritarian form of democracy, which means that it is less responsive to majority preferences.

The quality of this non-majoritarian democracy is open to question. For over three decades now, this questioning has taken the form of a debate over whether or not the EU suffers from a **democratic deficit**. There are two opposing viewpoints in this debate, as outlined in Section 10.2. One critique of EU democracy is based on showing that the leadership structure and the policy agenda are not very responsive to citizens' preferences. A major element of this position is the worry that national channels of accountability, for instance referendums, are inadequate means for citizens to have their say on the direction of integration. Another critical perspective on EU democracy is the normative claim that integration reduces the scope of the political alternatives available to citizens who may be dissatisfied with EU policies. This is because alternative directions potentially desired by voters, such as EU-level social–democratic market intervention or else the repatriation (that is, return) of powers to member states, are not practicable under the current system. The alternative perspective is that the current status quo is sufficiently democratic in light of the fact that the EU is not a sovereign state. Supporters of how the EU functions today are satisfied that, given its competences, the EU has an appropriately robust democratic system, including rigorous EU-level checks and balances and, indirectly, checks and balances via national politics.

The heated debate over the quality of EU democracy has not eclipsed the search for possible improvements to the current system. Enhancing democratic accountability involves a variety of possible options. As discussed in Section 10.3, these include measures to make the EU resemble a parliamentary democracy; adding a presidential element via direct election of the Commission president; encouraging **transnational parties** to replace fragmented national ones; and also mechanisms to improve indirect accountability via national political systems. The aim overall is to make the EU more responsive and accountable to citizens' preferences. However, these options entail a certain degree of risk in terms of disrupting the way the EU currently functions. More majoritarianism, as well as more national, and even cross-national political contestation over integration, could well challenge the status quo, something that has made political elites wary of further tinkering with the system. Nevertheless, as the process of integration continues, so will discussion of how to enhance democracy within the EU.

10.1   Democratic Accountability in the EU: Beyond Majoritarianism

The word "democracy" comes from an ancient Greek compound noun meaning "power/ rule of the people." This suggests two fundamental features of democracy: a community that decides together how to rule itself; and one in which every person can participate and have a say in governing. These principles are hard to implement in practice, especially in very large and complex societies where it is simply not possible for everyone to give his or her opinion on each important decision. Instead, modern democracy involves citizens delegating decision-making to parliaments and governments on the basis of elections. Elections reward political parties and politicians who win the most votes, yet this institutionalized form of democracy faces a key dilemma: how much governing power should be given on the basis of an electoral majority?

Central to this question is how far the rule of the people should be the rule of the majority (Bellamy 2007). All constitutional democracies place restrictions on the powers a winning majority can use to govern, in order to protect the rights of those who are not part of the majority. Most importantly, constitutions guarantee fundamental individual rights that no legislation can overturn, thereby limiting what can be done by a government elected by a majority of the people – a **majoritarian democracy**. For instance, a government winning a majority of votes can raise taxes on the rich or can restrict new immigration. Under a constitutional democracy guaranteeing property and citizenship rights, however, a government cannot simply confiscate the property of the rich or expel recent immigrants. Individual rights, which limit the scope of governmental action, are enforced by courts – unelected bodies that apply the constitution rather than following majority preferences.

The EU is no different, in that its decision-making institutions act within the constitutional framework of the treaties, which in turn limit exactly what kind of laws the Council of the EU and the Parliament can adopt. Indeed the EU itself also places fundamental constitutional limits on how member states treat their own citizens. To this end, the treaties contain a **suspension clause** that allows EU member states to withdraw Council voting rights from a government that "seriously and persistently" breaches liberty, democracy, respect for human rights and fundamental freedoms, and the rule of law (Article 7 TEU). It is the work of the EU Agency for Fundamental Rights to give

---

Box 10.1   Key Concept: European Elections as
Second-Order Contests

The first elections to the European Parliament were held in 1979, and since that time scholars have debated whether voters treat these as national or European electoral contests. Reif and Schmitt (1980) coined the phrase "second-order national contests" to describe a situation where national political issues dominated the agenda when electing MEPs. That is, instead of voting on the basis of where they stood on European integration and common European policies, citizens voted according to national issues, notably what they thought of their government. Whereas a first-order election is about the more important task of choosing a national government, the second-order interpretation suggests that European parliamentary elections are an alternative means to express one's opinion on government performance, not on EU business. Another sign that these elections are second-order contests is that turnout has always been roughly 20 percent lower than in national parliamentary elections (Hix and Høyland 2011, 147). In this context there is a significant amount of vote switching (Hix and Marsh 2007), so that national governing parties lose out to opposition and to minor parties (including anti-EU parties). Hence direct elections to an increasingly powerful parliament have not had the result that many expected: bringing together citizens around Europe to express what they want integration to achieve. Survey data suggest that some citizens do vote for MEPs according to parties' EU policies. However, the evidence is that EU issues matter far more in referendums on EU treaties. These "yes" or "no" situations are thus first-order contests about integration rather than about national government performance, as citizens are concerned in particular over whether integration benefits their country (Glencross and Trechsel 2011).

---

an expert opinion on whether this is the case. So far this suspension mechanism has never been used.

However, the significant difference between national governments and policy-making in the EU is that the body proposing legislation, the Commission, is unelected, while the Council of the EU represents governments elected by national electorates. The result is that the only institution representing a true EU-wide majority is the European Parliament. Yet elections for MEPs fail to excite voters even as the powers of this legislature have increased, which is why European parliamentary elections are often described, dismissively, as second-order contests (see Box 10.1 and **second-order elections** in Glossary). Hence the EU does not have a government elected by a popular majority. National and European elections have little direct impact on the composition of the Commission and its legislative agenda. This is because Commissioners are appointed for five years (they cannot be unilaterally recalled by a national government) and are obliged to be independent of national preferences or mandates. Moreover, the use of qualified majority voting (QMV) in the Council means that legislation that gets passed is subject to a super-majoritarian threshold, which is more than a simple majority. Given that there are also occasional instances where unanimity is used (as in treaty revision and enlargement), the result is a system that reconciles different political preferences rather than giving power to a legislative majority (Bellamy 2010).

Consequently, as a system of government, the EU has a much less majoritarian form of democracy than most member states do. Voting the Commission out of office or electing parties to carry out a particular legislative program at the EU-level is not an option. As a politically neutral body, insulated from electoral politics, commissioners do not have to take citizens' preferences into account in their day-to-day governing; in this respect they are unlike national governments, which are preoccupied by re-election and opinion polls. The Lisbon Treaty did introduce a **citizens' initiative** allowing a million EU citizens from across at least a quarter of the member states to petition the Commission to tackle a particular policy problem. However, a citizens' initiative does not create any legal obligation to propose legislation and must relate to a policy area where the Commission can actually initiate law. Hence petitions asking for an end to nuclear power in the EU or for the creation of a basic minimum income have been rejected, as the treaties do not grant the Commission the power to propose such legislation.

The ability of the majority to hold the EU system to account is thus limited. Instead, the EU relies on non-majoritarian forms of accountability based on inter-institutional checks and balances and on the rule of law (Moravcsik 2002). Non-majoritarian accountability is in fact quite common, as federal systems rely on this mechanism to reduce the legislative power of an aggregate majority, thereby preserving the autonomy of territorial sub-units (see Section 6.1).

10.1.1   Accountability without majoritarianism

One form of accountability beyond majoritarianism that exists in the EU concerns the quality of deliberation and representativeness involved in making law. That is, by bringing together a wide range of interests and perspectives within the Commission–Council–Parliament triangle, EU policy-making is able to draw on more expertise and find a better consensus position than in more majoritarian national systems. Citizens can explore for themselves which interest groups are active thanks to the EU Transparency Register, which lists over 5,000 groups and indicates what they lobby for in the EU. Indeed the evidence suggests that a multilateral and technocratic setting like the EU actually restricts the influence of special interests by comparison with their ability to shape government policy at the national level through campaign contributions and political networking (Keohane, Macedo, and Moravcsik, 2009). Commission consultations with interest groups and experts, combined with the increasing input from democratically elected MEPs (using the Parliament's power of amendment), result in inclusive policy-making. This inclusivity and focus on compromise is particularly important when it comes to creating legislation that favors the long-term interests of EU citizens but that could be blocked for short-term political reasons.

Indeed, in many EU countries, market liberalization would not have been possible without supranational decision-making. National politicians are often unwilling to introduce market competition because of the short-term electoral consequences, such as unemployment or opposition from unions and big companies unhappy with this reform. Of course, the fact that integration facilitates liberalization begs the question of whether EU re-regulation (i.e. common standards) is sufficient to offset the consequences of market deregulation (Føllesdal and Hix 2006). Compared with national governments, the EU has limited competences to establish social rights (health and safety at work, but not pensions or social security) and far fewer financial means to compensate those affected by increased market competition. So at the same time as national governments can no longer regulate markets as they like, there are limits as to the kind of regulation that is possible via the EU. This apparent mismatch is thus an inherent part of the debate over whether the EU is truly democratic (see Section 10.2).

Another way of understanding democratic accountability in the EU is to consider its regulatory outputs and how these correspond with – rather than respond to – citizens' preferences. Under the routine co-decision procedure used in the Ordinary Legislative Procedure (OLP), legislation that passes is inherently centrist, representing a consensus position. Policies favored by those at the outer reaches of the center-right or center-left do not make it into EU law, as exemplified by the failure of the liberalization of services (a strong center-right idea). Rather, legislation that gets adopted approximates to what the median or average voter favors (Crombez 2003). This is the product of a consensus-oriented decision-making system where there is no majority position powerful enough to ignore the concerns and interests of minorities. Under QMV, from 2014, a blocking minority of four countries representing 35 percent of the EU population is enough to prevent the Council from passing a law; so any measure needs to accommodate the preferences of a potentially blocking minority.

EU legislation can thus be said to be legitimate not because individuals have had an important say in expressing what they want EU institutions to do, but because what EU institutions decide corresponds to where most voters stand. Moreover, as these outputs relate to tackling shared problems that individual countries are less equipped to solve on their own, they can be said to have **output legitimacy**. This phrase, coined by the political scientist Fritz Scharpf (1999), relates to how policies can be legitimate by virtue of the benefits they produce. According to this logic, decisions are legitimate not because citizens have had a role in shaping them, but "because they effectively promote the common welfare of the constituency in question" (Scharpf 1999, 6). This contrasts with **input legitimacy** stemming from preferences expressed via political participation, namely citizens actually voting for parties with specific policies. This sense, that the EU system produces government for the people rather than being responsive to citizens' preferences and inputs – government by the people – is a major criticism of democracy in the EU.

Despite the absence of EU-level majoritarianism, there is an indirect majoritarian channel of accountability inherent in the EU system: national politics. Citizens can in principle use national elections (as well as potentially national referendums) to express their preferences regarding integration. This mechanism – like the retention of national vetoes in areas such as taxation, the multiannual financial framework (see Chapter 5, Glossary), foreign policy, and treaty reform – allows for indirect accountability (Moravcsik 2002). That is, voters can in theory threaten to sanction a national government (vote it out of office) when that government is willing to concede too much, say, by paying too much into the EU budget or by conferring new competences to the EU. A more extreme option is the possibility of withdrawing from the EU, which a national government is free to do should its citizens desire it. Whereas the EU system as a whole is not designed to be responsive to the will of the EU majority, national governments can pay heed to their own citizens' preferences on integration and act accordingly. The problem here, though, is that a single member state has very limited influence over policy-making under OLP, while the ability to pursue policy alternatives at the national level is constrained by EU rules. Hence there is a concern that integration prevents governments from being responsive to alternative policies that their citizens favor (see Section 10.2).

A final non-majoritarian accountability mechanism is a constitutional one. All EU legislation is subject to legal scrutiny by the CJEU, which makes sure everything is done within the competences defined in the treaties. Otherwise the CJEU can deem legislation to be incompatible with the subsidiarity principle. This is the principle according to which policy decisions should be taken at the level of government most appropriate for achieving the intended results (see Section 4.2). Some of the changes introduced by the Lisbon Treaty explicitly sought to develop democracy in the EU by linking the monitoring of subsidiarity to indirect channels of accountability rather than relying on the unelected CJEU. Hence the new yellow and orange card procedures allow national parliaments to object to the Commission's legislative proposals, and this gives national opinion more scope to shape EU policy-making (see Section 4.2). These changes are supposed to make enforcing subsidiarity a more political process instead of leaving it to the CJEU. The very fact that these measures – largely untested at the time of writing – were introduced suggests an ongoing concern with whether the EU system is sufficiently democratic. This often very heated debate involves arguing over whether there is a deficit of democracy in the EU, which in turn depends on how the nature and purpose of the EU are understood.

10.2   The Democratic Deficit Debate

The accusation that European integration suffers from a democratic deficit is a hoary and potent one. David Marquand (1979) identified the risk of a democratic deficit if national governments further transferred competences to the then EEC without strengthening parliamentary scrutiny at the European level. That is, national governments are (in theory) kept in check by national parliaments; but if governments confer decision-making responsibilities to the EU, then how are decisions taken at this level going to be accountable, and to whom? Federalists such as Marquand argued that increasing the power of the European Parliament was the only way to proceed, since the European Parliament is the only institution that represents the political preferences of the European people. However, the assumption that more integration requires a more parliamentary and majoritarian form of democracy is hotly contested. At the heart of the democratic deficit debate today is the question of whether or not the EU should be judged by the standard of a parliamentary model of democracy.

One immediate complication in this debate is the fact that democracy is very much about making power accountable to the people in whose name it is exercised. However, as the EU is a democratic system involving more than one people, there are multiple peoples in whose name power is exercised. That is why the EU has been labeled a *demoicracy* (see Chapter 6, Glossary) – that is, a democracy of multiple peoples. As it stands, these peoples seem to have chosen only to pool together certain competences, while others continue to be exercised at the national level. Indeed, the endurance of these separate national democratic communities has generated an important sub-branch of the democratic deficit debate, known as the "no-demos" problem. This issue concerns how essential the feeling of being a single people is for democracy and whether the lack of a feeling of European unity is a barrier to EU democracy or something that can develop over time (see Box 10.2).

What is not disputed is the fact that the EU system, precisely because it has no single demos to speak of currently, does not follow the standard majoritarian model of democracy (see Section 10.1). In this context, where one stands on the democratic deficit question usually hinges on whether the EU's non-majoritarian form of democracy is considered appropriate, given the EU's competences and the constraints that integration imposes on national governments. This gives rise to complex and heated arguments over whether the EU has found a suitable alternative to having a directly elected government.

However, determining the current quality of democratic accountability is not simply a technical or value-neutral question. Critics and supporters of the current EU system judge its democratic qualities from a normative perspective on what they believe European integration should or should not be able to achieve. This is why critics of EU democracy are concerned not just by a lack of responsiveness toward citizens (low input legitimacy) but also by the tendency of integration to narrow the policy choices available to citizens at both the EU and the national level. Hence one critique of EU democracy is essentially procedural, taking issue with how it functions, while another is normative, objecting to the kind of policies the EU system favors. Yet there are also those who believe that, given the unique complexities of crafting a legally binding system of governance across sovereign states, the EU is sufficiently democratic. Each of these three perspectives is examined in turn.

10.2.1   The procedural critique of EU democracy: A lack of responsiveness to citizens

Although the EU's non-majoritarian model of democracy shares certain similarities with federal systems, notably its reliance on bringing together a plurality of preferences across different communities (Coultrap 1999), there are extensive criticisms of how it operates. One major reason for challenging the democratic credentials of the EU is the

Box 10.2   Key Debate: The "No Demos" Problem

Dēmos is the ancient Greek word for "population," "people." The "no demos" problem thus concerns the implications that the absence of a single EU people has for the functioning of democracy in the EU. One side of the argument is premised on the claim that, since the EU is based on different national political communities, there can be no rule of the people in the EU. Democracy in this sense involves making sure that governing competences are where the people want them to be. This implies that pooling more competences presupposes a common identity, something that does not currently exist, as only a small minority of EU citizens – 10 percent – have a strong sense of an EU identity (Bellamy 2012). Similarly, majoritarian democracy in the EU can also be considered illegitimate, as it makes citizens subject to rule by a majority that they do not identify or feel solidarity with. Provisions (such as national vetoes) to respect national autonomy are thus justified from the "no demos" perspective. This conclusion is contested by those who argue that Europeans across member states actually share many cultural and political values, even though they do not speak a common language (Risse 2010). Moreover, the absence of an EU demos is something that could be overcome through identification with the EU's values and institutional system. The German philosopher Jürgen Habermas' (2001) contribution to this debate is to suggest that **constitutional patriotism** can provide a substitute for the national belonging found in member states. Pride in what integration represents and in how the EU reconciles the preferences of different peoples could therefore provide an overlapping sense of patriotism, which would make citizens accept the will of the majority even when they disagree with its content. Of course, constitutional patriotism is based on a high level of theoretical abstraction and presupposes that citizens can at times set aside national loyalties in the interest of Europe. Overall, the very presence of the "no demos" problem reflects the way in which European integration remains an ongoing political project without a fixed endpoint.

limited inputs citizens have into EU policy-making. This means that voting and public opinion do not matter much, either for determining EU policies or for sanctioning those responsible for them. Unlike federations, the EU has neither a mechanism for aggregating citizens' preferences (say, a presidential election or an EU-wide referendum) nor an integrated party system (see Section 6.1). From this perspective, the EU appears to be unresponsive to citizens and their policy preferences, while competences cannot be repatriated to the national level if EU policies prove ineffective.

These critics of EU democracy take issue with the adequacy of indirect accountability. Accountability via national political systems reflects the existence of multiple *dēmoi* (peoples) in the EU, each one capable of scrutinizing what happens in this non-majoritarian system. However, one noted feature of European integration has been the empowerment of national executives at the expense of national parliaments (Raunio 1999), which blunts the effectiveness of indirect accountability. National governments voting in the Council of the EU can take decisions that escape the control of their own parliaments, in that legislation adopted at the EU-level cannot be overridden by national law. Parliaments have a hard time determining exactly what governments say and do in both councils. Government leaders and ministers debate behind closed doors, and the records of what is said in these Brussels meetings are not made public (Føllesdal and Hix 2006). As a result, it is almost impossible for parliaments or the media to check whether governments are consistent in what they do and say in Brussels by comparison with what they say about the EU back home. Indeed, in his 2012 State of the Union address, Commission President José Manuel Barroso suggested that confidence in the EU was being undermined, as leaders agree on policy in Brussels only to express to a national audience their dissatisfaction with what was agreed.

The limited effectiveness of indirect accountability can further be seen in what happens in cases where a national referendum on an EU treaty has failed. Referendums are intended to be a way for citizens to have their say on important institutional and competence changes. Survey evidence suggests that, unlike in European Parliamentary elections, in referendums citizens are voting according to what they think of integration (Glencross and Trechsel 2011). In countries such as France, Denmark, the Netherlands, and Ireland, this had led to quite a few instances where citizens have rejected a proposed EU treaty. Treaties rejected by national electorates include the Maastricht Treaty, the Nice Treaty, the Constitutional Treaty, and the Lisbon Treaty. Yet in each case either citizens have been asked to vote again or the reforms contained in the rejected treaty were brought in via a new treaty, adopted by national parliaments – as happened with the failed Constitutional Treaty. As a result, this form of indirect accountability amounts in practice to accepting the diplomatic deals done by European political elites, as citizens do not have the power to unravel them.

Furthermore, political responsibility for what is decided via OLP is weak. The unelected Commission decides collectively whether to propose legislation, while consensus is required between governments in the Council as well as between major party groups in the European Parliament. What this means is that there is no mechanism for EU citizens to reject the existing leadership (that is, the Commission) and its policy agenda (Føllesdal and Hix 2006). Without electoral competition over who should lead and what policies should be pursued, the leadership and direction of EU policy-making is very difficult to challenge as there is no contest between a government and an opposition.

Some contestation over integration per se takes place when citizens vote for anti-EU parties, especially in European parliamentary elections. However, sending anti-EU representatives to the European Parliament has little impact on the Commission's legislative agenda – MEPs can only amend laws – and none on what competences the EU actually has, which is decided by national governments (Mair 2007). Moreover, voter turnout for the European Parliament – which citizens often treat as a second-order election (see Box 10.1) – is low overall by comparison with turnout for national parliamentary elections, as shown in Figure 10.1. Despite the increase in that legislature's decision-making powers, turnout has continued to decline (see Figure 10.2). These turnout figures thus

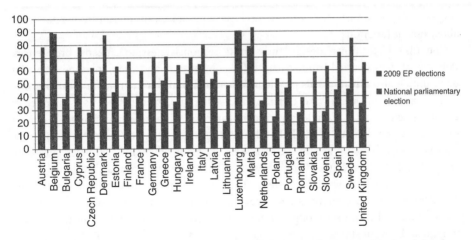

Figure 10.1 Voter turnout in the EU: European parliamentary elections and national elections. Source: Data from Norwegian Social Science Data Services, European Election Database (national election data valid as of September 2011), at www.nsd.uib.no/european_election_database/

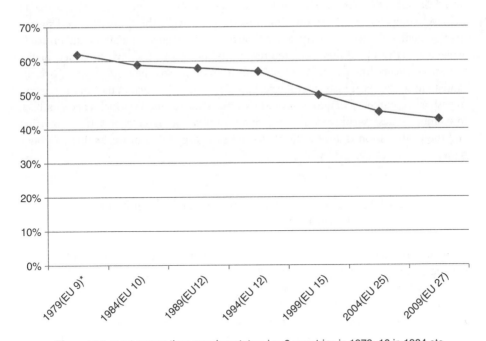

*Average turnout across then member states: i.e. 9 countries in 1979, 10 in 1984 etc.

Figure 10.2 Average voter turnout in elections for the European Parliament, 1979–2009. Source: Data from European Parliament, at http://www.europarl.europa.eu/aboutparliament/en/ 000cdcd9d4/Turnout-%281979-2009%29.html

suggest public dissatisfaction with the EU as well as a lack of interest in or knowledge about how it functions.

The EU's institutional design thus limits responsiveness to citizens' preferences. Policy blockages derived from the need for consensus – and even, in some cases, for unanimity – also illustrate this problem. When unanimity is the rule for treaty reform, there is a built-in bias toward retaining the status quo, even if there is a majority of countries against it, as a single government can simply block certain changes it objects to. This is especially true of the EU budget, for instance where the specter of a national veto is a huge bargaining chip (Gros 2008). Notably, when EU countries agreed to enlarge in 2004, net recipient countries such as Greece and Ireland threatened to use their veto power to block enlargement unless their own EU funding was maintained. The dependence on consensus also explains why reform of the expensive Common Agricultural Policy took so long to implement despite a majority of countries seeking to reduce these subsidies.

Even Majone, who is otherwise satisfied with the democratic control of EU regulation, sees the EU as unresponsive in the case of policy failure caused by the constraints on this institutional design. The high threshold for consensus and the inability to repatriate competences to the national level mean that ineffective policies can persist for a long time (Majone 2005). The Common Fisheries Policy, for instance, continues to be an EU-level competence despite the Commission not having the means to see fisheries management enforced properly. So, although national governments could probably achieve better results if they assumed responsibility for this task by using their navies to inspect catches, the treaties prevent them from doing so. The result is that, "over its more than twenty-year history, [fisheries] policy has largely failed in its aim of conserving fishery resources" (Majone 2006, 621). Competences could in principle be sent back to member states, but this would require all countries to agree during treaty revision and the Commission is always hostile to any such suggestion of weakening its policy remit.

10.2.2   The normative critique of EU democracy:
The narrowing of political alternatives

A second critique of EU democracy involves concern over the content of EU policy-making and not just over procedural weaknesses in responding to citizens. From this perspective, the quality of EU democracy is questionable because European integration narrows the political alternatives available to citizens. That is, the EU system has a negative effect on voter choice by constraining the democratic preferences of citizens. With only limited policy competences, the EU system cannot respond to some of the demands its citizens might have, while its existing rules actually hamper the ability for such policies to be pursued at the national level.

More concretely, while the EU has important powers to deregulate markets, the scope it has for re-regulating them is limited, given that it cannot raise taxes or interfere with social security or pension systems. This might be a democratically legitimate division of competences, as Majone claims (see Section 10.2.3). However, critics of the consequences of the EU system on democracy point out that EU market deregulation affects what member states can do independently to mitigate the effects of competition and to establish a social market (Bartolini 2005). The consequence is that the scope for national intervention in the market is reduced without the possibility of EU-level rules compensating for this reduction.

A basic example will bring this problem into relief. The four fundamental freedoms make it impossible for the Italian government to subsidize its car industry, as this constitutes unfair competition vis-à-vis other European manufacturers. However, enacting EU-level market intervention – to recreate what member states are no longer entitled to do – is impossible. That is, even with a majority of EU citizens in favor of subsidizing the European car industry in order to keep EU employment high and to maintain research in a strategic industry, the EU would not have the legal authority to do it. The same applies to a host of policy fields where governments have intervened for certain political goals, for example by allowing monopolies in railways and postal services in order to subsidize regional lines that make a loss, or in order to guarantee a universal postal coverage at a single price. Once governments have to introduce competition in these industries, there is no mechanism for the EU to re-regulate these markets via taxation or subsidies.

Normative critics of EU democracy thus claim the EU system is structurally biased against social market regulation, thereby limiting the policy choices available to EU citizens (Scharpf 1997). Of course, there is a possibility of left–right political competition within EU policy-making. However, this relates to "social regulation, rather than redistribution" (Hooghe and Marks 2009, 16). That is, political contestation takes place within a narrow framework, namely that of the policies relating to the regulation of the single market (see Chapter 7). Bigger questions surrounding whether to use the tax system to pursue redistributive policies (see Chapter 7, Glossary) in order to improve the welfare of the poor or reduce inequalities such as a minimum wage or income are off the table.

At the same time, national measures to create a social market must conform to the EU's four fundamental freedoms and to other rules. This problem of reduced national autonomy for maintaining a social market against neoliberal principles of free competition (see Box 5.2) is even more acute in the Eurozone. Governments there are legally bound to limit their deficits. According to the rules governing the euro, these governments have to balance their books – sometimes on the orders of the EU (see Chapter 12) – and this limits their discretion for deficit-financed welfare spending. Governments are formally free to decide how to tax their citizens and how to organize spending on pensions or social security. Yet in reality the Stability and Growth Pact and the excessive deficit procedure associated with it constrain what governments can do when it comes to how much tax they raise and how much they can spend. Once again, the net result is that membership of the EU limits the range of policy options available to national governments when they have to decide how to make the trade-off between equity and efficiency (see Section 7.1). In this way the EU affects how democracy is exercised at the national level, which helps explain the rise of popular mobilization against integration from the left of the political spectrum – a topic discussed in Section 11.2.

10.2.3   The case against a democratic deficit

Supporters of the status quo praise the EU as having achieved a degree of democratic accountability not present in any other international organization. In particular, no other international organization has a directly elected transnational legislature with the powers of the European Parliament. In combination with the legislative monopoly of the Commission, this results in a supranational system of governance where national governments' inputs are subject to unparalleled checks and balances. From this perspective, the current system is considered perfectly appropriate for the policy tasks conferred on the EU.

The most noted proponents of the position that the EU is sufficiently democratic for what it currently does are Giandomenico Majone and Andrew Moravcsik. The former argues that, as a regulatory state (see Box 7.2), the EU only has limited policy responsibilities concerning making markets more efficient. With these competences there is no need for an elected government and for a EU-level political mobilization of citizens, as these are appropriate only for a state with tax-raising powers that are used to redistribute resources between different groups (Majone 2002). Moreover, since EU citizens have never pushed for taxes to be decided at the EU-level and are reluctant to finance greater EU spending, it appears that the current division of competences is democratically legitimate. The EU engages in market regulation, while nation-states are responsible (through tax and spending decisions) for mitigating the consequences of market competition through welfare spending (Majone 2002).

Andrew Moravcsik has also defended the quality of democratic procedures in the EU. In terms of how it functions, he argues that

> constitutional checks and balances, indirect democratic control via national governments, and the increasing powers of the European Parliament are sufficient to ensure that EU policy-making is, in nearly all cases, clean, transparent, effective and politically responsive to the demands of European citizens. (Moravcsik 2002, 605)

Equally importantly, it is not just the institutional mechanism that is democratically robust, but also the constitutional settlement upon which the EU rests. By this Moravcsik (2006) means that citizens by and large have the EU system that they actually prefer.

One way of proving this is through the fact that fiscal policy, healthcare, pensions, policing, and education remain the responsibility of the member states. These competences are where citizens want them to remain: at the national level, responsive to the preferences of the national community. The EU's regulatory output has important effects on national decision-making, yet ordinary citizens are more concerned about the competences that member states still control. Consequently voters remain in the dark about the complex matters the EU is responsible for, and they "have little incentive to debate or decide" them (Moravcsik 2006, 226). This explains the low turnout for European parliamentary elections despite the increase in that legislature's decision-making powers (see Figure 10.1). This situation could change, should citizens desire another kind of EU system; but, as Moravcsik points out, since the Maastricht Treaty the EU's institutional design and competences have not changed dramatically (2006, 236).

The stability of the EU constitutional system is taken to be an indication of the fact – notwithstanding calls for changing the EU model (see Chapter 9) – that citizens are satisfied with the current arrangement. Expressions of dissatisfaction certainly exist, as shown by referendums rejecting the 2004 Constitutional Treaty (see Section 3.4). Moravcsik argues, however, that these are not motivated by hostility toward the EU's structure or policies; rather they reflect popular skepticism and disenchantment when EU issues become an ideological debate over greater or more reduced integration. What characterizes these referendums is an "exaggerated rhetoric that unsettles the larger population in the center of the EU political spectrum" (Moravcsik 2006, 237). How referendums on EU issues intersect with national politics is discussed in detail in Section 11.3.

Overall, the debate over a supposed democratic deficit in the EU does not simply take place between rival scholars. Concerns and complaints about the quality of EU democracy are present across member states. Hence it is not surprising in this context to encounter numerous recommendations for enhancing democracy within the EU. These need to be examined if we are to discover what they might offer as well as what pitfalls might surround them.

10.3   Enhancing Democracy in the EU

Treaty reform in the past two decades has sought to accomplish the hard task of having more democracy accompany more integration. This section sets out what further enhancements to the democratic functioning of the EU have been proposed within the context of the existing institutional architecture. More radical ideas about transforming the EU – notably proposals to make it a full-fledged federation, or else to roll back its competences and make it a confederation – were discussed in Chapter 9. Therefore the focus here is on introducing and analyzing suggestions for making the EU more democratic. The options currently on the table include making the EU resemble a parliamentary democracy, adding a presidential element via direct election of the Commission president, encouraging transnational parties to replace fragmented national ones, and taking measures to improve indirect accountability via national political systems.

10.3.1   Adding parliamentary or presidential features

Parliamentary government rests on the principle of accountability between an executive and a legislature made up of elected representatives of the people. There is an attenuated version of this executive–legislative connection in the current EU. A majority vote of MEPs is needed to approve the College of commissioners, and the European Parliament can censure – that is, throw out – this College by a two-thirds majority. In practice, as discussed in Section 10.2.1, these measures are insufficient to make the Commission's policy agenda responsive to the preferences of an EU majority. Hence one much discussed proposal to improve democracy in the EU is to transform relations between the Commission and the European Parliament.

What this could involve is allowing the European Parliament to choose between different possible candidates for the presidency of the Commission. Currently MEPs get to vote on a compromise candidate – one that ruffles few feathers – selected by using QMV in the Council. Instead, MEPs could select between official candidates with their own political programs concerning what the Commission should do and who would campaign on their platforms prior to European Parliamentary elections (Hix 2008). With rival candidates linked to rival European political groups, this would be a way of introducing more electoral competition into the EU system, thereby energizing these "second-order" elections.

Moreover, introducing electoral competition for the post of Commission president would also constitute a recognition of the fact that there are different political perspectives on what the European interest actually is, notably when it comes to market regulation. This would mark a change from treating the Commission as a neutral arbiter of what the European interest is. Making the Commission a more political body – politicizing it, in other words – and one with a policy mandate from the majority of MEPs would thus make its work more visible, thereby increasing the citizens' knowledge and interest. At the very least, the public would be able "to identify what the Commission President and the Commission stand for" (Bartolini and Hix 2006, 25). Indeed the Lisbon Treaty states that the President of the Commission must be appointed "taking into account the elections to the European Parliament" (Art. 17 TEU). This means that the main European parliamentary political groups are likely to propose their own candidates for the post during the 2014 European parliamentary elections.

Another mechanism for politicizing the Commission and for connecting it better to the citizens is to introduce direct elections for the president of the European Commission. Again, this idea rests on the proposed benefits of having more electoral competition within the EU system; but this would be based, however, on a presidential rather than a parliamentary democratic model. Having the Commission president elected by EU citizens would endow that figure with a political mandate to carry out certain policies within the remit of EU competences (Decker 2002). This **presidentialization** approach to enhancing EU democracy owes something to the American federal model. There the president is the expression of a political majority, a power base that has been essential for overcoming policy blockages and responding to citizens' policy priorities. Consequently, introducing presidentialism into the EU system is intended to add a majoritarian element, thus giving a more meaningful input to citizens and making outputs more responsive to their preferences.

10.3.2   Developing transnational parties and enhancing indirect accountability

Both the parliamentary and the presidential options are fundamentally connected to another feature for enhancing democracy in the EU: encouraging party political competition around European integration. A long-standing goal for improving the quality of EU democracy is the development of pan-European political parties. Political parties are a vital ingredient in democratic politics, as they offer citizens a choice between alternative policies and personalities for governing (Schattschneider 1960). Party competition provides voters not only with choice, but also with information, as the contest for office inevitably involves political debate, which is a way of mobilizing citizens – namely of getting them interested in politics. This kind of competition and the benefits it provides are in short supply when it comes to the politics of European integration. As explained in Box 10.1, European parliamentary elections tend to be lackluster, "second-order" affairs with lower participation than national elections. Citizens use them to express their level of satisfaction with their government rather than what they think the EU needs to do. Moreover, while party groups (families of like-minded national parties) exist in the European Parliament, political parties in member states are organized on national lines. This means that leaders, candidates, and issues are chosen at the national level, and this choice limits co-ordination outside the Parliament.

The development of transnational parties in the EU would be a positive move for democracy because it would make the EU system more responsive to citizens' preferences. If there were pan-European parties campaigning across the EU and if an EU-level party leadership structure were in place, citizens would find it easier to identify which party platform to support. A clear competition between EU-wide parties could also generate more interest in European Parliamentary elections. In addition, having transnational parties sitting in both the Council and the Parliament makes possible the coordination of decision-making across these two legislatures. That is, a majority of citizens across the member states could, by voting for the same parties, establish a controlling majority in both institutions. Such party coordination would make it easier for a majority of citizens to get the kind of legislation they desire, or else to block consistently Commission proposals they disapprove of. At the moment this is not possible since national parties are largely autonomous – meaning that parties of government sitting in the Council vote differently on EU legislation from their MEPs sitting in European party groups (Hix and Høyland 2011, 142).

Transnational parties can thus play a role in overcoming the fragmentation of politics across 28 member states: in federations, integrated party systems are associated with the centralization of politics and policy (see Section 6.1). With politicians and parties campaigning across national borders, this would naturally increase the visibility of EU policy issues as well as raise awareness of what the EU does. Indeed this explains why the EU is committed to financing the development of political parties at the European level, spending €31 million in 2012 on 13 parties. This commitment is enshrined in the treaties, as the Maastricht Treaty (Art. 41) specified that European political parties "are important as a factor for integration within the Union. They contribute to forming a European awareness and to expressing the will of the citizens of the Union."

A final suggestion for enhancing EU democracy concerns improving indirect accountability. This can take several forms, including better national parliamentary oversight regarding EU matters and changing how national referendums are used. The Lisbon Treaty, via its yellow and orange card procedures, explicitly acknowledged the benefits of increased national parliamentary participation in EU policy-making (see Section 4.2). These new measures accord with the EU principle of subsidiarity – that is, of ensuring that policy-making is not overly centralized at the EU-level. However, there are other benefits that stem from greater national parliamentary participation, especially making national governments more accountable for their EU-level decisions and improving national debate over EU policies (Auel 2007).

Certain countries already make extensive use of parliamentary control over national executives before ministers and heads of government participate in EU negotiations. This is visibly the case in Denmark, which has introduced *ex ante* controls on government ministers to ensure they negotiate according to strict guidelines approved by a parliamentary majority (see Box 10.3). All national parliaments have European affairs committees to scrutinize what the governments decide in Brussels. However, the Danish model is considered the most rigorous example – and one that could also be adopted elsewhere.

Some scholars also advocate organizing national referendums on EU treaties differently, so as to boost indirect accountability. Instead of *ad hoc* referendums left at the whim of national governments, one suggestion is to make treaty reform conditional on

---

Box 10.3   Case Study: Enhancing National Parliamentary Scrutiny: The Danish Example

The European Affairs Committee of the Danish parliament is responsible for overseeing what the Danish government does within the EU system. The basic principle behind its scrutiny of national ministers is to ensure that Danish EU policy is backed by a parliamentary majority. This counteracts the tendency for executives across the EU to gain power at the expense of national legislatures, as the latter are a step behind deals done in the councils. Before Danish ministers can agree to major proposed EU legislation, they must obtain a negotiating mandate from the Committee. The mandate relates to the government's negotiating strategy, that is, to what Denmark is prepared to accept or not when designing a new EU law, when settling the multiannual financial framework, when voting on a free trade agreement between the EU and another country, and so on (Finke and Melzer 2012). It is thus incumbent on the government minister to explain to the Committee what the advantages of this legislation are and what other member states in the Council think about it. In this way the Committee is fully informed about what is at stake and what is at play in EU legislative decision-making. For a mandate to be rejected – which happens rarely – committee members representing parties with a majority of seats must oppose it, forcing the government to revise its negotiating position. To minimize this risk, governments anticipate the kind of mandate the Committee will give, which means that the Danish negotiation position normally accommodates the Committee's preferences. Overall, national parliamentarians are kept well informed about EU decision-making, coalition and minority parties being able to ensure that government EU policy remains close to their preferences (Finke and Melzer 2012).

a set of referendums across all the member states. For a treaty to pass there would need to be a total majority of EU citizens in favor, as well as a majority of countries where the referendum was approved (Auer 2007). This idea is modelled on the Swiss "dual majority" principle, whereby constitutional amendment requires a majority of both cantons (territorial sub-units) and citizens. Treaty reform by dual majority would thus make the EU system reflect better what EU citizens desire, thereby endowing it with greater input legitimacy.

10.3.3   Obstacles to enhancing EU democracy

There are significant obstacles when it comes to realizing any of these four options for enhancing EU democracy. Among the parliamentary and the presidential options, it is the former that is more likely. This is because Hix's proposed tinkering with the election of the Commission president would not require full-blown treaty revision and is indeed encouraged by the wording of the Lisbon Treaty. By contrast, the presidential option requires revision of the treaties; this necessitates unanimity and is, in consequence, a more remote possibility. Indeed many national governments are wary of a directly elected Commission president, since the holder could overshadow them and increase the power of the Commission at the expense of the Council and of national autonomy. This wariness explains why member states opted for a low-visibility candidate when they appointed the first president of the European Council, Herman Van Rompuy (2009–2014), instead of going for a high profile (and divisive) figure such as former British Prime Minister Tony Blair. Nevertheless, the elected president option remains much discussed at the elite level, as illustrated by a 2012 report on the Future of Europe authored by 11 foreign ministers, which advocated presidentialization.

Other obstacles are present too when it comes to developing transnational parties. For one thing, national electorates are divided through the multiplicity of languages: no politician can campaign across all the member states speaking the language of each country. In this sense there will always be a linguistic fragmentation to how politics is debated in Europe, and some interpret it as a sign that the EU will never be based on a single demos (see Box 10.2). Moreover, there are legal constraints on transnational political participation. Since the Maastricht Treaty EU citizens are entitled to vote and be candidates in municipal and European elections wherever they happen to live. What the treaties do not provide, though, is the right for EU citizens to vote and be candidates in national elections wherever they reside. Citizens living in another EU country are not (as a rule) entitled to vote for the government of that country – a situation contradicting the idea that the EU is a shared political space where all its citizens can participate equally.

Another problem with the proposal of enhancing democracy by developing transnational parties in the EU concerns the ability to rely on such a transnational party system to link together majorities in the Council and in the Parliament. This connection is unlikely, as national and European electoral cycles are out of kilter, national elections being organized according to a completely different schedule from the European elections, which are held every five years. Consequently there is a low probability that a coherent majority of both member state governments and MEPs belonging to the same political family will sit at the same time in the European Parliament and in the Council (Magnette 2007).

Improving indirect accountability in line with the Danish model of national parliamentary scrutiny is a distinct possibility for most member states. However, further enhancing accountability through an increased use of referendums in national politics is by no means simple. Adopting the Swiss dual majority principle for passing treaty reform would entail a significant circumscription of member states' sovereignty, as some countries might be confronted with having to adopt a treaty that their citizens rejected. This goes against international law, whereby a state is only bound by treaties it has individually consented to (de Witte 2004). In a situation where a country rejected a treaty accepted by the rest of the member states, there could of course be a subsequent referendum for that country's citizens to decide whether to leave the EU. Linking referendum rejection of a treaty to an exit referendum could allow citizens to determine the level of integration they actually desire (Schmitter 2000), encouraging more differentiated integration (see Section 9.4).

However, the fact that national referendums have led precisely to the rejection of EU treaties illustrates the potential pitfall of enhancing EU democracy: it risks destabilizing the current system. In particular, introducing more majoritarianism – either through a more parliamentary government or through a directly elected president – risks creating policies that some member states will not wish to abide by. This could also create political rivals, at the EU level, to national heads of government, thereby reducing the status and authority of the latter. Similarly, opening up an intense, transnational political debate on what integration is for and how it should be organized is not free of consequences (Bartolini and Hix 2006). Introducing more political contestation into the EU system might well open up more space for parties to contest integration itself, or to seek a more radical policy agenda (anti-immigration, fiscal redistribution, and the like). These developments would pose a serious challenge to a consensus-based system designed to uphold the four fundamental freedoms and to regulate markets primarily for the sake of efficiency. Even introducing more national parliamentary oversight could constrain the ability of governments to find consensus positions, potentially disrupting decision-making. The then Italian Prime Minister Mario Monti, a former EU commissioner, thus caused a stir when he declared that, "if governments allow themselves to be fully bound by the decisions of their parliaments without protecting their own freedom to act, a break-up of Europe would be more probable than deeper integration" (quoted in Spiegel 2012).

Hence there are, paradoxically, many risks associated with enhancing EU democracy. Making more democracy coincide with more integration is not automatic. It requires institutional tinkering that makes national elites as well as the Commission worry about what these changes might mean. Given the progress registered in making the fundamental freedoms a reality and in conferring a great many competences upon the EU, political elites do not want to jeopardize these achievements. Consequently, the democratic deficit and what can be done about it seem certain to continue to be the subject of heated debate for the foreseeable future.

10.4   Concluding Summary

This chapter started by examining the nature of democracy within the EU. Contrary to the way democratic politics works in most member states, democracy in the EU functions on a non-majoritarian basis. Most noticeably, the EU does not have a directly elected government. Instead, accountability functions via inter-institutional checks and balances, and there are some further opportunities for controlling the EU via national politics. Overall, the result is a system designed to provide outputs in line with an overlapping majority of citizens' preferences but without these citizens having a direct say in the process. This has been described as resulting in output rather than input legitimacy.

Criticisms of this system abound; many scholars and politicians claim that the EU has a democratic deficit. This is contested by those who argue that the status quo is sufficiently democratic for the EU to fulfill its main tasks legitimately. The consensus culture – combined with governments' retention of vetoes, and even their ability to withdraw from the EU – is well suited for creating and regulating a single market. However, those who say that there is a deficit of democracy point to the fact that the EU is not very responsive toward its citizens. They cannot change the EU's leadership or reject its policy agenda, while countries whose citizens reject a treaty in a referendum are normally asked to vote again. In addition, there is a concern that integration narrows the political alternatives available to dissatisfied voters, as the EU's competences are fixed by treaties regardless of whether citizens would prefer the EU to do more or to do less.

Concerns about the quality of democracy in the EU correspond to suggestions for ensuring that more integration comes with more democracy. The goal of these proposals is to make the EU more responsive to the policies and type of integration that citizens desire. Suggestions here include making the EU more like a parliamentary democracy, adding a presidential element via direct election of the Commission president, encouraging transnational parties to replace fragmented national ones, and also enhancing mechanisms of indirect accountability via national political systems. These ideas have been considered seriously during previous treaty reform. Yet they come with various risks, as more democratic input from citizens could well disrupt the current consensus culture and institutional balance within the EU. As a result, more democratic reform is possible in theory but hard to implement in practice.

Guide to Further Reading

Bartolini, S., and S. Hix. 2006. "Politics: The Right or Wrong Sort of Medicine for the EU?" Notre Europe Policy Paper, No. 19.

A concise yet complex debate between two leading experts on EU democracy, examining the risks and promise of making the EU more democratic.

Schmitter, P. 2000. *How to Democratise the European Union . . . and Why Bother?* Lanham, MD: Rowman & Littlefield.

A clear and persuasive argument about the problems of EU democracy and how they can be resolved through institutional reform and the development of transnational parties.

Warleigh, A. 2003. *Democracy in the European Union*. London: Sage.

An effective and insightful overview of the democratic deficit debate in the EU, written so as to be accessible to undergraduate students.

Discussion Questions

1   What are the major features of majoritarian democracy and why are they not present in the EU system?

2   How does accountability function in the EU and what constitutes indirect accountability?

3   Why do some scholars deny that there is a democratic deficit in the EU?

4   How far are the EU's policies and competences responsive to citizens' preferences? Is it democratic to constrain what policies citizens can see implemented at the national or EU level?

5   What means of enhancing democracy in the EU is most likely to be implemented and what are the overall risks associated with this move?

Web Resources

This book is supported by a companion website, which can be found at www.wiley.com/go/glencross. There you will find a list of the web links referred to in this chapter wherever you see a "Web" icon in the page margins. In addition, you will find a list of further relevant online resources such as websites for EU institutions, political groups, archives, and think tanks, information on studying abroad, and biographies of key figures. You will also find self-assessment tools in the form of flashcards and independent study questions developed specifically for this chapter.

Glossary

Citizens' initiative

Petition procedure for requesting the European Commission to address a certain policy problem. It requires the signatures of 1 million EU citizens from at least a quarter of the member states; it does not create a legal obligation for the Commission to propose legislation.

Constitutional patriotism

Form of political allegiance based on an attachment to constitutional rights and values. This distinguishes it from patriotism based on national belonging, hence the suggestion that constitutional patriotism can unite EU citizens and justify more integration.

Democratic deficit

A long-standing complaint that the EU is insufficiently accountable and responsive to its citizens. The EU is often accused of being less democratic than its member states. However, some defend the status quo as the most accountable multinational political system.

Input legitimacy

Concept claiming that the legitimacy of public policies and political decisions is dependent on the ability of citizens to have an input into them – that is, to have their say and to vote on important issues.

Majoritarian democracy

Form of democracy in which majority will gets to set the legislative agenda, usually by electing representatives who have a parliamentary majority. Less majoritarian forms of democracy, common in federations, restrict what a legislative majority can accomplish, normally for the sake of protecting regional autonomy.

Output legitimacy

Concept claiming that public policies and political decisions can be legitimate even when voters have little input into them. Legitimacy in this case is the result of producing policies and decisions that benefit a majority of citizens even if the latter have had little say in formulating them.

Presidentialization

Strategy for enhancing democracy in the EU by having a directly elected president. This would give citizens a chance to vote on what kind of leader and political agenda they want for the EU.

Second-order election

Conceptual phrase, used to describe European parliamentary elections. The election is of "second-order" importance in the sense that citizens vote according to national issues, not according to what they think about European integration. Whereas a first-order election is about choosing a national government, European parliamentary elections are often said to be of a second order because citizens use them to express their opinions on government, not on EU business.

Suspension clause

A clause introduced in the 1997 Amsterdam Treaty whereby a member state can lose some of its EU rights, notably voting rights in the Council of the EU. This clause can be invoked by four fifths of member states, in response to serious and persistent breaches of liberty, democracy, respect for human rights and fundamental freedoms, and the rule of law.

Transnational parties

Political parties that operate and stand for election in more than one country, reflecting voters' shared values and policy preferences across borders. Developing such parties is considered a way to enhance democracy in the EU because competing EU-wide parties would help express European public opinion and generate more interest in European parliamentary elections. Currently parties are largely organized at the national level.

References

Auel, Katrin. 2007. "Democratic Accountability and National Parliaments: Redefining the Impact of Parliamentary Scrutiny in EU Affairs." *European Law Journal*, 13: 487–504. DOI: 10.1111/j.1468-0386.2007.00380.x

Auer, Andreas. 2007. "National Referendums in the Process of European Integration: Time for a Change." In Anneli Albi and Jacques Ziller, eds., *The European Constitution and National Constitutions: Ratification and Beyond*, 261–272. The Hague: Kluwer Law International.

Barroso, José Manuel. 2012. "State of the Union Address." Available at http://ec.europa.eu/soteu2012/ (accessed July 21, 2013).

Bartolini, Stefano. 2005. *Restructuring Europe: Centre Formation, System Building and Political Structuring between the Nation State and the European Union*. Oxford: Oxford University Press.

Bartolini, Stefano, and Simon Hix. 2006. "Politics: The Right or the Wrong Sort of Medicine for the EU?" Available at http://personal.lse.ac.uk/hix/Working_Papers/NotreEurope_Hix%20_Bartolini.pdf (accessed July 20, 2012).

Bellamy, Richard. 2007. *Political Constitutionalism: A Republican Defence of the Constitutionality of Democracy*. Cambridge: Cambridge University Press.

Bellamy, Richard. 2010. "Democracy without Democracy? Can the EU's Democratic 'Outputs' be Separated from the Democratic 'Inputs' Provided by Competitive Parties and Majority Rule?" *Journal of European Public Policy*, 17: 2–19. DOI: 10.1080/13501760903465256

Bellamy, Richard. 2012. "The Inevitability of the Democratic Deficit." In Andreas Dür and Hubert Zimmermann, eds., *Key Controversies in European Integration*, 54–71. Basingstoke: Palgrave Macmillan.

Coultrap, John. 1999. "From *Parliamentarism* to *Pluralism*: *Models* of *Democracy* and the *European Union's 'Democratic Deficit.'*" *Journal of Theoretical Politics*, 11: 107–135. DOI: 10.1177/0951692899011001005

Crombez, Christopher. 2003. "The Democratic Deficit in the European Union: Much Ado About Nothing?" *European Union Politics*, 4: 101–120. DOI: 10.1177/1465116503004001583

De Witte, Bruno. 2004. "Treaty Revision in the European Union: Constitutional Change through International Law." *Netherlands Yearbook of International Law*, 35: 51–84. DOI: 10.1017/S0167676804000510

Decker, Frank. 2002. "Governance beyond the Nation-State: Reflections on the Democratic Deficit of the European Union." *Journal of European Public Policy*, 9: 256–272.

Finke, Daniel, and Marius Melzer. 2012. "Parliamentary Scrutiny of EU Law Proposals in Denmark: Why Do Governments Request a Negotiation Mandate?" Working paper available at http://www.ihs.ac.at/publications/pol/pw_127.pdf (accessed July 20, 2013).

Føllesdal, Andreas, and Simon Hix. 2006. "Why There Is a Democratic Deficit in the EU: A Response to Majone and Moravcsik." *Journal of Common Market Studies*, 44: 533–562. DOI: 10.1111/j.1468-5965.2006.00650.x

Glencross, Andrew R., and Alexander Trechsel. 2011. "First or Second Order Referendums? Understanding the Votes on the EU Constitutional Treaty in Four EU Member States." *West European*

Politics, 34: 755–772. DOI: 10.1080/ 01402382.2011.572390

Gros, Daniel. 2008. "How to Achieve a Better Budget for the European Union." *CEPS Working Document, No. 289.* Available at http://aei.pitt.edu/id/eprint/9377 (accessed July 20, 2013).

Habermas, Jürgen. 2001. "Why Europe Needs a Constitution." *New Left Review*, 11, September/October.

Hix, Simon. 2008. *What's Wrong with the European Union and How to Fix It.* London: Polity.

Hix, Simon, and Bjørn Høyland. 2011. *The Political System of the European Union.* Basingstoke: Palgrave.

Hix, Simon, and Michael Marsh. 2007. "Punishment or Protest? Understanding European Parliament Elections." *The Journal of Politics*, 69: 495–510. DOI:10 .1111/j.1468-2508.2007.00546.x

Hooghe, Liesbet, and Gary Marks. 2009. "A Postfunctionalist Theory of European Integration: From Permissive Consensus to Constraining Dissensus." *British Journal of Political Science*, 39: 1–23.

Keohane, Robert, Stephen Macedo, and Andrew Moravcsik. 2009. "Democracy-Enhancing Multilateralism." *International Organization*, 63: 1–31. DOI: 10 .1017/S0020818309090018

Mair, Peter. 2007. "Political Opposition and the European Union." *Government and Opposition*, 42: 1–17. DOI: 10.1111/ j.1477-7053.2007.00209.x

Magnette, Paul. 2007. "Vers un changement de régime? " In Giuliano Amato, Hervé Bribosia, and Bruno de Witte, eds., *Genèse et destinée de la Constitution Européenne: Commentaire du Traité établissant une Constitution pour l'Europe à la lumière des travaux préparatoires et perspectives d'avenir*, 1065–1080. Brussels: Bruylant.

Majone, Giandomenico. 2002. "The European Commission: The Limits of Centralization and the Perils of Parliamentarization." *Governance*, 15: 375–392.

Majone, Giandomenico. 2005. *Dilemmas of European Integration: The Ambiguities and Pitfalls of Integration by Stealth.* Oxford: Oxford University Press.

Majone, Giandomenico. 2006. "The Common Sense of European Integration." *Journal of European Public Policy*, 13: 607–620. DOI: 10.1080/13501760600808212

Marquand, David. 1979. *Parliament for Europe.* London: Jonathan Cape.

Moravcsik, Andrew. 2002. "Reassessing Legitimacy in the European Union." *Journal of Common Market Studies*, 40: 603–624. DOI: 10.1111/1468-5965 .00390

Moravcsik, Andrew. 2006. "What Can We Learn from the Collapse of the European Constitutional Project?" *Politische Vierteljahresschrift*, 47: 219–241. DOI: 10.1007/s11615-006-0037-7

Raunio, Tapio. 1999. "Always One Step Behind? National Legislatures and the European Union." *Government and Opposition*, 34: 180–202. DOI: 10.1111/ j.1477-7053.1999.tb00477.x

Reif, Karlheinz, and Hermann Schmitt, 1980. "Nine Second-Order National Elections: A Conceptual Framework for the Analysis of European Election Results." *European Journal of Political Research*, 8: 3–44. DOI: 10.1111/j.1475-6765.1980 .tb00737.x

Risse, Thomas. 2010. *A Community of Europeans? Transnational Identities and Public Spheres.* Ithaca, NY: Cornell University Press.

Scharpf, Fritz W. 1997. "Economic Integration, Democracy and the Welfare State." *Journal of European Public Policy*, 4: 18–36.

Scharpf, Fritz W. 1999. *Governing in Europe: Effective and Democratic?* Oxford: Oxford University Press.

Schattschneider, Elmer E. 1960. *The Semi-Sovereign People: A Realist's View of Democracy in America.* New York: Holt, Rinehart & Winston.

Schmitter, Philippe. 2000. *How to Democratize the European Union: And Why*

Bother? Lanham, MD: Rowman & Littlefield.

Spiegel Online International. 2012. Interview with Italian Prime Minister Mario Monti, 6 August. Available at http://www.spiegel.de/international/europe/interview-on-the-euro-crisis-with-italian-prime-minister-mario-monti-a-848511.html (accessed March 15, 2012).

11

The Impact of European Integration on National Politics

Contents

Learning Objectives

- to identify evidence that European integration has become more salient in national politics;
- to analyze why citizens and politicians are increasingly contesting European integration;
- to distinguish between different types of Euroskepticism and to evaluate the policy recommendations associated with each;
- to interpret why governments hold referendums on EU issues;
- to analyze why the outcomes of referendums are hard to predict and their use is contested.

The Politics of European Integration: Political Union or a House Divided?, First Edition. Andrew Glencross.
© 2014 Andrew Glencross. Published 2014 by Blackwell Publishing Ltd.

11.0   Introduction: Political Adaptation to European Integration

Previous chapters have discussed how European integration has affected the legal and policy-making autonomy of EU member states. Governments have agreed to work together in various policy fields, even though this reduces their ability to act independently. This is exemplified by the legal power of the Court of Justice to strike down national laws that contravene EU treaties and legislation (see Section 4.4), or by the Stability and Growth Pact's restrictions on national budget deficits (see Section 5.2). On the surface, these may just look like technical and legal constraints affecting what national decision-makers can do. However, conforming to these EU rules has important political repercussions, as governments have to implement policies that might not be popular domestically. At the same time, opposition parties can gain votes by suggesting that they would negotiate alternative EU policies, or that they would even change their country's relationship to the EU. The result is that European integration is increasingly having political repercussions, as politicians and citizens at the national level debate the pros and cons of ever closer union.

The way in which integration has engendered political contestation at the national level is the subject of this chapter. Democratic politics in EU member states today has to adapt to a new political context, in which EU decisions and rules stand a good chance of being controversial and contested. This adaptation of national politics to the political realities of integration is a relatively recent phenomenon. As explained in 11.1, in the early years of integration national politics was relatively insulated from debates about how and why to pursue institutionalized cooperation among European states. Mainstream political parties generally supported greater integration – albeit with some internal splits – and citizens went along with this strategy. Yet the scope of the competences conferred to the EU and the volume of its regulations made integration a highly salient feature of national politics. This has led not only to more numerous splits within political parties over EU issues, but also to stronger opposition from ordinary citizens to integration itself.

Opposition to integration and the EU system it has generated is the multifaceted political ideology known as **euroskepticism**. This is examined in depth in Section 11.2, to show how this ideology manifests itself in different political contexts: European parliamentary elections, treaty ratification, and everyday national politics. Moreover, the analysis reveals the existence of different varieties of euroskepticism, notably hard and soft ones. Different versions of euroskepticism are associated both with different types of political party and with diverse proposals for how a country should participate in integration. Consequently, there is no single template for what it is that voters oppose about the contemporary EU.

One way for citizens to participate in shaping the direction integration takes is through referendums. These are held when governments solicit the opinion of voters to ratify a treaty or to decide on some other issue relating to integration. These votes are analyzed in Section 11.3, which focuses not only on why certain governments resort to referendums but also on the dynamics of these campaigns. In these cases governments and mainstream political parties often find it hard to get their message across about the need to ratify a treaty, making the outcome unpredictable. This unpredictability is increased by the way issues beyond the contents of the treaty at hand enter the political debate, feeding on both euroskepticism and a lack of knowledge about the EU among certain voters. Thus voters' rejection of treaties is associated with a campaign in which a variety of small parties and civil society groups from both ends of the political spectrum oppose integration for different reasons. Consequently it is hard to discern in a failed referendum a clear message about what voters would prefer integration to look like, a situation that calls into question the utility of asking citizens to vote on EU matters.

11.1   European Integration and National Politics: The End of the Permissive Consensus

The linkage between European integration and national politics works both ways. National governments provide important inputs into EU decision-making through participation in the Council of the EU and in the European Council. They also nominate individual commissioners and collectively choose the Commission president (albeit with the consent of the Parliament), thereby influencing the legislative program, although they cannot directly tell the Commission what laws to propose. In addition, governments play a role in holding the EU to account through national politics (see Section 10.1). At the same time, the development of common EU policies and the constitutionalization of the treaties are having a profound impact on national politics. This is because European integration limits what national governments are able to do autonomously in a wide – and increasing – variety of policy areas. These policy constraints limit the ability of national political parties to respond to some of the demands their citizens might have, for instance to limit immigration, to stimulate growth via public debt, or to promote national industries. As a result, these parties face problems such as whether to support integration as part of what they stand for, or how much to integrate EU issues into their national political debates and programs.

At the start of the European integration process, questions about how it should be organized and what policies should be pursued were kept largely separate from national politics. Diplomatic deals cut by political elites were thus insulated from publicity and public opinion. This context of a largely uninformed and yet trusting public has been described as a **permissive consensus** (Lindberg and Scheingold 1970). Citizens were permissive in the sense that they trusted their political elites to devise a mutually beneficial system that could secure peace, strengthen the state, and increase prosperity (see Chapter 1). The elite consensus was that economic integration could achieve all these goals. Crucially, European integration was not considered very relevant by comparison with more pressing domestic political questions about taxation, welfare spending, education, or foreign policy. This low salience helped sustain citizens' acquiescence in the scope and type of integration elites chose to pursue. Some, like Majone (2006), also claim that this emphasis on complex matters of economic integration such as the four fundamental freedoms was a deliberate ploy to foster an **integration by stealth**. From this perspective, the focus on pooling less salient aspects of sovereignty allowed the Commission and EU law to develop stealthily, outside the realm of domestic political contestation.

However, as the deepening of integration enlarged the number and scope of EU competences, the political salience of integration has grown. This has challenged both elite consensus and citizens' permissiveness toward greater integration. In particular, the growth of EU regulatory output and the resulting constraints on national autonomy have become a subject of contestation in national elections as well as in European parliamentary elections and during referendums on EU treaties. This trend, as well as that of increased media coverage, began with the 1992 Maastricht Treaty (Hooghe and Marks 2009), which was hugely contentious in many countries, especially in those that held referendums on it. Since that time, then, governments have had to contend with a changed political environment: parties, politicians, and the media are now very much involved in debating integration and the work of the EU.

In many ways, political parties preferred to keep national political debates separate from debates about European integration. This reflects the fact that the issues originally raised by integration were separate from the left–right divide (see Box 7.1), which has characterized Western European party politics since 1945 (Hooghe and Marks 2009). At least in the early years, the big questions raised by integration were related to its effects on sovereignty and national identity rather than to what national parties tended to fight over: government spending and taxation. In this sense, as an object of political contestation, the EU was considered separate from mainstream party political debate.

11.1.1   The emergence of a "constraining dissensus"

Nevertheless, during the era of the permissive consensus national elites were actively engaged in heated debates over European integration, even when the vast majority of the electorate was not. This can be seen from examples discussed in Part 1, including the debate over the European Defence Community (see Section 2.3) and the empty chair crisis (see Section 2.5). In fact, given these divisions among the European political elite, national parties were wary about competing with one another over what the EU should do or how it should be organized. They preferred not to make it a big political issue or politicize it. This is because parties, which in Europe are typically divided on left/right issues about government intervention in the economy and in society, are often internally split about how integration should occur (van der Eijk and Franklin, 2004). A notable example here is the French Socialist Party during the 2005 referendum on the EU Constitutional Treaty. Officially the party supported the constitution. However, a section of the party leaders actually led the "no" campaign against the treaty. Similar tension has existed in the British Labour Party, which in 1983 campaigned for withdrawal from the EEC, whereas in the late 1990s it advocated joining the euro if economic conditions were right.

These internal splits and reversals of position point to the dilemma that mainstream European political parties increasingly face when confronting European integration: the risk that integration undermines what they stand for. Center-left parties stand for the social market (see Box 5.2) as opposed to neoliberal free competition; yet they also promote a cosmopolitan identity rather than national loyalty. Hence, while these parties normally favor international cooperation and open borders, they are torn because of the threat that market liberalization poses to social market regulation (Kriesi, Grande, Lachat, Dolezal, Bornschier, and Frey 2006) – notably by triggering the risk of a race to the bottom in social standards (see Box 7.2). Center-right parties promote neoliberal competition but remain attached to national culture and identity. So they tend to prefer greater market liberalization, yet they worry about the consequences that open borders have on national social and cultural values (Kriesi et al. 2006). Consequently, these two main party families have opposing preferences when it comes to what integration should achieve. Center-right parties want the EU to promote and enforce deregulation while minimizing social regulation, whereas center-left parties favor counterbalancing deregulation with EU-wide social regulation.

Both ends of the political spectrum are thus disappointed and critical of integration when EU regulatory output fails to conform to their preferences. These disappointments have become more politically significant precisely as the EU's regulatory outputs extend to an increasing number of policy fields, undermining national autonomy. A particular problem occurs when these regulatory outputs are very different from what was the national norm. For instance, average EU social regulation (say, the Working Time Directive) is normally more constraining than pre-existing rules in the United Kingdom, whereas EU market deregulation (say, railways) is typically far more liberal than the prevailing norms in France (Hix 2008).

This discrepancy between national rules and those implemented by the EU has had effects on party support for integration. In the United Kingdom, the center-right Conservative Party has turned against the EU because of the growth of regulation on businesses. In France, by contrast, it is the Socialist Party that has become lukewarm toward greater integration, for fear that more market liberalization and stricter national balanced budget rules would be enforced. It is significant that parties from different sides of the left–right divide can find something to object to in EU policies. This reveals the way in which EU constraints on national regulatory and budgetary autonomy are opposed by center-left parties, while EU attempts at enhancing citizen rights and workers' rights across the single market are resisted by center-right parties. The former want nation-states to be able to have more leeway for pursuing their own version of the social market; the latter want to retain national sovereignty to pursue more neoliberal market policies.

Consequently, the insulation of national politics from questions about the merits of integration and how it should be organized is now over (Hooghe and Marks 2009). Parties are divided over what stance they should take on integration. At the same time they face electorates that question the need for further conferral of competences to the EU. The result is that parties and leaders are subject to a **constraining dissensus**, whereby what they can do at the EU level is increasingly scrutinized and challenged in national politics (Hooghe and Marks 2009).

Therefore the growing impact of EU policy-making on national autonomy reflects increased political contestation around integration. This shows that integration is more politically relevant than ever before. However, one area where integration has long been salient is that of the regions of EU member states. These territorial sub-units play an important role in European integration, as they are responsible for executing certain EU policies, especially for administering funds for regional development (see Section 5.1). More importantly, there is also a connection between European integration and the growth of regional parties that seek more policy competences in order to run their affairs more autonomously. Indeed some regions within EU member states seek to secede from their existing country and potentially to become EU members in their own right. This is why integration is sometimes considered a framework that actually encourages demands for greater regional autonomy within EU countries (see Box 11.1).

With European integration now a highly salient feature of national politics, political parties across member states face the challenge of responding to citizens' concerns or preferences about integration. In this context, mainstream parties not only find it harder

---

Box 11.1   Case Study: European Integration and the Growth of Regionalism

European integration has in many ways empowered the territorial sub-units of EU member states, such as Wales, Catalonia, or Flanders. Regions are officially involved in EU business, not only by distributing regional funds but also as participants in the Committee of the Regions. This is an advisory body that allows regional and locally elected representatives to give their thoughts on EU legislation with a regional dimension such as transport, employment, and the environment. Since the Maastricht Treaty it is also possible for federal member states (such as Germany, Austria, and Belgium) to send a minister of a regional government to represent their country in the Council when discussing a law with an important regional impact. Regions have also established more than 250 regional offices in Brussels to lobby for their interests. The net result is that Europe's regions have gained political and economic clout, especially in relation to their central governments (Hooghe and Marks 2001). This **Europe of the Regions** has been promoted by the European Commission as a way to make integration more popular at a local level by being responsive to the needs of regional actors. Nevertheless, some scholars point out that EU regulation curtails the legislative autonomy of certain regions, as EU legislation determines policies without the participation of regional governments (Jeffery 2005). As a result, regions are administrative agents of the EU rather than autonomous decision-makers. This helps explain the continuing claims for statehood among certain EU regions such as Scotland or Catalonia. European integration facilitates these claims, because the EU provides a large open market in which small states can thrive. At the same time, regions understand that statehood allows for full participation in the EU's intergovernmental institutions, where important decisions are made. However, the EU does not have a formal mechanism for regions seceding from a member state to join, which means, for example, that Spain could in theory block Catalonia from joining the EU, as accession always requires unanimity.

to persuade citizens about the merits of greater integration; they also face more numerous internal splits over EU policy and institutional reform. The challenge facing parties traditionally supportive of integration is compounded by the development of new parties – from both the left and the right – that explicitly oppose the EU and its current policies. These parties are responding to citizens' skepticism about the economic and political consequences of integration. Hence an important part of the new constraining dissensus surrounding European integration is the development of euroskepticism, which will now be examined.

11.2   Euroskepticism and Its Varieties

Euroskepticism, the political ideology opposing European integration – notably the current EU system – is a varied and complex phenomenon. The word itself seems to have come from British politics in the mid-1980s (Harmsen and Spiering 2004, 15–16) and to have become more widespread after British Prime Minister Margaret Thatcher's 1988 Bruges speech attacking the bureaucratic and institutional weaknesses of European integration. Today, however, euroskepticism is a pan-European affair – and one that manifests itself in different ways, depending on different critiques of integration advocated by various political parties.

These critiques can be divided into soft and hard variants of euroskepticism according to how hostile they are to the current system, and hence according to whether they advocate withdrawal from it. Different types of political party articulate different kinds of euroskepticism. At the same time, this political ideology is voiced in different political contexts, on the basis of the political opportunities that allow parties to profit from opposing integration. These opportunities arise during European parliamentary elections, treaty ratification, and national elections. Hence this section outlines when and where euroskepticism manifests itself before going on to explain what constitutes different types of euroskepticism.

11.2.1   When and where euroskepticism is expressed

One major arena in which euroskepticism has developed is that of European parliamentary elections. Here mainstream parties that support the status quo are challenged by parties fundamentally hostile to today's EU. Since the 2009 elections, for instance, there has been a bloc of MEPs from 11 member states that constitute the Europe of Freedom and Democracy party group. There is another group of 52 MEPs that constitutes the European Conservatives and Reformists Group. Both of these party groups are hostile   to the principle of an ever closer union and fundamentally opposed to governments that confer more competences to the EU. They have a cross-national membership, a fact that indicates the diffusion of anti-EU feeling across various member states, although both groups are dominated by British political parties. This confirms the long-standing trend whereby the United Kingdom is the country in which euroskepticism is most prevalent.

Anti-EU parties provide an outlet for euroskepticism that is not catered for by mainstream political parties. This is because the latter have traditionally been supportive – perhaps implicitly rather than explicitly – of the broad institutional status quo. Single-issue euroskeptic parties – that is, parties established just in order to protest against more integration – have emerged to challenge precisely this mainstream consensus. Such parties do better in European than in national elections. The United Kingdom Independence Party thus polled 16.5 percent of the national vote in the 2009 European elections, but only 3 percent in the 2010 general election. Another anti-EU party, the People's Movement against the EU, has been successful in Denmark, winning 7 percent of the vote in 2009 and gaining one MEP (out of only 13 Danish seats).

In the past, the success of single-issue euroskeptic parties was linked to second-order effects (see Box 10.1) based on opposing governing parties. That is, voting for anti-EU parties was associated with a general oppositional vote against the incumbent government. More recent research shows that opposition to government is not the driving force behind euroskepticism (Kriesi 2007). In this way European elections give a disgruntled minority the chance to voice its genuine hostility to the EU and integration more broadly. However, contesting integration by electing anti-EU MEPs remains more of a protest gesture than a way to shake up the system. MEPs are there to vote on legislation; they do not get to decide the legal and institutional contours of integration, and hence they cannot determine whether the EU gains more powers (Mair 2007).

Hence another moment when euroskepticism manifests itself is during periods of EU treaty ratification. These are periods when national parliaments – or, in the case of countries holding referendums, citizens – get a say in whether or not to accept a new EU treaty. Ratification decisions are fundamental to the development of integration, as new treaties normally mean new powers or new decision-making rules for the EU. Since the 1992 Maastricht Treaty, treaty ratification in general has become a hot topic in national politics regardless of whether there is a referendum. Opposition to a new EU treaty can expose splits – buried for the sake of concentrating on national issues – within a political party or a governing coalition. Referendums on an EU treaty (as well as on EU issues) have specific political dynamics, which is why they are studied in depth in Section 11.3.

A remarkable instance of the splits occasioned by treaty ratification happened in the governing British Conservative Party at the time of the Maastricht Treaty. A minority of euroskeptic members of parliament opposed the deal that their leader had negotiated and sought to derail ratification of the Maastricht Treaty. This revolt was only squashed when ratifying the treaty was turned into a vote of confidence in the government, albeit at the cost of weakening the government for the remainder of its term of office. Similar tensions surfaced in France in 2012, when the French Green Party, part of the governing coalition, officially opposed ratification of the Fiscal Compact (a treaty to be discussed in Chapter 12), which was designed to solve the Eurozone debt crisis.

Euroskepticism emerges in these ratification moments to dispute the direction integration is taking as well as the way in which the EU is organized. The idea behind opposition to an EU treaty is thus to generate support for a different kind of treaty reform, or to pave the way for a new legal relationship between a particular country and its EU partners. Nevertheless, in previous instances where treaty ratification has failed, the goals of the euroskeptics have not automatically been realized. Denmark was granted opt-outs from the euro and from the Common Security and Defence Policy after its citizens voted against ratifying the Maastricht Treaty, whereas the rejected Constitutional Treaty resurfaced as the Lisbon Treaty, being eventually ratified by all member states (see Section 3.4).

The fact that treaty ratification is becoming more and more politicized further underscores the demise of the permissive consensus era. Indeed this phenomenon points to the way in which EU issues, and thus euroskepticism, are more prevalent in national politics than ever before (Hooghe and Marks 2009). In some countries euroskepticism has always been more present. This is particularly true of the United Kingdom, often seen as an awkward EU member state and the only one that has held a referendum on whether to withdraw from the integration process (see Box 3.2). Its mainstream political parties tend to be less favorable to integration and supranationalism than their continental counterparts. This is illustrated by the fact that MEPs from Britain's Conservative Party sit with the small, explicitly euroskeptic European Conservatives and Reformists group rather than with the European People's Party, which brings together the major European center-right parties. However, euroskepticism is not just confined to a few countries, as public opinion polling suggests that citizens across the EU are critical of the current system of integration and lack trust in EU institutions (see Box 11.2).

In fact euroskepticism is also present in the national politics of non-EU countries such as Norway and Switzerland, whose elites have toyed with the idea of joining the club. This illustrates a trend found across Europe whereby political elites are less critical of integration and of the status quo in the EU than the average citizen is. Indeed, only a minority of the EU population – roughly 10 percent – has a strong sense of European identity, a feeling scholars associate with the economically mobile, more educated, and multilingual elites in politics or business (Fligstein 2008).

This does not mean that the remaining 90 percent are unambiguously against integration or against a European political identity, since only about a third of EU citizens express a purely national sense of identity. Rather the majority of EU citizens appear to be "situational" Europeans. These citizens approve of integration and are comfortable with being part of a larger political community according to circumstances such as specific policies or issues (Fligstein 2008).

This ambivalence toward integration among a large part of the population of the EU means that media coverage can play an important role in influencing attitudes toward the EU (Maier and Rittberger 2008). Given the linguistic diversity of Europe, the vast majority of citizens get their information about integration and the EU from language-specific media embedded in a national political and cultural context. It is thus important to note the presence of euroskepticism in the national media of some countries, such as the United Kingdom and Austria. Euroskepticism in the media is not necessarily linked to a political party with an anti-EU stance; rather it aims to capture and reflect the dissatisfaction or mistrust of ordinary people (see Figure 11.1). Again, this is especially true of the United Kingdom, where the best-selling daily newspaper, *The Sun*, is "vigorously and virulently Euroskeptic, conjuring up the image of the EU as a corrupt and untrustworthy predator, driven by a Franco-German plot to damage British economic interests, British security and British sovereignty" (Anderson 2004, 154). In the

Box 11.2   Key Concept: Public Opinion and the EU

Public opinion refers to what citizens think of a particular subject. In terms of the EU, this means what ordinary people think about integration, the EU's policies, and whether they trust its institutions. Data on public opinion are collected by the EU's own polling organization, **Eurobarometer**, created in 1973. This organization regularly conducts surveys across all member states, regularly asking citizens whether they consider EU membership to be a "good thing." These survey data are a unique resource used by analysts and scholars to understand public attitudes toward integration. The Commission also uses survey data to signal support for its policies or its proposed legislation. Traditionally, Eurobarometer's standard "is EU membership a good thing" question has revealed that citizens in countries that are large net contributors to the EU (such as Germany, Finland, and Sweden) consider the EU less beneficial than citizens in countries that are net recipients (McLaren 2005). Another key indicator of public attitudes to the EU is the level of trust citizens have in its institutions. Levels of trust have also tended to vary across member states, certain Eastern European countries being among those whose citizens find the EU most trustworthy, for example in proportions of 52 percent and 55 percent in Estonia and Bulgaria respectively (Eurobarometer 2012). This compares, across all member states, with an average of only 31 percent of citizens who trust the EU. Although data suggest that trust in national governments has also fallen in the past decades (see Figure 11.1), citizens' attitudes to the EU reveal how entrenched a critical perspective on the EU has become.

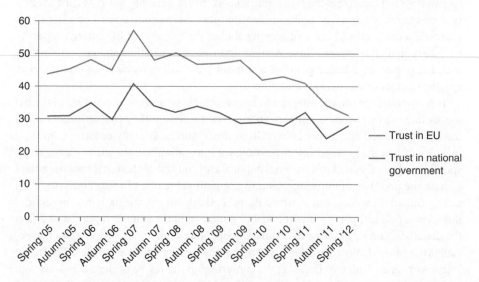

Figure 11.1   Citizens' "tendency to trust" the EU and national government. Source: Data from Eurobarometer 77, spring 2012

majority of other EU countries, especially where newspaper readership is lower, the mainstream print press is more sympathetic to integration, even if the citizens' interpretation of what the EU does for them and for their country is becoming more skeptical, as will be discussed.

11.2.2   Hard euroskepticism

As explained in Section 11.2.1, euroskepticism is an ideology that cuts across the traditional left/right divide in European politics. That is, it can be articulated both by parties of the left and by parties of the right, expressing frustration about how integration hampers the ideological goals of both ends of the political system. Yet there are different types of euroskepticism according to how far parties reject integration per se, as opposed to rejecting the way it is currently pursued through today's EU system. This variety suggests that there are separate explanations for different kinds of hostility toward European integration.

The most useful way of categorizing these varieties of euroskepticism is the hard versus soft distinction devised by Taggart (1998). Hard euroskepticism entails "principled opposition" to the EU as well as to European integration. The principle behind this opposition is that of wanting to withdraw from the EU or else completely revise the project by dismantling the current legal and institutional architecture. It is an extreme position, therefore, which contrasts with soft euroskepticism. The latter is best understood as "qualified opposition to the EU." This soft version is associated with objections to a particular EU policy or treaty that negatively affects national interests. Hence the major division within euroskepticism is between those who reject the benefits of integration, especially in the form of the EU, and those who support integration while still being critical of what the EU does and how it functions.

Hard euroskepticism, as manifested in single-issue parties such as the United Kingdom Independence Party or the Danish People's Movement Against the EU, is founded on a mixture of economic and democratic arguments against integration. The economic argument is that the costs of integration – contributions to the EU budget, but also the burden of applying EU rules – necessarily outweigh the benefits. This in itself is taken to be an immediate reason not to pursue any further integration but to seek an eventual exit from the EU. However, this kind of hostility is compounded by animosity toward the EU's democratic deficit. The principle here is that national governments, elected by and representative of a national people, should not be subject to implementing laws in which they have had little say. Hard euroskepticism thus stands for a strong defense of national sovereignty, which is best served by blocking new transfers of competences (for instance new treaties) and by trying to build a national mandate to withdraw. Since hard euroskeptic parties question the kind of formal electoral consent their citizens have given today's EU, they are often at the forefront of calls for referendums on treaties as well as on exiting the EU.

This focus on national democracy as the primary locus for decision-making is also connected to the defense of national borders and identity. From this perspective, European integration, with its dedication to open borders and its enlargement to new countries, is seen precisely as a threat to the integrity of national culture and to democracy. Hence hard euroskepticism is now also articulated by far-right political parties and by populist parties with an anti-immigration agenda (De Vries and Edwards 2009). A good example here is the French National Front, a far-right party that was very hostile to the EU Constitutional Treaty, considering it a threat to sovereignty and a prelude to further eastern enlargement. Similar kinds of extreme right-wing parties oppose the EU in Finland (True Finns), Belgium (the Flemish Bloc), Austria (the Freedom Party of Austria), and Denmark (the Danish People's Party). Hence this is a phenomenon common to West European member states, which experts link to the rise in immigration flows from Eastern Europe following the 2004 enlargement (De Vries and Edwards 2009).

The extreme left also vehicles outright hostility toward the EU. This opposition manifests itself through resistance to further integration "on the basis of the neoliberal character of the [EU] project and its negative influence on the welfare state" (De Vries and Edwards 2009, 9). Whereas the extreme right exploits fears about the dilution of national culture and identity, the extreme left version of euroskepticism tries to woo voters concerned about their economic well-being under more market competition. This is the case for Western European parties in Germany (Die Linke / The Left), in France (Le Parti communiste / The Communist Party, Le Parti de gauche / The Left Party), Italy (Partito della Rifondazione Comunista / The Communist Refoundation Party), and in Denmark (Socialistisk Folkeparti / The Socialist People's Party). These parties are worried that further integration will come at the cost of existing national social market regulation, that is, at the cost of undermining national efforts to compensate the losers of market competition. Hence hard euroskepticism – whether from a far-left or a far-right perspective – revolves around the question of maintaining national boundaries and independence (Kriesi et al. 2006).

However, the extreme left is torn over integration, as it ordinarily favors open borders for people and also realizes the possible benefits of using integration to tame global flows of capital and to change trade rules. Hence, while extreme right parties are against integration per se, extreme left parties often articulate their opposition to the EU as a call for pursuing a different kind of integration. This was the case during the Eurozone sovereign debt crisis, where extreme left parties opposed EU-mandated government budget cuts while advocating a different kind of European-wide solution rather than a return to national autonomy. In Greece notably, the hard left Coalition of the Radical Left (Syriza) won many votes in the 2012 national election with a platform of staying in the euro but without reducing government spending.

11.2.3   Soft euroskepticism

This tension over whether to reject all integration or else pursue a different kind of EU project is not present in genuine soft euroskepticism. This softer variety involves agreeing with the principle of pooling sovereignty for mutual gains while also criticizing elements of the current EU system (Taggart 1998). In other words, this criticism is targeted at elements of the EU that for some reason are seen as flawed or failing. This kind of criticism actually relates to two of the main planks of hard euroskepticism: the economic benefits of integration and the quality of democratic decision-making. This positioning reflects citizens' concerns that EU policies are sometimes too constraining on national autonomy or made in an opaque fashion, unresponsive to citizens' preferences.

Hence the soft version of euroskepticism seeks a better EU system, notably one that does more to ensure economic growth and is more democratic and transparent. In this way soft euroskepticism is more comfortable with the premise of integration: that weakening national boundaries and autonomy can be beneficial. It is this kind of euroskepticism that is filtering into mainstream political parties, which traditionally were "ideologically inclined to endorse further steps of integration both economically and politically" (Crum 2007, 65). One indication of this creeping soft euroskepticism can be seen in the growing opposition to net EU budget contributions in Germany, Sweden, and the Netherlands. Mainstream center-right and center-left parties in these countries have normally been in favor of integration, and yet the governments they have formed have become very critical of their large net EU budget contributions.

This opposition to the EU budget system among net contributor countries illustrates the fact that soft euroskepticism is a pragmatic creed. It lies between two extremes, neither seeing the EU and more integration as a means to solve all contemporary policy problems nor rejecting the EU outright. As a result, soft euroskepticism is associated with measures such as negotiating opt-outs (see Chapter 3, Glossary) on the basis of national interest, doing more to protect national interests generally, and limiting the drift toward more integration simply for the sake of integration.

Categorizing soft euroskepticism as a pragmatic, mid-range position is particularly useful for understanding public opinion on integration. Hence Kopecký and Mudde (2002) distinguish between "eurorejects," voters who oppose integration and the EU, "euroenthusiasts," who favor more integration, and "europragmatists," who want an EU that benefits their country and interests. In fact a pragmatic streak appears to explain differences in public opinion across member states on whether EU membership is considered beneficial, citizens of net contributor states being less likely to agree than those in net recipient countries (see Box 11.2). The presence of a multifaceted euroskeptic ideology in national politics is further illustrated by what happens when member states hold referendums on EU treaties, as discussed below.

11.3 National Referendums on EU Issues

Referendums are another way of ratifying an EU treaty (see Box 2.3). Instead of a national parliament voting on a treaty signed by its government, a referendum involves asking the people to decide. These votes are thus an exercise in what is known as **direct democracy**: asking the people for their opinion rather than delegating the decision to their elected representatives. National governments are free to decide whether to hold a referendum – there are no formal EU constraints on this practice – yet not all member states are constitutionally allowed to organize one for an international treaty. Germany and Italy outlaw this practice for fear of giving in to populist sentiment on vital issues of national interest; Ireland, by contrast, is legally obliged to hold a referendum when-ever there is a treaty change (see Section 3.4).

In the course of European integration various kinds of treaties have been subject to referendums. So were votes on whether a country should join the EEC/EU (like Norway in 1972 and 1994, Croatia in 2012), votes on whether a treaty of accession allowing another country to join should stand (France voted on accepting EEC enlargement in 1972), and also votes on whether a treaty changing EU decision-making and compe-tences should be accepted (Ireland and the Lisbon Treaty in 2011). Additionally, certain countries have held referendums on specific matters relating to integration; such were notably the Danish vote on whether to join the euro in 2000, followed by a referendum on the same issue in Sweden in 2003, and the UK vote on whether to leave the EEC in 1975. In total, national governments in member states and beyond have organized over 50 referendums on issues relating to EU integration (Hobolt 2009).

Consequently, these referendums are now an integral part of national politics. Indeed they have become the most important means whereby ordinary citizens participate in deciding upon and shaping the contours of European integration (Hooghe and Marks 2009). This is because referendums offer citizens a chance to debate the big EU issues – enlargement, decision-making, competences. At the same time, political leaders and parties have to articulate their preferences and visions regarding integration and where it is heading, something that mainstream parties have traditionally neglected to discuss in national politics. Hence the purpose of this section is to analyze the politics surrounding these votes and to assess what they mean for integration.

11.3.1   Why hold referendums?

As stated in Section 11.3 referendums involve giving citizens the choice to determine important issues relating to integration. It has almost become the norm for countries acceding to the EU to hold a referendum to ratify this move. In doing so, governments hope to ride a wave of pro-European sentiment that will bolster their domestic position. Hence nine of the ten countries joining in 2004 held such referendums, as did Croatia in 2012. Voting on treaties is less common – but it became more common after the Maastricht Treaty – and is done for different reasons. Yet it is a risky undertaking, as the recent record suggests that citizens are increasingly reluctant to go along with these deals. Since 2000, only six of the 11 referendums in member states (either on treaties or on joining the euro) have succeeded. This number includes **rerun referendums** in Ireland, where citizens were twice asked to vote again, on the Nice Treaty and on the Lisbon Treaty. Consequently it is important to consider why governments voluntarily resort to referendums (unlike in Ireland, where they are obligatory) and why they have lost them even though the odds seem stacked in their favor.

Most referendums on treaties are held when a government has sufficient votes to ratify the treaty via parliament, so this is not a question of bypassing parliament to pass a treaty. Rather national referendums on EU issues are, in theory, a way of connecting citizens to European integration. Asking citizens to vote provides democratic legitimacy to the process and outcome of integration by making their input count. This is in line with the rhetoric of bringing the EU closer to its citizens and making it more democratic, a position that emerged after the introduction of subsidiarity in the Maastricht Treaty. Democratic legitimacy was also at the heart of the debates surrounding the EU Constitutional Treaty, which is why four countries held referendums on that treaty. Indeed six more countries planned to do the same before the treaty's rejection by French and Dutch voters derailed the process.

However, there are also tactical political motives at play in the decision to hold a referendum. Traditionally, most European democracies, with the notable exception of Switzerland, have seldom relied on direct democracy. The growing use of referendums thus marks a departure from representative democracy, for which there are several causes. One is the intention to overcome an internal divide within a government over integration. A good example here is Britain's 1975 referendum on remaining in the EEC. It was held because the governing Labour Party was at odds over whether EEC membership was a good thing – as it was a socialist party, some of its leaders and many members were hostile to market liberalization (Smith 1999). Putting the issue to a national vote was a way to settle it without splitting the party for good, allowing the government to concentrate on the day-to-day running of the country.

Another reason to hold a referendum is for elected representatives to avoid taking decisions that could subsequently hurt them in a national election. This was certainly the case when British Prime Minister Tony Blair announced a plan for a national vote on the 2004 EU Constitutional Treaty. Originally against a referendum, Blair realized, as the negotiations dragged on, that with a general election scheduled for 2005 it would be useful to separate the EU Constitution from the election campaign (Dür and Mateo 2011). In a country with many eurosceptic voters, he did not want his party to suffer electorally by being responsible for ratifying an unpopular treaty.

It also appears that the fact of having held referendums before makes parties more willing to use direct democracy, so as not to disappoint voters who expect to have their say. This is the case in Denmark, where, even though there has always been sufficient support for parliamentary ratification of an EU treaty, parties do not wish to deprive the people of having their say (Buch and Hansen 2002). Moreover, in the case of the EU Constitutional Treaty, there was a contagion effect whereby, as one country announced it would hold a referendum, this created pressure for others to do the same. This meant that 10 of the 25 then member states were scheduled to have a referendum on this treaty after Tony Blair set the ball in motion with his 2004 referendum pledge. The framing of this treaty, initially penned by a constitutional convention (see Section 3.4) as a foundational document that could inspire constitutional patriotism (see Chapter 10, Glossary), obviously made it harder for governments to deny their citizens a say on its ratification (Moravcsik 2006).

Of course, only four countries actually voted as referendums elsewhere were abandoned, including in the United Kingdom, following rejections in France and the Netherlands. Although governing parties that signed the Lisbon Treaty pledged not to hold referendums on this successor to the Constitutional Treaty, many smaller parties and interest groups (pro-EU as well as anti-EU) campaigned for referendums across member states. Governing parties resisted these pressures for fear of another setback for reforming the EU, precisely because the political dynamics of referendum campaigns are uncertain and hard for elites to control.

11.3.2   The political dynamics of referendum campaigns

Ratification by referendum means citizens get to vote on a document negotiated by a national government. Consequently governments want to see citizens approve their handiwork, as a rejection of the treaty is an implicit disavowal of those who negotiated it. Similarly, governments in other member states will want a positive response when a treaty is subject to a referendum, as a single rejection will put reform on hold for all. In this way a host of important actors with access to significant political and financial resources are normally active to make sure citizens vote in favor of a treaty. Nevertheless, referendum campaigns are never a foregone conclusion, because the final decision lies with the voters, not with the government.

Perhaps the most important characteristic of referendum campaigns on European integration is thus the way in which these "shift the initiative to citizens and single-issue groups, and disarm party elites" (Hooghe and Marks 2009, 20). In the context of a "constraining dissensus," mainstream political parties have a hard task persuading voters to accept an EU treaty. A striking case in point is the Irish rejection of the Lisbon Treaty in 2008, even though the campaign in favor of it was supported by parties representing 90 percent of the seats in the legislature. Treaty rejections, as well as acceptances with very slim winning margins (for instance 51 percent in the French vote on the Maastricht Treaty), reveal a discrepancy between the preferences of political elites (governments and mainstream political parties) and those of ordinary people over European integration. This discrepancy makes referendum outcomes hard to predict.

One element of unpredictability surrounding referendums on EU issues is voter turnout. Unlike in European parliamentary elections, referendum turnout can be very high, as with the 89 percent who voted in Norway on EU accession on 1994. Referendum turnout can be higher even than for national elections (LeDuc 2002), although it can also be lower, as with the 35 percent who voted on the Nice Treaty in Ireland in 2001. In fact turnout fluctuates more in referendums than in national elections. Associated with this uncertainty over turnout is the possibility of large shifts in public opinion over the course of a campaign – larger than in national elections, where issues and debates are better known (LeDuc 2002). These shifts are the product of campaigns that invariably move away from the specific treaty at hand to debate the entire gamut of policies and problems associated with European integration.

The campaigns for the referendums on the EU Constitution and its successor, the Lisbon Treaty, illustrate well this tendency to debate matters far beyond the contents of a treaty. In the 2005 French referendum, for example, the campaign paid little attention to the actual details of EU institutional reform, even if this was one of the central components of the new treaty. Instead, opponents of the treaty managed to bring in other issues – such as immigration, the possibility of Turkish accession, and whether the EU charter of fundamental rights compromised French abortion law (Glencross 2009). These policy issues were tangential to the actual legal implications of the treaty – or indeed factually incorrect in the case of the fear that French abortion law could be altered. Yet the issues revealed voters' general concerns about integration and the direction it was taking. Similar fears were present during the Irish vote on the Lisbon Treaty.

A third of Irish voters incorrectly believed that the treaty would involve the amalgamation of the Irish army into an EU army and would overturn the country's prohibition on abortion, while over 40 percent thought that the treaty would compel the Irish government to raise its notoriously low corporation tax rate (Dehousse 2008).

These more general fears about the impact of integration are something that mainstream parties struggle to allay in referendum campaigns. Indeed the infiltration of policy and ideological issues into a campaign on a treaty dealing primarily with institutional reform raises the question of how the knowledge deficit (see Box 6.3) affects referendum campaigns. Here the empirical evidence suggests that both euroskepticism and voting "no" on an EU referendum are associated with lower income levels and less knowledge of how the EU functions (Gabel 1998). By contrast, urban and upper middle-class voters who declare themselves knowledgeable about the EU are more likely to ratify an EU treaty. However, referendum campaigns have been shown to lead to more media coverage and debate on European integration than is ordinarily the case in national politics. In this way, the use of direct democracy can open up a debate over integration that is ordinarily not very present. This means that referendums are a way of getting information about the EU across to voters and of suggesting in this way that these really are about integration and not second-order moments of anti-government protest (Hobolt 2009).

The debate on integration being made possible by resorting to direct democracy can lead to some surprising combinations of euroskepticism, with parties on both extremes of the political spectrum opposing an EU treaty. This was the case in France in 2005, where the far left and the far right helped mobilize voters against the EU Constitution by attacking its supposed neoliberal bias and its open immigration policy respectively. A similar dynamic existed in Ireland for the 2008 referendum. There a minor free market party opposed the Lisbon Treaty on the grounds that it created too much regulation, while another party that urged voters to reject the treaty was the radical nationalist party Sinn Féin, which wanted to protect Irish neutrality and welfare policy. Hence these opponents to treaty ratification used very different justifications for their position, yet they shared one major characteristic: defiance of the political establishment. This was obvious in the popular slogan of the Irish "no" movement against the Lisbon Treaty: "Don't Be Bullied" – a reference to the pressure from the government and other member states to ratify the treaty. Such pressure is commonplace in official government campaigns, as when Danish politicians asked their citizens not to jeopardize jobs by rejecting the euro, or when a former French president warned voters that rejecting the Maastricht Treaty would mean allowing a reunited Germany to dominate Europe (Criddle 1993).

Of course, the fact that this pressure has led to rerun referendums on treaties after voters have rejected them makes many question whether citizens should ever have their say on these issues (see Box 11.3). Nevertheless, the latter are a feature of the way national politics is adapting to European integration. Although only Ireland held a referendum on the Lisbon Treaty, the use of direct democracy to ratify future treaties remains on the agenda. This is especially the case in the United Kingdom, which in 2011 passed a law mandating that any new transfer of competences to the EU would have to be approved directly by the British people. In addition, politicians in both France and Austria have raised the possibility of holding referendums on allowing Turkey to join the EU. As a result, referendums are here to stay.

Box 11.3   Key Debate: Are National Referendums a Good Idea?

The rejection of EU treaties by voters in various national referendums highlights the risks of using direct democracy to determine a state's international relations. Ordinarily, EU member states rely on their parliaments (that is, on their representative democracy) to scrutinize and ratify international treaties. Yet EU treaties – highly complex legal documents – are increasingly put to a "yes or no" public vote. What happens in these cases is that referendum campaigns invariably shift away from the specific treaty at hand, to debate the entire gamut of policies and problems associated with European integration. While it might be appropriate for citizens to debate integration and to use a referendum to decide their country's level of involvement in the EU (Schmitter 2000), many analysts think referendums on a specific treaty reform are inappropriate. This is because deciding on a legal and institutional reform of the EU system is separate from the larger issue of what European integration is for and whether it is good for one's country (Dehousse 2006). By extension, the message coming from a referendum rejection is never very clear, given that the campaign debate involves so many issues beyond the technical details of the treaty. As a result, voters within and across member states can object to the same treaty on different grounds, making the message from what is supposed to be a simple question actually highly ambiguous. In the absence of a clear message, political leaders struggle to respond to citizens' preferences, thereby undermining the possibility of using referendums to pursue an alternative type of integration. Consequently, some scholars suggest that it is never a good idea for citizens to have a vote on this kind of international treaty (Moravcsik 2006).

11.4   Concluding Summary

European integration has not always been a salient feature of national politics. However, the era of the permissive consensus has disappeared in response to the increasing constraints that integration imposes on national autonomy. The result is increased contestation, within national politics, over integration and the EU, parties being torn over how to respond to citizens' dissatisfaction. Mainstream center-right and center-left parties are concerned when EU policies go against their ideological preferences for more market liberalization and more welfare protection respectively. At the same time new parties have emerged that explicitly oppose the EU and its current policies. As elites are split over how to pursue integration and citizens are wary about what the EU does, there is now a "constraining dissensus" in national politics.

Opposition to the EU is a manifestation of euroskepticism expressed during European parliamentary elections, moments of treaty ratification, and general national political debate. The ideology behind parties and politicians critical of the EU is varied.

Some are proponents of hard euroskepticism, which involves complete hostility toward pooling sovereignty. This hardline version can be expressed both by far-left parties, which are opposed to market liberalization, and by far-right parties, which reject any dilution of national sovereignty and identity. The latter oppose integration per se, while the former are amenable to adopting a radical alternative to the contemporary EU. The softer version of euroskepticism targets aspects of integration and of the current EU that for some reason are seen as flawed or failing. Hence this form of euroskepticism is associated with a pragmatic take on integration, in which voters want EU membership to be beneficial rather than a burden.

National debate and contestation over integration are particularly evident in moments when governments call a referendum on treaty ratification or another integration-related issue. Governments (except for Ireland) are not obliged to use this form of direct democracy, although they may do so in order to render ratification more legitimate or to avoid taking responsibility for an unpopular treaty. Normally there is a great deal of official backing for voters to pass a treaty. However, campaigns are volatile, making referendum outcomes hard to predict. Many issues beyond the scope of the treaty itself crop up, and minor parties from opposing ends of the political spectrum can mobilize opposition on the basis of citizens' fears or lack of understanding about integration. The political message from a failed referendum is thus unclear, as voters within and across member states can object to the same treaty on different grounds. Consequently referendums do not provide a clear message about what voters would prefer integration to look like. Nevertheless, there remains pressure from citizens and from euroskeptic parties to use direct democracy for deciding on integration issues.

Guide to Further Reading

Hobolt, S. B. 2009. *Europe in Question: Referendums on European Integration*. Oxford: Oxford University Press.

The most up-to-date and sophisticated analysis of the dynamics and outcomes of referendums on issues relating to integration.

McLaren, L. M. 2005. *Identity, Interests and Attitudes to European Integration*. Basingstoke: Palgrave.

An accessible and comprehensive analysis of public sentiment toward integration and of the factors driving public opinion.

Szczerbiak, A., and P. Taggart, eds. 2008. *Opposing Europe? The Comparative Party Politics of Euroscepticism*. Oxford: Oxford University Press.

A synoptic scholarly survey of the phenomenon of euroskepticism as a party political phenomenon, with different experts covering different countries and institutional settings.

Discussion Questions

1   What characterized the permissive consensus era and what evidence is there for its demise?

2   How widespread is euroskepticism across the EU and what parties advocate this ideology?
3   What is the difference between hard and soft euroskepticism and how does it translate into different policy recommendations?
4   For what reasons do governments decide to hold referendums on EU issues?
5   Is direct democracy a good way to decide on EU issues? What impact does this have on European integration?

Web Resources

This book is supported by a companion website, which can be found at www.wiley.com/go/glencross. There you will find a list of the web links referred to in this chapter wherever you see a "Web" icon in the page margins. In addition, you will find a list of further relevant online resources such as websites for EU institutions, political groups, archives, and think tanks, information on studying abroad, and biographies of key figures. You will also find self-assessment tools in the form of flashcards and independent study questions developed specifically for this chapter.

Glossary

Constraining dissensus
A situation in which European political elites not only are uncertain of whether to support more integration, but also face growing opposition to the EU from their citizens. This contrasts with the era of the permissive consensus.

Direct democracy
A form of democracy in which voters are asked to decide an issue for themselves rather than delegating the decision to elected representatives. Thus direct democracy is associated with referendums, that is, with a "yes or no" vote on a particular question (such as ratifying an EU treaty).

Eurobarometer
The EU's own polling organization, which regularly conducts surveys of public opinion on EU issues across member states.

Europe of the Regions
An expression used to refer to the way integration empowers the territorial sub-units of EU member states such as Wales, Catalonia, or Flanders. These sub-units have become important administrators of EU policies, providing regional leaders with more clout at the national and supranational level.

Euroskepticism
A political ideology that opposes European integration and the current EU system. Euroskepticism comes in different forms; extreme anti-EU hostility is labeled "hard" by comparison with a "soft" type, which is critical merely of certain flawed or failing aspects of integration.

Integration by stealth

A depiction of the early years of integration as deliberately focusing on technical and less salient aspects of pooling sovereignty, so as to expand supranationalism without contestation from domestic politics.

Permissive consensus

A reference to the early period of integration, when treaties and common policies were not very salient in national politics. Diplomatic deals cut by political elites were thus insulated from criticism, as citizens trusted their leaders, who in turn shared a consensus for more integration.

Rerun referendums

A rerun referendum is a referendum on an EU treaty that is held a second time because voters rejected it the first time. This has happened in Denmark and Ireland, whose voters rejected ratification of certain EU treaties. Rerun referendums arise because of pressure from other governments to ratify treaties.

References

Anderson, Peter J. 2004. "A Flag of Convenience? Discourse and Motivations of the London-Based Eurosceptic Press." In Robert Harmsen and Menno Spiering, eds., *Euroscepticism: Party Politics, National Identity and European Integration*, 151–170. Amsterdam: Rodopi.

Buch, Roger, and Kasper M. Hansen. 2002. "The Danes and Europe: From EC 1972 to Euro 2000 – Elections, Referendums and Attitudes." *Scandinavian Political Studies*, 25: 1–26. DOI: 10.1111/1467-9477.00061

Criddle, Byron. 1993. "The French Referendum on the Maastricht Treaty September 1992." *Parliamentary Affairs*, 46: 228–238.

Crum, Ben. 2007. "Party Stances in the Referendums on the EU Constitution." *European Union Politics*, 8: 61–82. DOI: 10.1177/1465116507073286.

De Vries, Catherine E., and Erica E. Edwards. 2009. "Taking Europe to Its Extremes: Extremist Parties and Public Euroscepticism." *Party Politics*, 15: 5–28. DOI: 10.1177/1354068808097889

Dehousse, Renaud. 2006. "The Unmaking of a Constitution: Lessons from the European Referenda." *Constellations*, 13: 151–164. DOI: 0.1111/j.1351-0487.2006.00447.x

Dehousse, Renaud. 2008. "One No Too Many." *European Union Studies Association Review*. Available at http://www.eustudies.org/publications_review_fall08.php#forum-4 (accessed July 20, 2013).

Dür, Andreas, and Gemma Mateo. 2011. "To Call or Not to Call? Political Parties and Referendums on the EU's Constitutional Treaty." *Comparative Political Studies*, 44: 468–492. DOI: 10.1177/0010414010393476

Eurobarometer. 2012. "Public Opinion in the European Union." Standard Eurobarometer, 77 (spring). Available at http://ec.europa.eu/public_opinion/archives/eb/eb77/eb77_first_en.pdf (accessed July 20, 2013).

Fligstein, Neil. 2008. *Euroclash: The EU, European Identity, and the Future of Europe*. Oxford: Oxford University Press.

Gabel, Matthew. 1998. "Public Support for European Integration: An Empirical Test of Five Theories." *Journal of Politics*, 60: 333–354. DOI: 10.2307/2647912

Glencross, Andrew. 2009. "The Difficulty of Justifying EU Integration as a Consequence of Depoliticization: Evidence from the 2005 French Referendum." *Government and Opposition*, 44: 243–261. DOI: 10.1111/j.1477-7053.2009.01287.x

Harmsen, Robert, and Menno Spiering. 2004. "Introduction: Euroscepticism and the Evolution of European Political Debate." In Robert Harmsen and Menno Spiering, eds., *Euroscepticism: Party Politics, National identity and European integration*, 13–35. Amsterdam: Rodopi.

Hix, Simon. 2008. "Towards a Partisan Theory of EU Politics." *Journal of European Public Policy*, 15: 1254–1265. DOI: 10.1080/13501760802407821

Hobolt, Sara Binzer. 2009. *Europe in Question: Referendums on European Integration*. Oxford: Oxford University Press.

Hooghe, Liesbet, and Gary Marks. 2001. *Multi-Level Governance and European Integration*. Oxford: Rowman & Littlefield.

Hooghe, Liesbet, and Gary Marks. 2009. "A Postfunctionalist Theory of European Integration: From Permissive Consensus to Constraining Dissensus." *British Journal of Political Science*, 39: 1–23.

Jeffery, Charlie. 2005. "Regions and the European Union: Letting Them in, and Leaving Them Alone." In Stephen Weatherill and Ulf Bernitz, eds., *The Role of Regions and Sub-national Actors in Europe*, 33–45. Oxford: Hart.

Kopecký, Petr, and Cas Mudde. 2002. "The Two Sides of Euroscepticism: Party Positions on European Integration in East Central Europe." *European Union Politics*, 3: 297–326. DOI: 10.1177/1465116502003003002

Kriesi, Hanspeter. 2007. "The Role of European Integration in National Election Campaigns." *European Union Politics*, 8: 83–108. DOI: 10.1177/1465116507073328

Kriesi, Hanspeter, Edgar Grande, Romain Lachat, Marin Dolezal, Simon Bornschier, and Timotheos Frey. 2006. "Globali-zation and the Transformation of the National Political Space: Six European Countries Compared." *European Journal of Political Research*, 45: 921–956. DOI: 10.1111/j.1475-6765.2006.00644.x

LeDuc, Lawrence. 2002. "Referendums and Elections: How Do Campaigns Differ?" In David M. Farrell and Rüdiger Schmitt-Beck, eds., *Do Political Campaigns Matter? Campaign Effects in Elections and Referendums*, 137–153. London: Routledge.

Lindberg, Leon, and Stuart Scheingold. 1970. *Europe's Would-Be Polity: Patterns of Change in the European Community*. Cambridge, MA: Harvard University Press.

Maier, Jürgen, and Berthold Rittberger. 2008. "Shifting Europe's Boundaries: Mass Media, Public Opinion and the Enlargement of the EU." *European Union Politics*, 9: 243–267. DOI: 10.1177/1465116508089087

Mair, Peter. 2007. "Political Opposition and the European Union." *Government and Opposition*, 42: 1–17. DOI: 10.1111/j.1477-7053.2007.00209.x

Majone, Giandomenico. 2006. "The Common Sense of European Integration." *Journal of European Public Policy*, 13: 607–620. DOI: 10.1080/13501760600808212

McLaren, Lauren M. 2005. *Identity, Interests and Attitudes to European Integration*. Basingstoke: Palgrave Macmillan.

Moravcsik, Andrew. 2006. "What Can We Learn from the Collapse of the European Constitutional Project?" *Politische Vierteljahresschrift*, 47: 219–241. DOI: 10.1007/s11615-006-0037-7

Schmitter, Philippe. 2000. *How to Democratize the European Union: And Why Bother?* Lanham, MD: Rowman & Littlefield.

Smith, Julie. 1999. "The 1975 Referendum." *Journal of European Integration History*, 5: 41–56.

Taggart, Paul. 1998. "A Touchstone of Dissent: Euroscepticism in Contemporary Western European Party Systems." *Euro-

pean Journal of Political Research, 33: 363–388. DOI: 10.1111/1475-6765 .00387

van der Eijk, Cees, and Mark Franklin. 2004. "Potential for Contestation on European Matters in National Elections in Europe." In Gary Marks, ed., *European Integration and Political Conflict*, 32–50. Cambridge: Cambridge University Press.

12

Integration and Democracy in the Shadow of the Eurozone Debt Crisis

Learning Objectives

- to identify structural problems with the design of EMU;
- to analyze the impact of the 2008 global financial crisis on government finances in the Eurozone;
- to evaluate why bailouts were provided and what consequences result from their terms;
- to identify the changes in EMU wrought by the Fiscal Compact and banking union;
- to evaluate why the democratic basis of the EU response to the sovereign debt crisis is contested;
- to identify alternative policy responses and analyse why these have not been pursued;
- to evaluate the significance of the debate over where responsibility for the sovereign debt crisis ultimately lies.

The Politics of European Integration: Political Union or a House Divided?, First Edition. Andrew Glencross.
© 2014 Andrew Glencross. Published 2014 by Blackwell Publishing Ltd.

Timeline of Key Events 12.1: The Eurozone Crisis (2008–2013)

September 2008	US Investment bank Lehman Brothers files for bankruptcy, triggering global credit crunch
Late 2008	Massive intervention from US Federal Reserve and European Central Bank to provide liquidity for banking system
October 2009	New Greek government dramatically revalues size of budget deficit
May 2010	Greece shut out of international bond market, followed by EU-IMF bailout package (€110 billion)
May 2010	European Central Bank begins bond-buying program to bring down interest on debt in Italy and Spain
November 2010	Ireland shut out of international bond market, followed by EU-IMF bailout package (€85 billion)
April/May 2011	Portugal shut out of international bond market, followed by EU-IMF bailout package (€78 billion)
November 2011	Greek prime minister proposes referendum on bailout terms but is forced to withdraw idea under pressure from France and Germany
February 2012	Treaty establishing the European Stability Mechanism signed, creating a €500 billion permanent bailout fund
February/March 2012	Greek creditors forced to take €100 billion "haircut" (i.e. loss) on their debt holdings
March 2012	EU countries (except United Kingdom and Czech Republic) sign Treaty on Stability, Coordination and Governance in the Economic and Monetary Union
May 2012	Ireland holds referendum successfully ratifying new EU treaty
June 2012	Spanish government declares intention to seek EU financing to help its banking sector
	Government of Cyprus requests emergency EU funding
September 2012	German Constitutional Court rejects legal challenge to European Stability Mechanism
September 2012	European Central Bank unveils new program of bond purchases for Eurozone sovereign debt
January 2013	Treaty on Stability, Coordination and Governance in the Economic and Monetary Union enters into force
March 2013	Cyprus negotiates an EU-IMF bailout on condition of a special levy on savers' deposits

12.0   Introduction: The Eurozone Crisis as a Challenge to Democracy and Integration

The Eurozone crisis, which occurred after the 2008 financial crisis, is a multifaceted policy problem. It relates primarily to the stability of economic and monetary integration – in other words to the survival of the euro – but also has wide-ranging economic and political consequences. The collapse of financial institutions in the US in 2008 and a wave of bank losses that affected European-based institutions generated a huge concern over government debt in the EU. Governments had to provide emergency loans to banks or to take on their debt in order to prevent them from going bankrupt and harming the rest of the economy. In this context, there was great uncertainty over how to rescue the banking system and how to fund dramatic increases in national debt. Eurozone policy makers confronted serious dilemmas about whether to provide financial support – and, if so, how – to governments that were no longer able to fund their deficits and were facing the possibility of leaving the euro. These choices had an enormous impact on the direction that integration took, raising the vital question of how far such decisions, which affect citizens' economic well-being as much as the future of the EU, can be taken democratically.

As explained in Section 12.1, European monetary integration was pursued for both economic and political reasons. Moreover, the rules behind the single currency precluded the possibility of bailing out governments in financial difficulty. The mechanism for avoiding this situation was the Stability and Growth Pact, supposed to enforce budgetary rigor across the Eurozone. Yet the 2008 financial crisis sparked not only a banking crisis but also a sovereign debt crisis, as governments in several Eurozone countries struggled to find the funds to rescue their insolvent banks. This problem highlighted the fact that monetary union was not accompanied by a **banking union**: that is, national governments remained responsible for regulating and rescuing banks from bad debts. The size of the latter was so huge that governments in Greece, Ireland, Portugal, and Cyprus could not afford to borrow such sums on the financial markets. In this context, Eurozone countries had to decide whether to find a way to give emergency funding or else let these governments withdraw from the euro, risking unpaid debts and a new round of huge bank losses.

The decision to bail out these governments – which was accomplished by providing them with enough funding to make up for the shortfall between tax revenue and spending – was taken because this was the less costly option. Consequently, the most important aspect of the bailout concerns the terms under which funding was provided. The discussion in Section 12.2 shows how, within the Eurozone, Germany took the lead in determining the conditions under which other countries gave emergency financial assistance. To reassure the financial markets and taxpayers asked to guarantee the bailouts, German Chancellor Angela Merkel successfully pushed for new EU treaties designed to establish a permanent bailout mechanism, accompanied by measures to improve national fiscal responsibility. These innovations were further accompanied by an evolution in the operation of the European Central Bank (ECB) and by gradual progress toward an eventual EU banking union.

How the EU responded to the crisis is an ongoing source of controversy. There was, in the first place, criticism of the democratic legitimacy of designing bailouts that require public spending cuts alongside fundamental socio-economic reform. Similarly, experts and politicians called into question whether these bailouts were the right solution and argued over where blame for the crisis lies. All three controversies are treated one by one in Section 12.3 and made to reveal the complexity of the politics behind the sovereign debt crisis. In particular, the political division that became apparent in the Eurozone is one between the northern countries asked to provide bailout funds and the southern countries in need of them. Northern countries blamed their southern neighbors for not being fiscally responsible enough, while their southern neighbors complained about being locked into a currency union that made their firms uncompetitive.

Reflecting on what the sovereign debt crisis means for the future of integration, the chapter concludes by showing how both the crisis and the EU's response illustrate fundamental characteristics of contemporary European integration. In the face of an unexpected emergency, national politicians took the lead and pressed ahead with more integration. The results depend on national acceptance not just of the bailout provisions, but also of the enforcement of debt brakes (national legal limits on budget deficits) mandated by the new EU treaty. This means that democratic politics at the national level will continue to have a fundamental influence on EU affairs. Yet the fact that arguments over how to resolve the crisis dominated national as well as EU politics clearly demonstrates the end of the separation between national and EU politics, at least for countries with the euro.

12.1   The Causes of the Eurozone Crisis

The introduction of the euro was a logistical success, as the euro smoothly replaced national currencies in physical and digital transactions and became a major world currency, second only to the US dollar. Firms from other countries doing business in the Eurozone used this currency for trade, while central banks and financial institutions sought to hold euro-denominated national debt as a safe investment. Yet, even before its launch, the euro project was called into question (Feldstein 1997). There were many doubts surrounding the economic and political benefits of economic and monetary union (EMU). Of particular concern was the design of EMU, which relied on having an independent central bank without a central government – that is, without integrated tax and spending policies – in what might not be an optimum currency area (see Section 5.2). While the crisis afflicting the Eurozone since 2009 might not be a straightforward vindication of these doubts, structural issues to do with how EMU was designed play a large role in explaining the difficulty the EU faced in responding to the crisis. This response is the subject of Section 12.2; in the present section the focus is on understanding the design of EMU and the unfolding of the Eurozone crisis in the wake of the 2008 global financial crisis.

12.1.1   Benefits and concerns surrounding the European Monetary Union (EMU)

Politically, the driving force behind EMU was the desire to cement ever closer integration after the end of the Cold War by tying a reunited Germany into unprecedented institutional cooperation in Europe (Feldstein 1997). In economic terms, the creation of the euro was sold on the basis of the benefits this would bring to trade and investment by eliminating the costs of currency exchange and by making price competition easier, which is anti-inflationary. However, EMU did not involve just making business easier for firms. Its mechanism rested on rules for fiscal stability – the Stability and Growth Pact (SGP; see Box 5.1) – that would prevent governments from borrowing too much on the back of a strong currency. In order to meet these conditions, Ireland, Portugal, and Spain reorganized their public finances so as to lower the total public debt below the 60 percent of GDP allowed by the Maastricht Treaty (Lane 2012). Italy and Greece never achieved this target but were nonetheless admitted into the euro, while France and Germany broke the terms of the Stability and Growth Pact with impunity, in the mid-2000s, by running up annual deficits above the permitted 3 percent threshold.

Nevertheless, the prelude to the introduction of the euro saw an improvement in the fiscal positions of states that traditionally struggled to rein in public debt. Italy, most notably, enjoyed a virtuous circle as the interest rates of prospective Eurozone countries converged on the lower German one – the economic core of EMU. This made it easier to balance budgets, as the cost of servicing national debt decreased substantially (Marsh 2009, 205). The period after the launch of the euro was also beneficial for states accustomed to paying a higher rate of interest on debt. Although individual governments were responsible for their own debt, financial markets were not overly worried about differences in public finances because the SGP set national limits on Eurozone debt. As a result, countries such as Greece and Italy continued to pay low interest on their debt, which investors ostensibly regarded as a safe investment, like that of Germany (Lane 2012).

However, there is a less visible feature of EMU: having a shared currency ultimately puts pressure on participating governments to adopt more liberalizing policies for improving national competitiveness (Hall 2012). A single currency does more than just complete a single market – the "one market, one money" slogan the Commission advocated. In addition, monetary integration adds impetus to deregulate in areas beyond formal EU competence or where EU legislation is hard to adopt – for example taxes on labor, services, employment contracts. This pressure comes from being locked into a common currency, which makes **currency devaluation** no longer an option. In this context, a government in a country whose goods or services become less competitive than those of another country – either by being more expensive or by being poorer in quality – cannot suddenly level the playing field by lowering the value of its currency. Under a shared currency, competitiveness has to come instead by changing costs – most obviously by lowering the salaries, or by improving productivity through investment and innovation (Marsh 2009, 246). This is a longer term form of adjustment to differences in productivity than devaluation, but economists consider it a better means of achieving lasting and stable growth, as recurrent devaluations scare off investment and discourage entrepreneurship. Politically, however, lowering production costs is very challenging, as it translates into breaking union power, lowering wages, and reducing employment rights. These kinds of measures are precisely what the EU has asked for in return for the loans given to countries such as Greece in order to plug gaps in their public finances, as discussed in Section 12.2.

From the start, some EU member states, namely the UK, Denmark, and Sweden, refused to accept this euro bargain. Interestingly, these countries all experienced significant recessions in the early 1990s resulting in currency devaluations, and, in response, they introduced various measures designed to reduce government spending and to

increase competitiveness. More importantly, governments and citizens in all three countries were reluctant to relinquish national control over interest rates and the (emergency)
possibility of currency devaluation in return for gains in trade and in fighting inflation.
Indeed, evidence for the euro's success on these terms is mixed. Trade in the Eurozone
increased by 10–15 percent within half a decade (Sadeh 2012), but overall economic
growth was actually very similar among Eurozone and non-euro EU countries in the
decade before the financial crisis (Sadeh 2012, 229). Moreover, while the ECB managed
to accomplish its statutory goal of achieving an inflation rate of 2 percent or less during
this decade, non Eurozone countries such as Sweden and the United Kingdom also
achieved this rate (Sadeh 2012, 237–238). Yet the problem with EMU is less that it
disappointed expectations about stimulating growth than that it failed to prompt productivity gains across the Eurozone. Imbalances in competitiveness and productivity
made the Eurozone weak in the face of an unexpected crisis, which came in the form
of a worldwide banking crisis that began in the United States.

12.1.2   The global financial crisis' effect on the Eurozone

The collapse of several banking institutions in the US in 2008 led to a wave of private
debt defaulting: individuals no longer able to repay loans and mortgages caused enormous losses for banks. The wave affected European-based financial institutions, which
were also exposed to these defaults. In this economic climate, banks immediately became
wary of lending to one another. Indeed the banking crisis was so severe that many
important financial institutions were threatened with **insolvency** (that is, with having
debts outweigh their assets). With no Eurozone-wide mechanism for rescuing banks
from insolvency, it was up to national governments to step in and lend to the banks,
even if this meant additional national debt.

Banks, pension funds, and sovereign wealth funds (strategic financial reserves held
notably by oil-exporting countries) lend money to governments that need to finance the
shortfall between revenue and spending through borrowing. Suddenly governments
were asking these institutions for enormous amounts of money – to be repaid through
future taxation – in order to recapitalize the banks that had been affected by huge debt
write-offs (this money was to be repaid through future taxation). Investors thus became
concerned about government debt in the Eurozone. The concern reflects the sheer
amount of debt taken on by governments to bail out banks otherwise threatened with
bankruptcy – an amount that potentially affected governments' future ability to reim-
burse national debt. Given the sums involved, this fear about national solvency was
perfectly understandable. In Ireland, rescuing the banks cost 40 percent of GDP (Shambaugh 2012) – a necessary evil, as a banking collapse would be even more severe, wiping
out customer savings, freezing the flow of credit in the economy, and even raising the
risk of civil strife.

When countries intervened to protect their banks from insolvency, they did so in a
context in which the banking sector had grown enormously since the creation of the
euro. Bank lending had increased as EMU facilitated lending within the Eurozone, while
lower interest rates allowed individuals to borrow more for consumption (mortgages,

credit cards, and so on). These developments illustrate the risk of having a shared currency without a banking union to coordinate the regulation of banks (for instance the way they make loans) and their rescue in crisis moments (say, by guaranteeing deposits or by injecting capital to prevent insolvency). In the EU, banking regulation and recapitalizing banks are the responsibility of member states, unlike in federal systems such as the United States, where the federal government alone is responsible (Shambaugh 2012).

The consequence of investors' fears about national solvency was to freeze up the credit available to certain governments desperate to cover the difference between spending and tax revenue. Such shortfalls existed not just because of the need to cover bank losses, but also because of a dramatic slowdown in the world economy. In times of economic recession, tax revenue from companies and individuals falls, while spending on welfare (notably unemployment) increases, hurting public finances. Consequently the predicament facing Eurozone countries was either to borrow money from other Eurozone countries or else to go bust by failing to make payments on national debt or by not paying salaries, pensions, and other liabilities.

These concerns about the solvency of Eurozone countries first surfaced in Greece in late 2009. After the general election of October 2009, the new Greek government dramatically announced that its annual budget deficit would be nearly 13 percent of GDP. This represented twice the previous government's estimate and four times the amount allowed by the Stability and Growth Pact. Immediately afterwards, Greece's total debt was re-evaluated at around 130 percent of GDP, more than twice the statutory 60 percent limit inscribed in the EU treaties. This revelation left financial markets reeling and meant that, to attract buyers for 10-year government **bonds**, Greece had to pay an interest rate 4 percent higher than the market rate for equivalent German debt. As financial institutions were faced with this shocking news, their fears about the state of government finances spread. Soon after Greece, Ireland and Portugal started having to pay a much higher rate of interest, too, when selling government bonds – that is, when taking on debt to cover shortfalls between spending and revenue. This higher interest rate represents the greater risk associated with financing Irish or Greek debt by comparison with financing German debt: the cheapest rate was available to the government most likely to repay its debt.

Greece's debt situation is by far the most catastrophic in the Eurozone (Greece has run budget deficits of around 5 percent per annum from 2001 to 2008, by comparison with an EU average of 2 percent) and is largely explicable through domestic factors (Featherstone, 2011). By contrast, Ireland before 2008 was cutting its overall public debt to GDP ratio, as was Spain. Yet these countries were badly hit by the global recession, as well as by the collapse of house prices following an unsustainable construction and financing bubble – both of which lowered tax revenue while forcing up public spending on unemployment assistance. At the same time countries across the Eurozone also had to borrow to finance the recapitalization of banks that had made bad loans. Higher interest rates on debt in 2010/11 thus came at the worst possible time for Greece, Ireland, and Portugal – countries with precarious public finances during a severe global recession. This generated a vicious circle, as higher interest rates on public debt meant higher government deficits (more money needs to be spent to service the debt), which in turn require more debt to be issued at a higher interest rate. Three Eurozone countries,

> ## Box 12.1   Key Concept: Sovereign Default
>
> A sovereign (that is, a sovereign state) is in default when it cannot or will not pay back its debts in full. History is littered with examples of governments that have defaulted; there have been 320 such defaults since 1800 (Reinhart and Rogoff 2009), and they bring a variety of consequences. Failure to repay debt is certainly not a cost-free option: a sovereign that defaults will face enormous problems borrowing money again, while the domestic economy will suffer, as banks write off their holdings of government debt and foreign investors withdraw. This scenario occurred in Argentina in 2002, when the country ceased making payments on its debt. Politically, however, this may be a lesser price to pay than introducing tax hikes or making huge spending cuts. The **International Monetary Fund (IMF)** acts as a lender of last resort to governments in this predicament precisely because the effects of a default are most damaging, both internally and externally, as foreign creditors (for example pension funds) lose out. IMF support comes with conditions attached, so as to ensure that the emergency funding is eventually paid back (this enables it to help other countries in the future). Yet national debt totaling more than 120 percent of GDP is considered "unsustainable" under IMF rules. This was the situation facing Greece in 2012, which is why the IMF and the EU agreed to a partial write-off of its debt. At €100 billion (out of a total debt of approximately €350 billion), this is the largest sovereign default in history, although Greece itself is no stranger to default, having defaulted in the 1830s, in 1893, and in the 1930s (Featherstone 2011).

Greece, Ireland, and Portugal, found themselves in this position within the space of a year, risking a sovereign default (see Box 12.1) or an exit from the Eurozone if other members had not provided them with emergency loans – a process discussed below in Section 12.2.

12.2   The Travails of Formulating an EU Response

A Eurozone bailout of countries in financial difficulty was not supposed to happen. Article 125 of the Lisbon Treaty states that heavily indebted countries will not have their debts paid by others. More importantly, the SGP was designed to prevent governments from getting into this situation. However, it was in fact easier to accrue such debts, given the lower interest rates available to countries such as Greece and Italy in the first decade of the euro, although Ireland and Spain, which later on had similar debt issues, kept within the SGP rules. Politically, in the midst of a severe economic shock, it was never going to be easy to find a solution that required governments to take on huge financial commitments to keep the Eurozone intact. In particular, there was a split between governments in a healthy fiscal state (low annual debt and easily sustainable total debt) and ones worried about their own finances. This tension, coupled with the sheer size of the funding required and the speed at which market fears spread, made for a protracted response to the Eurozone sovereign debt crisis.

12.2.1 Deciding whether to provide a bailout and on what terms

As the cost of issuing new debt in Greece, Ireland, and Portugal became prohibitively expensive, or insufficient to cover their spending commitments, the policy choice was a binary one: leave the euro or negotiate a bailout. A country could in principle leave the single currency, although there is no official legal mechanism for this (Deo, Donovan, and Hatheway 2011). This would offer two potential advantages for resolving fiscal difficulties. A new national currency would be much weaker than the euro, boosting exports and hence growth. Being sovereign over one's currency also gives governments the ability simply to create money to service debts and to pay for public spending. In this scenario a central bank issues new money to cover government spending by buying government debt directly from the government. Technically, EU law prohibits all member states from financing their deficits via central bank credits (Article 104 of the Maastricht Treaty), but in a crisis situation a government may well consider this option. This explains why the ECB was designed to be completely independent and aloof from political considerations, so as to be completely focused on fighting inflation – although the Eurozone crisis has led to some changes in its monetary policy (see Box 12.2).

Creating money is an extreme measure and one traditionally believed to generate high inflation, which hurts ordinary citizens' standard of living and drives up interest rates, imperiling government finances over time. Devaluation will also have an inflationary effect in countries heavily reliant on imports, as the latter become much more expensive. Additionally, citizens will anticipate a decision to leave EMU and are likely to withdraw their euros while they still can – a situation known as a "run on the bank," which can only undermine the domestic banking system further. Politically and economically, therefore, exiting the euro would be very costly, especially in countries like Greece, which rely on energy imports and have weak export sectors.

The costs of Greece (or any other country) leaving the euro would not be borne just by its firms and citizens. Banks across the rest of the Eurozone that lent money to Greek companies and individuals would suddenly see their loans converted into a new and weak national currency. Hence creditors would be left with repayments in a depreciating currency; as a result, banks in the EU would be exposed to a new round of bad debt. Another concern surrounding a withdrawal from the euro is the contagion effect, whereby financial markets would speculate on who might be next out of the single currency, speculation likely to trigger instability and runs on banking systems across the Eurozone. This kind of contagion already occurred over the course of 2010–2012. Investors concerned about Greek sovereign debt became wary about lending money to Ireland and Portugal, which meant that these countries had to issue debt at higher and higher rates of interest, until the rate became unaffordable. The same process forced up interest rates in Spain and Italy in 2011. Thus, even if the Greek economy is very small,

Box 12.2   Case Study: The Evolving Role of the ECB

Based in Frankfurt (Germany), the ECB has it as its principal aim (according to the EU treaties) to keep inflation at or below 2 percent a year. This objective was a key demand of the German government, which was only prepared to accept EMU on the basis of establishing an independent central bank that would be serious about preventing inflation (Marsh 2009). When the ECB was established, countries participating in the euro provided gold and foreign exchange reserves totaling €41 billion so as to be able to intervene if necessary to stabilize the currency against the dollar, yen, and so on. Although the ECB is designed to be apolitical, the Eurozone sovereign debt crisis saw EU politicians place great pressure on the ECB to do more to resolve the crisis. One measure that the ECB took was to inject money into the fragile EU banking sector by providing €500 billion in low-interest loans in December 2011. This move aimed to encourage lending to companies, stimulate consumption and get banks to buy Eurozone debt so as to drive down interest rates on repayments. Nevertheless, politicians in countries struggling to afford high interest repayment on their debt (like Italy and Spain) argued that the ECB should buy up government bonds in massive quantities, in order to drive down the interest charged. This pressure bore fruit with the launch, at the beginning of 2013, of Outright Monetary Transactions (OMT), a scheme for buying government debt from countries that agree in return to implement reforms so as to balance their books. To offset the risk of inflation – an unlimited bond-buying spree would be the equivalent of printing money – the ECB is "sterilizing" the purchases. This involves selling off assets (for example other countries' bonds) equivalent to the sum of the bonds bought via OMT, so that no new money is created. Nevertheless, bond buying via sterilization is controversial and was rejected by the German representative on the ECB board. Should the ECB run out of assets to sell to sterilize bond buying, it will need to ask Eurozone countries for more.

representing less than 3 percent of Eurozone GDP, the financial repercussions of this country exiting the euro are estimated to give the astronomical sum of €1 trillion (Moravcsik 2012, 61). Consequently there were good reasons why Eurozone governments decided to proceed with bailout packages for countries that could no longer borrow on the international financial markets. The major problem was devising the terms for such a deal.

Determining the conditions on which to provide a bailout, first for Greece and then for Ireland and Portugal, posed a question of leadership and legitimacy. The president of the Commission as well as the new president of the European Council entered the fray at various points. However, the source of these emergency loans was the member states, complemented by monies from the IMF. Since national governments and their taxpayers would have to guarantee the funds, it was national leaders who played the decisive role in devising the terms of the bailouts. In particular, the German chancellor, Angela Merkel, played the most prominent role as leader of the Eurozone's major economic power and as the greatest financial contributor to these schemes.

Merkel's proposed solution involved giving emergency funding to countries frozen out of the financial markets in return for dramatic domestic economic and fiscal reforms. For instance, the agreement with Ireland spelled out which taxes should be raised and where public spending should be cut, notably by reducing public service employment. The objective behind the measures is to balance government spending quickly, so that within the space of a few years that government may be able to borrow again on the markets, at reasonable interest rates, and eventually accrue a surplus to reduce overall debt. Bailout funds are provided in tranches, as a team of EU and IMF economists monitored public finances in order to check whether governments stick to the terms of the deal. Attaching these kinds of conditions is in fact standard practice for IMF emer- gency loans to countries in currency and financial crises, although critics argue about the utility and legitimacy of these agreements (Collier and Gunning 1999). Indeed Eurozone countries requiring emergency funding experienced waves of protests at having government spending and taxation decisions imposed from outside, as will be discussed in Section 12.3. For European integration, this form of top-down economic management constitutes an historic turning point: never before has the EU been so implicated in deciding on national tax and spending policies.

The IMF provided some of the funds for Greece, Ireland (here Denmark, the United Kingdom, and Sweden provided extra bilateral funding), and Portugal; but its resources were insufficient for those governments' needs. This is why the EU needed to create from scratch a temporary funding mechanism to cover €80 billion for Greece (accompanied by a further €100 billion in February 2012), €67.5 billion for Ireland, and €52 billion for Portugal. This gave rise to thorny legal questions, since the EU treaties did not specify any mechanism for bailing out a Eurozone country and this meant that any funding arrangement would have to be temporary, unless the treaties were formally changed.

Given the risk that uncertainty over public finances would spread to countries such as Italy and Spain (as in fact happened by late 2011), Merkel pressed for the creation of a permanent bailout fund. The plan was to reassure markets about the long-term commitment to the single currency by creating a €500 billion fund called the **European Stability Mechanism (ESM)** and designed to provide loans to governments experienc- ing financial trouble. Establishing the ESM required a new treaty, which was signed at a European Council summit in February 2012; but Eurozone creditors, led by Germany, demanded a counterpart. This came in the form of a Treaty on Stability, Coordination and Governance in the Economic and Monetary Union (also known as the Fiscal Compact), designed to create more robust rules for ensuring national fiscal discipline.

12.2.2   The Fiscal Compact and moves toward a banking union

Negotiations over the Fiscal Compact were swift but not without complications, the impetus being again provided by German Chancellor Angela Merkel. Her overriding concern was that a new treaty would reassure German public opinion that the EU bailout mechanism was being accompanied by serious measures to prevent future crises requiring contributions from German taxpayers. Indeed the most important of these measures was inspired by recent German legislation designed to make it constitutionally impossible to run up government debt in the long term.

At the heart of the "Fiscal Compact" – so called because it specifies new rules on how governments should manage their finances – is the creation of binding national commitments to run balanced budgets. These rules for balanced budgets are modeled on the *Schuldenbremse* ("debt brake") that Germany introduced in 2009, intending it to produce a balanced budget by 2020 (Switzerland has had one since 2001). The Fiscal Compact compels its signatories to pass national laws limiting budget deficits to 0.5 percent of GDP (the United Kingdom and the Czech Republic have not signed it). This figure is calculated in terms of the business cycle, permitting temporary spending rises during recessions. All the countries using the euro had to ratify the treaty, which entered into force on January 1, 2013. Eurozone countries had a major incentive to introduce a national debt break immediately into law: from March 2013 loans made by the ESM are conditional on a member state adopting the national debt brakes mandated by the Fiscal Compact.

Although this treaty does not give the EU competence to control how countries actually enforce their national debt brakes, the Court of Justice is empowered to verify whether member states actually pass this legislation within the specified one-year timeframe. Financial penalties of up to 0.1 percent of GDP can be imposed on governments that fail to adopt this legislation. An additional constraint imposed on signatories is the obligation, for countries with a total debt of more than 60 percent of GDP, to reduce this debt by one twentieth per year until they reach a position below the 60 percent threshold. This commitment only becomes binding 3 years after an annual budget deficit has returned to below 3 percent of GDP. Taken together, these commitments are supposed to remove the likelihood of governments running up new debts and to reassure financial markets, eventually lowering interest rates on debt.

However, the new treaty does not significantly enhance the EU's ability to control national governments' fiscal decisions. The Fiscal Compact relies instead on getting member states to make the provisions of the SGP binding under national law. There was a suggestion of empowering the European Commission's monitoring ability by giving the Commission the right to veto national budgets that do not conform to EU debt rules. Again, this was an idea originating in Germany and supported by countries such as Finland and Austria, which managed to keep control of government finances even amid global recession. A majority of other member states successfully opposed this move toward enhanced supranational budgetary control – an unsurprising opposition, given the number actually in breach of the rules at the time (see Figure 5.1). Consequently there are fears that the supranational mechanism for enforcing fiscal rigor will again be too weak, meaning that the system will be reliant on national enforcement via debt brake legislation. In any case, the operation of debt brakes will take time, as member states are expected to use transitional arrangements to bring deficits down gently while the commitment to pay back 1/20 of total debt over 60 percent of GDP can only be enforced after a 3-year period – that is, not before 2016 (Dullien 2012).

Since the Fiscal Compact is only a long-term measure for fixing debt, EU leaders also took gradual steps toward creating a banking union. These moves were designed to make it possible to deal with more immediate matters and to resolve problems that were the primary cause of many Eurozone countries' bad debts. Starting in 2009, the European Commission proceeded to "stress tests" on EU banks, in order to check whether the latter have sufficient assets to cope with bad debts. Since 2010, this is now the responsibility of the European Banking Authority. This independent agency increased the capital requirements for banks in 2011, obliging banks to hold more safe assets as a percentage of their loans. The purpose of this measure was to restore confidence in inter-bank lending by preventing rogue banks from making risky loans. In addition, in December 2012 the EU agreed to give the ECB the power to supervise the EU's banks from 2014 on, so as to prevent risky lending practices or unsustainable business models. This is a major step in the direction of breaking the link between bank losses and sovereign **liquidity** problems of the kind that necessitated bailouts in Ireland and Portugal.

Indeed the link between bank bailouts and sovereign debt was further illustrated by the case of Spain. Its total public debt was low – it was below the 60 percent threshold prior to the 2008 financial crisis – but Spanish banks were badly affected by a housing boom and bust that resulted in unpaid loans to the estimated value of €60 billion. As a result, in June 2012 the Spanish government officially declared that it needed EU help to support its banking system, something the country could no longer afford to do. This meant that Spain became the fourth country to receive emergency EU funding, although in this instance the funding was specifically earmarked to rescue the banking sector. In the same month the government of Cyprus also requested emergency EU funding and began negotiations for the fifth EU-IMF bailout to help with the cost of a bank bailout. Between 2008 and 2012 the Cypriot public debt rose from 50 percent to 85 percent, while the banking sector swelled to a figure eight times larger than GDP; hence the country could not afford to re-capitalize its banks. Cyprus' bailout was particularly controversial, as the EU and the IMF made it conditional on raising funds via a special levy on savers' deposits.

In November 2012 the European Commission approved a €37 billion euro package for four heavily indebted Spanish banks, in return for major restructuring that involved significant branch closures and job losses. This was another milestone, as it moved the Eurozone closer to a system of mutual bank support, although other aspects of a banking union – such as a commonly funded bank deposit guarantee – remain under discussion to date. Ultimately the intention is to counteract the fact that, as one economist put it, EU "banks are international in life, but national in their death" (Goodhart 2009, 16). However, this move involves mutualizing financial risks across member states, which is highly controversial – as indeed are many aspects of the EU response to the Eurozone crisis.

12.3   Criticism and Controversies Surrounding the EU Response

Responding to the Eurozone crisis was a politically fraught affair. This was bound to be the case, given the need for large financial guarantees to bail out governments unable to borrow on the markets. Yet the controversy and criticism surrounding how the EU dealt with the aftermath of the financial crisis involves more than just wrangling over money. Three separate concerns are central to the politics of the Eurozone sovereign debt crisis: the issue of how democratic the decision-making process was; that of whether the measures taken were the right ones; and the question where the blame should lie for the origins of the crisis. This section explores all three concerns one by one.

12.3.1   Democratic decision-making?

Decision-making in a crisis is a test for any political system. When the repercussions of the 2008 financial crisis struck the Eurozone, the problem was not just the EU's ability to take decisions but also its ability to elicit democratic approval for tough choices. Of course, the quality of democracy in the EU has increasingly been open to question (see Chapter 10). Yet the sovereign debt crisis posed this question in much starker terms than ever before. This was because the governments of some countries had to commit public funds in order to make up for shortfalls in the budgets of other countries, in return for major socio-economic reforms that went beyond anything conducted under the Ordinary Legislative Procedure. Both moves met with deep domestic opposition: citizens from the creditor countries were skeptical about the wisdom of providing bailouts, and there were mass protests against socio-economic reforms being imposed in recipient countries such as Greece and Spain.

In this context the interplay of national and EU politics was crucial, as politicians had to satisfy domestic public opinion while also making decisions for the broader European interest. The case of Germany illustrates well the dilemma. Chancellor Angela Merkel knew that her citizens were very wary about providing emergency loans to Greece – a skepticism that fits exactly with the notion of a "constraining dissensus" discussed in Section 11.1. German public opinion blamed government economic mismanagement for Greece's debt problems – mismanagement exemplified by the fact that full pension rights were based on 35 years' contributions, 10 less than in Germany. Merkel thus wanted to design a bailout deal that would convince her national voters that the EU was serious about reforming how countries run their economies. In addition, she was concerned that the German Constitutional Court would rule that financial support for Greece and others was illegal unless a new treaty overturned the Lisbon Treaty's "no bailout" clause (Paterson 2011).

Consequently, German domestic preferences were central to how Merkel approached solving the sovereign debt crisis. The insistence on getting a deal that satisfied these preferences engendered some hostility from other EU member states, concerned as they were that their voices were not being heard. Hence this attitude on the part of the German leader raised the specter of a German-run Europe. At the popular level, anxiety about German dominance had the effect that street protests in Greece or Portugal against reforms introduced to satisfy EU creditors were invariably accompanied by anti-Merkel slogans and allusions to Nazi-era Germany. These demonstrations were also a manifestation of domestic opposition to EU-imposed socio-economic reforms, notably tax increases, reduced pension or unemployment benefits, and public sector layoffs. Such measures, an essential part of the terms of the Eurozone bailouts, were portrayed as an imposition of **austerity** coming from external creditors without the approval of national voters. When, in November 2011, the Greek prime minister proposed a national referendum on the terms of the EU bailout, European leaders successfully applied diplomatic pressure for him to abandon this plan, which led to his eventual resignation. EU leaders were afraid that voters would reject the deal, thereby unraveling their attempts to solve the crisis.

Another indication of the external constraints facing member states' ability to decide their own affairs came from Italy. Having a very large public debt – namely one of over €2 trillion – Italy has long been preoccupied with interest rates, since small variations have large effects on the cost of servicing its outstanding debt. In late 2011 financial markets rapidly lost confidence in the Italian government's ability to reform its public finances. This was not just the result of contagion, as fears about government finances spread from Greece to other countries, but also a damning verdict on the inability of Prime Minister Silvio Berlusconi to carry out the numerous pledges to reform the Italian state (Jones 2012). As pressure to improve Italian public finances was also coming from European leaders, namely Angela Merkel and Nicolas Sarkozy, as well as from the ECB, Berlusconi lost his parliamentary majority and resigned. In his place came, without a new election, a non-partisan government led by former EU Commissioner Mario Monti. The aim of this move was to allow experts – a so-called technocratic government above partisan politics (see Chapter 9, Glossary) – to stabilize the country's finances and to reassure financial markets until the elections of 2013. External actors such as markets and powerful EU member states thus seriously constrain the policy choices available to voters in weaker EU countries.

The Italian example is also emblematic of government instability across the EU since 2008. That is, governing parties have found it extremely difficult to win in re-election campaigns, as shown by the electoral defeat of ruling parties in France, Finland, Greece, Ireland, Portugal, Slovakia, and Spain. In many of these cases electoral unpopularity was directly linked to a government's implementation of socio-economic reforms and moves toward fiscal rigor. Moreover, in the Netherlands, the government of Mark Rutte fell in April 2012 when his coalition failed to get parliamentary support for budget cuts aimed at conforming with the Stability and Growth Pact. Yet a change in government does not affect a member state's legal obligations: ruling parties and coalitions still have to meet EU budget rules or, in the case of recipients of bailouts, meet the terms of these agreements. Consequently popular resentment against austerity has not led to a change in policy direction; this reveals just how constrained economic sovereignty has become. Nevertheless, there was a heated debate over whether public belt-tightening was the most appropriate solution to the crisis.

12.3.2   The right response?

Opinions among experts and politicians differed considerably over the best way to resolve the sovereign debt crisis. As an alternative to the existing bailout mechanism, radical proposals involving changing the nature of debt and of the ECB have been floated. Here the central concern is that the emphasis on fiscal responsibility, often

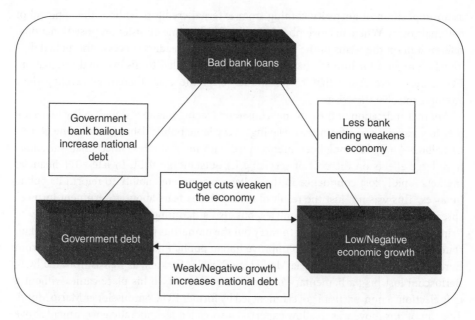

Figure 12.1 The vicious cycle of government debt and weak growth in the Eurozone

pejoratively labeled "austerity," is counterproductive. This is because the sudden implementation of tax raises and spending cuts forces an economy to contract. The kinds of cuts that are being asked of Eurozone countries are indeed drastic: a reduction of the budget deficit by 11 percent of GDP in Greece within 3 years, a 9 percent cut in Ireland over 5 years, or six percentage points in Portugal in 3 years (Hall 2012). For countries facing liquidity and even solvency problems, a recession – in other words a fall in overall GDP – exacerbates these woes, creating a vicious cycle (Shambaugh 2012). A shrinking economy means lower tax receipts and hence a bigger budget deficit, while at the same time increasing the debt to GDP ratio, as illustrated in Figure 12.1.

According to some experts, one way to break this cycle would be for the ECB to act as a lender of last resort in the bond markets. This move targets the high interest rate on national debt, which has caused such budgetary problems for certain countries in the Eurozone. High interest rates on debt, which indicate low market confidence in a country's economy and fiscal position, leave governments facing even greater budget shortfalls on top of those caused by recession. This situation contrasts with the virtuous circle prior to the creation of the euro, when diminishing interest rates on debt – a sign of the various markets' confidence that monetary integration would improve fiscal responsibility – helped cut deficits. The argument here is that, if the ECB promised financial markets unlimited funds to buy national debt within the Eurozone, then interest rates on debt would stabilize at an affordable level (De Grauwe 2011).

The ECB already functions as the lender of last resort to the Eurozone's banks: it provided huge sums when these banks suddenly began to stop lending to one another and to businesses (see Box 12.2). Acting as a financial backstop for Eurozone public debt would reassure creditors holding government bonds (banks, pension funds, and the like) that they would always find a buyer – the ECB – for their holding of Greek or Italian debt. In this way the risk involved in lending money to these governments would be much lower, allowing financial markets to provide credit at an affordable rate. This move could thus break the contagion effect, in which worries about one country's debt spread to others. With lower interest rates on debt, the shortfall in public finances in countries such as Greece, Ireland, or Spain would also be lower, and this would bring less severe spending cuts of the kind that lower overall growth (Hall 2012).

Currently, direct purchases of government debt by the ECB are not permissible under the EU treaties. Direct central bank purchases of government debt are considered highly inflationary, and the mandate of the ECB, in line with the preferences of the German government when it agreed to abandon its own currency, is to fight inflation. Yet critics of this orthodoxy suggest that purchasing government debt already held by private creditors does not have the inflationary consequences of financing deficits through the method of printing money (De Grauwe 2011). The former does not involve allowing governments to spend above their tax revenues – a policy that diminishes the real value of money, thereby creating inflation – but rather provides reassurance for bondholders, encouraging them to lend.

Interestingly, both the US Federal Reserve and the Bank of England responded to the 2008 financial crisis by pursuing this policy of buying vast quantities of their own government's debt back from creditors. The risk in the Eurozone is that massive bond buying would saddle the ECB with debts, creating huge liabilities for taxpayers should a country default, just as holders of Greek debt lost €100 billion in 2010. Starting in 2013, the ECB was permitted to buy huge quantities of government debt from private bondholders; this shows an evolution in the orthodoxy of Eurozone central banking (see Box 12.2). The message was underscored by Mario Draghi, the president of the ECB, who in 2012 declared that "the ECB is ready to do whatever it takes to preserve the euro."

A second, growth-focused alternative to the bailout system involves changing the way governments issue debt in the Eurozone. The euro was originally designed as one currency with seventeen national debts. Given the liquidity problems facing countries within the Eurozone – that is, their ability to borrow in order to finance deficits during a global slump – the suggestion is to move toward a single Eurozone debt. This is a very radical proposal in that mutualizing debt means that taxpayers from countries with sound finances become responsible for paying debts accrued by those of others. In other words, this kind of arrangement, dubbed "**fiscal union**," involves real financial solidarity across member states. The Eurozone bailouts do involve some such solidarity, but one resting on "guarantees for borrowing rather than direct transfers of funds" (Hall 2012, 364). By contrast, a single Eurozone debt entails that all taxpayers share the responsibility for servicing and, eventually, repaying the debts accrued by other national governments.

This kind of solidarity is not a very attractive proposition for taxpayers from countries such as Germany, Finland, Austria, or the Netherlands, which are already net contributors to the EU budget. However, from the perspective of countries struggling with large debts, such as Greece and Italy, a fiscal union would be a huge advantage, as it would remove obstacles to borrowing cheaply. For this very reason policy-makers fear that mutualizing debt would remove the incentives for these governments to reform their public finances. Consequently a full fiscal union is not an immediately realizable goal. Rather, an idea often floated during the Eurozone crisis was to create a new kind of debt: Eurobonds. These would be an important stepping stone toward full fiscal union and could be used during the crisis to reduce borrowing costs or to finance growth-inducing public spending. To avoid the problem that cheap borrowing will hinder fiscal reform in certain countries, one Eurobond scheme involves issuing a Blue Bond covering national debt up to 60 percent of GDP, while a separate Red Bond would be issued by national governments for borrowing above that rate (Delpla and Weizsäcker 2010). Blue Bonds, being more secure, would be much cheaper to finance than Red Bonds, providing a strong incentive for governments to balance their books. The heated debate that ensued from proposals to change government borrowing in the Eurozone pitted southern Eurozone countries against northern ones (see Box 12.3), thereby highlighting a further dividing line in the politics of the sovereign debt crisis: who exactly is to blame?

12.3.3   Who is to blame?

Divisions in the Eurozone over how to respond to the sovereign debt crisis reveal the socio-economic as much as political differences between member states. The core areas of prosperity, centered around Germany and its immediate neighbors, are characterized by intensive capital investment, highly skilled labor, and export-led growth. This contrasts with the southern periphery, typified by Greece and Portugal but also by southern Italy, which is reliant on low-cost labor and dependent on demand-led growth (Hall 2012). Joined together under a common currency, the less competitive countries of the Eurozone lost the ability to devalue their currency. This allowed firms from more competitive countries to gain market share, to invest more, and then to adapt better to changes in the global economy. Moreover, German firms benefited from lower unit labor costs (the ratio of pay to productivity) relative to the Eurozone because of high capital investment as well as weak domestic demand, more flexible working practices, and low government spending (Moravcsik 2012, 59). The result was that companies in Germany became up to 25 percent more competitive than their counterparts in Italy, Spain, Greece, and Portugal (Moravcsik 2012, 59). As a result, the design of the single currency itself is often identified as the ultimate cause of the fiscal problems besetting weaker Eurozone countries. However, finding a single culprit for the sovereign debt crisis risks overlooking a complex set of political and economic causes.

Given that the sovereign debt crisis relates to governments within the Eurozone having to borrow large sums and to accumulate high debts, it is necessary to examine the role played by national governments. One common accusation here is that the countries requiring bailouts have been profligate or at best careless about their finances. In fact governments' fiscal performance in the Eurozone is very mixed. Ireland and Spain abided by the terms of the Stability and Growth Pact up until the 2008 financial crisis, which is more than can be said for France and Germany (Lane 2012). Yet both

Box 12.3   Key Debate: The Eurozone Split over Eurobonds

The core idea behind reforming the existing Eurozone debt system by issuing Eurobonds is to have all countries using the euro guarantee repayment of euro-denominated debt. Each government would contribute proportionally to servicing and paying off the Eurobonds issued; this would imply fiscal union, which is actually the same principle involved in the Eurozone's European Stability Mechanism – a €500 billion permanent bailout fund established in September 2012. Yet there is great reluctance to issue Eurobonds in many northern European countries. Governments there would be expected not only to guarantee the debt of other countries, but also to pay a higher interest rate on borrowing, as the risk associated with Eurobonds would be greater than, say, for individual German or Finnish debt. This is a very hard deal to sell to taxpayers, as politicians in northern Europe worry about voters punishing them at the ballot box to support such schemes. Governments that have implemented tough measures to become fiscally responsible also expect member states in southern Europe to tighten their belts before benefiting from Eurobonds. This is illustrated by German Chancellor Angela Merkel's comment in 2011 that "member states face many years of work to atone for past sins" (quoted in Hall 2012, 368). Moreover, populist parties such as the True Finns in Finland have garnered support by opposing Eurozone bailouts as propping up failing economies, a policy that goes against national interest. Such rhetoric thus exemplifies the "no demos" quandary underlying the Eurobonds split (see Box 10.2). Fiscal union amounts to financial solidarity, which is a core component of being a single political community. Yet voters and politicians in many member states currently oppose this development. Consequently the Eurobonds debate is part of a wider debate over how much European integration citizens want and whether solidarity across member states can trump national interests.

Ireland and Spain experienced huge housing booms facilitated by the cosy links between developers and politicians responsible for urban planning, and these booms generated massive bank losses as house prices collapsed during the post-2008 recession. This suggests that more could have been done at the national level to dampen such speculative construction and selling. Admittedly, these governments lacked a major policy tool for deflating the property bubble because the interest rate is set by the independent ECB. Ireland and Spain thus could not raise interest rates to discourage credit-based construction. Moreover, the credit that financed this housing boom often came from banks in northern Europe – banks in Germany and the Netherlands that would also be facing huge losses without government bailouts to those supposedly profligate countries (Moravcsik 2012, 59).

The major outlier in the Eurozone, though, is Greece. Despite the Eurozone rules, Greece's fiscal performance was very poor even before the financial crisis. The evidence points to Greece's exceptional place among pre-2004 accession countries: it ranks lowest in terms of competitiveness and has the worst rate of corruption (Featherstone 2011). Greek governance is sorely hampered by massive tax evasion and an inability to identify the total number of civil servants, whose ranks are swollen through endemic political patronage. The net result is an inability to balance spending and taxation, which explains why, when public borrowing was cheap (as during the first decade of the euro), governments resorted to accumulating debt. Of course, this response is not in itself a Greek peculiarity; Italy's debt tops €2 trillion, while France last ran a balanced budget in 1974.

Greece is thus an extreme example of the difficulty that a number of member states experience in trying to control their budgets. In the first decade of the euro, a global credit boom fuelled domestic consumption, helping growth, which in turn helped public finances (more tax receipts) – which also benefited from cheaper borrowing costs. Consequently governments faced few pressures to reform their public finances, especially as the SGP was laxly enforced. Nevertheless, some countries have been able to implement sweeping fiscal reforms of their own accord, without supranational pressure. This was the case of Sweden in the 1990s: owing to public sector layoffs and a significant reduction in welfare provision, the budget deficit went from 10 percent of GDP in 1993 to less than 2 percent in 1997 (Anderson 2001). Similarly, throughout the 2000s Germany pursued major welfare reforms and introduced a debt brake to control federal as well as regional spending.

However, the institutional capacity and the political will to implement such costly reforms varies across the EU. This can be seen from the political debates across member states on how to resolve the sovereign debt crisis. The 2012 French presidential election, for instance, was won by a center-left politician with an anti-austerity platform. Greek politics also saw a fierce battle over whether to go along with the terms of the bailouts. The socialist party Syriza, which became the second biggest parliamentary party after the 2012 election, strongly opposed EU-imposed cuts in public spending, although ultimately a coalition of parties supporting the bailout was able to form a government.

Despite these national divergences in coming to terms with fiscal problems, responsibility for the sovereign debt crisis is a shared affair. All Eurozone countries are tied together in a closely knit political and economic sphere, which means that actions and inaction in one country have significant repercussions elsewhere. The willingness and ability to implement a series of bailouts alongside a permanent bailout fund suggest that, at the policy level, mutual responsibility eventually triumphed over the tendency to attribute blame. Yet the terms of these bailouts clearly indicate that wealthier northern European countries expect their southern neighbors to become more like them. This is by no means impossible. Ireland's ability to start borrowing on the financial markets already in July 2012 indicates that rapid fiscal improvement is possible – and Ireland was followed by Portugal in early 2013. However, the longer the sovereign debt crisis hovers over the EU, the more difficult it will be to overcome divisions and recrimination.

12.4 Conclusion: What the Crisis Means for the Future of Integration

Instead of providing a concluding summary, this chapter ends by reflecting on what the sovereign debt crisis means for the future of integration. First, though, it is important to note how both the crisis and the EU's response to it illustrate fundamental characteristics of contemporary European integration. Never before have complicated EU policy debates played such a central role in national politics, as is shown by government instability in the face of meeting EU budget rules. This tendency is compelling evidence of the Europeanization of national politics – for better or for worse (see Chapter 7, Glossary). Equally, the response to the crisis, notably the evolution of the ECB's role and the scrapping of the "no bailout" policy, shows the EU's capacity for flexibility (Moravcsik 2012). As is the historical trend, an unexpected situation revealed incompleteness in the stage of integration reached – the construction of monetary union without a banking union – and forced policy-makers to respond. At the time of writing, however, there is no full banking union, which means that the Eurozone remains vulnerable to the problem of bad bank debt leading to sovereign debt crises.

National leaders were at the forefront of deciding the EU response to the sovereign debt crisis, relegating the Commission and the Parliament – but not the ECB – to secondary roles. This largely intergovernmental approach is understandable because it is national governments that have to secure parliamentary and constitutional approval for bailouts and for austerity measures. Nevertheless, in a new departure for integration, it was one country in particular that set the agenda. Germany, the economic powerhouse of the Eurozone and the biggest contributor to bailout packages, played a central role in determining that indebted countries would need to implement austerity. Many governments saw their macro-economic policy options greatly constrained in order for them to meet the conditions for reforming the Eurozone instituted by German Chancellor Angela Merkel.

Citizens and politicians confronted with the *fait accompli* of the Fiscal Compact and of the ESM thus complained about the lack of democratic inputs into the EU response to the debt crisis. Only Irish voters got to vote on the new Fiscal Compact, in a referendum that passed in May 2012. Indeed, EU leaders even put pressure on the Greek government not to hold a referendum on the bailout provision. Equally, national electorates have discovered how much economic sovereignty is a cooperative affair, limiting the autonomy of national governments, notably the ability to accommodate their citizens' tax and spending preferences. In Italy a temporary technocratic government had to be formed to reassure financial markets by reducing public spending. Moreover, governments implementing fiscal reforms have been voted out of office across the EU, even though their successors have to meet the same terms, whether in the form of the SGP or in separate bailout agreements.

Given that the debt brakes introduced via the Fiscal Compact rely on national legal implementation, successfully solving the sovereign debt crisis is crucially dependent on national acceptance of fiscal reform. National acquiescence cannot be taken for granted, as demonstrated by trends both within the countries providing bailouts and in those receiving them. In the former there is skepticism about financial solidarity, while in the latter there is popular resistance to this form of supranational economic intervention. In this context, divisions within the EU, namely the north/south split, have become apparent – and so have splits in national politics, as voters in Spain and Greece debate whether to accept the terms of the bailouts. These trends point both to the continued evolution of euroskepticism and to its growing importance within national political spheres more and more preoccupied with integration issues.

The sovereign debt crisis thus highlights the problem of economic and political solidarity across the EU. Mutual financial guarantees were necessary to preserve the single currency, but national electorates in creditor countries did not welcome this move – a clear indicator of the domestic political obstacles to creating a fiscal union. Moreover, many citizens in countries that require a bailout have objected to having to meet conditions imposed at the demand of other EU member states. The crisis also raised another issue of solidarity and unity across the EU by reinforcing the distinction between those outside of the single currency and those using the euro. The Eurozone area has strengthened its informal system of cooperation, the **Eurogroup** (euro-area finance ministers), which appoints a president and meets before the Council's ECOFIN meetings to present a united Eurozone front on economic and finance policy. However, the luster of the euro has dimmed, dampening the enthusiasm for adopting the single currency among certain post-2004 accession countries. These countries are legally obliged to join eventually. Estonia did so in 2011, yet Bulgaria postponed its timetable for euro membership several times, even though it meets the criteria.

Equally importantly, moves toward a banking union and more economic coordination for the EU triggered added wariness toward integration among British euroskeptical parties. It was to appease euroskeptical elements in his Conservative Party that British Prime Minister David Cameron refused to sign the Fiscal Compact in 2011. This opposition left the United Kingdom very isolated, as did its reluctance to establish greater supranational banking regulation for fear of hurting the financial interests of the City of London. Indeed in 2013 Prime Minister Cameron announced his intention, if re-elected in 2015, of renegotiating the UK's relationship with the EU and then subjecting this deal to an "in or out" referendum on staying in the EU. Around this time opinion polls suggested that 70 percent of Britons were "not very" or "not at all" attached to the EU. Whether this trend of seeking alternative arrangements spreads – Sweden and the Czech Republic also objected to joining the new banking union – will determine whether the EU will experience enhanced differentiated integration (see Section 9.4).

Overall, the sovereign debt crisis is perhaps the toughest challenge the EU has faced. In light of this, the choice to move toward a banking union is a clear signal that European political elites still supported more integration to resolve the vulnerability of the single currency. How much longer this tendency to resolve internal crises through greater integration will continue depends not just on what financial burden voters in creditor states will accept in exchange for keeping the euro intact. The commitment to greater integration is also conditional on the acquiescence of voters in the countries that have been bailed out, as well as in those where fundamental socio-economic reform is necessary to balance the budget. With the demise of the permissive consensus era, these voters' enthusiasm for the euro cannot be taken for granted; hence neither can national politicians' ability to persuade citizens to choose more integration. Thus accomplishing a banking union – let alone moving toward fiscal union – to strengthen monetary integration cannot be taken for granted and may be accompanied by further internal differentiation. In this context, the politics of European integration should prove a continuing source of contestation, frustration, but also inspiration.

Guide to Further Reading

Hall, P. 2012. "The Economics and Politics of the Euro Crisis." *German Politics*, 21: 355–371. DOI: 10.1080/09644008.2012.739614

A study from a political economy perspective showing the fundamental institutional and policy problems that resulted from joining together different kinds of economies under a single currency.

Lane, P. R. 2012. "The European Sovereign Debt Crisis." *The Journal of Economic Perspectives*, 26: 49–67. DOI: http://dx.doi.org/10.1257/jep.26.3.49

A clearly written overview of the fundamental economic processes behind the sovereign debt crisis.

Sadeh, T. 2012. "The End of the Euro Mark 1: A Sceptical View of European Monetary Union." In Hubert Zimmerman and Andreas Dür, eds., *Key Controversies in European Integration*, 121–129. Basingstoke: Palgrave.

A provocative take on the economic incompatibilities undermining the Eurozone, resulting in the prediction that weaker economies will leave the euro.

Discussion Questions

1   How was the design of EMU intended to prevent the need for bailouts and how well did this mechanism function?
2   Why did bad bank loans trigger a crisis of confidence in government debt among several Eurozone countries and why were particular countries affected?
3   What does the Fiscal Compact seek to achieve and how far does it change national fiscal autonomy?
4   How democratically legitimate has the EU response to the Eurozone crisis been and what political debates did it trigger in both creditor countries and bailout recipients?
5   Why is responsibility for the sovereign debt crisis in dispute? Does attributing blame matter for how to pursue institutional reform?

Web Resources

This book is supported by a companion website, which can be found at www.wiley .com/go/glencross. There you will find a list of the web links referred to in this chapter wherever you see a "Web" icon in the page margins. In addition, you will find a list of further relevant online resources such as websites for EU institutions, political groups, archives, and think tanks, information on studying abroad, and biographies of key figures. You will also find self-assessment tools in the form of flashcards and independent study questions developed specifically for this chapter.

Glossary

Austerity
Normally a term of criticism, used to denounce spending cuts and tax rises intended to compensate for government deficits. Critics of austerity measures claim that the latter depress growth, thereby making budget crises worse.

Banking union
A system in which banks operating across different jurisdictions are nonetheless subject to common regulatory rules and are protected by a common scheme to prevent insolvency. This implies financial solidarity across borders, because banks are tied together, especially in a currency union like the Eurozone. The system also implies centrally organized powers designed to monitor whether banks play by the rules.

Bonds
A bond is a debt instrument; it pays interest and is sold by companies and governments to finance their spending. Although government bonds are normally considered safe investments, interest rates on them differ according to how good a country's finances are judged to be by investors. Small changes in interest on bonds have large repercussions on public finances in countries with very large debts (like Italy).

Currency devaluation
Devaluation occurs when a government withdraws from a currency union (or a fixed exchange rate system), causing a significant fall in the value of the national currency on global markets. This makes exports cheap and hence more competitive, but devaluation comes at a price: it makes imports more expensive and reduces domestic demand.

Eurogroup
Informal meeting of finance ministers from member states using the euro. The group meets prior to the Council's ECOFIN configuration meetings in order to devise a common approach of Eurozone countries to economic and financial policy.

European Stability Mechanism (ESM)
A permanent bailout fund endowed with €500 billion, established in 2012, with capital provided by member states. It issues emergency loans to EU countries on condition that they have ratified the 2012 Treaty on Stability, Coordination, and Governance (also known as the Fiscal Compact).

Fiscal union
The principle that financial responsibility (e.g. for bank bailouts and debt) is shared between a group of countries. Fiscal union thus works on the basis of pooling fiscal

powers so that tax and spend decisions are taken collectively, which is a major step in closer integration.

Insolvency

The inability to pay back, in full, one's debt as well as the interest upon it; this can happen to governments as well as to private firms such as banks. When a government is insolvent, investors will no longer lend it money; they will often lose money as debt goes unpaid.

International Monetary Fund (IMF)

International organization established in 1945 for the purpose of overseeing global financial stability. It performs an essential stabilizing role by providing emergency loans to countries that are suddenly unable to borrow on financial markets. Its funds come from member states, and loans are conditional upon governments implementing major socio-economic reforms.

Liquidity

The ability to pay back short-term debt on time, as originally agreed. Banks and governments can both face sudden liquidity problems – for example when they become wary of lending to one another, or when tax revenue falls sharply. In these cases short-term credit extension is needed to pay back debt on time and to maintain market confidence. Failure to secure emergency credit can in turn trigger insolvency.

References

Anderson, Karen M. 2001. "The Politics of Retrenchment in a Social Democratic Welfare State: Reform of Swedish Pensions and Unemployment Insurance." *Comparative Political Studies*, 34: 1063–1091. DOI: 10.1177/0010414001034009005

Collier, Paul, and Jan Willem Gunning. 1999. "The IMF's Role in Structural Adjustment." *The Economic Journal*, 109: F634–F651. Available at http://www.jstor.org/stable/2566066 (accessed July 20, 2013).

De Grauwe, Paul. 2011. "The European Central Bank: Lender of Last Resort in the Government Bond Markets?" CESifo Working Paper Series No. 3569. Available at SSRN: http://ssrn.com/abstract=1927783 (accessed July 20, 2013).

Delpla, Jacques, and Jakob von Weizsäcker. 2010. "The Blue Bond Proposal." Bruegel Policy Briefs, No. 2010/03 (May). Available at http://aei.pitt.edu/13911/1/1005 -PB-Blue_Bonds.pdf (accessed July 20, 2013).

Deo, Stephane, Paul Donovan, and Larry Hatheway. 2011. "Euro Break-up: The Consequences." *UBS Investment Research Global Economic Perspectives.* Available at http://bruxelles.blogs .liberation.fr/UBS%20fin%20de%20l% 27euro.pdf (accessed July 20, 2013).

Dullien, Sébastien. 2012. "Reinventing Europe: Explaining the Fiscal Compact." Available at http://ecfr.eu/content/ entry/commentary_reinventing_europe _explaining_the_fiscal_compact (accessed July 20, 2013).

Featherstone, Keith. 2011. "The *JCMS* Annual Lecture: The Greek Sovereign Debt Crisis and EMU: A Failing State in a Skewed Regime." *Journal of Common Market Studies*, 49: 193–217. DOI: 10.1111/j.1468-5965.2010 .02139.x

Feldstein, Martin. 1997. "The Political Economy of the European Economic and Monetary Union: Political Sources of an Economic Liability." *Journal of Economic Perspectives*, 11: 23–42. DOI: 10.1257/jep.11.4.23

Goodhart, Charles. 2009. "Procyclicality and Financial Regulation." *Banco de España Revista de Estabilidad Financiera*, 16: 11–20. Available at http://www.bde.es/f/webbde/Secciones/Publicaciones/InformesBoletinesRevistas/RevistaEstabilidadFinanciera/09/May/Fic/ief0116.pdf (accessed July 20, 2013).

Hall, Peter A. 2012. "The Economics and Politics of the Euro Crisis." *German Politics*, 21: 355–371. DOI: 10.1080/09644008.2012.739614

Jones, Erik. 2012. "Italy's Sovereign Debt Crisis." *Survival: Global Politics and Strategy*, 54: 83–110. DOI: http://dx.doi.org/10.1080/00396338.2012.657545

Lane, Philip R. 2012. "The European Sovereign Debt Crisis." *The Journal of Economic Perspectives*, 26: 49–67. DOI: http://dx.doi.org/10.1257/jep.26.3.49

Marsh, David. 2009. *The Euro: The Politics of the New Global Currency*. New Haven, CT: Yale University Press.

Moravcsik, Andrew. 2012. "Europe After the Crisis: How to Sustain a Common Currency." *Foreign Affairs* (May/June). Available at http://www.foreignaffairs.com/articles/137421/andrew-moravcsik/europe-after-the-crisis (accessed July 20, 2013).

Paterson, William E. 2011. "The Reluctant Hegemon? Germany Moves Centre Stage in the European Union." *Journal of Common Market Studies*, 49: 57–75. DOI: 10.1111/j.1468-5965.2011.02184.x

Reinhart, Carmen M., and Kenneth S. Rogoff. 2009. *This Time Is Different: Eight Centuries of Financial Folly*. Princeton, NJ: Princeton University Press.

Sadeh, Tal. 2012. "The End of the Euro Mark I: A Sceptical View of European Monetary Union." In Hubert Zimmermann and Andreas Dür, eds., *Key Controversies in European Integration*, 121–129. Basingstoke: Palgrave Macmillan.

Shambaugh, Jay C. 2012. "The Euro's Three Crises." *Brookings Papers on Economic Activity*. Available at http://www.brookings.edu/~/media/Files/Programs/ES/BPEA/2012_spring_bpea_papers/2012_spring_BPEA_shambaugh.pdf (accessed July 20, 2013).

Index

Page numbers followed by an asterisk indicate material in the glossary; page numbers in italics denote in-text box material; page numbers in bold refer to tables and figures.